New Perspectives on

Microsoft® Office PowerPoint® 2003

CourseCard Edition

Comprehensive

D1372616

THOMSON

COURSE TECHNOLOGY™

Australia • Canada • Mexico • Singapore • Spain • United Kingdom • United States

What does this logo mean?

It means this courseware has been approved by the Microsoft® Office Specialist Program to be among the finest available for learning Microsoft Office Word 2003, Microsoft Office Excel 2003, Microsoft Office Access 2003, and Microsoft Office PowerPoint® 2003. It also means that upon completion of this courseware, you may be prepared to take an exam for Microsoft Office Specialist qualification.

What is a Microsoft Office Specialist?

A Microsoft Office Specialist is an individual who has passed exams for certifying his or her skills in one or more of the Microsoft Office desktop applications such as Microsoft Word, Microsoft Excel, Microsoft PowerPoint, Microsoft Outlook®, Microsoft Access, or Microsoft Project. The Microsoft Office Specialist Program is the only program in the world approved by Microsoft for testing proficiency in Microsoft Office desktop applications and Microsoft Project.* This testing program can be a valuable asset in any job search or career advancement.

More Information:

To learn more about becoming a Microsoft Office Specialist, visit www.microsoft.com/officespecialist

To learn about other Microsoft Office Specialist approved courseware from Course Technology, visit **www.course.com/newperspectives/teacherslounge**

New Perspectives on

Microsoft® Office PowerPoint® 2003

CourseCard Edition

Comprehensive

Beverly B. Zimmerman
Brigham Young University

S. Scott Zimmerman
Brigham Young University

THOMSON

COURSE TECHNOLOGY™

Australia • Canada • Mexico • Singapore • Spain • United Kingdom • United States

THOMSON

COURSE TECHNOLOGY

New Perspectives on Microsoft® Office PowerPoint® 2003—Comprehensive, CourseCard Edition
is published by Course Technology.

Senior Managing Editor:
Rachel Goldberg

Senior Product Managers:
Kathy Finnegan, Karen Stevens

Senior Technology Product Manager:
Amanda Young Shelton

Product Manager:
Brianna Hawes

Associate Product Manager:
Emilie Perreault

Editorial Assistant:
Shana Rosenthal

Marketing Manager:
Joy Stark

Developmental Editor:
Katherine T. Pinard

Production Editors:
Jennifer Goguen, Kelly Robinson

Composition:
GEX Publishing Services

Text Designer:
Steve Deschene

Cover Designer:
Nancy Goulet

Cover Artist:
Ed Carpenter
www.edcarpenter.net

Preface

Real, Thought-Provoking, Engaging, Dynamic, Interactive—these are just a few of the words that are used to describe the New Perspectives Series' approach to learning and building computer skills.

Without our critical-thinking and problem-solving methodology, computer skills could be learned but not retained. By teaching with a case-based approach, the New Perspectives Series challenges students to apply what they've learned to real-life situations.

Our ever-growing community of users understands why they're learning what they're learning. Now you can too!

See what instructors and students are saying about the best-selling New Perspectives Series:

> "I have used books from the New Perspectives series for about ten years now. I haven't been able to find anything else that approaches their quality when it comes to covering intermediate and advanced software application topics."
> —Karleen Nordquist, College of St. Benedict & St. John's University

...and about New Perspectives on Microsoft Office PowerPoint 2003:

> "Helpful tips and hints for delivering effective presentations are offered throughout the book. The authors truly emphasize the fact that the PowerPoint software is a tool to use and a presentation is only as interesting as its presenter."
> — Candice Spangler, Columbus State Community College

> "The new 'Managing Your Files' tutorial covers all the basic skills students need to have a good working knowledge of files and file management. It is clear, concise, and easy to understand."
> —Mary Logan, Delgado Community College

> "New Perspectives PowerPoint 2003 is an excellent text for helping students master the skills necessary for developing dynamic presentations. Step-by-step examples integrated with tips for effective presentations are reinforced with exercises and cases relevant to today's world. Students will definitely be able to use all the features of PowerPoint after finishing this text."
> — Kathleen Bent, Cape Cod Community College

www.course.com/NewPerspectives

Why *New Perspectives* will work for you

Context

Each tutorial begins with a problem presented in a "real-world" case that is meaningful to students. The case sets the scene to help students understand what they will do in the tutorial.

Hands-on Approach

Each tutorial is divided into manageable sessions that combine reading and hands-on, step-by-step work. Screenshots—now 20% larger for enhanced readability—help guide students through the steps. **Trouble?** tips anticipate common mistakes or problems to help students stay on track and continue with the tutorial.

Review

In New Perspectives, retention is a key component to learning. At the end of each session, a series of Quick Check questions helps students test their understanding of the concepts before moving on. And now each tutorial contains an end-of-tutorial summary and a list of key terms for further reinforcement.

Assessment

Engaging and challenging Review Assignments and Case Problems have always been a hallmark feature of the New Perspectives Series. Now we've added new features to make them more accessible! Colorful icons and brief descriptions accompany the exercises, making it easy to understand, at a glance, both the goal and level of challenge a particular exercise holds.

Reference

While contextual learning is excellent for retention, there are times when students will want a high-level understanding of how to accomplish a task. Within each tutorial, Reference Windows appear before a set of steps to provide a succinct summary and preview of how to perform a task. In addition, a complete Task Reference at the back of the book provides quick access to information on how to carry out common tasks. Finally, each book includes a combination Glossary/Index to promote easy reference of material.

Student Online Companion

This book has an accompanying online companion Web site designed to enhance learning. This Web site includes:
- Internet Assignments and Lab Assignments for selected tutorials
- Student Data Files and PowerPoint presentations
- Microsoft Office Specialist Certification Grids

Certification

The logo on the front of this book means that this book has been independently reviewed and approved by ProCert Labs. If you are interested in acquiring Microsoft Office Specialist certification, you may use this book as courseware in your preparation. For more information on this certification, go to www.microsoft.com/officespecialist.

Review

Apply

Reference Window

Task Reference

www.course.com/NewPerspectives

New Perspectives offers an entire system of instruction

The New Perspectives Series is more than just a handful of books. It's a complete system of offerings:

New Perspectives catalog
Our online catalog is never out of date! Go to the catalog link on our Web site to check out our available titles, request a desk copy, download a book preview, or locate online files.

Coverage to meet your needs!
Whether you're looking for just a small amount of coverage or enough to fill a semester-long class, we can provide you with a textbook that meets your needs.

- Brief books typically cover the essential skills in just 2 to 4 tutorials.
- Introductory books build and expand on those skills and contain an average of 5 to 8 tutorials.
- Comprehensive books are great for a full-semester class, and contain 9 to 12+ tutorials.
- Power Users or Advanced books are perfect for a highly accelerated introductory class or a second course in a given topic.

So if the book you're holding does not provide the right amount of coverage for you, there's probably another offering available. Go to our Web site or contact your Course Technology sales representative to find out what else we offer.

Instructor Resources
We offer more than just a book. We have all the tools you need to enhance your lectures, check students' work, and generate exams in a new, easier-to-use and completely revised package. This book's Instructor's Manual, ExamView testbank, PowerPoint presentations, data files, solution files, figure files, and a sample syllabus are all available on a single CD-ROM or for downloading at www.course.com.p

How will your students master Microsoft Office?
SAM (Skills Assessment Manager) 2003 helps you energize your class exams and training assignments by allowing students to learn and test important computer skills in an active, hands-on environment. With SAM 2003, you create powerful interactive exams on critical Microsoft Office 2003 applications, including Word, Excel, Access, and PowerPoint. The exams simulate the application environment, allowing your students to demonstrate their knowledge and to think through the skills by performing real-world tasks. Designed to be used with the New Perspectives Series, SAM 2003 includes built-in page references so students can create study guides that match the New Perspectives textbooks you use in class. Powerful administrative options allow you to schedule exams and assignments, secure your tests, and run reports with almost limitless flexibility. Find out more about SAM 2003 by going to www.course.com or speaking with your Course Technology sales representative.

Distance Learning
Enhance your course with any of our online learning platforms. Go to www.course.com or speak with your Course Technology sales representative to find the platform or the content that's right for you.

www.course.com/NewPerspectives

About This Book

This book covers the basic to more advanced features of Microsoft PowerPoint 2003, from planning and creating a presentation, to applying complex animation and sound effects and integrating slides with other Microsoft programs.

- New! Now includes a free, tear-off PowerPoint 2003 CourseCard that provides students with a great way to have PowerPoint skills at their fingertips.
- By popular demand, this book now includes a new tutorial on file management!
- Updated for the new software! This book includes coverage of new PowerPoint 2003 features, including using the new Research task pane, saving a presentation to a CD, and saving a presentation as a single Web page.
- The two "Presentation Concepts" tutorials at the beginning of the book provide a solid foundation and detailed information on planning, developing, and giving a presentation.
- Students also learn how to apply and modify text and graphic objects, integrate PowerPoint with other programs, collaborate with workgroups, apply advanced special effects, and create special types of presentations.
- For PowerPoint 2003, there is increased emphasis on understanding graphics—including tables, diagrams, shapes, and clip art images—and how to use them effectively in a presentation.
- Many of the Reference Windows contain helpful tips for how to use PowerPoint slide components, including text, graphics, transitions, and special effects, to create and deliver professional-looking and successful presentations.

Features of the New Perspectives series include:

- Large screenshots offer improved readability.
- Sequential page numbering makes it easier to refer to specific pages in the book.
- The Tutorial Summary and Key Terms sections at the end of each tutorial provide additional conceptual review for students.
- Meaningful labels and descriptions for the end-of-tutorial exercises make it easy for you to select the right exercises for your students.

Acknowledgments

The authors would like to thank the following reviewers for their valuable feedback on this project: Kathleen Bent, Cape Cod Community College; Michael Feiler, Merritt College; Shui-lien Huang, Mt. San Antonio College; Glen Johansson, Spokane Community College; Mary Logan, Delgado Community College; Candice Spangler, Columbus State Community College, and Kathy Winters, The University of Tennessee at Chattanooga. Also we give special thanks to Rachel Goldberg, Senior Managing Editor; Kathy Finnegan and Karen Stevens, Senior Product Managers; Kelly Robinson and Jen Goguen, Production Editors; Emilie Perreault, Associate Product Manager; Shana Rosenthal, Editorial Assistant; John Bosco and John Freitas, Quality Assurance Managers; Harris Bierhoff and Susan Whalen, Quality Assurance Testers; Steven Freund, Dave Nuscher, and Rebekah Tidwell for their work on the Instructors Resources; and the staff at GEX. Thank you all for your expertise, enthusiasm, and vision for this book. Finally, we would like to thank Katherine T. Pinard, our Developmental Editor, for her shepherding this project to completion. Her experience, knowledge, and attention to detail have been invaluable in helping bring this project to fruition. She has been a delight to work with.

Beverly B. Zimmerman
S. Scott Zimmerman

www.course.com/NewPerspectives

Brief Contents

Presentation Concepts Tutorials — PRES 1

Tutorial 1 Planning and Developing Your Presentation . . . . PRES 3
Planning a Presentation for a Nonprofit Agency — PRES 3

Tutorial 2 Giving Your Presentation . . . . PRES 41
Selecting Visuals and Practicing Your Presentation — PRES 41

File Management — FM 1

Managing Your Files. . . . . FM 3
Creating and Working with Files and Folders in Windows XP — FM 3

Office — OFF 1

Using Common Features of Microsoft Office 2003 . . . . OFF 3
Preparing Promotional Materials — OFF 3

PowerPoint—Level I Tutorials — PPT 1

Tutorial 1 Creating a Presentation . . . . PPT 3
Presenting Information About Humanitarian Projects — PPT 3

Tutorial 2 Applying and Modifying Text and Graphic Objects. . . . . PPT 41
Presenting and Preparing for an Expedition to Peru — PPT 41

PowerPoint—Level II Tutorials — PPT 91

Tutorial 3 Presenting a Slide Show . . . . PPT 91
Customizing and Preparing a Presentation — PPT 91

Tutorial 4 Integrating PowerPoint with Other Programs and
Collaborating with Workgroups. . . . . PPT 149
Presenting Information About an Annual Banquet — PPT 149

PowerPoint—Level III Tutorials — PPT 187

Tutorial 5 Applying Advanced Special Effects in Presentations . . . . PPT 187
Adding More Complex Sound, Animation, and Graphics to a Presentation — PPT 187

Tutorial 6 Creating Special Types of Presentations . . . . PPT 231
Giving Presentations with Transparencies, 35mm Slides, Posters, and Banners — PPT 231

Additional Case 1 Creating a Presentation on Local Folklore — ADD 1

Additional Case 2 Creating a Presentation for the Director
of a Museum or Hall of Fame — ADD 5

Glossary/Index. . . . . REF 1

Photo Credits. . . . . REF 9

Task Reference. . . . . REF 10

Microsoft Office Specialist Certification Grid. REF 14

Table of Contents

Preface V

Presentation Concepts
Read This Before You Begin . . . . PRES 2

Tutorial 1   **PRES 3**

Planning and Developing Your Presentation . . . **PRES 3**
Planning a Presentation for a Nonprofit Agency . . . PRES 3

Session 1.1 . . . . **PRES 4**
Planning Your Presentation . . . . PRES 4
Determining the Purpose of Your Presentation . . . . PRES 4
    Giving Informative Presentations . . . . PRES 5
    Giving Persuasive Presentations . . . . PRES 5
    Giving Demonstrations or Training Presentations . . . . PRES 6
Determining the Outcome of Your Presentation . . . . PRES 8
    Writing Purpose and Outcome Statements . . . . PRES 8
Analyzing Your Audience's Needs and Expectations . . . . PRES 9
Assessing the Situation for Your Presentation . . . . PRES 11
Selecting Appropriate Media . . . . PRES 13
    Using a Chalkboard, Whiteboard, or Notepad . . . . PRES 13
    Using a Flip Chart . . . . PRES 14
    Using Posters . . . . PRES 14
    Using Black-and-White or Color Overheads . . . . PRES 15
    Using Handouts . . . . PRES 16
    Using 35mm Slides . . . . PRES 16
    Using Electronic On-Screen Presentations . . . . PRES 17
Session 1.1 Quick Check . . . . PRES 19

Session 1.2 . . . . **PRES 20**
Focusing Your Presentation . . . . PRES 20
    Identifying Your Main Ideas . . . . PRES 21
    Organizing Your Presentation . . . . PRES 21
Developing an Introduction . . . . PRES 22
    Gaining Your Audience's Attention . . . . PRES 23
    Using Anecdotes . . . . PRES 23
    Using Statistics and Quantitative Data . . . . PRES 23
    Using Quotations, Familiar Phrases, and Definitions . . . . PRES 24
    Using Questions . . . . PRES 24
    Commenting About the Audience or Occasion . . . . . PRES 24
    Using Audience Participation . . . . PRES 24
    Stating Your Purpose Statement . . . . PRES 25
    Establishing a Rapport with Your Audience . . . . PRES 26
    Providing an Overview of Your Presentation . . . . PRES 26
    Avoiding Common Mistakes in an Introduction . . . . . . PRES 26
Developing the Body of Your Presentation . . . . PRES 27
    Gathering Information . . . . PRES 27
Organizing Your Information . . . . PRES 30
    Organizing Information Inductively . . . . PRES 30

Organizing Information Deductively . . . . PRES 31
Organizing Information Chronologically . . . . PRES 32
Organizing Information Spatially . . . . PRES 32
Organizing Information by Problem and Solutions . . . . PRES 33
Supporting Your Main Points . . . . PRES 33
Providing Transitions . . . . PRES 33
Developing Your Summary or Conclusion . . . . PRES 34
Session 1.2 Quick Check . . . . PRES 35
Tutorial Summary . . . . PRES 36
Key Terms . . . . PRES 36
Review Assignments . . . . PRES 36
Case Problems . . . . PRES 37
Quick Check Answers . . . . PRES 40

Tutorial 2   **PRES 41**

Giving Your Presentation . . . . **PRES 41**
Selecting Visuals and Practicing Your Presentation PRES 41

Session 2.1 . . . . **PRES 42**
Understanding the Benefits of Using Visuals in
Your Presentation . . . . PRES 42
Selecting Appropriate Visuals for Your Purpose . . . . PRES 44
    Using Tables . . . . PRES 44
    Using Graphs . . . . PRES 46
    Using Charts . . . . PRES 47
    Using Illustrations . . . . PRES 49
Selecting Appropriate Visuals for Your Audience . . . . . . PRES 51
Selecting Appropriate Visuals for Your Situation . . . . . . PRES 52
Creating Effective Visuals . . . . PRES 52
Making the Most of Your Visuals . . . . PRES 53
    Using a Storyboard . . . . PRES 53
    Effectively Presenting Visuals . . . . PRES 54

Session 2.2 . . . . **PRES 56**
Choosing an Appropriate Delivery Method . . . . PRES 56
    Giving a Written or Memorized Presentation . . . . PRES 57
    Giving an Extemporaneous Presentation . . . . PRES 58
    Giving an Impromptu Presentation . . . . PRES 59
Preparing for Questions from the Audience . . . . PRES 60
Overcoming Nervousness . . . . PRES 61
Practicing Your Presentation . . . . PRES 63
Improving Your Delivery . . . . PRES 64
    Establishing Eye Contact . . . . PRES 64
    Using a Pleasant, Natural Voice . . . . PRES 65
Using Proper Grammar and Pronunciation . . . . PRES 66

Using Non-verbal Communication . . . . .PRES 66
    Checking Your Appearance and Posture . . . . .PRES 66
    Using Natural Gestures and Movement . . . . .PRES 67
    Avoiding Annoying Mannerisms . . . . .PRES 67
Giving Collaborative or Team Presentations . . . . .PRES 68
Setting Up for Your Presentation .PRES 70
Using a Facilities Checklist . . . . .PRES 71
Session 2.2 Quick Check . . . . .PRES 73
Tutorial Summary . . . . .PRES 73
Key Terms . . . . .PRES 74
Review Assignments . . . . .PRES 74
Case Problems . . . . .PRES 75
Quick Check Answers . . . . .PRES 79

File Management   FM 1

Read This Before You Begin. . . . . FM 2

Managing Your Files   FM 3

Creating and Working with Files and Folders in
Windows XP . . . . .FM 3

Organizing Files and Folders . . . . .FM 4
    Understanding the Need for Organizing Files and Folders . .FM 5
    Developing Strategies for Organizing Files and Folders . . . . .FM 6
    Planning Your Organization . . . . .FM 7
Exploring Files and Folders . . . . .FM 7
    Using Windows Explorer . . . . .FM 9
    Navigating to Your Data Files . . . . .FM 10
Working with Folders and Files . . . . .FM 12
    Creating Folders . . . . .FM 12
    Moving and Copying Files and Folders . . . . .FM 14
    Naming and Renaming Files . . . . .FM 16
    Deleting Files and Folders . . . . .FM 17
Working with Compressed Files .FM 18
Quick Check . . . . .FM 20
Tutorial Summary . . . . .FM 21
Key Terms . . . . .FM 21
Review Assignments . . . . .FM 21
Case Problems . . . . .FM 22
SAM Assessment and Training . . . . .FM 24
Lab Assignments . . . . .FM 24
Quick Check Answers . . . . .FM 24

Office   OFF 1

Read This Before You Begin . . . . .OFF 2

Using Common Features of   OFF 3
Microsoft Office 2003

Preparing Promotional Materials . . . . .OFF 3

Exploring Microsoft Office 2003 . . . . .OFF 4
    Integrating Office Programs . . . . .OFF 5
Starting Office Programs . . . . .OFF 5
    Switching Between Open Programs and Files . . . . .OFF 8
Exploring Common Window Elements . . . . .OFF 9
Using the Window Sizing Buttons .OFF 9
Using Menus and Toolbars . . . . .OFF 11
    Viewing Personalized Menus and Toolbars . . . . .OFF 11
Using Task Panes . . . . .OFF 14
    Opening and Closing Task Panes . . . . .OFF 14
    Navigating Among Task Panes . . . . .OFF 15
Using the Research Task Pane . . . . .OFF 16
Working with Files . . . . .OFF 18
    Creating a File . . . . .OFF 19
    Saving a File . . . . .OFF 19
    Closing a File . . . . .OFF 21
    Opening a File . . . . .OFF 22
Getting Help . . . . .OFF 23
    Using ScreenTips . . . . .OFF 23
    Using the Type a Question for Help Box . . . . .OFF 23
    Using the Help Task Pane . . . . .OFF 25
    Using Microsoft Office Online .OFF 27
Printing a File . . . . .OFF 29
Exiting Programs . . . . .OFF 30
Quick Check . . . . .OFF 31
Tutorial Summary . . . . .OFF 31
Key Terms . . . . .OFF 31
Review Assignments . . . . .OFF 31
SAM Assessment and Training . . . . .OFF 32
Quick Check Answers . . . . .OFF 32

PowerPoint

Level I Tutorials. . . . . .PPT 1
Read This Before You Begin . . . . .PPT 2

Tutorial 1   PPT 3
Creating a Presentation . . . . PPT 3

Presenting Information About Humanitarian Projects . .PPT 3

Session 1.1 . . . . .PPT 4
What Is PowerPoint? . . . . .PPT 4
Opening an Existing PowerPoint Presentation . . . . .PPT 5

Switching Views and Navigating a Presentation . . . . .PPT 6
Viewing a Presentation in Slide Show View . . . . .PPT 7
Planning a Presentation . . . . .PPT 10
Using the AutoContent Wizard . . . . .PPT 10
Session 1.1 Quick Check . . . . .PPT 13

Session 1.2 . . . .**PPT 13**
Modifying a Presentation . . . . .PPT 13
   Editing Slides . . . . .PPT 14
   Deleting Slides . . . . .PPT 17
   Adding a New Slide and Choosing a Layout . . . . .PPT 19
   Promoting, Demoting, and Moving Outline Text . . . . . . .PPT 21
   Moving Slides in Slide Sorter View . . . . .PPT 23
Checking the Spelling and Style in a Presentation . . . . .PPT 24
   Checking the Spelling . . . . .PPT 24
   Using the Style Checker . . . . .PPT 25
   Using the Research Task Pane . . . . .PPT 27
Creating Speaker Notes . . . . .PPT 29
Previewing and Printing a Presentation . . . . .PPT 30
Session 1.2 Quick Check . . . . .PPT 33
Tutorial Summary . . . . .PPT 33
Key Terms . . . . .PPT 33
Review Assignments . . . . .PPT 33
Case Problems . . . . .PPT 34
Internet Assignments . . . . .PPT 40
SAM Assessment and Training . . . . .PPT 40
Quick Check Answers . . . . .PPT 40

Tutorial 2   **PPT 41**
Applying and Modifying Text and Graphic Objects **PPT 41**
Presenting and Preparing for an Expedition to Peru . .PPT 41

Session 2.1 . . . .**PPT 42**
Planning a Presentation . . . . .PPT 42
Creating a New Presentation from a Design Template . . . . . .PPT 42
Applying a Design Template . . . . .PPT 44
Understanding Graphics . . . . .PPT 45
   Inserting Clip Art . . . . .PPT 46
   Resizing Clip Art . . . . .PPT 47
   Recoloring Clip Art . . . . .PPT 48
Modifying the Design Template in the Slide Master . . . . . . .PPT 50
Inserting and Modifying a Bitmap Image on a Slide . . . . . . .PPT 52
Modifying Text on a Slide . . . . .PPT 55
   Modifying the Format of Text on a Slide . . . . .PPT 55
   Resizing a Text Box on a Slide .PPT 57
Applying a Second Design Template . . . . .PPT 58
Adding and Modifying Tab Stops . . . . .PPT 60
Inserting Footers and Slide Numbers . . . . .PPT 62
Session 2.1 Quick Check . . . . .PPT 65

Session 2.2 . . . .**PPT 66**
Creating a Table in a Slide . . . . .PPT 66
Creating a Diagram on a Slide . . . . .PPT 69
Creating and Manipulating a Shape . . . . .PPT 72
Inserting Text Boxes . . . . .PPT 74
   Adding Text to the Diagram . . . . .PPT 74
   Rotating and Moving Text Boxes . . . . .PPT 75
Adding a Summary Slide . . . . .PPT 77
Session 2.2 Quick Check . . . . .PPT 79
Tutorial Summary . . . . .PPT 79
Key Terms . . . . .PPT 79
Review Assignments . . . . .PPT 79
Case Problems . . . . .PPT 81
Internet Assignments . . . . .PPT 86
SAM Assessment and Training . . . . .PPT 86
Quick Check Answers . . . . .PPT 87

PowerPoint
Level II Tutorials . . . . **PPT 89**
   Read This Before You Begin . . . . **PPT 90**

Tutorial 3   **PPT 91**
Presenting a Slide Show . . . . **PPT 91**
Customizing and Preparing a Presentation . . . . . . .PPT 91

Session 3.1 . . . .**PPT 92**
Planning the Presentation . . . . .PPT 92
Inserting Slides from Another Presentation . . . . .PPT 92
Creating a Custom Design Template . . . . .PPT 95
   Creating a Custom Color Scheme . . . . .PPT 95
   Creating a Custom Background .PPT 97
   Modifying Fonts and Bullets . . . . .PPT 99
   Adding a Background Image . . . . .PPT 101
   Saving a Custom Design Template . . . . .PPT 104
   Using a Custom Design Template . . . . .PPT 105
Applying Graphics and Sounds to Your Presentation . . . . . . .PPT 106
   Adding a Digital Photo to a Slide . . . . .PPT 107
   Adding a Movie . . . . .PPT 108
   Adding Sound Clips . . . . .PPT 110
Adding a Textured Background . . . . .PPT 112
Session 3.1 Quick Check . . . . .PPT 113

Session 3.2 . . . .**PPT 114**
Creating a Chart (Graph) . . . . .PPT 114
Building and Modifying an Organization Chart . . . . .PPT 119
Applying Special Effects . . . . .PPT 124
   Adding Slide Transitions . . . . .PPT 125
   Applying a Built-In Animation Scheme . . . . .PPT 126

Applying Custom Animation . . . . .PPT 128
Using the Pointer Pen to Mark Slides During a Slide Show . .PPT 133
Hiding Slides . . . . .PPT 134
Preparing the Presentation to Run on Another Computer . . .PPT 136
Session 3.2 Quick Check . . . . .PPT 138
Tutorial Summary . . . . .PPT 138
Key Terms . . . . .PPT 138
Review Assignments . . . . .PPT 138
Case Problems . . . . .PPT 140
Internet Assignments . . . . .PPT 146
Lab Assignments . . . . .PPT 146
SAM Assessment and Training . . . . .PPT 146
Quick Check Answers . . . . .PPT 146

Tutorial 4   **PPT 149**

**Integrating PowerPoint with Other Programs
and Collaborating with Workgroups . . . . PPT 149**
Presenting Information About an Annual Banquet . . .PPT 149

Session 4.1 . . . .**PPT 150**
Planning the Presentation . . . . .PPT 150
Applying a Template from Another Presentation . . . . .PPT 150
Using Integration Techniques: Importing, Embedding,
and Linking . . . . .PPT 152
Importing and Exporting a Word Outline . . . . .PPT 154
    Importing the Word Outline . . . . .PPT 154
    Exporting the Outline to Word .PPT 155
Importing Graphics . . . . .PPT 157
Embedding and Modifying a Word Table . . . . .PPT 158
Linking and Modifying an Excel Chart . . . . .PPT 161
Session 4.1 Quick Check . . . . .PPT 165

Session 4.2 . . . .**PPT 165**
Creating and Editing Hyperlinks .PPT 165
Adding Action Buttons . . . . .PPT 169
Viewing a Slide Show with Embedded or Linked Objects . . . .PPT 171
Publishing Presentations on the World Wide Web . . . . .PPT 173
    Publishing the Web Pages . . . . .PPT 174
    Viewing a Presentation in a Web Browser . . . . .PPT 175
Sharing and Collaborating with Others . . . . .PPT 177
Session 4.2 Quick Check . . . . .PPT 178
Tutorial Summary . . . . .PPT 178
Key Terms . . . . .PPT 178
Review Assignments . . . . .PPT 179
Case Problems . . . . .PPT 180
Internet Assignments . . . . .PPT 183
SAM Assessment and Training . . . . .PPT 184
Lab Assignments . . . . .PPT 184
Quick Check Answers . . . . .PPT 184

PowerPoint

Level III Tutorials . . . . PPT 185
   Read This Before You Begin . . . . PPT 186

Tutorial 5   **PPT 187**

**Applying Advanced Special Effects
in Presentations** . . . . **PPT 187**
Adding More Complex Sound, Animation, and
Graphics to a Presentation . . . . .PPT 187

Session 5.1 . . . .**PPT 188**
Planning the Presentation . . . . .PPT 188
Using PowerPoint Slides as Picture Objects . . . . .PPT 188
    Pasting a PowerPoint Slide into a Word Document . . . . .PPT 189
    Pasting Slides into Another Slide as Pictures . . . . .PPT 191
Applying Complex Animation and Sound Effects . . . . .PPT 196
    Animating a Background Object . . . . .PPT 196
    Animating a Process Diagram .PPT 197
    Downloading Clips from Microsoft Office Online . . . . . .PPT 201
    Applying the Downloaded Motion and Sound Clips . . . .PPT 203
    Inserting a CD Audio Track into a Slide . . . . .PPT 206
    Adding Action Buttons to a Slide . . . . .PPT 208
    Recording a Narration . . . . .PPT 209
Manipulating Background Objects . . . . .PPT 211
Session 5.1 Quick Check . . . . .PPT 212

Session 5.2 . . . .**PPT 213**
Setting up a Self-Running Presentation . . . . .PPT 213
    Setting the Slide Timing Manually . . . . .PPT 213
    Rehearsing and Recording the Slide Timing . . . . .PPT 214
    Applying Kiosk Browsing . . . . .PPT 215
Adding Illustrations and Callouts .PPT 217
Creating and Editing a Custom Show . . . . .PPT 221
Session 5.2 Quick Check . . . . .PPT 223
Tutorial Summary . . . . .PPT 223
Key Terms . . . . .PPT 223
Review Assignments . . . . .PPT 223
Case Problems . . . . .PPT 225
Internet Assignments . . . . .PPT 230
SAM Assessment and Training . . . . .PPT 230
Quick Check Answers . . . . .PPT 230

Tutorial 6 .... **PPT 231**

Creating Special Types of Presentations ...... **PPT 231**
Giving Presentations with Transparencies,
35mm Slides, Posters, and Banners .... PPT 231

Session 6.1 .... **PPT 232**
Creating a design Template for Overheads .... PPT 232
    Preparing the Template .... PPT 233
    Using a Digital Image as a Bullet .... PPT 235
    Adding Background Objects to the Slide Masters ...... PPT 236
Creating a Design Template for 35mm Slides .... PPT 239
    Setting up the Template for 35mm Slides .... PPT 239
    Adding a Picture Background to the Slide Masters ..... PPT 241
Making Overhead Transparencies .... PPT 243
Preparing 35mm Slides .... PPT 245
Saving a Presentation as an RTF Outline .... PPT 246
Session 6.1 Quick Check .... PPT 247

Session 6.2 .... **PPT 247**
Creating a Poster Presentation .... PPT 247
    Creating a Multiple-Page Poster Presentation .... PPT 248
    Creating a Banner .... PPT 249
    Creating a Single-Page Poster .... PPT 251
Reviewing a Presentation and Comparing Revisions .... PPT 253
    Reviewing a Presentation .... PPT 254
    Merging and Comparing Presentations .... PPT 256
    Reviewing Changes .... PPT 257

Publishing a Web Presentation with Custom Action Buttons ....PPT 259
Session 6.2 Quick Check .... PPT 263
Tutorial Summary .... PPT 264
Key Terms .... PPT 264
Review Assignments .... PPT 264
Case Problems .... PPT 265
Internet Assignments .... PPT 269
SAM Assessment and Training .... PPT 269
Quick Check Answers .... PPT 270

Additional Case 1
Creating a Presentation on Local Folklore .... ADD 1

Additional Case 2
Creating a Presentation for the Director of a Museum or
Hall of Fame .... ADD 5

Glossary/Index .... **REF 1**

Photo Credits .... **REF 9**

Task Reference .... **REF 10**

Microsoft Office Specialist Certification Grid .... **REF 14**

New Perspectives on
Presentation Concepts

Tutorial 1   PRES 3
Planning and Developing Your Presentation
Planning a Presentation for a Nonprofit Agency

Tutorial 2   PRES 41
Giving Your Presentation
Selecting Visuals and Practicing Your Presentation

Objectives

Session 1.1
- Write a statement of purpose for your presentation and determine your desired outcome
- Analyze the needs and expectations of your audience
- Assess the situation in which you'll give your presentation
- Select an appropriate medium for your presentation

Session 1.2
- Limit your topic to provide focus
- Outline the general organization of a presentation
- Develop an effective introduction, body, and conclusion

Student Data Files

There are no student Data Files needed for this tutorial.

Planning and Developing Your Presentation

Planning a Presentation for a Nonprofit Agency

Case

Giving Presentations for YES!

As a student at Rocky Mountain State College, you recently obtained an internship with Youth Essential Services (YES!), a private, nonprofit organization serving school-aged children with physical and mental disabilities in the Colorado Springs area. The mission of YES! is to provide developmentally challenged youth with training and motivational programs to help them function effectively in society. Presently, the organization serves between 1100 and 1300 young people each month.

Kenna McNaughton, executive director of YES!, says that you'll make many oral presentations as part of your internship. Some of these presentations will be brief and informal, such as communicating pertinent information to the YES! staff, or providing training to volunteers. Other presentations will be lengthy and formal, such as reporting on the status of programs to the Board of Directors, or requesting funds from potential donors. Sometimes you'll need to convey your entire message in an oral format; other times your presentation might supplement a written document, such as a financial statement or a wrap-up report for a successful project. Sometimes you'll give your presentation as part of a group or team; other times you'll give your presentation alone. The success of your internship—and of many of the organization's programs—will depend upon the quality of your presentations.

In this tutorial, you'll plan your presentation by determining the purpose and outcome of your presentation and analyzing the needs and expectations of your audience. You'll assess the situation for giving your presentation and select appropriate media. In addition, you'll focus and organize your presentation and develop an introduction, body, and conclusion for your presentation.

Planning Your Presentation

You should plan an oral presentation the same way you would plan a written document—by considering your purpose, audience, and situation. Oral presentations, however, differ from written documents in the demands placed upon your audience, so you'll need to apply special techniques to ensure a successful presentation.

Planning a presentation in advance will improve the quality of your presentation, make it more effective and enjoyable, and, in the long run, save you time and effort. As you plan your presentation, you should determine why you're giving the presentation, who will be listening to the presentation, and where the presentation will take place.

Figure 1-1	➤ Planning saves time

Specific questions you should ask yourself about the presentation include:

- What is the purpose of this presentation?
- What type of presentation do I need to give?
- Who is the audience for my presentation, and what do they need and expect?
- What is the situation (location and setting) for my presentation?
- What is the most appropriate media for my presentation?

Answering these questions will help you create a more effective presentation, and will enable you to feel confident in presenting your ideas. The following sections will help you answer these questions in planning your presentation.

Determining the Purpose of Your Presentation

Your purpose in giving a presentation will vary according to each particular situation, so the best way to determine your purpose is to ask yourself why you're giving this presentation and what you expect to accomplish. Common purposes for giving presentations include to inform, to persuade, and to demonstrate or train. We'll now consider these types of presentations.

Giving Informative Presentations

Informative presentations provide your audience with background information, knowledge, and specific details about a topic that enable them to make informed decisions, form attitudes, or increase their expertise on a topic.

Examples of informative presentations include:

- Academic or professional conference presentations
- Briefings on the status of projects
- Reviews or evaluations of products and services
- Reports at company meetings
- Luncheon or dinner speeches
- Informal symposia

Provide background and details ◄ **Figure 1-2**

Informative presentations can address a wide range of topics and are given to a wide range of audiences. For example, you might want to educate students at Rocky Mountain State College about the goals and programs of YES!, or you might want to inform YES! staff members about plans for next month's sports activity. Or, you might want to tell parents of youth participating in YES!-sponsored activities about the organization of the Board of Directors. Your main goal in each instance is to provide useful and relevant information to your intended audience.

Giving Persuasive Presentations

Although every presentation involves influencing an audience to listen and be interested in a specific topic, some presentations are more persuasive than others. **Persuasive presentations** are presentations with the specific goal of influencing how an audience feels or acts regarding a particular position or plan.

Examples of persuasive presentations include:

- Recommendations
- Sales presentations
- Action plans and strategy sessions
- Motivational presentations

Figure 1-3 ▶ **Influence your audience**

Persuasive presentations also cover a wide range of topics and are given to a wide range of audiences. In addition, persuasive presentations are usually designed as balanced arguments involving logical as well as emotional reasons for supporting an action or viewpoint. For example, you might want to persuade students at Rocky Mountain State College to volunteer their time in community service. Or, you might want to recommend a particular fundraising activity to YES! administrators. Or, you might want to motivate parents of YES! participants to apply for additional services for their children. Your goal in each of these persuasive presentations is to convince your audience to accept a particular plan or point of view.

Giving Demonstrations or Training Presentations

Demonstrations are a specific type of presentation that shows an audience how something works or helps them to understand a process or procedure. Examples of demonstration presentations include:

- Overviews of products and services
- Software demonstrations
- Process explanations

For example, you might want to demonstrate to volunteers from Rocky Mountain State College how to give encouragement and support to handicapped youth at athletic events. Or, you might want to show YES! staff members how the new accounting software handles reimbursements. Or, you might want to show parents of YES! participants how to fill out a transportation release form. In each of these presentations, your goal is to show how something works so your audience understands the process.

Training presentations provide audiences with an opportunity to learn new skills, or to be educated on how to perform a task, such as how to operate a piece of equipment. Training presentations usually differ from demonstrations by providing listeners with hands-on experience, practice, and feedback, so they can correct their mistakes and improve their performances.

Examples of training presentations include:

- Employee orientation (completing job tasks such as running the copy machine)
- Seminars and workshops
- Educational classes and courses

Show how to perform a task ◀ **Figure 1-4**

For example, you might want to provide training to volunteers from Rocky Mountain State College on how to manage conflict during team sports. Or, you might want to present a seminar to the YES! staff on how to write an effective grant proposal. Or, you might want to teach parents of YES! participants how to help their children with basic life skills, such as counting money. In all of these presentations, your goal is to assist your audience in learning and practicing new abilities and skills.

Sometimes you may have more than one purpose for your presentation. For instance, you need to inform the YES! staff of the newly revised policy on transporting participants to organized activities. In addition to explaining the new policy, you'll need to persuade your co-workers of the importance of following the new guidelines. You might also need to answer any questions they have about how to implement certain aspects of the policy.

Having too many purposes can complicate your presentation and keep you from focusing on the specific needs of your audience. For that reason, you should try to limit your presentation to one main purpose, and one or two secondary purposes.

Purposes for Giving Presentations

Reference Window

Type of Presentation	Goal of Presentation	Examples
Informative	Present facts and details	Academic or professional conferences, status reports, briefings, reviews of products and services, luncheon or dinner speeches, informal symposia
Persuasive	Influence feelings or actions	Recommendation reports, sales presentations, action plans and strategy sessions, motivational presentations
Demonstrations or Training	Show how something works; provide practice and feedback	Overviews of products and services, software demos, process explanations, employee orientation, seminars and workshops, educational courses

In addition to determining your purpose for a presentation, you should also consider the needs of your audience. Effective presentations are those that enable listeners to achieve their goals. We will now consider how to determine what the audience should gain or learn from your presentation.

Determining the Outcome of Your Presentation

Your goal in giving a presentation should be to help your listeners understand, retain, and use the information you present. So, you should determine the **outcome** or what you want to happen as a result of giving your presentation or what you want the audience to do as a result of hearing your presentation. Focusing on the outcome of your presentation—what you want your listeners to think or do after listening to your message—forces you to make your presentation more audience-oriented. By addressing the needs of your listeners, you'll worry less about yourself and more about how to make your presentation effective for your audience.

Writing Purpose and Outcome Statements

Writing down the purpose and outcome of your presentation helps you to analyze what the presentation will involve, and enables you to create a more effective presentation. When you write down the purpose and desired outcomes of your presentation, you should use just two or three sentences. A good statement of your purpose and desired outcomes helps you later as you write the introduction and conclusion for your presentation.

Consider the following examples of purpose statements and outcomes:

- Purpose: To demonstrate the newly purchased arm pads and leg braces for moderately handicapped youth participating in YES! activities. Outcomes: Staff members will understand that the new equipment can decrease the number of injuries to participants. Staff members will want to use the new equipment at next month's field day.
- Purpose: To inform teachers of intellectually handicapped children in the community about the goals and programs of YES! Outcomes: Teachers will want eligible students to participate in YES! sponsored activities. Teachers will know the eligibility criteria for participation, and how to refer their students to our organization.

In both of these examples, the presenter stated a specific purpose with specific outcomes.

Reference Window	**Questions for Determining Your Purpose and Outcomes**

- Why am I giving this presentation?
- What is the primary purpose of this presentation?
- What are the secondary purposes of this presentation?
- What should the audience know or do as a result of this presentation?

Your supervisor, Kenna, asks you to give a presentation about YES! to student leaders at Rocky Mountain State College. Your written purpose might be: To inform student leaders of the goals and programs of YES!. Your written outcome might be: Student leaders will want to create an official partnership between YES! and Rocky Mountain State College so that students can receive course credit for their volunteer work with the agency.

Figure 1-5 provides a basic worksheet for helping you determine the purpose and outcomes of this and other presentations.

Purpose and Outcomes worksheet ◄ **Figure 1-5**

Purpose and Outcomes
Worksheet

Why are you giving this presentation?
_____
_____
_____

What is the primary purpose of your presentation? Check one and explain it.
☐ Provide useful and relevant facts and details
_____
_____

☐ Persuade or influence how audience feels or acts
_____
_____

☐ Show how something works or demonstrate a procedure
_____
_____

☐ Provide hands-on experience, practice, and feedback
_____
_____

What are the secondary purposes for your presentation? Check and explain all that apply.
☐ Provide useful and relevant facts and details
_____

☐ Persuade or influence how audience feels or acts
_____

☐ Show how something works or demonstrate a procedure
_____

☐ Provide hands-on experience, practice, and feedback
_____

☐ Other
_____

What should the audience know, feel, or do as a result of your presentation?
_____
_____
_____

What other outcomes are there for your presentation?
_____
_____
_____

Next you'll analyze what your audience will need and expect from your presentation.

Analyzing Your Audience's Needs and Expectations

The more you know about your listeners, the more you'll be able to adapt your presentation to their needs. By putting yourself in your listeners' shoes, you'll be able to visualize your audience as more than just a group of passive listeners, and you can anticipate what they need and expect from your presentation. Anticipating the needs of your audience will also increase the chances that your audience will react favorably to your presentation.

When you give a presentation to YES! employees, your audience consists of professionals, such as counselors, therapists, and support staff. Audiences in these categories typically are interested in specifics related to their job functions, as well as how your desired outcomes will impact their workload, fulfill their goals and objectives, and affect their budget. In addition, YES! coworkers usually want a less formal presentation than audiences outside your organization.

When you give your presentation at Rocky Mountain State College, your audience will consist of other students and interested faculty and administrators. They will expect to learn: how student involvement in community service benefits the campus community; how community service experiences can supplement what students learn in the classroom; how a partnership between YES! and Rocky Mountain State College would function; and what the administrative costs would be for the university.

Other characteristics of your audience that you'll want to consider include their **demographic characteristics**; that is, features such as age, gender, level of education, and familiarity with your topic.

Figure 1-6	Adapt to the needs of your audience

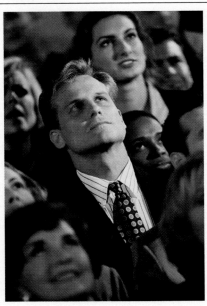

Examples of how demographic characteristics can affect your presentations include:

- **Age**: People of different age groups may vary in terms of attention span and the way they relate to examples. A presentation on the educational impact of student involvement in community service would be appropriate for college students, but probably not for elementary-school students. Moreover, young children have shorter attention spans and generally can't sit for as long as adults. Presentations to young children should be divided into short sessions interspersed with physical activity.
- **Gender**: It's important to fairly represent both genders by avoiding male pronouns (he, his) to represent both sexes, and by using examples that show both men and women performing all jobs at work and at home.
- **Education**: Audiences with specialized training expect examples that use terms and concepts from their field. Audiences with more education expect a higher level of technicality than audiences with less education.
- **Familiarity with the topic**: Audiences familiar with your topic won't need as many definitions and explanations as audiences not familiar with your topic.

In addition to analyzing general features and characteristics of your audience, you should also consider how your audience will use the information that you present. YES! administrators attending a presentation on potential fundraising activities need to know how much money other organizations have raised, and how much the fundraising activity itself would cost, in order to estimate their net profit.

Understanding the needs and expectations of your audience helps you adapt the content of your presentation to a particular audience, and enables you to address their concerns. By anticipating questions your listeners might ask about your topic, you can address those questions and concerns in your presentation. Finally, understanding the needs and concerns of your audience assures that your presentation is useful, interesting, and relevant.

Questions for Analyzing Your Audience

- Who will be listening to my presentation (peers, superiors, subordinates, visitors)?
- What does the audience expect me to talk about?
- What general characteristics or demographics do I know about the audience (age, gender, education level, knowledge of the topic)?
- What does the audience need to know about the topic of the presentation (general background or overview, details, cost estimates)?
- How will listeners use this information (make decisions, perform a task)?
- What are the major concerns or objections to my point of view (too expensive, too difficult)?
- What do I want the audience to think, know, or do as a result of this presentation?

In your presentation about YES!, you realize that your audience will be your peers. They will vary in their experience with your topic, but most of them will be familiar with volunteerism. The biggest concern of college students is that involvement in service activities with YES! might be too time-consuming. You'll need to address that concern in your presentation.

Figure 1-7 provides a basic worksheet for helping you analyze the needs and expectations of your audience for this and other presentations.

Audience Analysis worksheet ◄ **Figure 1-7**

Audience Analysis Worksheet

Who will be listening to your presentation? Check all that apply.
☐ Peers
☐ Superiors
☐ Subordinates
☐ Strangers

What do they expect you to talk about?
_____
_____

What general characteristics do you know about the audience?
Age _____
Gender _____
Education _____
Experience with topic _____
Other _____

What does your audience need to know about the topic? Check and explain all that apply.
☐ General background or overview _____
☐ Details _____
☐ Cost estimates _____
☐ Other _____

How will your listeners use this information? Check and explain all that apply.
☐ Make decisions _____
☐ Perform a task _____
☐ Form an opinion _____
☐ Increase understanding _____
☐ Other _____

What are your audience's biggest concerns or objections? Check and explain all that apply.
☐ Too expensive _____
☐ Too difficult _____
☐ Other _____

What do you want your audience to think, know, or do as a result of this presentation?
_____
_____
_____

Assessing the Situation for Your Presentation

Many of your presentations will involve speaking on the same subject to different audiences and in different settings. Planning an effective presentation will be a matter of learning to adapt your content to your **situation**, the unique setting, time frame, or circumstances (such as the size of your audience) for your presentation. The more you know about the situation for your presentation, the better you can adapt your presentation to different audiences.

Probably the most important aspects to consider are how much time you'll have, and whether someone else will speak before or after you. Giving a presentation along with other presenters means you'll have to watch your time closely so you don't infringe on someone else's time. It can also mean that you'll have to cut your presentation short if someone uses part of your time. Even if you're the sole speaker, it's wise to make back-up plans in case your time limit changes just before you speak.

| Figure 1-8 | **Setting and locations affect expectations** |

The setting for a presentation can affect audience expectations, and hence will dictate the appropriate level of formality. That's why it's important to know where your presentation will occur, including the size and shape of the room, and the seating arrangement. The small conference room with a round table and moveable chairs at YES! headquarters would call for a much more informal presentation than the large rectangular lecture hall with fixed seating at Rocky Mountain State College.

You'll also need to adapt your presentation according to the size of your audience. Four or five co-workers at YES! would probably expect to be able to interrupt your presentation and ask questions or express their own views, whereas the large audience at Rocky Mountain State College would not. The setting for your presentation and the size of your audience also influence the method and equipment you use to give your presentation, and the size of your visuals. Students in large rooms often sit toward the back of the room, far away from your visuals. So you will need to increase the size of your visuals in your presentation at Rocky Mountain State College, or use an overhead, slide, or computer projection system. On the other hand, if your audience at YES! headquarters is fewer than ten people, you might be able to use a laptop computer screen for your visuals.

Questions for Analyzing the Situation for Your Presentation

- How much time will I have for my presentation?
- Will I be speaking alone or with other people?
- How large will the audience be?
- How formal or informal will the setting be?
- What will the room be like, and how will it be arranged?
- What equipment will be available for my presentation (chalkboard, overhead projector, slide projector, computer projection system)?
- Do I have the skills to operate available equipment?
- Who will be available to assist me in case of an equipment failure?
- How much time will I have to set up for my presentation?
- What other aspects must I consider (temperature, extraneous noises)?
- Who will be available to assist me with room temperature, lights, or extraneous noise problems?

Now you need to decide what kind of presentation methods you'll use in your presentation.

Selecting Appropriate Media

As you plan your presentation, you'll need to select the **media**, or presentation methods, you'll use to support and clarify your presentation. Media commonly used for oral presentations include:

- Chalkboard
- Whiteboard
- Notepad and easel
- Flip chart
- Posters
- Black-and-white or color overheads
- Handouts
- 35mm slides
- Computer-projected visuals, such as PowerPoint slides.

In selecting appropriate media for your presentation, it's important to fit the media to your particular purpose, audience, and situation. Every medium allows you to provide support for the points you'll make in your presentation, and help your audience see and hear your ideas. Each medium, however, has its own strengths and limitations. We'll consider those now.

Using a Chalkboard, Whiteboard, or Notepad

Chalkboards, whiteboards, or large paper notepads work well for small meetings and informal discussions, and are especially helpful in stressing important points from your presentation, or in recording comments from the audience. These media usually require little advance preparation, other than bringing along a piece of chalk or a marker, and they come in portable forms.

Figure 1-9	Chalkboards emphasize main points

On the other hand, these media have disadvantages, including the difficulty of speaking to your audience while you write or draw. If your handwriting is difficult to read, it can detract from your presentation, as can poor spelling. In addition, these media are only effective for writing a few words or short phrases, or making simple drawings.

Using a Flip Chart

Flip charts, previously prepared pictures and visuals that are bound together and shown one at a time, can be used in both formal and informal settings. Using a flip chart allows you to highlight the main points of your presentation, and present information in an appropriate sequence. Flip charts work best when used in a small, well-lighted room.

Figure 1-10	Flip charts show sequence

The disadvantages of flip charts are that they are too small to be seen in large rooms or by large audiences, they require significant advance preparation, and they are cumbersome.

Using Posters

Posters, written summaries of your presentation that can be displayed on stationary blackboards or attached to the walls of a room, are effective for letting audiences refer to your presentation before or after the event. Posters are especially prevalent at academic or professional conferences, and presenters often stand by their posters to answer questions from the audience.

Posters provide visual summaries **Figure 1-11**

Because posters usually contain professional lettering, as well as technical graphics and illustrations, they can't be easily revised, and they do require advance preparation.

Using Black-and-White or Color Overheads

Overheads, transparent sheets that enable text and visuals to be projected onto a screen, are used frequently, but equipment for showing them must be available. Creating overheads can be as simple as copying your presentation notes onto the overhead transparencies. Overheads do require some advance preparation, however, or they look amateurish or uninteresting. In addition, overheads are ineffective if the lettering is too small or too dense.

Overheads focus attention **Figure 1-12**

Overheads allow for flexibility in your presentation as they can quickly be reorganized or adjusted, as necessary. You can also draw on overheads using a transparency marker during your presentation.

Using Handouts

Handouts, sheets of paper summarizing key points of your presentation or numerical data, give your listeners something to take with them following your presentation. Handouts can assist your listeners in understanding difficult concepts, and can also alleviate the difficulties of taking notes.

Figure 1-13 ▶ **Handouts alleviate note taking**

Although handouts are helpful, they require advance preparation to look professional. Also, be careful that your handouts don't detract from your presentation by enticing your audience to pay more attention to them than your presentation.

Using 35mm Slides

Using **35mm slides**, photographic transparencies that are projected onto a screen, requires advance preparation, so you must allow enough time to take pictures, and have them developed into professional-looking slides. Slides are especially good for presentations in a formal setting, in large rooms, or with large audiences. Slides require that you turn the lights down, however, which makes it difficult for you to see your presentation notes, for the audience to take notes, and for some people to stay awake. In addition, using slides forces you to choose between facing your audience and standing at a distance from the slide projector, or standing behind the slide projector and talking to the backs of your audience.

You can increase the effectiveness of your slide presentation by using a hand-held remote to advance your slides, and a laser pointer to draw attention to important aspects of the slides. Or, you could give the presentation in tandem with someone else—you as the presenter and the other person as the operator of the equipment.

Using Electronic On-Screen Presentations

Electronic on-screen presentations (presentations created with Microsoft PowerPoint, Corel Presentations, or other presentation software and projected onto a screen) allow you to create professional-looking presentations with a consistent visual design. They also enable you to incorporate other media into your presentations, such as photographs, sound, animation, and video clips. Electronic on-screen presentations are also easy to update or revise on the spot, and can easily be converted into other media, such as overheads, posters, or 35mm slides.

Incorporate other media ◄ **Figure 1-15**

Electronic on-screen presentations require special equipment such as a computer projection system which may not always be available. And, sometimes you must present your computer presentation in a darkened room, making it difficult for you to see your notes and for your listeners to take notes. You can reduce the difficulty by asking someone else to operate the computer equipment for you.

In addition, electronic on-screen presentations require advance preparation and set up to ensure compatibility of the computer, the projection system, and the disk containing your presentation files. Moreover, many presenters create on-screen presentations that are too elaborate, rather than being simple and straightforward.

Reference Window

Strengths and Weaknesses of Presentation Media

Type of Medium	Strengths	Weaknesses	Audience Size	Advance Preparation	Formality
Chalkboard, Whiteboard or Notepad	Enables audience input; good for summarizing; adaptable	Must write and talk simultaneously, requires good handwriting and spelling	Small	None required	Informal
Flip chart	Can highlight main points and sequence information	Too small to be seen in large room	Small	Required	Formal and Informal
Posters	Can be referred to following your presentation; good for displaying other materials	Can't be easily revised; needs explanation	Medium, Large	Required	Formal and Informal
Overheads	Equipment readily available; adaptable; can draw on	Often boring, uninteresting, or ineffective	Medium, Large	Required	Formal and Informal
Handouts	Alleviates taking notes; can be referred to later	Can distract from your presentation	Small, Medium, Large	Required	Formal and Informal
35mm slides	Good for formal presentations in large rooms	Difficult to see your notes and to advance slides; require special equipment	Large	Extensive preparation	Formal
Electronic on-screen slides	Incorporates media; good for formal presentations in large rooms	May be too elaborate or distracting; require special equipment	Small, Large	Extensive preparation	Formal

Since every medium has its disadvantages, you might want to use more than one medium in your presentation. At the college, you'll give your presentation in a room that isn't equipped with a computer projection system, but does have a large chalkboard and overhead projector. So you might want to create a poster displaying photographs of YES! activities and participants, show an overhead transparency explaining how the partnership between YES! and the university would work, and prepare a handout containing information on YES! service projects.

No matter what media you use, your goal should be to keep your presentation simple and to adapt it to the purpose, audience, and situation of each unique situation.

Figure 1-16 provides a basic worksheet for helping you assess the situation and media for this and other presentations.

Situation and Media Assessment worksheet ◄ **Figure 1-16**

Situation and Media Assessment
Worksheet

How much time will you have for your presentation and the setup? _____

How large will your audience be? _____

How formal will the setting be? _____

What will the room be like and how will it be arranged? _____

What equipment will be available for your presentation? Check all that apply.
☐ Chalkboard
☐ Whiteboard
☐ Notepad and easel
☐ Stationary posterboard
☐ Overhead projector
☐ Slide projector
☐ Computer projection system

What other aspects must you consider for your presentation?
Temperature _____
Lighting _____
Noise and distractions _____
Other _____

Who will assist you with the equipment and other situational aspects?
Friend or colleague _____
Media or custodial staff _____
Other _____

How will you introduce yourself and your qualifications?
_____
_____
_____

What media will be appropriate for your presentation? Check appropriate media and explain.
☐ Chalkboard _____
☐ Whiteboard _____
☐ Notepad and easel _____
☐ Flip chart _____
☐ Poster _____
☐ Black-and-white or color overheads _____
☐ Handouts _____
☐ 35mm slides _____
☐ Computer Projected visuals, such as PowerPoint slides _____

Session 1.1 Quick Check

Review

1. Define and give examples for the following types of presentations:
   a. informative presentation
   b. persuasive presentation
   c. demonstration or training session
2. In two or three sentences, describe how knowing the education level of an audience would affect a presentation on trademarks and copyright laws.
3. List at least two important questions you should ask as part of assessing the presentation situation.

4. Consider the following presentations. In each instance, list two media that would be effective for that presentation, and explain why you think those media would be effective. Then list two media that would be ineffective for that presentation and explain why.
   a. a presentation at the local hardware store to eight to 10 homeowners on how to successfully remodel a kitchen
   b. a presentation at a hotel ballroom to 40 to 50 convention planners on why they should hold their next convention in Colorado Springs
   c. a presentation to two or three administrative staff at a local business on how to conduct a successful Web conference
5. List two media that are useful for recording comments from the audience.
6. If you want to use sound and animation in your presentation, which medium should you use?

Session 1.2

Focusing Your Presentation

Once you determine your purpose, analyze your audience's needs and expectations, and assess the particular situation in which you'll give your presentation, you need to plan the content of your presentation. You should begin by identifying the major points or main ideas that are directly relevant to your listeners' needs and interests, and then focus on those.

One of the biggest problems every presenter faces is how to provide **focus**, that is, narrowing the topic to make it manageable. Your tendency will be to want to include every aspect of a topic, but trying to cover everything usually means that you'll give your audience irrelevant information and lose their interest. Focusing on one aspect of a topic is like bringing a picture into focus with your camera—it clarifies your subject and allows you to emphasize interesting details. Failing to focus in presentations, like in photography, always brings disappointment to you and your audience.

How you focus your topic will depend upon the purpose, audience, and situation for your presentation. Remember, the narrower the topic, the more specific and interesting the information will be. Strategies for focusing or limiting your presentation topic are the same as those you would use to limit the scope of any written document—focus on a particular time or chronology, geography or region, category, component or element, segment or portion of a procedure, or point of view.

- **Time or chronology**: Limiting a topic by time means you focus on a few years, rather than trying to cover the entire history of a topic. Unfocused: The history of Egypt from 640 to 2000. Focused: The history of Egypt during the Nasser years (1952–1970).
- **Geography or region**: Limiting a topic by geography or region means you look at a topic as it relates to a specific location. Unfocused: Fly fishing. Focused: Fly fishing in western Colorado.
- **Category or classification**: Limiting a topic by category means you focus on one member of a group or on a limited function. Unfocused: Thermometers. Focused: Using bimetallic-coil thermometers to control bacteria in restaurant-prepared foods.
- **Component or element**: Limiting a topic by component or element means you focus on one small aspect or part of an organization or problem. Unfocused: Business trends. Focused: Blending accounting practices and legal services, a converging trend in large businesses.

- **Segment or portion**: Limiting a topic by segment or portion means you focus on one part of a process or procedure. Unfocused: Designing, manufacturing, characterizing, handling, storing, packaging, and transporting of optical filters. Focused: Acceptance testing of optical filters.
- **Point of view**: Limiting a topic by point of view means you look at a topic from the perspective of a single group. Unfocused: Employee benefits. Focused: How employers can retain their employees by providing child-care assistance and other nontraditional benefits.

Reference Window

Ways to Limit Your Topic

- Time or chronology
- Geography or region
- Category or classification
- Component or element
- Segment or portion of a process or procedure
- Point of view or perspective

In your presentation about YES! at Rocky Mountain State College, you'll need to limit your topic. You decide to discuss only current programs needing volunteers, not past or future programs. You'll also limit your presentation to service opportunities in the Colorado Springs area, and not include opportunities at the YES! satellite programs throughout the state. In addition, you'll only present information on volunteer programs, not fundraising, budgeting, or legal functions. Further, you'll only discuss how student volunteers assist with recreation therapy, not physical therapy. Finally, you'll approach your topic from a student volunteer's perspective.

Identifying Your Main Ideas

As you identify your **main ideas**, or key points of your presentation, you should phrase them as conclusions you want your audience to draw from your presentation. This helps you to continue to design your presentation with the listener in mind.

Your main ideas for your presentation about YES! at Rocky Mountain State College include:

1. University students and their communities benefit when students volunteer with non-profit organizations such as YES!.
2. Students learn as they participate in service that meets a community need.
3. Students can apply what they learn in the classroom to help solve many social and economic problems in the community.
4. A formal partnership between YES! and the university would assist students in obtaining course credit for their service with nonprofit organizations.

You're now prepared to consider the content and organization of your presentation. In the sections that follow, you'll formulate the general organization of your presentation.

Organizing Your Presentation

Once you've finished planning your presentation, you'll need to assemble the content or ideas of your presentation, and organize them in a logical manner. There are many different ways to organize or arrange your presentation, depending upon your purpose, the needs of your audience, and a particular speaking situation. In general, all good presentations start with an effective introduction, continue with a well-organized body, and end with a strong conclusion. See Figure 1-17.

Figure 1-17 ▶ **Introduction, body, and conclusion**

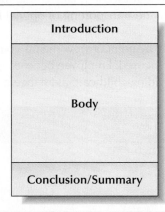

The **introduction**, or opening statements of a presentation, enables you to gain your listeners' attention, establish a relationship with your audience, and preview your main ideas. The body of your presentation is where you'll present pertinent information, solid evidence, and important details. The conclusion allows you to restate your main points, suggest appropriate actions, and recommend further resources.

Reference Window | **General Organization of Presentations**

- Introduction
  - Gains and keeps attention of audience
  - Creates a favorable impression
  - Establishes your credibility
  - Provides overview of presentation
- Body
  - Follows main points of presentation
  - Provides evidence and support for main points
  - Presents research in adequate detail
  - Shows relevance of data
- Conclusion
  - Restates main points of presentation
  - Suggests appropriate action
  - Recommends ways of finding additional data

In the next section, you'll learn how to develop the introduction to your presentation.

Developing an Introduction

Your introduction is the most important part of your entire presentation because it provides your listeners' first impression of you and your presentation, and sets the tone for the rest of your presentation. An effective introduction enables you to gain your listeners' attention, establish a rapport with your audience, and provide your listeners with an organizational overview or preview of your presentation.

Gaining Your Audience's Attention

Your first task in giving an effective presentation is to gain and keep your audience's attention. Even if your audience is interested in your topic, they can be easily distracted, so it's important to create an effective introduction that will immediately grab their attention. Here are some ways to gain your audience's attention:

- Anecdotes, stories, or personal experiences
- Surprising statistics or relevant data
- A quotation, familiar phrase, or definition
- Rhetorical questions or unresolved issues and problems
- Comments about the audience or occasion
- Audience participation
- Statement of your topic

Using Anecdotes

Think back to a presentation you attended recently. What do you remember most about it? Isn't it a story or experience that sticks out most in your mind? **Anecdotes**, short stories or experiences that demonstrate a specific point, help you to gain your listeners' attention because they draw the listener into your topic and make the topic more personal. Sharing a personal experience helps your audience relate to you as a real person and makes your topic more relevant.

You could begin your presentation at Rocky Mountain State College by relating your personal experience in meeting Chad, a handicapped youth who you helped:

"During my junior year at Rocky Mountain State College, I volunteered to help out at a Sports Camp sponsored by a local nonprofit organization called YES!. At the Sports Camp, I met Chad, a 14-year-old who suffers from cerebral palsy. Chad didn't have a lot of friends and spent his time after school alone, playing computer games. During camp, I helped Chad learn to play basketball. Now he spends some of his time after school playing basketball with other kids he met at camp. I'm glad I could help Chad and other kids become more confident and make new friends. But I benefited, also. My Recreation Management major now has new meaning. I see how the things I learn in class can be applied in the real world to help kids like Chad."

Using Statistics and Quantitative Data

Interesting statistics and quantitative data relating to the needs of your audience can increase the listeners' interest in knowing more about your topic. Make sure, however, that the statistics and data you use are current, accurate, and easily understood.

In your presentation at Rocky Mountain State College you could refer to interesting and related data:

"Last year, Coloradoans showed their commitment to solving some of our community's problems by donating $827,000 to more than 85 nonprofit organizations in the state. But money isn't the only donation these nonprofits need. Many of them would benefit greatly from a generous donation of your time."

Using Quotations, Familiar Phrases, and Definitions

Short quotes, familiar phrases, or definitions can effectively gain your audience's attention because they lead into the rest of your talk. You could use the following quotation to introduce your presentation at Rocky Mountain State College:

"'A man of words and not of deeds is like a garden full of weeds.' That simple adage could describe our students who currently can't take advantage of opportunities for experiential learning, because Rocky Mountain State College has no academic internship programs or partnerships with local service organizations."

Using Questions

Asking questions to introduce your topic can be effective if the questions are thought-provoking and the issues are important. **Rhetorical questions**—questions you don't expect the audience to answer—are especially effective. You should exercise caution, however, and not use too many questions. You should also be aware that someone in the audience might call out humorous or otherwise unwanted answers to your questions, detracting from the effectiveness of your introduction, and putting you in an awkward position.

Some examples of rhetorical questions you could use in your presentation at Rocky Mountain State College include:

"Why have colleges and universities across the country begun to establish partnerships with local nonprofit organizations? [Pause] What are the benefits of volunteerism for college students? [Pause] What can we as student leaders do to receive course credit while solving some of the problems in the Colorado Springs community?"

Commenting About the Audience or Occasion

Comments about the audience or occasion enable you to show your enthusiasm about the group you're addressing, as well as about your topic. Remember, however, that your comments should be brief and sincere. Referring to the occasion can be as simple as:

- "I'm happy you've given me an opportunity to express my views about creating a partnership between Rocky Mountain State College and local nonprofit organizations."
- "As you know, Joni de Paula, our student-body president, has invited me to tell you about my experience as an intern with YES!, a local nonprofit organization."
- "As student leaders at Rocky Mountain State College, you're probably interested in the growing movement in higher education to give students college credit for their work in solving local community problems."

Using Audience Participation

Audience participation, allowing your audience to be actively involved in your presentation, encourages the audience to add their ideas to your presentation, rather than to simply sit and listen. Audience participation is especially effective in small group settings or situations where you're attempting to find new ways to approach ideas. Audience participation can also consist of asking for volunteers from the audience to help with your demonstration, or asking audience members to give tentative answers to an informal quiz or questionnaire, and then adjusting your presentation to accommodate their responses.

Audiences remember participation **Figure 1-18**

In your presentation at Rocky Mountain State College, you might ask a few members of the audience to express their feelings about their volunteer efforts in the past.

Stating Your Purpose Statement

Simply stating your purpose statement works well as an introduction if your audience is already interested in your topic, or your time is limited. Most audiences, however, will appreciate a more creative approach than simply stating, "I'm going to persuade you to support a partnership between Rocky Mountain State University and YES!, a local non-profit organization." Instead, you might say something like, "My purpose is to discuss a situation that affects almost every student at Rocky Mountain State University."

Because you'll be giving many presentations throughout your career, you'll want to be on the lookout for ideas for effective introductions. You might want to keep a presentations file for collecting interesting stories and quotations that you can use in preparing future presentations.

Ways to Gain Your Audience's Attention

Reference Window

Method for Gaining Attention	Strength of Method
Anecdote or personal experience	Helps audience relate to you as a real person
Surprising statistic or relevant data	Increases audience interest in topic
Quotation, familiar phrase or definition	Leads in well to remainder of presentation
Rhetorical question or issue	Gets audience thinking about topic
Comment about the audience or occasion	Enables you to show your enthusiasm
Audience participation	Encourages audience to add their own ideas
Statement of the topic	Works well if audience is already interested

Establishing a Rapport with Your Audience

The methods you use to gain your audience's attention will determine whether you establish a **rapport** with the audience; in other words, decide how the audience responds to you and to your presentation. It's important, then, that whatever you do in your introduction creates a favorable impression with your audience, and helps you establish credibility.

If your audience is unfamiliar with you or no one formally introduces you, you should introduce yourself and provide your credentials to establish a rapport with your audience. Be careful not to spend much time on this, however, or to distance yourself from your audience by over-emphasizing your accomplishments.

In your presentation at Rocky Mountain State College, you might start out by simply saying, "Hi. I'm _____, a senior at RMSC and a Recreation Management major."

Providing an Overview of Your Presentation

One of the most important aspects of an introduction is to provide your audience with an overview of your presentation. Research indicates that **overviews**, sometimes called advance organizers or previews, prepare your audience for each point that will follow, and provide them with a structure for plugging in your main points. Overviews help your audience understand and remember your presentation because by providing a verbal road map of how your presentation is organized.

Overviews should be brief and simple, stating what you plan to do and in what order. After you've given your audience an overview of your presentation, it's important that you follow that same order.

Avoiding Common Mistakes in an Introduction

An inadequate introduction can ruin the rest of your presentation no matter how well you've prepared. So you should allow yourself plenty of time to carefully plan your introductions. In addition, you should consider these guidelines to avoid common mistakes:

- Don't begin by apologizing about any aspect of your presentation, such as how nervous you are, or your lack of preparation. Apologies destroy your credibility and guarantee that your audience will react negatively to what you present.
- Check the accuracy and currency of your stories, examples, and data. Audiences don't appreciate being misled, misinformed, or manipulated.
- Steer clear of anything potentially vulgar, ridiculing, or sexist. You won't be respected or listened to once you offend your audience.
- Don't use gimmicks to begin your presentation, such as making a funny face, singing a song, or ringing a bell. Members of your audience won't know how to respond and will feel uncomfortable.
- Avoid trite, flattering, or phony statements, such as, "Ladies and gentlemen, it is an unfathomable honor to be in your presence." Gaining respect requires treating your audience as your equal.

- Don't coerce people into participating. Always ask for volunteers. Putting reluctant members of your audience on the spot embarrasses everyone.
- Be cautious when using humor. It's difficult to predict how audiences will respond to jokes and other forms of humor; therefore, you should avoid using humor unless you know your audience well.

Once you've introduced your topic, you're ready to develop the body of your presentation.

Developing the Body of Your Presentation

To develop the **body**, the major points and details, of your presentation, you'll need to gather information on your topic, determine the organizational approach, add supporting details and other pertinent information, and provide transitions from one point to the next.

Gathering Information

Most of the time, you'll give presentations on topics about which you're knowledgeable and comfortable. Other times, you might have to give presentations on topics that are new to you. In either case, you'll probably need to do research to provide additional information that is effective, pertinent, and up-to-date.

You can find additional materials on your topic by consulting:

- Popular press items from newspapers, radio, TV, and magazines. This information, geared for general audiences, provides large scale details and personal opinions that may need to be supplemented by additional research.

Using newspapers and magazines ◀ **Figure 1-19**

- Library resources such as books, specialized encyclopedias, academic journals, government publications, and other reference materials. You can access these materials using the library's card catalog, indexes, computer searches, and professional database services.

Figure 1-20 ▷ **Using information in libraries**

- Corporate documents and office correspondence. Since using these materials might violate your company's nondisclosure policy, you might need to obtain your company's permission, or get legal clearance beforehand.

Figure 1-21 ▷ **Using corporate documents**

- Experts and authorities in the field, or other members of your organization. Talking to other people who are knowledgeable about your topic will give you additional insight.

Talking to experts and authorities ◄ **Figure 1-22**

- Interviews, surveys, and observations. If you do your own interviews, surveys, and observations, be prepared with a list of specific questions, and always be respectful of other people's time.

Interviewing and surveying ◄ **Figure 1-23**

- Internet sources. The Web has become an excellent place to find information on any topic. Be sure, however, to evaluate the credibility of anything you obtain from these sources.

Figure 1-24 ▶ **Using the Internet**

For your presentation at Rocky Mountain State College, you located the following additional information: an article from the Colorado Springs Daily Scribe entitled, "YES! Helps Children Meet Their Challenges;" a book from the RMSC library entitled, *A Guidebook for Providing Opportunities for Experiential Education in Higher Education*; the YES! organization's latest annual report; an informal survey of 25 current interns showing their attitudes toward establishing a partnership between YES! and RMSC; and printouts of the YES! Web page describing the organization's funding sources and current activities.

After you fully research your topic, you're ready to organize the information in an understandable and logical manner so that your listeners can easily follow your ideas.

Organizing Your Information

You should choose an organizational approach for your information based upon the purpose, audience, and situation of each specific presentation. Sometimes your company or supervisor might ask you to follow a specific organizational pattern or **template** in giving your presentations. Other times you might be able to choose your own organizational approach. Some common approach options include: inductive, deductive, chronological, spatial, and problem-solution organizational patterns.

Organizing Information Inductively

When you begin with the individual facts and save your conclusions until the end of your presentation, you are using **inductive organization**. See Figure 1-25. Inductively organized presentations usually are more difficult to follow because the most important information may come at the end of a presentation. Inductive organization can be useful, however, when your purpose is to persuade your audience to follow an unusual plan of action, or you feel your audience might resist your conclusions.

Inductive organization ◀ Figure 1-25

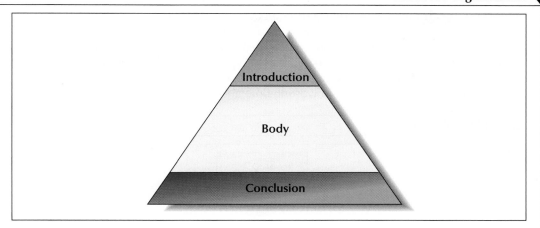

If you thought student leaders at Rocky Mountain State College would resist your recommendation (that $600,000 from student fees be allocated to the operating budget of a new Student Community Involvement Center), you would probably want to first present your reasons for making that recommendation.

Organizing Information Deductively

Deductive organization means that you present your conclusions or solutions first, and then explain the information that led you to reach your conclusions. See Figure 1-26. Deductive organization is the most common pattern used in business because it presents the most important or bottom-line information first.

Deductive organization ◀ Figure 1-26

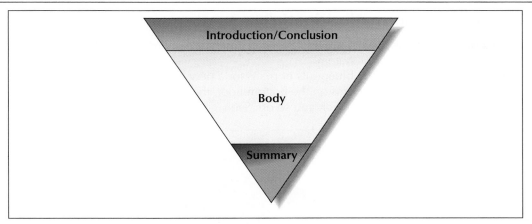

Deductive organization works well for informative presentations because it allows your audience to know your recommendations at the beginning of the presentation when their attention level is highest. Organizing your presentation at Rocky Mountain State College in a deductive manner would mean that you would begin by stating your opinion that student leaders should support an official partnership between the university and YES!, and then supporting that view with further information.

Organizing Information Chronologically

When you use **chronological organization**, you organize things according to a time sequence. See Figure 1-27. Chronological organization works best when you must present information in a step-by-step fashion, such as demonstrating a procedure, or training someone to use a piece of equipment. Failing to present sequential information in the proper order (such as how to bake a cake, or conduct a soil analysis) can leave your listeners confused, and might result in wasting time and resources.

Figure 1-27 ▶ **Chronological organization**

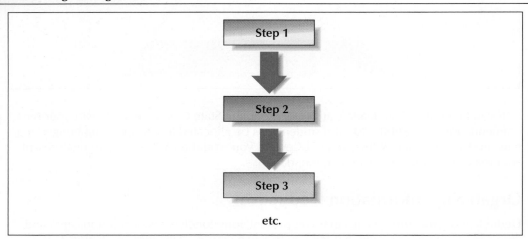

If you were explaining to administrators how to answer a Request for Proposal (RFP) to obtain government funding for YES! activities, you would need to explain how to complete the process in a specified sequence.

Organizing Information Spatially

Spatial organization is used to provide a logical and effective order for describing the physical layout of an item or system.

If you were describing the blueprints or plans for a new building for YES!, you would begin by describing all the rooms on the bottom floor, then proceed to the next floor and describe all the rooms on that floor, and so on. See Figure 1-28.

Figure 1-28 ▶ **Spatial organization**

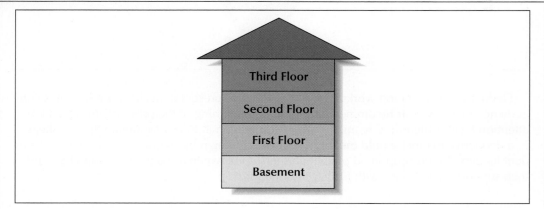

Organizing Information by Problem and Solutions

Problem-solution organization consists of presenting a problem, outlining various solutions to the problem, and then explaining the solution you recommend. Problem-solution presentations work best when your purpose is to recommend a specific action or solution over several alternative actions or solutions.

Reference Window

Ways to Organize Your Presentation

Organizational Pattern	Explanation of Pattern	Type of Presentation
Deductive	Present conclusions or solutions first	Informative presentations
Inductive	Present conclusions or solutions last	Persuasive presentations
Chronological	Order by time sequence	Demonstrations and training
Spatial	Order by space or position	Physical layouts
Problem-solution	Present problem and various solutions, then recommend solution	Persuasive presentations

Supporting Your Main Points

In every presentation, it's important to keep the information simple and relevant. Research has shown that our short-term memory limits what we can recall to a maximum of seven chunks of information, and that we remember specific, concrete details long after we remember generalities or unrelated pieces of information.

You should, therefore, support the main points of your presentation with evidence in the form of specific reasons, explanations, examples, data, or agreement of experts. In addition, you should try to intersperse difficult concepts with easier-to-understand material, and try to move from what your audience already understands to new information.

Providing Transitions

In any presentation, you need to provide **transitions**, organizational signposts that indicate the organization and structure of your presentation. Transitions enable your listeners to realize that you're shifting gears or moving to a new topic. Effective transitions help your audience mentally summarize what you have discussed previously and prepare themselves for what you'll discuss next. Transitions also enable you to pause briefly to check your notes or to reestablish eye contact with your audience.

Appropriate transitions include words that indicate you will provide examples, make additional points, compare similar concepts, discuss results, or make recommendations. Transitions may include:

Using Transitions

Purpose	Word or Phrase
Provide examples	For example, For instance, To illustrate
Make additional points	In addition, Furthermore, Next, Now I will discuss
Establish order	First, Second, Third
Compare	Likewise, In the same manner, Let's consider another
Discuss results	Consequently, Therefore, Thus
Summarize	In brief, To conclude, To move to my last point, Finally
Recommend	I'd like to suggest, What do we do now?

Now that you've developed an effective body for your presentation by supporting your main points with adequate details and creating effective transitions, you're ready to develop a conclusion or summary.

Developing Your Summary or Conclusion

The ending or final part of your presentation should take the form of a summary or **conclusion**. Summaries and conclusions are valuable because they help your listeners remember important information from your presentation and allow you to reemphasize your main points. Your conclusion leaves your audience with a final impression of you and your presentation, so you don't want to leave your conclusion to chance. Plan to spend as much time on the conclusion as you did on your introduction.

The following suggestions will help you create an effective summary or conclusion:

- Use a clear transition to move into your conclusion. This will signal your audience that you're moving from the body of your presentation to the closing statements.
- Recap or restate the key ideas of your presentation. Repeating the main points of your presentation will help your audience remember what you covered.
- Review the relevancy or importance of what you said. Don't introduce new ideas; simply remind your audience why they should care about your topic.
- If appropriate, suggest a clear action step or plan. If your purpose was to persuade your audience to take a specific action, you should use your conclusion to suggest what the audience should do now.
- If possible, suggest where your audience can find additional resources by providing important phone numbers, addresses, e-mail addresses, or Web addresses.
- Relate your conclusion to your introduction. Some experts suggest writing your conclusion at the same time you write your introduction to assure that they both provide the same focus. Whenever you write your conclusion, compare it to your introduction to make sure they are complementary.
- Don't end with an apology or trite statement like "I see my time is up, so I'll quit." When you're finished, say "Thank you," and sit down.

In your presentation at Rocky Mountain State College, you could conclude your presentation by stating, "Now that you've seen how a formal partnership between YES! and the university would work, I'd like to briefly summarize the main points I've made today. First, university students and the communities in which they live both benefit when students volunteer with nonprofit organizations. Second, students become active learners as they apply what they learn in the classroom to help solve community problems. Finally, it's important to establish a formal partnership between these nonprofit organizations and the university so that students can obtain course credit for their work. By allocating $600,000 from student fees toward the operating budget of a new Student Community Involvement Center, you can help students take advantage of opportunities for experiential learning, while helping Chad and the 1300 other young people like him."

Figure 1-29 provides a basic worksheet for helping you determine the focus and organization for this and other presentations.

Focus and Organization worksheet | **Figure 1-29**

Focus and Organization
Worksheet

How will you focus your presentation?
Time or chronology _____
Geography or region _____
Category or classification _____
Component or element _____
Segment or portion _____
Point of view _____

What are your main ideas for your presentation?
_____
_____
_____

How will you gain your audience's attention?
Anecdote, story, or personal experience _____
Statistic or relevant data _____
Quotation, familiar phrase, or definition _____
Rhetorical question, issue, or problem _____
Comment about audience or situation _____
Audience participation _____
Statement of topic _____

How will you establish a rapport with your audience?
_____
_____

Where can you find additional information about your presentation?
Newspapers or magazines _____
Library resources _____
Corporate documents _____
Experts and authorities _____
Interviews and surveys _____
Internet sources _____

How will you organize your information? Check one and then explain it.
☐ Inductively ☐ Deductively ☐ Chronologically ☐ Spatially ☐ Problem/Solution
_____
_____

How will you support your main points?
_____
_____

What transitions will you use?
_____
_____

How will you conclude or summarize your presentation?
_____
_____

Session 1.2 Quick Check

Review

1. List three methods for focusing your topic.
2. Determine which methods have been used to focus the following topics: (a) Creating E-commerce Solutions for Small Business Owners (b) How to Submit Winning Bids: Obtaining Government Contracts.
3. Why should you phrase the main ideas of your presentation as conclusions you want your audience to draw?
4. What are the three basic parts of every presentation, and what is the purpose of each part?
5. List one advantage for each of the following ways to gain your audience's attention: (a) personal experience (b) statistics or data (c) rhetorical questions.
6. List four places to find additional materials on a topic.

7. What is the difference between organizing your presentation deductively and inductively, and when would you use each of these organizational patterns?
8. Give an example of a transitional phrase you could use to indicate that you're moving to your next main point.

Review

Tutorial Summary

In this tutorial, you learned how to plan your presentation by determining the purpose and outcome of your presentation and how to analyze the needs and expectations of your audience. You learned how to assess the situation for giving your presentation and how to select appropriate media. In addition, you learned how to focus and organize your presentation and how to develop an effective introduction, body, and conclusion for your presentation.

Key Terms

35mm slides
anecdote
audience participation
body
chronological organization
conclusion
deductive organization
demographic characterisitcs
demonstration
electronic on-screen
    presentation

flip chart
focus
handouts
inductive organization
informative presentation
introduction
main ideas
media
outcome
overheads
overview

persuasive presentation
posters
problem-solution
    organization
rapport
rhetorical question
situation
spatial organization
template
training presentation
transition

Practice

Practice the skills you learned in the tutorial using the same case scenario.

Review Assignments

While you're preparing your presentation to student leaders at Rocky Mountain State College, your supervisor, Kenna McNaughton, decides to have you give three presentations at Kennedy High School, also in Colorado Springs.

The first presentation will be a 30-minute, informative presentation on the value of community service. You'll give this presentation, as part of a school assembly, to over 200 students in a large, computer-equipped auditorium with fixed seating.

The second presentation will be a 15-minute, persuasive presentation to teachers on giving credit for service assignments. You'll give this presentation as part of a faculty in-service meeting, to approximately 35 teachers in a faculty lounge with small tables and movable chairs.

The third presentation will be a 50-minute presentation for Senior class officers on how to plan a successful service project. You'll give this presentation as part of a leadership training session, to about six students in a medium-sized classroom with movable desks. Do the following:

1. Complete a Purpose and Outcomes Worksheet for the three types of presentations.
2. Explain differences and similarities between the three groups in terms of the following demographic features: age, gender, and level of education. Then complete an Audience Analysis Worksheet for the three types of presentations.

3. Explain how the settings for these presentations will affect your audience's expectations and the appropriate level of formality. Then complete a Situation and Media Assessment Worksheet for the three types of presentations.
4. Determine appropriate and inappropriate media for each of the three presentations.
5. Give an example of how you could focus the topic for the first presentation by limiting it by geography or region.
6. Give an example of how you could focus the second presentation by limiting it by point of view.
7. Give an example of how you could focus the third presentation by limiting it by category or classification.
8. Prepare an introduction for the first presentation using a story or anecdote. (You may create a fictional anecdote.)
9. Prepare an introduction for the second presentation using rhetorical questions.
10. Prepare an introduction for the third presentation using some kind of audience participation.
11. List two places to find additional information on the topics of each of these presentations.
12. Determine an appropriate organizational pattern for each of the three presentations.
13. Complete a Focus and Organization Worksheet for each of the three presentations.

Case Problem 1

Apply

Apply the skills you learned to prepare three presentations for a company marketing home security products.

Safelee Home Security Products Sudhir Raguskus is director of marketing for Safelee Home Security Products. The company currently markets a new line of home security systems that includes hardware (alarms, automated lighting, and deadbolt locks) and monitoring services. Sudhir asks you to help prepare presentations for his company. Do the following:

1. Complete a Purpose and Outcomes Worksheet for each of these audiences: (a) sales personnel (b) potential clients (c) public safety officials who will be notified by Safelee in cases of emergency
2. Explain the differences and similarities between the above three groups in terms of the following demographic features: age, level of education, and familiarity with the subject. Complete an Audience Analysis Worksheet for each of the three presentations.
3. Explain the likely settings for these presentations and how these will affect your audience's expectations and dictate the appropriate level of formality.
4. Determine appropriate and inappropriate media for each of the three presentations. Complete a Situation and Media Assessment Worksheet for each of the three presentations.
5. Give an example of how to focus or limit each presentation.
6. Identify three main ideas of your presentation to potential clients.
7. Prepare an appropriate introduction for each presentation. (Some of your introductory information may be fictional.)
8. Determine how to establish a rapport with public safety officials.
9. List two places to find additional information on the topics of each of these presentations.
10. Determine an appropriate organizational pattern for each of the three presentations.
11. Write an effective conclusion for each of the three presentations.
12. Complete a Focus and Organization Worksheet for each of the three presentations.

Research

Use the Internet to research the American Cancer Society and prepare a presentation with another student.

Case Problem 2

American Cancer Society The American Cancer Society is a well-known nonprofit organization with chapters in nearly every state and county. Working with another member of the class, create a team presentation to inform your classmates about the goals and programs of the American Cancer Society organization in your area. Obtain information about the organization by searching the Internet.

1. Decide on a type of presentation.
2. Complete a Purpose and Outcomes Worksheet.
3. Define your audience according to their general demographic features of age, gender, level of education, and familiarity with your topic.
4. Explain how the demographic characteristics of your audience will affect your presentation. Then complete an Audience Analysis Worksheet.
5. Describe the setting for your presentation and the size of your audience. Then complete a Situation and Media Assessment Worksheet.
6. Select appropriate media for your presentation and explain why they are appropriate. Explain why other media are inappropriate.
7. Show two ways to focus your presentation and limit the scope of your topic.
8. Each of you should select a method for gaining your audience's attention and write an introduction using that method. Discuss the strengths of each method for your particular audience.
9. Create an advance organizer, or overview.
10. Identify at least two sources for information on your topic and consult those sources. For one of your sources, connect to the Internet and go the American Cancer Society's Web site at **www.cancer.org**. To find a second source, use a search engine and try searching for information on "American Cancer Society goals." Print out at least one page of information that supports the main points of your presentation.
11. Select an appropriate organizational pattern for your presentation. Explain why that pattern is appropriate.
12. Identify four transitional phrases that you'll use.
13. Write a summary for your presentation recapping the key ideas.
14. Complete a Focus and Organization Worksheet.

Apply

Apply the skills you learned to prepare a presentation about a recent event such as a concert, sports event, or movie.

Case Problem 3

EVENTix EVENTix owns and operates transactional kiosks that sell mall gift certificates and event/entertainment tickets. Konda Cameron, marketing director for EVENTix, asks you to prepare several presentations about EVENTix. Do the following:

1. Think of the most recent event (such as a concert, sports event, or movie) that you attended. Complete a Purpose and Outcomes Worksheet for a presentation to participants of the event, trying to convince them that they should purchase future events tickets from EVENTix.
2. Complete a Purpose and Outcomes Worksheet for a presentation to participants of the event, explaining how to obtain tickets from an EVENTix kiosk.
3. Complete a Purpose and Outcomes Worksheet for a presentation to participants of the event, informing them of other events for which EVENTix sells tickets.
4. Konda asks you to present information about EVENTix's gift certificate programs at a retailers convention. You'll give your 15-minute presentation in the ballroom of a hotel to over 300 conference attendees. Describe how your presentation will be influenced by this situation. Complete an Audience Analysis Worksheet.
5. Determine appropriate media for the convention presentation if no on-screen technology is available.

6. Complete a Situation and Media Assessment Worksheet.
7. Give an example of how to focus your topic for this particular audience.
8. Create an appropriate attention-getting introduction for your presentation. Explain why other attention getters might be inappropriate.
9. Determine an appropriate organizational pattern.
10. Complete a Focus and Organization Worksheet.

Case Problem 4

Research

Research and analyze how another person has used or failed to use the principles you learned in this tutorial in an oral presentation.

Analyzing an Oral Presentation Attend or read a presentation, lecture, or speech and, if possible, obtain a transcript of the presentation. For example, you might hear a political speech or attend an academic presentation. Make copies of your notes or the complete transcript of the presentation for your teacher. Do the following:

1. Complete a Purpose and Outcomes Worksheet.
2. Describe the audience for the presentation, including any general demographics that you can determine. Complete an Audience Analysis Worksheet.
3. Describe where the presentation was given, including the setting and the number of people attending the presentation.
4. Describe the media the speaker used for the presentation. Explain whether or not you feel the media were appropriate, and whether other media would have been more effective. (For instance, if overheads were used, would it have been more effective to use an online electronic presentation?) Complete a Situation and Media Assessment Worksheet.
5. Identify how the speaker established a rapport with the audience.
6. Describe any mistakes the speaker may have made in apologizing to the audience, or failing to consider the needs of the audience. How could these mistakes have been prevented?
7. Determine the structure of the presentation. If you have a written copy of the presentation, mark the introduction, body, and conclusion on the copy.
8. Describe how the speaker gained the audience's attention.
9. Identify whether the speaker provided an overview, or preview, of the presentation. If you have a written copy of the presentation, underline any overviews or previews.
10. Identify the major points in the presentation. If you have a written copy of the presentation, underline the details the presenter used to support these major points.
11. Identify the organizational pattern used in the presentation. Explain whether or not you think the organizational pattern was effective, or if another organizational pattern might have been better.
12. Identify any transitional phrases the speaker used.
13. Describe how the speaker ended the presentation. Explain whether or not you felt the ending was effective.
14. Complete a Focus and Organization Worksheet.
15. Interview a professional in your field and ask about the types of presentations he or she gives. Organize these into the types of presentations given above. Explain your findings.

Quick Check Answers

Session 1.1

1. a. explains background information, knowledge, and details about a topic; academic and professional conference presentations, briefings, reviews, reports, meetings, luncheon or dinner speeches, informal symposia.
    b. convinces audience to feel or act a certain way; recommendations, sales, action plans, strategy sessions, motivational speeches.
    c. demonstrations: show how something works; product and services overviews, computer software demonstrations. Training sessions: give hands-on practice and feedback on performance; employee orientation, seminars, workshops, classes, courses.
2. Audiences with specialized education, such as lawyers, would expect you to use specialized terms; audiences with less education would need more explanations and definitions.
3. How much time will I have? Will I be speaking alone? How large of an audience? How formal or informal of a setting? What will the room be like? How will the room be arranged? What equipment will be available? How much time will I have to set up? What other aspects must I consider? Will I need to introduce myself?
4. a. effective: flip chart, poster, handout; they work with small informal groups and don't require additional equipment. Ineffective: 35mm slides and computer-projected visuals; they're better for larger, more formal presentations.
    b. effective: posters, black-and-white or color overheads, 35mm slides, computer-projected visuals; they're better for large groups where visuals need to be enlarged, and for formal presentations.
    c. chalkboard, whiteboard, notepad, handout; they're best for small groups where audience involvement is important.
5. chalkboard, whiteboard, notepad
6. computer-projected slides

Session 1.2

1. by time or chronology, geography or region, category or classification, component or element, segment or portion, point of view
2. (a) category, component, point of view (b) category, component, segment
3. True
4. introduction (to gain and keep attention, create favorable impression, establish credibility, present overview), body (provide evidence and support for main points, present research, show relevance), conclusion (restate main points, suggest action, recommend additional sources)
5. (a) draw audience into the topic, makes topic more personal and relevant, helps audience relate to you as a person (b) increase interest in topic (c) address thought-provoking and important issues
6. popular press, library resources, corporate documents, experts, interviews, surveys, observations, Internet
7. deductive: presents conclusions first and reasoning second; informative presentations. inductive: presents reasons first, conclusions last; persuasive presentations, or when audience will resist conclusions
8. in addition, furthermore, next, now I will discuss

Objectives

Session 2.1
- Select and create appropriate and effective visuals
- Present your visuals effectively

Session 2.2
- Choose an appropriate delivery method
- Prepare for questions from the audience
- Overcome your nervousness and control your speaking anxiety
- Improve your delivery
- Analyze your non-verbal communication
- Give a collaborative presentation
- Set up for your presentation

Giving Your Presentation

Selecting Visuals and Practicing Your Presentation

Case

Giving Your Presentation at Rocky Mountain State College

Joni de Paula, student body president at Rocky Mountain State College (RMSC), invites you to talk about your experiences as a YES! intern with members of the RMSC Student Senate as part of their deliberations over a proposed partnership with local nonprofit organizations. You planned and organized your presentation; now you'll prepare to give it.

In this tutorial, you'll learn the benefits of using visuals in your presentations, and how to select and create appropriate visuals. You'll also choose an appropriate method for delivering your presentation, and learn ways to improve your delivery. Finally, you'll learn how to set up for your presentation.

Student Data Files

There are no student Data Files needed for this tutorial.

Understanding the Benefits of Using Visuals in Your Presentation

It's much more difficult for people to understand and remember what they hear versus what they see. You can help your listeners comprehend and retain the ideas from your presentation by supplementing your presentation with effective **visuals**, including tables, charts, graphs and illustrations. The old adage, "A picture is worth a thousand words" especially applies to presentations because listeners understand ideas faster when they can see and hear what you're talking about. Using visual aids to supplement your presentation does the following:

- increases your audience's understanding. Visuals are especially helpful in explaining a difficult concept, displaying data, and illustrating the steps in a process.
- helps listeners remember information. Audiences will remember information longer when you use visuals to highlight or exemplify your main points, review your conclusions, and explain your recommendations.
- highlights your organization. Visuals can serve the same purpose as headings in a printed manuscript by allowing your audience to see how all the parts of your presentation fit together. Visuals can also help you preview and review main points, and differentiate between the main points and the sub-points.
- adds credibility to your presentation. Speakers who use visuals in their presentation are judged by their audiences as more professional and better prepared, as well as more interesting.
- stimulates and maintains your listeners' attention. It's much more interesting to see how something functions, rather than just hear about it. Giving your listeners somewhere to focus their attention keeps them from being distracted or bored.
- varies the pace of your presentation. Visuals enable you to provide sensory variety in your presentation, and keep your presentation from becoming monotonous.
- keeps you on track. Visuals not only benefit your audience, but also help you by providing a means for remembering what you want to say, and for staying on track.

In your presentation at Rocky Mountain State College, if you want to present information showing how the number of students involved in internships has dramatically increased in the last few years, you could simply read a summary of the numbers, as shown in Figure 2-1.

Figure 2-1 ▶ **Written summary**

Internship Data Presented in Verbal Format

"In the fall of 1993, the number of students at Rocky Mountain State College involved in internships, hit an unprecedented peak at 90. Then for the next three years, it fell almost steadily, dropping to 87 in 1994, 76 in 1995, 66 in 1996, and 43 in 1997. There was a slight upsurge in 1998 to 50, then another little drop in 1999 to 42. Then in 2000, the tide seemed to turn, as the number of interns began to go up, first to 52, then to 60 in 2001. In the four years from 2002 to 2006, the number of students opting for an internship more than doubled, as the number grew from 66 to 86 in 2002 and 2003. In 2004, the number of interns stood at 95, increasing to 113 in 2005 and 120 in 2006."

But reading a long series of numbers would be difficult for your audience to understand, and it would be boring. By using visuals, you can present the same data in a format that's easier to understand, and more interesting. You can present the data in tabular format, as shown in Figure 2-2.

Tabular summary ◄ **Figure 2-2**

Internship Data Presented in Visual Format

Year	Number of Interns
1993	90
1994	87
1995	76
1996	66
1997	43
1998	50
1999	42
2000	52
2001	60
2002	66
2003	86
2004	95
2005	113
2006	120

Or, you might want to create a graph instead, as shown in Figure 2-3.

Graphical summary ◄ **Figure 2-3**

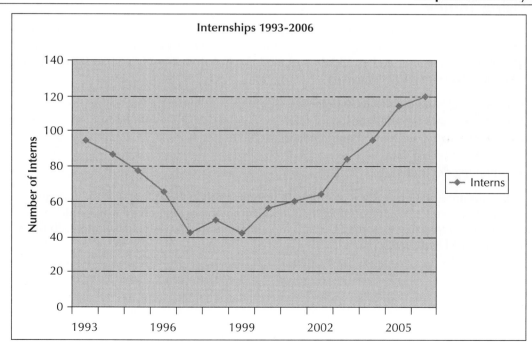

Using visuals improves the quality of your presentation, and enables your audience to better understand your presentation. Visuals add information, clarification, emphasis, variety, and even pizzazz to your presentation.

You can choose from many types of visuals for your presentations: tables (text and numerical), graphs (bar and line), charts (pie, organizational, flow), and illustrations (drawings and diagrams, maps, and photographs). In the past, creating visuals was expensive, but the recent development of inexpensive computer software allows you to quickly and inexpensively create tables and graphs, scan photographs, resize drawings, and download visuals from the Internet for your presentation.

To effectively use visuals in your presentations, you'll need to ask yourself which visuals are best for your particular purpose, audience, and situation. You should also ask yourself which visuals you can create effectively.

Reference Window

Selecting Appropriate Visuals

- Which visuals are suitable for my purpose and desired outcomes?
- Which visuals would my audience understand?
- Which visuals work best for the situation in which I'll give my presentation?
- Which visuals can I create effectively?

Answering these questions to the best of your ability will increase the chances that your visuals will be effective.

Selecting Appropriate Visuals for Your Purpose

The following sections provide suggestions to help you select appropriate visuals—tables, graphs, charts, or illustrations—for your particular purpose.

Using Tables

Tables are a visual method of organizing words and numerical data in horizontal rows and vertical columns. Tables are especially useful in informative presentations where your purpose is to provide your audience with specific information in a systematic and economical manner. Tables are also effective in:

- making facts and details accessible
- organizing data by categories
- summarizing results and recommendations
- comparing sets of data
- facilitating decisions

In your presentation at RMSC, you might want to explain the many benefits students receive as a result of volunteering in their local communities. You could use a table to summarize and emphasize the broad benefits as well as the specific benefits within each main category. See Figure 2-4.

Benefits of Academic Volunteerism	
Category	**Specific Benefits**
Develops civic values	Focus on relationships, rather than content Understand other cultures and needs Gain sense of ethical duty
Improves professional development	Develop problem-solving skills Improve rhetorical skills Practice professional skills
Inspires students	Develop personal philosophy Become aware of learning Increase involvement

Or, perhaps you want to show the number of students who completed internships in one year. You could use a table to make those numbers more accessible to your audience. Using a table allows you to organize the number of interns according to semester, and the student's year in school. See Figure 2-5.

Number of Students Completing an Internship During the School Year 2005-2006 (by Semester)				
	Fall	**Summer**	**Winter**	**Total**
Freshman	0	2	2	4
Sophomore	1	6	3	10
Junior	11	13	13	37
Senior	15	14	15	44
Total	27	35	33	95

In both instances, using a table (Figures 2-4 and 2-5) allows you to organize the information so that your audience can quickly see and understand your presentation.

Using the Table feature of your word processor, you can create professional-looking tables. Remember to follow these suggestions to make your tables more effective:

- Keep the table simple. Limit the amount of text and numerical data you use. Dense text is difficult to read, and complex numbers are difficult to understand.
- Use a descriptive title and informative headings. Use a title that explains what you're summarizing or comparing, and label rows and columns so your readers know what they're looking at.
- Remove excess horizontal and vertical lines. To simplify your table, use as few vertical and horizontal lines as possible.
- Use shading and emphasis sparingly. Shading and textual features, such as bolding, italics, and underlining, can be distracting. Don't use heavy shading, and keep textual variety to the main headings.
- Align numbers by place value.
- Keep all numbers consistent in value and number of significant digits.

Whether or not you use a table in your presentation will depend on your purpose. Although tables are good for showing exact numbers (such as, how many Juniors completed an internship during fall semester), they're not as good for showing trends (for instance, the increase or decrease over the past five years in the number of internships).

Using Graphs

Graphs show the relationship between two variables along two axes or reference lines: the independent variable on the horizontal axis, and the dependent variable on the vertical axis. Like tables, graphs can show a lot of information concisely. Graphs are especially useful in informative presentations when you're showing quantities, or in persuasive presentations when you're comparing similar options using factors such as cost. Graphs are also effective for:

- comparing one quantity to another
- showing changes over time
- indicating patterns or trends

Common graphs include bar graphs and line graphs. **Column** and **bar graphs**, graphs that use horizontal or vertical bars to represent specific values, are useful in comparing the value of one item to another over a period of time, or a range of dates or costs. In your presentation at RMSC, suppose you want to show the difference between the number of men and women completing internships with nonprofit agencies over the past 13 years. By using a column or bar graph, you could easily compare the differences between students. See Figure 2-6.

Figure 2-6 ▶ **Column graph**

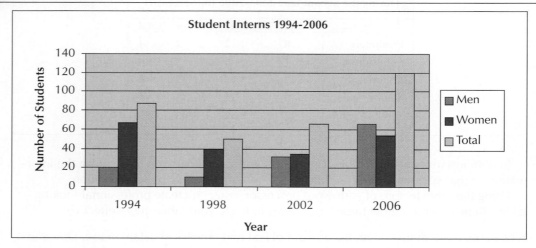

Line graphs, graphs that use points to represent the specific values and then join the points by a line, are especially effective for illustrating trends. You should use them instead of bar graphs when you have large amounts of information, and exact quantities don't require emphasis. Suppose you want to show the number of youths participating in YES!-sponsored activities during the first six months of each of the last three years (2004-2006). Using a column or bar graph would require 18 columns or bars. A more effective way to show the data would be a line graph, as shown in Figure 2-7. Your audience would immediately recognize that, while the number of youth participants has fluctuated in other years, it currently remains constant.

Line graph ◄ **Figure 2-7**

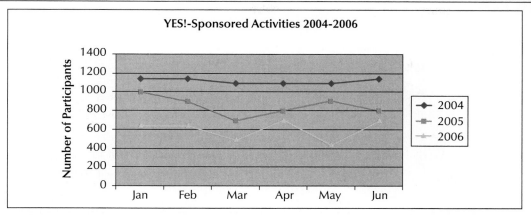

Whether or not you use a graph in your presentation will depend on your purpose. If you choose to use a graph, follow these guidelines:

- Keep graphs simple, clear, and easy to read. Limit the number of comparisons to no more than five.
- Compare values that are noticeably different. Comparing values that are similar means that all the bars will appear identical, and all the lines will overlap.
- Make each bar or line visually distinct. Use a different pattern, shade, or color for each line or bar in a group, and keep bars the same width.
- Label each line and bar. Remember that you're trying to help your listeners understand and use the information.
- Label both axes.

You can create simple bar graphs and line graphs by using the graphing feature of your spreadsheet or database program, or the chart feature of your word-processing or presentations program.

Using Charts

The terms chart and graph often are used interchangeably; however, they are distinct. **Charts** are visuals that use lines, arrows, and boxes or other shapes to show parts, steps, or processes. While charts show relationships, they don't use a coordinate system like graphs. Charts are especially helpful in presentations where your goal is to help your listener understand the relationships between the parts and the whole. Common charts include pie charts, organizational charts, and flowcharts.

Pie charts, charts that are shaped like a circle or pie, are best for showing percentages or proportions of the parts that make up a whole. Pie charts allow your listeners to compare the sections to each other, as well as to the whole. Pie charts can be created to display either the percentage relationship or the amount relationship.

Whether or not you use a pie chart in your presentation will depend on your purpose. In your presentation at RMSC, you want to explain how nonprofit organizations, such as YES!, provide assistance to the residents of the Colorado Springs area. You could do that by using a pie chart to show what percent of the agency's budget is allotted to its priority programs, such as self-sufficiency training. See Figure 2-8. Or, you could create the pie chart to show the amounts spent on each type of program.

Figure 2-8 | **Pie chart**

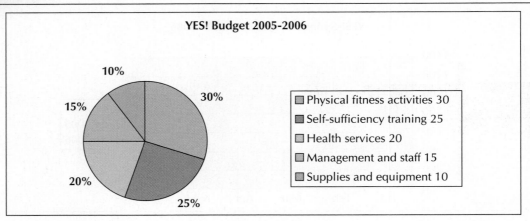

General suggestions for creating effective pie charts include:

- Keep slices of the pie relatively large. Comparisons of more than eight sections are difficult to see and differentiate. If necessary, combine several small sections into a section titled, "Other."
- Use a descriptive title for the whole and label each segment. Help your audience understand what you're comparing in terms of the whole, as well as each section of the pie. Keep all labels horizontal so they can be read easily.
- Make sure the parts add up to 100 percent.
- Begin the largest section at the top of the pie. The largest section should begin at the 12 o'clock position. The other sections should get smaller as they move around the pie clockwise, except for the "Other" section, which is usually the last section.
- Use a normal flat pie chart, unless it has fewer than five slices. In other words, you should not display the pie chart with 3D perspective, pulled-out pie slices, or in donut format. These effects can detract from seeing the pie as a whole, and can make the chart difficult to read.

You can create simple pie charts by entering your data into a spreadsheet program and then using the graphing feature of that program, or you can use a program such as Microsoft Chart directly in Word, PowerPoint, or other applications software.

Organizational charts, charts that show relationships using boxes and lines in a horizontal and vertical pattern, are effective for showing hierarchy such as the structure of a company or other organization or illustrating the relationship between departments. In your presentation at Rocky Mountain State College, you could show the structure of the YES! organization by creating an organizational chart, as shown in Figure 2-9.

Organizational chart ◄ **Figure 2-9**

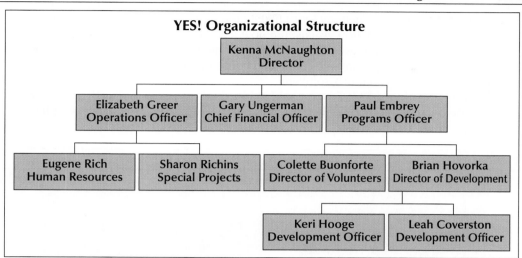

You can create organizational charts using the Organization Chart feature in Microsoft applications. There are also a number of software applications designed specifically for creating charts.

Flowcharts, charts that use lines, arrows, and boxes or other shapes to show sequence, are useful for describing the steps in a procedure, or stages in a decision-making process. Flowcharts are especially effective in demonstrations and training presentations because they can visually supplement verbal instructions, and show the results of alternative decisions. See Figure 2-10.

Flowchart ◄ **Figure 2-10**

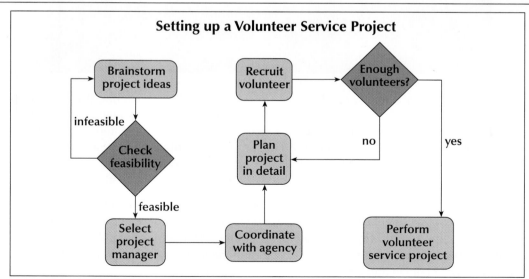

Using Illustrations

Illustrations, pictorial ways to represent parts and processes, consist of diagrams, drawings, maps, photographs, and clip art. Illustrations are especially helpful in showing relationships that aren't numerical. **Diagrams** and **line drawings** are simple illustrations using lines and shapes to represent parts, objects and processes, and can be used to show how to assemble a piece of equipment, or how the parts of an item or process are related to each other. **Maps** show spatial relationships (position and location) in a geographic area. **Photographs** show what something looks like. In the past, it was difficult to obtain and use photographs in presentation visuals, but now it is relatively easy because of digital cameras and scanners. Moreover, you can improve the quality of your photographs by removing blemishes, enhancing the colors and contrast, cropping, and making other modifications with photo-editing software.

In your presentation at RMSC, you could scan a picture (or take one with a digital camera) of student interns. You could then use photo-editing software to enhance the picture, enlarge it, and use it on a poster. See Figure 2-11.

Figure 2-11 ▶ **Photograph**

Clip art consists of collections of easy-to-use images that have been bundled with computer programs or purchased separately. Although clip art is readily available, not all clip art images are the same quality. Whenever you use clip art, you should make sure the image is professional-looking and appropriate for your presentation. There are also many Web sites that offer free still and animated clips, as well as sound clips.

General guidelines for using illustrations in your presentations include:

- Use illustrations to supplement your main points. You should use illustrations, especially photographs, in a presentation because they convey meaning, not because they look pretty.
- Make diagrams and drawings accurate. New computer technology enables you to retrieve, edit, and even alter an image. Distorting the image can make it harder for your listeners to recognize and accurately interpret the illustration.
- Provide scale and focus. Crop or trim photographs to emphasize what is important and eliminate unnecessary details.
- Abide by all copyright laws. Illustrations, including photographs and clip art, retrieved from the Internet are subject to copyright laws. Make sure you understand and abide by copyright laws.
- Avoid plagiarism. If you use someone else's chart, diagram, illustration, or photograph, give proper credit.

In summary, selecting an appropriate visual for your purpose is a matter of knowing the strengths and weaknesses of each type of visual. If you want your audience to know facts and figures, a table might be sufficient; however, if you want your audience to make a particular judgment about the data, a bar graph, line graph, or pie chart might be better. If you want to show processes and procedures, diagrams are better than photographs.

The following Reference Window summarizes the strengths of each type of visual for the particular purposes you may have in your presentations. Use this summary to help you decide which visual is appropriate for a particular type of information and purpose.

Selecting Appropriate Visuals for Your Purpose

Reference Window

Purpose	Table	Bar graph	Line graph	Pie chart	Flowchart	Org. chart	Drawing	Photo	Map
Summarize costs	X	X	X	X					
Relate parts to whole	X				X	X		X	X
Illustrate trends		X	X	X					
Demonstrate cause and effect		X	X						
Compare alternatives	X	X	X	X				X	
Summarize advantages/ disadvantages	X								
Provide chronology	X	X	X		X		X		
Follow procedure/ work flow					X				
See parts and apparatus	X						X	X	
Explain organization	X					X			
Show spatial relationship							X		X

Selecting Appropriate Visuals for Your Audience

Now that you know the purpose of each type of visual, you also need to understand how to choose a visual based on your audience. In analyzing whether a visual is appropriate for a particular audience, a general guideline to follow is that audiences familiar with the topic prefer visuals they can interpret themselves, such as flowcharts, graphs, and diagrams. On the other hand, audiences unfamiliar with the topic need help interpreting the information. Visuals for these audiences should consist of basic tables, graphs, and simple diagrams.

In addition, non-expert audiences generally have a harder time interpreting numerical data than words, so try to avoid numerical visuals. On the other hand, if you can't avoid numerical data, plan to devote extra time during your presentation to explain the numerical data. Likewise, non-expert audiences unfamiliar with certain types of images need additional help interpreting those images. For example, if you show an apparatus, equipment, or machine to non-experts, you must explain in detail what they are seeing and why it's important.

Selecting Appropriate Visuals for Your Situation

You not only have to select different visuals for different purposes and audiences, you also have to select visuals based on your situation. Selecting visuals that are appropriate for your situation involves determining which visuals work best for the medium, equipment, and room setup where you'll give your presentation. If the room doesn't have a slide projector or overhead transparency projector, you might find it difficult to use photographs. If you're limited to using a chalkboard, white board, or notepad, you might not have time to create a complex table. In such cases, you might have to provide the complex tables or graphs in posters or handouts. Flowcharts may be effective on a flip chart in a small, well-lit room; however, flip charts aren't effective in a large room, or with large audiences. Maps also are difficult to use in presentations unless they are enlarged or projected, and then they usually need a lot of explanation for the audience to understand them.

No matter which visual you select, be sure everyone in your audience can see, and make sure the medium you use to display the visual enables your audience to understand and correctly interpret your visual.

Now that you've determined which visuals are appropriate for your presentation, you'll need to determine whether you can create them yourself or, need to have someone else create them for you.

Creating Effective Visuals

Even though computer programs now make it easier to create visuals, such as graphs and illustrations, you may still need to use a technical illustrator or graphic artist to create specialized diagrams and drawings. In analyzing whether to create visuals yourself or obtain the help of a professional, you should consider what your audience will expect, how much time you have to prepare your visuals, whether you have the expertise and equipment necessary to create the visuals, and whether you have the budget to hire an illustrator or artist.

Reference Window	**Questions for Determining Whether You Can Create Visuals**

- What are the expectations for my visuals?
- How much time will I have to prepare the visuals?
- Do I have adequate knowledge or expertise to create the visuals?
- What computer equipment and other production resources do I have available for creating my own visuals?
- How much money is budgeted to hire a technical illustrator or graphic artist?

If you decide to create your own visuals, be aware of the difficulties involved. You should consider the following guidelines (in addition to the suggestions presented earlier for each type of visual):

- Keep your visuals simple. Remember that "less is more" when it comes to creating effective visuals.
- Make your visuals professional-looking. Shabby-looking or amateurish visuals will detract from your presentation and from your credibility.
- Keep your visuals consistent. Keep titles to all of your visuals consistent in size and color so your audience can quickly recognize what your visuals are about.
- Use color sparingly and purposefully. Use the brightest color for the most important information, or to indicate patterns. Don't add color just to make things "look good," or you may end up with something garish.

Of course, one alternative to preparing visuals yourself, or hiring someone to prepare them for you, is to purchase CDs of photographs and clip art, or download images from the Internet. But be aware of copyright laws. As a student, you fall under copyright "fair use" rules, which means that you can, for educational purposes only, use copyrighted material on a one-time basis without getting permission from the copyright holder. On the other hand, if you work for a not-for-profit or for-profit company, much stricter copyright laws apply. Learn the copyright laws and abide by them.

Once you've created your visuals or obtained them from some other source, you'll need to plan how to manage and present your visuals during your presentation. The following section will help you understand how to use your visuals.

Making the Most of Your Visuals

Effective visuals can become ineffective if they aren't presented successfully. You'll need to prepare everything beforehand, and then plan how you'll integrate your visuals into your presentation. Perhaps the easiest way to figure out how to present visuals in your presentation is to create a simple storyboard showing the points you want to discuss, and the visual you want to accompany each point.

Using a Storyboard

A **storyboard** is a table or map of instructions and visuals that explains how to complete a process or describe a series of events. Storyboards are used in the motion picture industry to map the narrative of a movie with the particular camera shots and special effects that are to accompany that narrative. You can adapt the same storyboarding technique in planning your presentation. Simply take a piece of paper and fold it in half lengthwise. On the left side of the page, briefly describe your presentation point, or write down a heading from your outline. Then on the right side of the page, list or sketch the visual or visuals that you want to accompany that point. You can also include any physical movements or gestures that you want to make, such as pointing to a particular part of a slide or overhead. Figure 2-12 shows a sample storyboard for your presentation at Rocky Mountain State College.

Figure 2-12	Storyboard

Benefits of Academic Volunteerism

The first category is Civic Values. Students develop their ability to center on relationships rather than content. They develop an understanding of other cultures and needs, as well as a sense of ethical duty toward society.

Show table listing civic values.

The second category is Professional Development. Students develop problem-solving skills, critical-thinking skills, and writing skills.

Show photo of students performing skills.

The third category is Personal Inspiration. Students develop a sense of who they are and of responsibility for their own actions. They become involved participants rather than just academic observers.

Show table listing types of attributes that students develop.

A storyboard like the one in Figure 2-12 can help you choose and use the best possible visuals for your presentation.

Effectively Presenting Visuals

In addition, you should follow these simple guidelines for effectively presenting your visuals:

- Use visuals to support your ideas, not just as attention getters or gimmicks. Most visuals work best when they supplement your ideas, rather than being tacked on at the beginning or end of your presentation. However, in a formal setting, you should begin your presentation with a slide or overhead showing your name, the title of your presentation, and your company logo.
- Display the visual as you discuss it. Use your storyboard to indicate when you want to display the visual, and then remove the visual when you're through discussing it. Don't let your visuals get ahead or behind of your verbal presentation.
- Stand to the side, not in front, of the visual. Avoid turning your back on your audience as you refer to a visual. Talk directly to your audience, rather than turning toward or talking at the visual.
- Introduce and interpret the visual. Explain to your audience what they should be looking at in the visual and point to what is important. But don't get sidetracked and spend all your time explaining the visual.
- Avoid using too many visuals. Present your material in simple, digestible amounts instead of overwhelming your audience with too much information.
- Turn off the equipment when you're finished.

Figure 2-13 provides a basic worksheet for helping you select appropriate visuals and determining whether you can create them.

Presentation Visuals worksheet | **Figure 2-13**

Presentation Visuals Worksheet

Which visuals are suitable for your purpose and desired outcomes?
- ☐ **Text table**
- ☐ **Numerical table**
- ☐ **Bar graph**
- ☐ **Line graph**
- ☐ **Pie chart**
- ☐ **Organizational chart**
- ☐ **Flowchart**
- ☐ **Diagram**
- ☐ **Illustration**

Which visuals would your audience expect and understand?
- ☐ **Text table**
- ☐ **Numerical table**
- ☐ **Bar graph**
- ☐ **Line graph**
- ☐ **Pie chart**
- ☐ **Organizational chart**
- ☐ **Flowchart**
- ☐ **Diagram**
- ☐ **Illustration**

Which visuals work best for the situation in which you'll give your presentation?
- ☐ **Text table**
- ☐ **Numerical table**
- ☐ **Bar graph**
- ☐ **Line graph**
- ☐ **Pie chart**
- ☐ **Organizational chart**
- ☐ **Flowchart**
- ☐ **Diagram**
- ☐ **Illustration**

Which of the visuals you checked above could you create effectively?

_____
_____
_____
_____

How much time will you have to prepare the visuals?_____

What knowledge or expertise do you have to create these visuals?

_____
_____

What computer equipment and other production resources are available for creating these visuals?

_____
_____

How much money has been budgeted to hire help in creating these visuals?_____

Now that you've determined which visuals would be appropriate for your presentation and how to integrate them into your presentation, you're prepared to plan how to deliver your presentation.

Session 2.1 Quick Check

1. Define the purpose for each of the following visuals:
   a. table
   b. graph
   c. chart
   d. illustration
2. Describe a strength and weakness of each of the following visuals:
   a. table
   b. graph
   c. chart
   d. illustrations
3. If you want to show how the number of students in your major has increased in the last five years, which of the following visuals would be appropriate: (a) table, (b) bar graph, (c) line graph, (d) pie chart?
4. If you want to show what percent of your monthly budget goes to housing, which of the following visuals would be appropriate: (a) table, (b) bar graph, (c) line graph, (d) pie chart?
5. If you want to show the managerial structure of your company, which of the following visuals would be appropriate: (a) table, (b) pie chart, (c) organization chart, (d) flowchart?
6. If you want to show the procedure for getting money from an ATM, which of the following visuals would be appropriate: (a) organization chart, (b) flowchart, (c) map, (d) photograph?
7. If you want to show where the Student Senate meets, which of the following visuals would be appropriate: (a) flowchart, (b) map, (c) drawing, (d) photograph?
8. What is a storyboard and how would you use it to make your presentation more effective?

Session 2.2

Choosing an Appropriate Delivery Method

The **delivery method** is your approach for the presentation—written out and read word for word, using a simple outline or notes, or off-the-cuff. Questions you should ask yourself in choosing a delivery method include those that will enable you to determine what is the most appropriate method for your purpose, audience, and situation.

Reference Window

Questions to Ask in Determining an Appropriate Delivery Method

- What delivery method is the most appropriate for my purpose?
- What delivery method will my audience expect?
- What delivery method is the most appropriate for this setting and situation?

You could present the information you prepared in several different ways. Common delivery methods include:

- written or memorized delivery, reading your entire presentation or repeating it from memory
- extemporaneous delivery, giving your presentation from brief notes or an outline
- impromptu delivery, speaking without notes and without rehearsal

Each type of presentation has its own advantages and disadvantages. You should select the delivery method that is appropriate for your purpose, audience, and situation. The following sections will help you determine which type of presentation is best.

Giving a Written or Memorized Presentation

Giving a **written** or **memorized presentation** involves completely writing out your presentation and then reading it word for word, or memorizing it in advance.

Written presentation   ◄   **Figure 2-14**

Written or memorized presentations are especially effective when you are:

- unfamiliar with the topic or have a highly complex topic
- interested in using specific words for persuading or informing your audience
- addressing a large, unfamiliar, or formal audience
- speaking with a group, or under a strict time limit
- extremely nervous or anxious
- inexperienced in public speaking

Written or memorized presentations don't leave a lot to chance, so they work well in formal settings when you must stick to a topic and stay on time. They're also helpful if you think you'll forget what you prepared, or become nervous and tongue-tied as a result of your inexperience with the topic, or with giving presentations. Written or memorized presentations often are given on certain occasions, such as formal paper sessions at academic or professional conferences.

On the other hand, written or memorized presentations take a long time to prepare, and once you've memorized your presentation, it's not easy to alter it in response to changes in time limits or audience questions. Perhaps the biggest drawback to written or memorized presentations is that it's difficult to sound natural while reading your presentation, or reciting it from memory. So your listeners may lose interest.

For your presentation to the RMSC Student Senate, you're one of several speakers presenting your ideas to the entire Senate. You also have a strict time limit of 12 minutes. In this instance, you want to give a written or memorized presentation so that you can cover everything you want to say in the fewest possible words.

Giving an Extemporaneous Presentation

Extemporaneous presentations involve speaking from a few notes or an outline. Extemporaneous presentations are more flexible than written or memorized presentations, and are ideal for speaking in a more informal setting.

| Figure 2-15 | Extemporaneous presentation |

Extemporaneous presentations are ideal when you are:

- familiar with the topic or audience
- presenting to a medium-sized group, or in an informal setting
- giving a shorter presentation, or have a flexible time limit
- seeking audience participation or questions
- experienced in public speaking

Speaking extemporaneously works well when you're using media requiring no advance preparation, such as chalkboards, white boards, and notepads. An extemporaneous delivery also allows you to have a more natural-sounding presentation, or to adapt your presentation for audience questions or participation.

On the other hand, when you give an extemporaneous presentation, you may have a tendency to go over your time limit, leave out crucial information, or lack precision in explaining your ideas to your listeners. In addition, speaking extemporaneously can make you appear less credible if you have a tendency toward nervousness or anxiety.

Suppose that following your presentation at RMSC, you're asked to speak for 20-30 minutes before a subcommittee of the Student Senate. In that instance, you would probably want to use an extemporaneous delivery so you could speak more naturally and allow members of the subcommittee to ask questions.

Giving an Impromptu Presentation

Impromptu presentations involve speaking without notes, an outline, or memorized text. Impromptu presentations are more flexible than either written, memorized, or extemporaneous presentations; however, they're also more difficult to make effective.

Impromptu presentation ◀ **Figure 2-16**

Impromptu presentations work best when you're in the following situations:

- very familiar with your topic and audience
- speaking to a small, intimate group, or in an in-house setting
- asked to speak at the spur of the moment
- more interested in getting the views of your audience than in persuading them

Generally, you should be wary of impromptu presentations because you leave too much to chance. Speaking without notes may result in taking too much time, saying something that offends your audience, or appearing unorganized. If you think you might be asked to speak impromptu, jot down some notes beforehand so you'll be prepared.

Kenna McNaughton, your supervisor, will probably ask you to take 2–3 minutes during the next YES! staff meeting to discuss your presentation at Rocky Mountain State College. You'll want to write down a few notes so you'll be more focused, but you don't need to do extensive planning.

Reference Window

Three Delivery Methods

Method	Preparation	Audience	Situation	Strengths
Written or memorized	much advance preparation	Large	Formal setting; complex or unfamiliar topic; unfamiliar with audience; definite time limit; inexperienced presenter	Effective when exact wording is important; helps overcome nervousness
Extemporaneous	Some advance preparation	Medium, small	Informal setting; familiar with topic and audience; flexible time limit; experienced presenter	Allows more natural presentation; enables audience participation
Impromptu	Little advance preparation, but difficult to give	Small	Informal setting; very familiar with topic and audience; shorter time limits; experienced presenter	Allows flexibility; enables audience participation; spur of the moment

No matter which method of delivery you choose, you'll need to decide whether you want your audience to have an opportunity to ask questions. Preparing for questions from the audience is an important part of giving an effective presentation.

Preparing for Questions from the Audience

Some professional speakers suggest that you should savor the idea of questions from the audience, rather than trying to avoid them. The absence of questions, they argue, may actually indicate that your audience had no interest in what you said, or that you spoke too long. Adopting the attitude that interested listeners will have questions enables you to anticipate and prepare for the questions your audience will ask.

Interested listeners have questions **Figure 2-17**

Things you should consider in preparing for questions include:

- Announce a specific time limit for questions and stick to it. When you want to end, simply state, "We have time for one more question."
- Realize that your audience will ask questions about the information in your presentation that is new, controversial, or unexpected.
- Listen carefully to every question. If you don't understand the question, ask to have it rephrased.
- Repeat the question to make sure everyone in the audience heard it.
- Keep your answers brief. If you need additional time, arrange for it after your presentation.
- If you can't answer a question, admit it, and move on.
- Don't be defensive about hostile questions. Treat every person's question as important and respond courteously.

In your presentation at RMSC, you anticipate that your audience will have questions, such as the following: "What other schools allow their students to receive college credit for working with nonprofits?" "How would a partnership between RMSC and YES! facilitate students receiving credit?" "How would allowing credit for internships affect the number of hours for graduation?" You begin immediately to plan how to answer such questions.

Now that you've determined which type of presentation you want to give, and you're prepared to answer questions from your audience, it's time to think about an almost universal problem—overcoming nervousness.

Overcoming Nervousness

Just thinking about speaking in front of other people may cause your heart to beat faster and your palms to sweat. You aren't alone. Feeling nervous about giving a presentation is a natural reaction. But you don't need to let your nervousness interfere with you giving a successful presentation. Being nervous is not all bad, because it means your adrenalin is flowing, and you'll have more energy and vitality for your presentation. In most instances, your nervousness will pass once you begin speaking.

Sometimes, however, nervousness arises from feelings of inadequacy, or from worrying about problems that could occur during a presentation. The best way to overcome these concerns is to carefully plan and prepare your presentation, and then practice it so you can relax and not worry.

| Figure 2-18 | Plan, prepare, and practice |

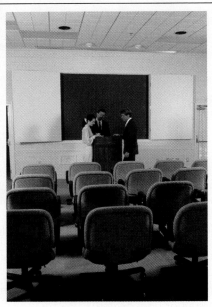

Other things you can do to overcome your nervousness include:

- Focus your presentation on your listeners' needs, not on yourself. When you focus your mind on meeting the needs of your audience, you begin to forget about yourself and how the audience might respond to you.
- Think positively about your presentation. Be optimistic and enthusiastic about your opportunity to gain experience. Visualize yourself as calm and confident.
- Work with your nervousness. Realize that some nervousness is normal and will help make your presentation better. Remember, your audience isn't nearly as concerned about your nervousness as you are.
- Give yourself plenty of time before your presentation. Arrive early to avoid rushing around before your presentation. Devote a few minutes beforehand to relax and review your presentation notes.
- Talk to people beforehand. It's easier to talk to people you know than to complete strangers. If you think of your audience as friends who want you to succeed, you'll gain new confidence in presenting your ideas to them.
- When you first stand up, look at your audience and smile. Then take a few slow breaths to calm yourself before you begin to speak.
- Don't expect everything to be perfect. Have back up plans in case something goes wrong, but handle problems with grace and a sense of humor.
- Observe other presenters. Make a list of the things they do that you like, and try to implement those things into your own presentations.

In preparation for your presentation to the RMSC Student Senate, you decide to meet a few of the Senators beforehand. After meeting a few of the students who represent your class of seniors, you realize that they're concerned with many of the same questions you had, such as how to gain valuable real-world experiences. You realize that they're interested in obtaining helpful information from your presentation that will enable them to make an informed decision in the Student Senate.

Practicing Your Presentation

The most effective way to overcome your nervousness and deliver a smooth presentation is to practice, practice, practice. Begin by simply rehearsing the key points of your presentation in your mind. Then rehearse your presentation in front of a few close friends. Ask your friends what you can do to improve your presentation. Pay special attention to what they say about key aspects of your presentation, such as your introduction, main points, and conclusion. Then rehearse your presentation again.

Practicing gives you confidence ◄ Figure 2-19

As you rehearse, use your visual aids and try to speak at the same pace you'll use when giving your presentation. Ask someone to time your presentation. By practicing your presentation until you're comfortable with every aspect of it, you'll go a long way toward reducing the apprehension that comes with feeling unprepared. Practicing your presentation will help you feel more confident as a speaker.

Practicing Your Presentation

Reference Window

- Practice in front of a few friends and a sample of your presentation audience.
- Ask your friends to give you suggestions on how to improve your presentation.
- Time your presentation using the speaking pace you'll use during your presentation.
- Practice with your visual aids.
- Pay particular attention to your introduction, main points, and conclusion.

In an effort to prepare for your presentation to the Student Senate you ask another intern to listen to what you prepared. She says she's not clear on how working with YES! has helped you develop problem-solving skills. You make a note to add another example to support that main point.

The next sections will help you learn how to improve your delivery by establishing eye contact and using a pleasant, natural speaking voice.

Improving Your Delivery

No matter how well you prepare your presentation, you won't be successful if your delivery is ineffective. No one enjoys a presentation when the speaker refuses to look up, or drones on endlessly in a monotone voice. The best presentations are those where the presenter appears confident and speaks naturally in a conversational manner.

As you practice your presentation, remember to project yourself as a confident and qualified speaker. Two ways that help you appear confident are establishing eye contact with your listeners and speaking in a natural voice.

Establishing Eye Contact

One of the most common mistakes beginners make is failing to establish eye contact with their audience. Speakers who keep their eyes on their notes, stare at their visuals, or look out over the heads of their audience create an emotional distance between themselves and their listeners.

A better method is to look directly at your listeners, even if you have to pause to look up. To establish eye contact, you should look at individuals, not just scan the audience. Focus on a particular member of the audience for just a second or two, then move on to someone else until you eventually get to most of the people in the audience or, if the audience is large, to most parts of the presentation room. You can usually judge how things are going by your audience's reaction, and make adjustments accordingly.

Figure 2-20 ▶ **Establish eye contact**

Establishing Eye Contact

- Look directly at your listeners.
- Look at individuals; don't just scan the audience.
- Focus on a particular person, then move on to someone else.
- Eventually look at most of the people or most areas of the audience.

As part of your presentation at RMSC, you'll want to look directly at each member of the Student Senate. That will enable you to create a personal connection with your audience, and see how they're responding to your presentation.

Using a Pleasant, Natural Voice

Most successful presenters aren't blessed with the deep voice of a professional news broadcaster or the rich, full voice of an opera singer; however, they use a pleasant, natural voice to make their presentations more interesting.

Use your natural voice ◄ **Figure 2-21**

Consider these suggestions for making your voice more pleasant and appealing:

- Use your natural speaking voice and a conversational manner. Think of talking to your audience as you would to a friend or teacher. That will allow you to use a voice that is more natural and easy to listen to.
- Vary the pitch, rate, and volume of your voice. Overcome monotony by emphasizing important words, pausing at the end of lengthy sentences, and slowing down during transitions. However, don't let the volume of your voice drop at the end of sentences.

- Stand up straight. Improving your posture allows you to project your voice by putting your full strength behind it.
- Learn to relax. Relaxing will improve the quality of your voice by keeping your muscles loose and your voice more natural.
- Practice breathing deeply, which gives you adequate air to speak properly.

Using Proper Grammar and Pronunciation

One of the best ways to be seen as a credible speaker is to use proper grammar and pronunciation. To assure you're pronouncing a word correctly, check its pronunciation in a dictionary. Some common problems in pronunciation include:

- mispronunciations caused by dropping a letter, such as "liberry" instead of library, and "satistics" instead of statistics
- mispronunciations caused by adding a letter or inserting the wrong letter, such as "acrost" instead of across, "learnt" instead of learned, or "stadistics" instead of statistics
- colloquial expressions, such as "crick" instead of creek, or "ain't" instead of isn't or aren't
- lazy pronunciation caused by dropping the final letters, such as "speakin" rather than speaking
- filler words, such as "a," "um," "like," and "ya know."

As part of your presentation to the Student Senate, you wonder how to pronounce the word "data." You look it up in your dictionary and find that the preferred pronunciation is "dāta," not "dăta".

Using Non-verbal Communication

Nonverbal communication is the way you convey a message without saying a word. Most nonverbal communication deals with how you use your body to communicate—how you look, stand, and move.

Checking Your Appearance and Posture

Your appearance creates your audience's first impression of you, so make sure your dress and grooming contribute to the total impression you want to convey to your audience. Dress appropriately for the situation, and in a manner that doesn't detract from your presentation.

For your presentation at the RMSC Student Senate, you should wear nicer clothing than you wear to class. This might mean dress slacks and shirt for a man, and a skirt and blouse, or dress, for a woman. For a formal presentation, you should wear business attire, such as a suit and tie for man and a suit or tailored dress for a woman.

Dress appropriately | **Figure 2-22**

An important part of how you communicate is your posture. Refrain from slouching as your audience may interpret that to mean that you don't care or you're insecure. Stand tall and keep your hands at your side, except to change overheads. Don't bend over or stretch up to speak into the microphone; adjust the microphone for your height.

Using Natural Gestures and Movement

The gestures or movements you make with your hands and arms will depend on your personality and your delivery method. It's important to choose gestures that are natural for you, so ask someone else whether your gestures are distracting. Informal presentations lend themselves to more gestures and movement than formal presentations where you're standing in front of a microphone on a podium. But giving a formal presentation doesn't mean you should hide behind the lectern, or behave like a robot. Even formal presentations allow for gestures that are purposeful, spontaneous, and natural.

In your presentation at the RMSC Student Senate, you plan to stand at the podium. But during a staff meeting at YES!, you would stand closer to your coworkers, and would probably be more animated.

Avoiding Annoying Mannerisms

Be aware of your unique **mannerisms**, recurring or unnatural movements of your voice or body, that can be annoying, such as raising your voice and eyebrows as if you are talking to children; playing with keys, a pen, or equipment; or fidgeting, rocking, and pacing. All of these mannerisms can communicate nervousness, as well as detract from your presentation.

Your Non-verbal Communication

Eyes	Establish eye contact by looking directly at listeners and focusing on a particular person.
Voice	Use your natural speaking voice and a conversational manner. Vary the pitch, rate, and volume of your voice. Breathe deeply.
Appearance and Posture	Stand tall and keep your hands at your sides.
Gestures	Use natural gestures.
Movement	Avoid recurring movements that can be annoying, and mannerisms, such as rocking and pacing.

After you practice your presentation to the RMSC Student Senate in front of a friend, she points out that you kept clicking the clip on your pen. You make a note to leave your pen in your backpack during your presentation.

Giving Collaborative or Team Presentations

Collaborative presentations, giving your presentation as part of a group or team, are a common occurrence. Since much of the work in business and industry is collaborative, it's only natural that presentations often are given as a team. The benefits of collaborative presentations include:

- giving more people valuable experience. Collaborative presentations involve more people and give each member of a team experience in communicating ideas.
- providing more workers with exposure and the rewards of a task accomplished.
- allowing for a greater range of expertise and ideas.
- enabling more discussion.
- presenting greater variety in presentation skills and delivery styles.

Figure 2-23	**Team presentation**

A successful collaborative or team presentation depends on your group's ability to plan thoroughly and practice together. The following suggestions are meant to help you have a successful group presentation:

- Plan for the transitions between speakers.
- Observe time constraints.
- Show respect for everyone and for his or her ideas.

- Involve the whole team in your planning.
- Be sensitive to personality and cultural differences.

Figure 2-24 provides a basic worksheet for practicing and delivering your presentation.

Presentation Delivery worksheet ◄ **Figure 2-24**

Presentation Delivery Worksheet

What delivery method is the most appropriate for your purpose, audience, and situation?
- ☐ Written or memorized delivery chronology
- ☐ Extemporaneous delivery
- ☐ Impromptu delivery

What questions will your audience probably ask?

_____
_____
_____
_____

What are your audience's needs?

_____
_____
_____
_____

What do you enjoy most in a presentation? How can you implement this in your own presentation?

_____
_____
_____
_____

Team Preparation
  Transitions between speakers _____
  Time allotted for each speaker _____

Rehearsal Checkoff
- ☐ Practiced presentation in front of friends or sample audience.
- ☐ Asked friends for suggestions and feedback on presentation.
- ☐ Timed your presentation. How long was it? _____
- ☐ Practiced with visual aids.
- ☐ Gave particular attention to introduction, main points, and conclusion.

- -

Evaluation by Your Sample Audience

Established eye contact with audience	☐ excellent	☐ good	☐ needs improvement
Used natural voice	☐ excellent	☐ good	☐ needs improvement
Used conversational manner	☐ excellent	☐ good	☐ needs improvement
Varied pitch, rate, and volume of voice	☐ excellent	☐ good	☐ needs improvement
Stood up straight	☐ excellent	☐ good	☐ needs improvement
Appeared relaxed	☐ excellent	☐ good	☐ needs improvement
Used proper grammar and pronunciation	☐ excellent	☐ good	☐ needs improvement
Well dressed and groomed	☐ excellent	☐ good	☐ needs improvement
Used natural gestures and movements	☐ excellent	☐ good	☐ needs improvement
Free of annoying mannerisms	☐ excellent	☐ good	☐ needs improvement

Setting Up for Your Presentation

Even the best-planned and practiced presentation can fail if your audience can't see or hear your presentation, or if they're uncomfortable. That's why it's important to include the **setup** or physical arrangements for your presentation as an important element of preparation. Of course, there are some things over which you have no control. If you're giving your presentation as part of a professional conference, you can't control whether the room you're assigned is the right size for your audience. Sometimes (but certainly not always) you can't control what projection systems are available, the thermostat setting in the room, or the quality of the speaker system. But you can control many of the things that could interfere with or enhance the success of your presentation, if you consider them in advance.

You've probably attended a presentation where the speaker stepped up to the microphone only to find that it wasn't turned on. Or, the speaker turned on the overhead projector to find that the bulb was burned out. Or, the speaker had to wait while the facilities staff adjusted the focus on the slide projector. Much of the embarrassment and lost time can be prevented if the speaker plans ahead and makes sure the equipment works.

Figure 2-25 ▶ **Setting up for the presentation**

But even when the equipment works, it might not work the same as your equipment. One way to prevent this problem is to use your own equipment, or practice in advance with the available equipment. When you must use the available equipment but can't practice with it in advance, you should prepare for the worst and plan ahead.

Here are a few suggestions for planning ahead:

- Contact the facilities staff before your presentation to make sure they have the equipment you need. Also make sure the equipment is scheduled for the time and place of your presentation.
- Make sure your equipment is compatible with the facilities at your presentation site. For instance, what version is the software installed on the computer you'll use?
- Take backup supplies of chalk, markers, and extension cords.
- If you plan to use visuals requiring a sophisticated projection system, bring along other visuals, such as overhead transparencies or handouts, as a backup in the event that the computer or slide projector fails.
- If possible, arrive early and test equipment. Allow yourself enough time before your presentation to practice with the equipment and contact technical staff if problems occur.
- Use a Facilities Checklist to help you anticipate and prevent problems.

Not all of the facilities are under your control. In your presentation at RMSC, you will have access to the facilities staff, but you won't be authorized to change things like temperature settings, or the arrangement of chairs. On the other hand, during your staff meetings at YES!, you can move the chairs away from the table and into a semicircle, or you can adjust the temperature controls to make the room more comfortable.

Using a Facilities Checklist

Using a Facilities Checklist, a list of things to bring or do to set up for your presentation, will help you ensure that your audience is comfortable and your equipment works. Planning ahead will also help you prevent many of the problems that may arise. The Facilities Checklist divides the areas you should consider in setting up your presentation into the following categories: room, layout, equipment, and presentation materials. See Figure 2-26.

Figure 2-26 ▶ Facilities Checklist

Facilities Checklist	
Room	☐ Is the room the right size?
	☐ Is the lighting adequate?
	☐ Is the ventilation working properly?
	☐ Is the temperature setting comfortable?
	☐ Are there distracting noises?
Layout	☐ Are the chairs arranged how you want them?
	☐ Are the stand, podium, and microphone set up properly?
	☐ Is the lighting set properly for your type of visuals?
Equipment	☐ Is the electricity on?
	☐ Are there needed extension cords?
	☐ Are all the light bulbs functioning?
	☐ Does the overhead projector, slide projector, or computer projector work properly?
	☐ Is the microphone working with its volume properly adjusted?
	☐ Is the microphone adjusted to the right height?
	☐ Are electrical cords arranged so you don't get entangled in them or trip over them?
	☐ For large presentation rooms, are there microphones set up in the audience for questions and comments, and do they all work properly?
Presentation Materials	☐ Do you have all your visuals (slides, overheads, electronic presentation, handouts, demonstration items)?
	☐ Do you have a pointer?
	☐ If you're using a laser pointer, is it working properly?
	☐ Is a tripod available for your poster or notepad?
	☐ Are there thumbtacks, pins, or tape for your poster or sign?
	☐ Are your slides properly loaded into the slide projector carousel or slide tray?
	☐ Do you have a chalkboard, white board, or notepad?
Supporting Services	☐ Do you have drinking water?
	☐ Does the audience have notepaper and pens?
	☐ Does the entrance to the presentation room give information about the speaker or session being held there?
	☐ Do you know how to handle audiovisual, lighting, or sound problems in the event something goes wrong?
Skills	☐ Do you know how to work the audiovisual equipment?
	☐ Do you know how to adjust the house lights?
	☐ Do you know how to use the mobile microphone?
	☐ Do you know how to adjust the microphone volume?
	☐ Do you know how much room you have on the podium so you don't fall off?

In considering the room in which you'll give your presentation, you'll want to check whether the room is properly ventilated, adequately lighted, and free from distracting noises, such as clanking of dishes in the kitchen, hammering and sawing by work crews, or interference from the speakers in adjacent rooms.

In considering the layout of the room, you'll want to make sure the chairs are arranged so that everyone in the audience can see and hear your presentation. You'll also want to make sure the microphone stand provides enough room for your notes, or that the equipment, such as the overhead projector, is close enough that you won't have to walk back and forth to your notes.

In considering the equipment, you'll want to check to make sure all the needed equipment is available and functioning properly. You'll also want to make sure you have adequate space for your equipment and access to electrical outlets. You might want to make arrangements for extra bulbs for the projector or overhead, or bring your own.

In considering the presentation materials, you'll want to make sure that you have chalk or markers for the chalkboard and white board, an easel to support your visuals, or thumbtacks you can use to mount your visuals on the wall or a poster board. You'll also want to make sure you have a glass of water in case your throat gets dry.

As you go through the Facilities Checklist, you find that everything you need is available in your presentation room at Rocky Mountain State College. You feel confident knowing that you have done everything possible on your part to prepare for your presentation. When the presentation time comes, you deliver your message with a natural, clear voice, and keep eye contact with your audience. Your audience responds favorably to your presentation, asks meaningful questions for which you are prepared, and compliments you on a job well done. Your presentation is a success in every way.

Session 2.2 Quick Check

Review

1. List and define three common presentation delivery methods.
2. Which delivery method(s) are appropriate if you must speak under a strict time limit and want to use specific wording in your presentation?
3. Which delivery method(s) are appropriate if you're asked to speak on the spur of the moment?
4. Which delivery method(s) are appropriate if you want audience participation?
5. True or False. You should avoid questions from the audience because it shows that your audience didn't pay attention to your presentation.
6. List the most important way to overcome nervousness about giving a presentation.
7. Define non-verbal communication and give one example.
8. Give an example of a filler word you should avoid in your presentation.

Tutorial Summary

Review

In this tutorial, you learned the benefits of using visuals in your presentation and how to select the most appropriate visual for your purpose. You learned the strengths and weaknesses of visuals such as tables, graphs, charts, and illustrations and how to select the most appropriate visuals for your presentation. You learned how to create and present effective visuals. You also learned how to choose an appropriate delivery method for giving your presentation, how to prepare for questions from the audience, and how to overcome nervousness. You learned ways to practice your presentation and improve your delivery, including using proper grammar and pronunciation and non-verbal communication. You learned how to give a collaborative or team presentation. Finally, you learned how to set up for your presentation and to use a facilities checklist.

Key Terms

bar graph	flowchart	nonverbal communication
chart	graph	organizational chart
clip art	illustration	photograph
collaborative presentation	impromptu presentation	pie chart
column graph	line drawing	setup
delivery method	line graph	storyboard
diagram	mannerism	table
extemporaneous	map	visual
presentation	memorized presentation	written presentation

Practice

Practice the skills you learned in the tutorial to prepare three presentations for another nonprofit organization.

Review Assignments

Tanner Granatowski is an intern for Business With a Heart, another nonprofit organization in the Colorado Springs area. Business With a Heart matches people willing to donate goods, time, or talents with those in desperate need. The nonprofit company also partners with local businesses to distribute goods, similar to food banks. You're asked to help Tanner prepare and give three presentations for Business With a Heart.

The first presentation will be a 20-minute presentation to members of the local Chamber of Commerce (approximately 40 people). Your purpose in this presentation is to inform the Chamber of the goals and purposes of Business With a Heart. The presentation will take place in the large banquet hall of the new Colorado Springs City Center, which is fully equipped with the latest technology.

The second presentation will be a 10-minute presentation to 10 members of the Board of Directors of The Henderson Foundation, a national foundation that gives money to non-profit organizations. Your purpose in this presentation is to persuade the Board of Directors to donate $400,000 to help Business With a Heart expand its programs. The presentation will take place in the 100-year-old foundation board room. It has electricity, but no computer projection equipment.

The third presentation will be a 40-minute presentation to five members of the staff at Business With a Heart. Your purpose in this presentation is to show staff members how to contact local business owners over the phone to find out if they are interested in donating their excess goods. The presentation will take place in a small staff room. Do the following:

1. Explain the differences and similarities between the three presentations in terms of your audience. Complete an Audience Analysis Worksheet for each presentation.
2. Explain how your purpose and the type of information you will present in each presentation will affect the visuals that you would use.
3. Explain the differences and similarities between the three presentations in terms of the presentation situation. Complete a Situation and Media Assessment Worksheet for each presentation.
4. Explain how your purpose and the type of information you will be presenting in each of these presentations will affect the visuals that you use. Complete a Presentation Visuals Worksheet for each presentation.
5. Give an example of how you would use a numerical table in one presentation.
6. Give an example of how you would use a graph in one presentation.
7. Give an example of how you would use a chart in one presentation.

8. Give an example of how you would use an illustration in one presentation

9. Explain how your purpose, audience, and situation would affect the delivery method you would use for each presentation. Complete a Presentation Delivery Worksheet for each presentation.

10. Create a storyboard showing an idea and visual for one presentation.

11. List two questions you think the audience might ask for each presentation.

12. Give an example of how your nervousness might vary for the presentations. Explain what you would do to overcome your nervousness.

13. Describe what you would wear for each presentation.

14. Using the Facilities Checklist, describe one aspect you can control and one you can't control for each presentation.

Apply

Apply the skills you learned to create a new presentation for a company that plans corporate retreats.

Case Problem 1

Wyoming ESCAPE Wyoming ESCAPE is a Jackson Hole-based company that plans corporate retreats, taking advantage of Wyoming's beautiful scenery and recreation. Wyoming ESCAPE provides activities to help harried workers and executives unwind and play team-enhancing games—everything from ropes courses to river raft races in the summer, and snowman building and cross-country skiing in the winter. The staff at Wyoming ESCAPE asks you to help them prepare for three presentations.

The first presentation will be a 20-minute presentation to sales personnel (approximately 15 people). Your purpose in this presentation is to inform the sales staff about the activities you provide so that they can market the retreats. The presentation will take place at company headquarters in a large conference room. The conference room does not have a computer projection system, but does have a slide projector.

The second presentation will be a 10-minute presentation to approximately 45 potential participants. Your purpose in this presentation is to persuade your audience to consider Wyoming ESCAPE for their corporate retreat, and to contact your sales staff for further details. The presentation will take place at a national human resources conference in the ballroom of a large hotel. The hotel has a computer projection system, as well as a slide projector.

The third presentation will be a 40-minute presentation to five staff members who'll conduct the activities. Your purpose in this presentation is to demonstrate how to conduct several new activities that will be used during corporate retreats. The presentation will take place in a small conference room. There is no slide projector or computer projection system in the conference room, but there is a large white board.

Do the following:

1. Complete a Purpose and Outcomes Worksheet for each presentation.

2. Explain the differences and similarities between the audiences for the three presentations, including any general demographics that you can determine. Complete an Audience Analysis Worksheet for each presentation.

3. Explain how the settings for these presentations would probably affect your audience's expectations and the appropriate level of formality.

4. Determine appropriate and inappropriate media for each presentation. Complete a Situation and Media Assessment Worksheet for each presentation.

5. Complete a Focus and Organization Worksheet to determine an appropriate organizational pattern and organize the text in your presentation accordingly.

6. Explain how your purpose, audience, and setting would affect the visuals you would use. Complete a Presentation Visuals Worksheet for each presentation.

7. Give an example of a visual you could use to show sales personnel that the number of participants has decreased in the last year.
8. Give an example of a visual you could use to convince potential participants that they would enjoy attending Wyoming ESCAPE.
9. Give an example of a visual you could use to show the staff a new game for the retreat.
10. Create a storyboard showing an idea and visual for one presentation.
11. Using a Presentation Delivery Worksheet, specify which delivery method you would use for each presentation, and list one question you think the audience might ask for each presentation. Also explain how your level of nervousness might differ for each presentation, and what you would do to overcome your nervousness.
12. Using a Facilities Checklist for each presentation, list two set up details you would want to check for each presentation.

Research

Prepare three presentations using information you have found from the Internet or other research resources.

Case Problem 2

FamilyOrigins.biz   Tamar Ruest works for FamilyOrigins.biz, a company that allows family members to speak to each other free-of-charge over the Internet, share stories and photographs through personal Web pages, and obtain genealogy-related supplies over the Internet, such as government reports, printed family histories, and forms for creating a family tree. Obtain information for your presentation by going to various genealogy sites on the Internet such as **http://www.Ancestry.com**, **http://www.familysearch.org**, **http://www.MyFamily.com** or any other genealogy resource. You're asked to create three presentations.

The purpose of the first presentation is to inform your listeners of the success of FamilyOrigins.biz. Your presentation will be given to 50 attendees at a genealogy conference held in a large conference room in a local motel. There is no computer projection system or slide projector available at the motel, but your company has an overhead projector you could take to the conference.

The purpose of the second presentation is to persuade your audience of the need for genealogy. Your audience consists of 15 members of your family (or someone else's) attending a family reunion held at an outdoor pavilion at a local state park. There is an electrical outlet at the pavilion, but no slide projector, computer projection system, or blackboard.

The third presentation, demonstrating how to download the form to create a family tree, will be given to your classmates. You should base your media selection upon the facilities at your school and classroom.

Do the following:

1. Complete a Purpose and Outcomes Worksheet for each presentation.
2. Explain the differences and similarities between the above three groups in terms of their age, level of education, and familiarity with the subject. Complete an Audience Analysis Worksheet for each presentation.
3. Explain how the settings for these presentations would affect your audience's expectations and the appropriate level of formality. Complete a Situation and Media Assessment Worksheet for each presentation.
4. Determine appropriate and inappropriate media for each presentation.
5. Complete a Focus and Organizational Worksheet to determine an appropriate organizational pattern and organize the text in your presentation accordingly.
6. Explain how your purpose, audience, and setting for each presentation would affect the visuals you would use.

7. Complete a Presentation Visuals Worksheet for each presentation, giving an example of an appropriate visual for each presentation.
8. Create a storyboard showing an idea and visual for one presentation.
9. Using a Presentation Delivery Worksheet, identify which delivery method you would use for each presentation. List two questions you think the audience might ask for each presentation. Explain how your level of nervousness might differ for each presentation, and what you would do to overcome your nervousness.
10. Complete a Facilities Checklist for each presentation, determining two things you should check for each presentation.

Apply

Apply the skills you learned in the tutorial to create a presentation about your favorite fairy tale or nursery rhyme.

Case Problem 3

Kids Kreative Communication   Kids Kreative Communication sells fairy tale and nursery rhyme software that teaches young children to read, including online coloring books and stories that use a particular child's name. You're asked to give some presentations for Kids Kreative.

The purpose of the first presentation is to demonstrate how a particular software program works. Your audience will be five elementary school teachers who will use the software at a local elementary school. Your presentation will be given in the school's computer classroom, which has a white board and a computer projection system.

The purpose of the second presentation is to interest approximately 40 elementary school principals attending a national teaching convention in the complete line of Kids Kreative software. Your presentation will be given in a hotel conference room which has an overhead projector and a slide projector.

The purpose of the third presentation is to inform 10 programmers at Kids Kreative of some of the needs of current software users. Your presentation will be given at Kids Kreative headquarters, in a small conference room which has an overhead projector and a white board.

Do the following:

1. Complete a Purpose and Outcomes Worksheet for each presentation.
2. Explain the differences and similarities between the above three groups in terms of their age, level of education, and familiarity with the subject. Complete an Audience Analysis Worksheet for each presentation.
3. Explain how the settings for these presentations would affect your audience's expectations and the appropriate level of formality. Complete a Situation and Media Assessment Worksheet for each presentation.
4. Determine appropriate and inappropriate media for each presentation.
5. Complete a Focus and Organization Worksheet to determine an appropriate organizational pattern, and organize the text in your presentation accordingly.
6. Explain how your purpose, audience, and setting for each presentation would affect the visuals you would use. Complete a Presentation Visuals Worksheet for each presentation.
7. Create a storyboard showing an idea and a visual for one presentation.
8. Using a Presentation Delivery Worksheet, specify which delivery method you would use for each presentation. List one question you think the audience might ask for each presentation. Explain how your level of nervousness might differ for each presentation, and what you would do to overcome your nervousness.
9. Complete a Facilities Checklist for each presentation, determining which items on the checklist would apply to each presentation.

Research

Create a collaborative presentation using resources on leadership and teambuilding from the Internet.

Case Problem 4

Flores High Performance Seminars   Juanita Flores owns Flores High Performance Seminars, a company providing monthly seminars and training on coaching, leadership, teambuilding, and presentations. Juanita asks you to give a presentation to your class on one of these topics. Working with one or two other members of the class, create a five to seven minute presentation for your classmates. You could get ideas for your presentation by going to various sites on the Internet. Simply type the words teambuilding, leadership, coaching, or training into your search engine. After you have organized your materials, do the following:

1. Decide what type of presentation you'll give.
2. Complete a Purpose and Outcomes Worksheet for your presentation.
3. Define your audience according to their general demographic features of age, gender, level of education, and familiarity with your topic. Complete an Audience Analysis Worksheet for your presentation.
4. Assess the situation for your presentation by describing the setting and size of your audience. Complete a Situation and Media Assessment Worksheet.
5. Select appropriate media for your presentation and explain why they are appropriate.
6. Complete a Focus and Organization Worksheet and organize the text in your presentation accordingly.
7. Show two ways you could focus your presentation and limit the scope of your topic.
8. Select a method for gaining your audience's attention, and write an introduction using that method.
9. Create an advance organizer or overview for your presentation.
10. Identify at least two sources for information on your topic and consult those sources. Include at least one source from the Internet.
11. Select an appropriate organizational pattern for your presentation.
12. Identify four transitional phrases that you'll use in your presentation.
13. Write a summary for your presentation recapping the key ideas.
14. Complete a Presentation Visuals Worksheet.
15. Create an appropriate visual for your presentation.
16. Using the Presentation Delivery Worksheet, decide on an appropriate presentation style. Write a list of questions you think your classmates will ask.
17. Practice your presentation in front of another group in your class, and ask them to complete the evaluation part of the Presentation Delivery Worksheet.
18. Complete a Facilities Checklist for your presentation.
19. Set up your classroom.
20. Give your presentation to your classmates.

Quick Check Answers

Session 2.1

1. a. organize information in horizontal rows and vertical columns
   b. show the relationship of two variables along a horizontal and a vertical axis
   c. show the relationship of variables without using a coordinate system
   d. show relationships that aren't numerical
2. a. table (strengths): effective for making facts and details accessible, organizing data by categories, summarizing results and recommendations, and comparing sets of data; (weaknesses): not effective for showing change across time, trends, procedures, or spatial relationships.
   b. graph (strengths): effective for comparing one quantity to another, showing changes over time, and indicating patterns or trends; (weaknesses): not effective for showing organizational hierarchy, procedures or work flow, parts and wholes, or spatial relationships.
   c. chart (strengths): effective for comparing parts to the whole, explaining organizations, and showing chronology, procedures, and work flow; (weaknesses): not effective for showing changes over time or percentages.
   d. illustration (strengths): effective for showing how things appear, the assembly and relationship of parts and processes to each other, and spatial relationships; (weaknesses): not effective for summarizing data, providing chronology, or showing processes.
3. a., b., and c.
4. d.
5. c.
6. b.
7. b., c., and d.
8. technique from movie industry showing dialogue and accompanying camera shots and special effects; list idea you're discussing on left side of sheet and the accompanying visual on the right side of the sheet.

Session 2.2

1. written or memorized presentation—write out presentation and read it word for word or memorize it; extemporaneous presentation—speak from a few notes or outline; impromptu presentation—speak without notes or outline, or off-the-cuff.
2. written or memorized presentation
3. impromptu presentation
4. extemporaneous presentation, impromptu presentation
5. False; questions probably mean your audience listened and was interested in what you had to say.
6. planning, preparation, and practice
7. conveying a message without talking; appearance, posture, body movement, gestures, and mannerisms.
8. "uh," "um," "you know," "er," "a," "like"

New Perspectives on
Managing Your Files

Creating and Working with Files and Folders in Windows XP

FM 3

Read This Before You Begin

To the Student

Data Files

To complete the Managing Your Files (FM) tutorial, you need the starting student Data Files. Your instructor will either provide you with these Data Files or ask you to obtain them yourself.

The Managing Your Files tutorial requires the folder named "FM" to complete the Tutorial, Review Assignments, and Case Problems. You will need to copy this folder from a file server, a standalone computer, or the Web to the drive and folder where you will be storing your Data Files. Your instructor will tell you which computer, drive letter, and folder(s) contain the files you need. You can also download the files by going to www.course.com; see the inside back or front cover for more information on downloading the files, or ask your instructor or technical support person for assistance.

If you are storing your Data Files on floppy disks, you will need **two** blank, formatted, high-density disks for this tutorial. Label your disks as shown, and place on them the folders indicated.

▼**FM Data Disk 1: Tutorial**
    FM\Tutorial folder
▼**FM Data Disk 2: Exercises**
    FM\Review folder
    FM\Cases folder

When you begin this tutorial, refer to the Student Data Files section at the bottom of the tutorial opener page, which indicates which folders and files you need for the tutorial. Each end-of-tutorial exercise also indicates the files you need to complete that exercise

Course Labs

The Managing Your Files tutorial features an interactive Course Lab to help you understand file management concepts. There are Lab Assignments at the end of the tutorial that relate to this lab. Contact your instructor or technical support person for assistance in accessing the labs.

To the Instructor

The Data Files and Course Labs are available on the Instructor Resources CD for this title. Follow the instructions in the Help file on the CD to install the programs to your network or standalone computer. See the "To the Student" section above for information on how to set up the Data Files that accompany this text.

You are granted a license to copy the Data Files and Course Labs to any computer or computer network used by students who have purchased this book.

System Requirements

If you are going to work through this book using your own computer, you need:

• **Computer System** This tutorial assumes a typical installation of Microsoft Windows XP Professional (although the Microsoft Windows XP Home version is acceptable as well).

• **Data Files** You will not be able to complete the tutorials or exercises in this book using your own computer until you have the necessary starting Data Files.

• **Course Labs** See your instructor or technical support person to obtain the Course Lab software for use on your own computer.

www.course.com/NewPerspectives

Objectives

- Develop file management strategies
- Explore files and folders
- Create, name, copy, move, and delete folders
- Name, copy, move, and delete files
- Work with compressed files

Lab

Using Files

Student Data Files

Managing Your Files

Creating and Working with Files and Folders in Windows XP

Case

Distance Learning Company

The Distance Learning Company specializes in distance learning courses for individuals who want to participate in college-level classes to work toward a degree or for personal enrichment. Distance learning is formalized education that typically takes place using a computer and the Internet, replacing normal classroom interaction with modern communications technology. The company's goal is to help students gain new skills and stay competitive in the job market. The head of the Customer Service Department, Shannon Connell, interacts with the Distance Learning Company's clients on the phone and from her computer. Shannon, like all other employees, is required to learn the basics of managing files on her computer.

In this tutorial, you'll help Shannon devise a strategy for managing files. You'll learn how Windows XP organizes files and folders, and you'll examine Windows XP file management tools. You'll create folders and organize files within them. You'll also explore options for working with compressed files.

▼**FM folder**

▽ **Tutorial folder**

Agenda.doc
Holiday.bmp
New Logo.bmp
Proposal.doc
Resume.doc
Salinas members.eml
Stationery.bmp
Vinca.bmp

▽ **Review folder**

Billing Worksheet.wk4
Car Savings Plan.xls
Commissions.xls
Contracts.xls
Customer Accounts.xls
Filenames.pps
Personal Loan.doc
Speech.wav
Water lilies.jpg

▽ **Cases folder**

Invoice Feb.xls
Invoice Jan.xls
Invoice March.xls
Painting Class -
  Agenda.doc
Painting Class -
  Questionnaire.doc
Painting Class - Teaching
  Manual.doc
Paris.jpg
Vegetables.jpg

Using Files

Organizing Files and Folders

Knowing how to save, locate, and organize computer files makes you more productive when you are working with a computer. A **file**, often referred to as a **document**, is a collection of data that has a name and is stored in a computer. Once you create a file, you can open it, edit its contents, print it, and save it again—usually using the same program you used to create it. You organize files by storing them in **folders**, which are containers for your files. You need to organize files so you can find them easily and work efficiently.

A file cabinet is a common metaphor for computer file organization. A computer is like a file cabinet that has two or more drawers—each drawer is a storage device, or **disk**. Each disk contains folders that hold documents, or files. To make it easy to retrieve files, you arrange them logically into folders. For example, one folder might contain financial data, another might contain your creative work, and another could contain information you're collecting for an upcoming vacation.

A computer can store folders and files on different types of disks, ranging from removable media such as **floppy disks**, **Zip disks**, and **compact discs (CDs)** to **hard disks**, or fixed disks, which are permanently stored in a computer. Hard disks are the most popular type of computer storage because they can contain many gigabytes of data—millions of times more data than a floppy disk—and are economical.

To have your computer access a removable disk, you must insert the disk into a **drive**, which is a computer device that can retrieve and sometimes record data on a disk. See Figure 1. A hard disk is already contained in a drive, so you don't need to insert it each time you use the computer.

Figure 1	Computer drives and disks

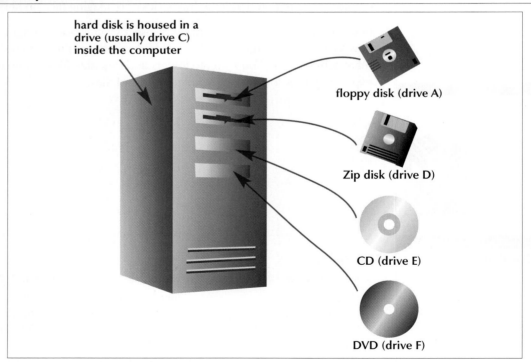

hard disk is housed in a drive (usually drive C) inside the computer

floppy disk (drive A)

Zip disk (drive D)

CD (drive E)

DVD (drive F)

A computer distinguishes one drive from another by assigning each a drive letter. The floppy disk drive is drive A. (Most computers have only one floppy disk drive—if your computer has two, the second one is called drive B.) The hard disk is usually assigned to drive C. The remaining drives can have any other letters, but are usually assigned in the order that the drives were installed on the computer—so your CD drive might be drive D or drive F.

Understanding the Need for Organizing Files and Folders

Windows XP stores thousands of files in many folders on the hard disk of your computer. These are system files that Windows XP needs to display the desktop, use drives, and perform other operating system tasks. To ensure system stability and find files quickly, Windows organizes the folders and files in a hierarchy, or **file system**. At the top of the hierarchy, Windows stores folders and important files that it needs when you turn on the computer. This location is called the **root directory**, and is usually drive C (the hard disk). The term "root" refers to another popular metaphor for visualizing a file system—an upside-down tree, which reflects the file hierarchy that Windows uses. In Figure 2, the tree trunk corresponds to the root directory, the branches to the folders, and the leaves to files.

Windows file hierarchy ◄ **Figure 2**

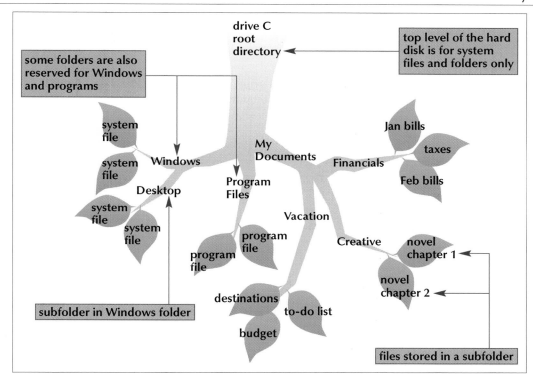

Note that some folders contain other folders. An effectively organized computer contains a few folders in the root directory, and those folders contain other folders, also called **subfolders**.

The root directory, or top level, of the hard disk is for system files and folders only—you should not store your own work here because it could interfere with Windows or a program. (If you are working in a computer lab, you might not be allowed to access the root directory.)

Do not delete or move any files or folders from the root directory of the hard disk—doing so could mean that you cannot run or start the computer. In fact, you should not reorganize or change any folder that contains installed software, because Windows XP expects to find the files for specific programs within certain folders. If you reorganize or change these folders, Windows XP cannot locate and start the programs stored in that folder. Likewise, you should not make changes to the folder that contains the Windows XP operating system (usually named Windows or Winnt).

Because the top level of the hard disk is off limits for your files—the ones that you create, open, and save on the hard disk—you must store your files in subfolders. If you are working on your own computer, you should store your files within the My Documents folder. If you are working in a computer lab, you will probably use a different location that your instructor specifies. If you simply store all your files in one folder, however, you will soon have trouble finding the ones you want. Instead, you should create folders within a main folder to separate files in a way that makes sense for you.

Likewise, if you store most of your files on a removable disk, such as a Zip disk, you need to organize those files into folders and subfolders. Before you start creating folders, whether on a hard disk or removable disk, you should plan the organization you will use.

Developing Strategies for Organizing Files and Folders

The type of disk you use to store files determines how you organize those files. Figure 3 shows how you could organize your files on a hard disk if you were taking a full semester of distance learning classes. To duplicate this organization, you would open the main folder for your documents, create four folders—one each for the Basic Accounting, Computer Concepts, Management Skills II, and Professional Writing courses—and then store the writing assignments you complete in the Professional Writing folder.

Figure 3	Organizing folders and files on a hard disk

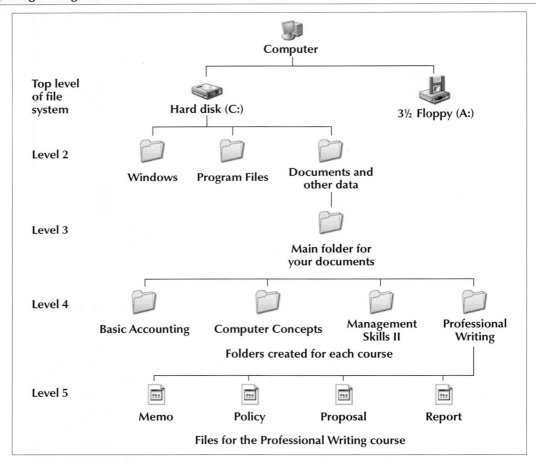

If you store your files on removable media, such as a floppy disk, Zip disk, or rewritable CD, you can use a simpler organization because you do not have to account for system files. In general, the larger the medium, the more levels of folders you should use because large media can store more files, and therefore need better organization. For example, you could organize your files on a 100 MB Zip disk. In the top level of the Zip disk, you could create folders for each general category of documents you store—one each for Courses, Creative, Financials, and Vacation. The Courses folder could then include one folder for each course, and each of those folders could contain the appropriate files.

You could organize these files on 1.44 MB floppy disks. Because the storage capacity of a floppy disk is much less than that of a Zip disk, you would probably use one floppy disk for your courses, another for creative work, and so on. If you had to create large documents for your courses, you could use one floppy disk for each course.

If you work on two computers, such as one computer at an office or school and another computer at home, you can duplicate the folders you use on both computers to simplify transferring files from one computer to another. For example, if you have four folders in your My Documents folder on your work computer, you would create these same four folders on your removable media as well as in the My Documents folder of your home computer. If you change a file on the hard disk of your home computer, you can copy the most recent version of the file to the corresponding folder on your removable media so that it is available when you are at work. You also then have a **backup**, or duplicate copy, of important files that you need.

Planning Your Organization

Now that you've explored the basics of organizing files on a computer, you can plan the organization of your files for this book by writing in your answers to the following questions:

1. How do you obtain the files for this book (on a floppy disk from your instructor, for example)? _____

2. On what drive do you store your files for this book (drive A, C, D, for example)? _____

3. Do you use a particular folder on this drive? If so, which folder do you use? _____

4. Is this folder contained within another folder? If so, what is the name of that main folder? _____

5. On what type of disk do you save your files for this book (hard disk, floppy disk, Zip disk, CD, or network drive, for example)? _____

If you cannot answer any of these questions, ask your instructor for help.

Exploring Files and Folders

Windows XP provides two tools for exploring the files and folders on your computer—Windows Explorer and My Computer. Both display the contents of your computer, using icons to represent drives, folders, and files. However, by default, each presents a different view of your computer. **Windows Explorer** shows the files, folders, and drives on your computer, making it easy to navigate, or move from one location to another within the file hierarchy. **My Computer** shows the drives on your computer and makes it easy to perform system tasks, such as viewing system information.

The Windows Explorer window is divided into two sections, called **panes**. The left pane, also called the **Explorer bar** or **Folders pane**, shows the hierarchy of the folders and other locations on your computer. The right pane lists the contents of these folders and other locations. If you select a folder in the left pane, for example, the files stored in that folder appear in the right pane. The My Computer window is also divided into panes—the left pane, called the task pane, lists tasks related to the items displayed in the right pane.

If the Folders pane in Windows Explorer showed all the folders on your computer at once, it could be a very long list. Instead, Windows Explorer allows you to open drives and folders only when you want to see what they contain. If a folder contains subfolders, an expand icon ⊞ appears to the left of the folder icon. (The same is true for drives.) To view the folders contained in an object, you click the expand icon. A collapse icon ⊟ then appears next to the folder icon; click the collapse icon to close the folder. To view the files contained in a folder, you click the folder icon, and the files appear in the right pane. See Figure 4.

Figure 4 **Viewing folder contents in Windows Explorer**

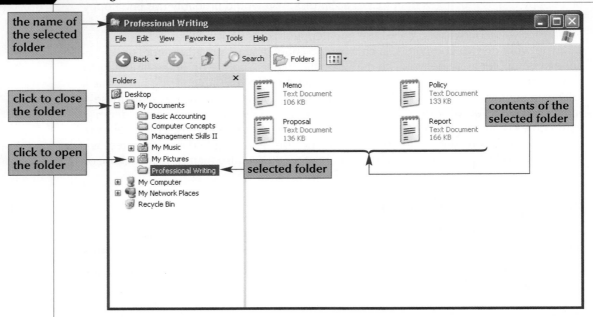

Using the Folders pane helps you navigate your computer and orients you to your current location. As you move, copy, delete, and perform other tasks with the files in the right pane of Windows Explorer, you can refer to the Folders pane to see how your changes affect the overall organization.

Like Windows Explorer, My Computer also lets you view, organize, and access the drives, folders, and files on your computer. Instead of using the Folders pane, however, you can navigate your computer in four other ways:

- **Opening drives and folders in the right pane:** To view the contents of a drive or folder, double-click the drive or folder icon in the right pane of the My Computer window. For example, to view the contents of the Professional Writing folder as shown in Figure 5, you open the My Documents folder and then the Professional Writing folder.
- **Using the Standard Buttons toolbar:** Click the buttons on the Standard Buttons toolbar to navigate the hierarchy of drives, folders, subfolders, and other objects in your computer.
- **Using the Address bar:** By clicking the Address bar list arrow, you can view a list of drives, folders, and other locations on your computer. This gives you a quick way of moving to an upper level of the Windows XP file system without navigating the intermediate levels.
- **Using the task pane:** The Other Places area of the My Computer task pane lists links you can click to quickly open folders or navigate to other useful places.

By default, when you first open My Computer, it shows all the drives available on your computer, whereas Windows Explorer shows the files, folders, and drives on your computer. However, by changing window settings, you can make the two tools interchangeable. You can change settings in the My Computer window to show the Folders pane instead of the task pane. If you do, you have the same setup as Windows Explorer. Likewise, if you close the Folders pane in the Windows Explorer window, the task pane opens, giving you the same setup as in the My Computer window.

Viewing folder contents in My Computer ◄ **Figure 5**

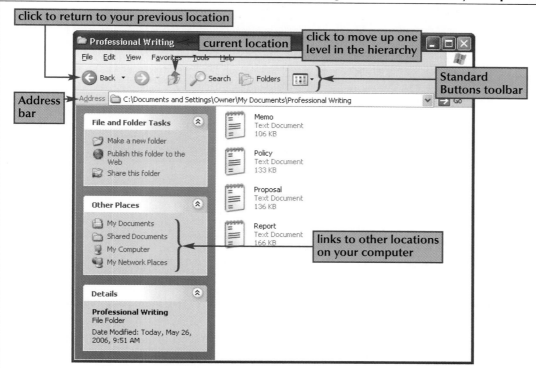

Shannon prefers to use Windows Explorer to manage her files. You'll use Windows Explorer to manage files in the rest of this tutorial.

Using Windows Explorer

Windows XP also provides a folder for your documents—the **My Documents folder**, which is designed to store the files and folders you work with regularly. On your own computer, this is where you can keep your data files—the memos, videos, graphics, music, and other files that you create, edit, and manipulate in a program. If you are working in a computer lab, you might not be able to access the My Documents folder, or you might be able to store files there only temporarily because that folder is emptied every night. Instead, you might permanently store your Data Files on removable media or in a different folder on your computer or network.

When you start Windows Explorer, it opens to the My Documents folder by default. If you cannot access the My Documents folder, the screens you see as you perform the following steps will differ. However, you can still perform the steps accurately.

To examine the organization of your computer using Windows Explorer:

▶ **1.** Click the **Start** button on the taskbar, point to **All Programs**, point to **Accessories**, and then click **Windows Explorer**. The Windows Explorer window opens.

▶ **2.** Click the **expand** icon ⊞ next to the My Computer icon. The drives and other useful locations on your computer appear under the My Computer icon, as shown in Figure 6. The contents of your computer will differ.

| Figure 6 | Viewing the contents of your computer |

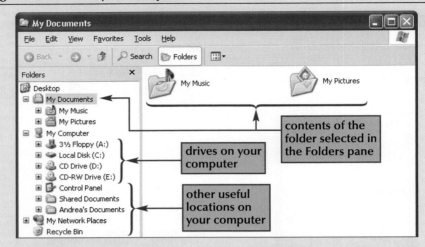

3. Click the **expand** icon ⊞ next to the Local Disk (C:) icon. The contents of your hard disk appear under the Local Disk (C:) icon.

   Trouble? If you do not have permission to access drive C, skip Step 3 and read but do not perform the remaining steps.

   My Documents is still the selected folder. To view the contents of an object in the right pane, you can click the object's icon in the Folders pane.

4. Click **Documents and Settings** in the Folders pane. Its contents appear in the right pane. Documents and Settings is a built-in Windows XP folder that contains a folder for each user installed on the system.

You've already mastered the basics of navigating your computer with Windows Explorer. You click expand icons in the left pane until you find the folder that you want. Then you click the folder icon in the left pane to view the files it contains in the right pane.

Navigating to Your Data Files

The **file path** is a notation that indicates a file's location on your computer. The file path leads you through the Windows file system to your file. For example, the Holiday file is stored in the Tutorial subfolder of the FM folder. If you are working on a floppy disk, for example, the path to this file is as follows:

A:\FM\Tutorial\Holiday.bmp

This path has four parts, and each part is separated by a backslash (\ ):

- **A**: The drive name; as you've learned, drive A is the name for the floppy disk. If this file were stored on the hard disk, the drive name would be C.
- **FM**: The top-level folder on drive A.
- **Tutorial**: A subfolder in the FM folder.
- **Holiday.bmp**: The full filename with the file extension.

If someone tells you to find the file A:\FM\Tutorial\Holiday.bmp, you know you must navigate to your floppy disk drive, open the FM folder, and then open the Tutorial folder to find the Holiday file. My Computer and Windows Explorer can display the full file path in their Address bars so you can keep track of your current location as you navigate.

You can use Windows Explorer to navigate to the Data Files you need for the rest of this tutorial. Refer back to the information you provided in the "Planning Your Organization" section and note the drive on your system that contains your Data Files. In the following steps, this is drive A, the floppy disk drive. If necessary, substitute the appropriate drive on your system when you perform the steps.

To navigate to your Data Files:

1. Make sure your computer can access your Data Files for this tutorial. For example, if you are using a floppy disk, insert the disk into the floppy disk drive.

   Trouble? If you don't have the Data Files, you need to get them before you can proceed. Your instructor will either give you the Data Files or ask you to obtain them from a specified location (such as a network drive). In either case, be sure that you make a backup copy of your Data Files before you start using them, so that the original files will be available on your copied disk in case you need to start over because of an error or problem. If you have any questions about the Data Files, see your instructor or technical support person for assistance.

2. In the Windows Explorer window, click the **expand** icon + next to the drive containing your Data Files, such as 3½ Floppy (A:). A list of the folders on that drive appears.

3. If the list of folders does not include the FM folder, continue clicking the **expand** icon + to navigate to the folder that contains the FM folder.

4. Click the **FM** folder. Its contents appear in the Folders pane and in the right pane of the Windows Explorer window. The FM folder contains the Cases, Review, and Tutorial folders, as shown in Figure 7. The other folders on your system might vary.

Navigating to the FM folder | **Figure 7**

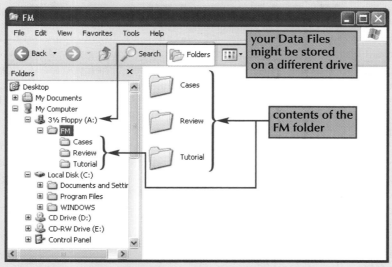

5. In the left pane, click the **Tutorial** folder. The files it contains appear in the right pane. You want to view them as a list.

6. Click the **Views** button 🔡 on the Standard Buttons toolbar, and then click **List**. The files appear in List view in the Windows Explorer window. See Figure 8.

Figure 8 | Files in the Tutorial folder in List view

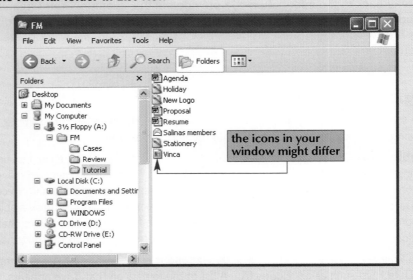

The file icons in your window depend on the programs installed on your computer, so they might be different from the ones shown in Figure 8.

Leave the Windows Explorer window open so you can work with the files in the Tutorial folder.

Working with Folders and Files

After you devise a plan for storing your files, you are ready to get organized by creating folders that will hold your files. You can do so using My Computer or Windows Explorer. For this tutorial, you'll create folders in the Tutorial folder. When you are working on your own computer, you will usually create folders within the My Documents folder.

Examine the files shown in Figure 8 again and determine which files seem to belong together. Holiday, New Logo, and Vinca are all graphics files containing pictures or photographs. The Resume and Stationery files were created for a summer job hunt. The other files were created for the Salinas neighborhood association project to update a playground.

One way to organize these files is to create three folders—one for graphics, one for the job hunt files, and another for the Salinas files. When you create a folder, you give it a name, preferably one that describes its contents. A folder name can have up to 255 characters, except / \ : * ? " < > or |. With these guidelines in mind, you could create three folders as follows:

- **Graphics folder**: Holiday, New Logo, and Vinca files
- **Job Hunt folder**: Resume and Stationery files
- **Playground folder**: Agenda, Proposal, and Salinas members files

Shannon asks you to create three new folders. Then you'll move the files to the appropriate subfolder.

Creating Folders

You've already seen folder icons in the windows you've examined. Now, you'll create folders in the Tutorial folder using the Windows Explorer menu bar.

Creating a Folder Using Windows Explorer

- In the left pane, click the drive or folder where you want to create a folder.
- Click File on the menu bar, point to New, and then click Folder (*or* right-click a blank area in the folder window, point to New, and then click Folder).
- Type a name for the folder, and then press the Enter key.

Now you can create three folders in your Tutorial folder as you planned—the Graphics, Job Hunt, and Playground folders. The Windows Explorer window should show the contents of the Tutorial folder in List view.

To create folders using Windows Explorer:

1. Click **File** on the menu bar, point to **New** to display the submenu, and then click **Folder**. A folder icon with the label "New Folder" appears in the right pane, and the expand icon appears next to the Tutorial folder because it now contains a subfolder. See Figure 9.

Creating a folder in the Tutorial folder ◄ **Figure 9**

folder name is selected and ready for you to replace

Trouble? If the "New Folder" name is not selected, right-click the new folder, click Rename, and then continue with Step 2.

Windows uses "New Folder" as a placeholder, and selects the text so that you can replace it with the name you want.

2. Type **Graphics** as the folder name, and then press the **Enter** key. The new folder is named "Graphics" and is the selected item in the right pane.

You are ready to create a second folder. This time you'll use a shortcut menu to create a folder.

3. Right-click a blank area next to the Graphics folder, point to **New** on the shortcut menu, and then click **Folder**. A folder icon with the label "New Folder" appears in the right pane with the "New Folder" text selected.

4. Type **Job Hunt** as the name of the new folder, and then press the **Enter** key.

5. Using the menu bar or the shortcut menu, create a folder named **Playground**. The Tutorial folder contains three new subfolders.

Now that you've created three folders, you're ready to organize your files by moving them into the appropriate folders.

Moving and Copying Files and Folders

If you want to place a file into a folder from another location, you can either move the file or copy it. **Moving** a file removes it from its current location and places it in a new location you specify. **Copying** places the file in both locations. Windows XP provides several techniques for moving and copying files. The same principles apply to folders—you can move and copy folders using a variety of methods.

Reference Window

Moving a File or Folder in Windows Explorer or My Computer

- Right-click and drag the file you want to move to the destination folder.
- Click Move Here on the shortcut menu.

or

- Click the file you want to move, and then click Move this file in the File and Folder Tasks area.
- In the Move Items dialog box, navigate to the destination folder, and then click the Move button.

Shannon suggests that you continue to work in List view so you can see all the files in the Tutorial folder, and then move some files from the Tutorial folder to the appropriate subfolders. You'll start by moving the Agenda, Proposal, and Salinas members files to the Playground folder.

To move a file using the right mouse button:

1. Point to the **Agenda** file in the right pane, and then press and hold the *right* mouse button.

2. With the right mouse button still pressed down, drag the **Agenda** file to the **Playground** folder. When the Playground folder icon is highlighted, release the button. A shortcut menu opens.

3. With the left mouse button, click **Move Here** on the shortcut menu. The Agenda file is removed from the main Tutorial folder and stored in the Playground subfolder.

   Trouble? If you release the mouse button before dragging the Agenda file to the Playground folder, the shortcut menu opens, letting you move the file to a different folder. Press the Esc key to close the shortcut menu without moving the file, and then repeat Steps 1 through 3.

4. In the right pane, double-click the **Playground** folder. The Agenda file is in the Playground folder.

5. In the left pane, click the **Tutorial** folder to see its contents. The Tutorial folder no longer contains the Agenda file.

The advantage of moving a file or folder by dragging with the right mouse button is that you can efficiently complete your work with one action. However, this technique requires polished mouse skills so that you can drag the file comfortably. Another way to move files and folders is to use the File and Folder Tasks links in the task pane of the Windows Explorer or My Computer window. Although using the File and Folder Tasks links takes more steps, some users find it easier than dragging with the right mouse button.

You'll move the Resume file to the Job Hunt folder next. First, you'll close the Folders pane so that the task pane replaces it.

To move files using the File and Folder Tasks area:

1. Click the **Folders** button on the Standard Buttons toolbar. The task pane replaces the Folders pane, so that this window now resembles the My Computer window. Switch to List view, if necessary.

2. Click the **Resume** file to select it. The task pane links change so that they are appropriate for working with files.

3. In the File and Folder Tasks area, click **Move this file**. The Move Items dialog box opens. See Figure 10.

Move Items dialog box ◀ **Figure 10**

use the expand and collapse icons to navigate your computer

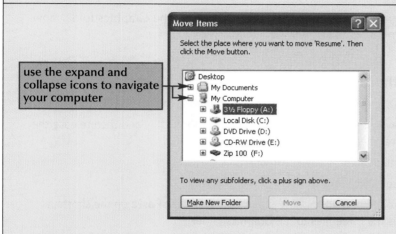

4. Click the **expand** icon ⊞ next to the drive containing your Data Files. Continue clicking **expand** icons ⊞ to navigate to the Tutorial folder provided with your Data Files.

5. Click the **Job Hunt** folder.

6. Click the **Move** button. The Move Items dialog box closes; Windows moves the Resume file to the Job Hunt folder, and then displays the contents of the Tutorial folder, which no longer contains the Resume file.

   You'll move the Stationery file from the Tutorial folder to the Job Hunt folder.

7. Click the **Stationery** file in the Tutorial window, and then click **Move this file** in the File and Folder Tasks area. The Move Items dialog box opens again, with the Job Hunt folder already selected for you.

8. Click the **Move** button.

   You can also copy a file using the same techniques as when you move a file—by dragging with the right mouse button or by using the File and Folder Tasks links. Another easy way to copy a file is to use the file's shortcut menu. You can copy more than one file at the same time by selecting all the files you want to copy, and then clicking them as a group. To select files that are listed together in a window, click the first file in the list, hold down the Shift key, click the last file in the list, and then release the Shift key. To select files that are not listed together, click one file, hold down the Ctrl key, click the other files, and then release the Ctrl key.

Reference Window	**Copying a File or Folder in Windows Explorer or My Computer**

- Click the file or folder you want to copy, and then click Copy this file or Copy this folder in the File and Folder Tasks area.
- In the Copy Items dialog box, navigate to the destination folder, and then click the Copy button.

or

- Right-click the file or folder you want to copy, and then click Copy on the shortcut menu.
- Navigate to the destination folder.
- Right-click a blank area of the destination folder window, and then click Paste on the shortcut menu.

You'll copy the three graphics files from the Tutorial folder to the Graphics folder now. It's easiest to select multiple files in List view or Details view.

To copy files using the shortcut menu:

▶ **1.** In the Tutorial window, switch to List view, if necessary, and then click the **Holiday** file.

▶ **2.** Hold down the **Ctrl** key, click the **New Logo** file, click the **Vinca** file, and then release the **Ctrl** key. Three files are selected in the Tutorial window.

▶ **3.** Right-click a selected file, and then click **Copy** on the shortcut menu.

▶ **4.** In the right pane, double-click the **Graphics** folder to open it.

▶ **5.** Right-click the background of the Graphics folder, and then click **Paste** on the shortcut menu. Windows copies the three files to the Graphics folder.

▶ **6.** Switch to List view, if necessary.

Now that you are familiar with two ways to copy files, you can use the technique you prefer to copy the Proposal and Salinas members files to the Playground folder.

To copy the two files:

▶ **1.** In the Graphics folder window, click the **Back** button on the Standard Buttons toolbar to return to the Tutorial folder.

▶ **2.** Use any technique you've learned to copy the **Proposal** and **Salinas members** files from the Tutorial folder to the Playground folder.

You can move and copy folders in the same way that you move and copy files. When you do, you move or copy all the files contained in the folder. You'll practice moving and copying folders in the Case Problems at the end of this tutorial.

Naming and Renaming Files

As you work with files, pay attention to **filenames**—they provide important information about the file, including its contents and purpose. A filename such as Car Sales.doc has three parts:

- **Main part of the filename:** The name you provide when you create a file, and the name you associate with a file
- **Dot:** The period (.) that separates the main part of the filename from the file extension
- **File extension:** Usually three characters that follow the dot in the filename

The main part of a filename can have up to 255 characters—this gives you plenty of room to name your file accurately enough so that you'll know the contents of the file just by looking at the filename. You can use spaces and certain punctuation symbols in your filenames. Like folder names, however, filenames cannot contain the symbols \ / ? : * " < > | because these characters have special meaning in Windows XP.

A filename might display an **extension**—three or more characters following a dot— that identifies the file's type and indicates the program in which the file was created. For example, in the filename Car Sales.doc, the extension "doc" identifies the file as one created by Microsoft Word, a word-processing program. You might also have a file called Car Sales.xls—the "xls" extension identifies the file as one created in Microsoft Excel, a spreadsheet program. Though the main parts of these filenames are identical, their extensions distinguish them as different files. You usually do not need to add extensions to your filenames because the program that you use to create the file adds the file extension automatically. Also, although Windows XP keeps track of extensions, not all computers are set to display them.

Be sure to give your files and folders meaningful names that will help you remember their purpose and contents. You can easily rename a file or folder by using the Rename command on the file's shortcut menu.

Shannon recommends that you rename the Agenda file in the Playground folder to give it a more descriptive filename—that file could contain the agenda for any meeting. The Agenda file was originally created to store a list of topics to discuss at a meeting of the Salinas neighborhood association. You'll rename the file "Salinas Meeting Agenda."

To rename the Agenda file:

1. Click **Tutorial** in the Other Places menu, and then double-click the **Playground** folder.

2. In the Playground window, right-click the **Agenda** file, and then click **Rename** on the short-cut menu. The filename is highlighted and a box appears around it.

3. Type **Salinas Meeting Agenda**, and then press the **Enter** key. The file now appears with the new name.

   Trouble? If you make a mistake while typing and you haven't pressed the Enter key yet, press the Backspace key until you delete the mistake, and then complete Step 3. If you've already pressed the Enter key, repeat Steps 1 through 3 to rename the file again.

   Trouble? If your computer is set to display file extensions, a message might appear asking if you are sure you want to change the file extension. Click the No button, right-click the Agenda file, click Rename on the shortcut menu, type "Salinas Meeting Agenda.doc", and then press the Enter key.

All the files that originally appeared in the Tutorial folder are now stored in appropriate subfolders. Shannon mentions that you can streamline the organization of the Tutorial folder by deleting the files you no longer need.

Deleting Files and Folders

You should periodically delete files and folders you no longer need so that your main folders and disks don't get cluttered. In My Computer or Windows Explorer, you delete a file or folder by deleting its icon. Be careful when you delete a folder, because you also delete all the files it contains. When you delete a file from a hard disk, Windows XP removes the filename from the folder, but stores the file contents in the Recycle Bin. The **Recycle Bin** is an area on your hard disk that holds deleted files until you remove them permanently; an icon on the desktop allows you easy access to the Recycle Bin. If you change your mind and want to retrieve a file deleted from your hard disk, you can use the Recycle Bin to recover it or return it to its original location. However, after you empty the Recycle Bin, you can no longer recover the files that were in it.

When you delete a file from a floppy disk or another disk on your network, it does not go into the Recycle Bin. Instead, it is deleted as soon as its icon disappears—and you cannot recover it.

Shannon reminds you that because you copied the Holiday, New Logo, Proposal, Salinas members, and Vinca files to the Graphics and Playground folders, you can safely delete the original files in the Tutorial folder. As with moving, copying, and renaming files and folders, you can delete a file or folder in many ways, including using a shortcut menu or the File and Folder Tasks menu.

To delete files in the Tutorial folder:

▶ **1.** Use any technique you've learned to navigate to and open the **Tutorial** folder.

▶ **2.** Switch to List view (if necessary), click **Holiday** (the first file in the file list), hold down the **Shift** key, click **Vinca** (the last file in the file list), and then release the **Shift** key. All the files in the Tutorial folder are now selected. None of the subfolders should be selected.

▶ **3.** Right-click the selected files, and then click **Delete** on the shortcut menu. Windows XP asks if you're sure you want to delete these files.

▶ **4.** Click the **Yes** button.

So far, you've worked with files using Windows Explorer and My Computer, but you haven't viewed any of their contents. To view file contents, you open the file. When you double-click a file in Windows Explorer or My Computer, Windows XP starts the appropriate program and opens the file.

Working with Compressed Files

If you transfer files from one location to another, such as from your hard disk to a removable disk or vice versa, or from one computer to another via e-mail, you can store the files in a **compressed (zipped) folder** so that they take up less disk space. You can then transfer the files more quickly. When you create a compressed folder, Windows XP displays a zipper on the folder icon.

You compress a folder so that the files it contains use less space on the disk. Compare two folders—a folder named My Pictures that contains about 8.6 MB of files and a compressed folder containing the same files, but requiring only 6.5 MB of disk space. In this case, the compressed files use about 25 percent less disk space than the uncompressed files.

You can create a compressed folder using the Compressed (zipped) Folder command on the New submenu of the File menu or shortcut menu in Windows Explorer or My Computer. Then you can compress files or other folders by dragging them into the compressed folder. You can open files directly from a compressed folder, or you can extract the files first. When you **extract** a file, you create an uncompressed copy of the file and folder in a folder you specify. The original file remains in the compressed folder.

If a different compression program has been installed on your computer, such as WinZip or PKZip, the Compressed (zipped) Folder command does not appear on the New submenu. Instead, it is replaced by the name of your compression program. In this case, refer to your compression program's Help system for instructions on working with compressed files.

Shannon suggests you compress the files and folders in the Tutorial folder so you can more quickly transfer them to another location.

To compress the folders and files in the Tutorial folder:

1. In Windows Explorer, navigate to the Tutorial folder.

2. Right-click a blank area of the right pane, point to **New** on the shortcut menu, and then click **Compressed (zipped) Folder**. A new compressed folder with a zipper icon appears in the Tutorial window. See Figure 11. Your window might appear in a different view.

Creating a compressed folder **Figure 11**

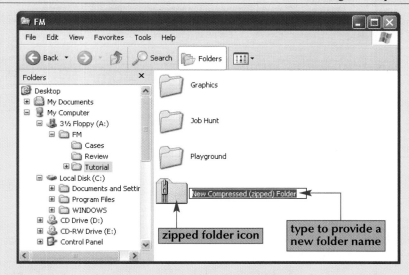

Trouble? If the Compressed (zipped) Folder command does not appear on the New sub-menu, a different compression program is probably installed on your computer. Click a blank area of the Tutorial window to close the shortcut menu, and then read but do not perform the remaining steps.

3. Type **Final Tutorial files**, and then press the **Enter** key. Windows XP creates the compressed folder in the Tutorial folder.

4. Click the **Graphics** folder in the right pane, hold down the **Shift** key, click the **Playground** folder in the right pane, and then release the **Shift** key. Three folders are selected in the Tutorial window.

5. Drag the three folders to the **Final Tutorial files** compressed folder. Windows XP copies the files to the folder, compressing them to save space.

You open a compressed folder by double-clicking it. You can then move and copy files and folders in a compressed folder, though you cannot rename them. If you want to open, edit, and save files in a compressed folder, you should first extract them. When you do, Windows XP uncompresses the files and copies them to a location that you specify, preserving them in their folders as appropriate.

To extract the compressed files:

1. Right-click the **Final Tutorial files** compressed folder, and then click **Extract All** on the shortcut menu. The Extraction Wizard starts and opens the Welcome to the Compressed (zipped) Folders Extraction Wizard dialog box.

2. Click the **Next** button. The Select a Destination dialog box opens.

▶ **3.** Press the **End** key to deselect the path in the text box, press the **Backspace** key as many times as necessary to delete "Final Tutorial files," and then type **Extracted**. The last three parts of the path in the text box should be "\FM\Tutorial\Extracted." See Figure 12.

Figure 12	▶ Select a Destination dialog box

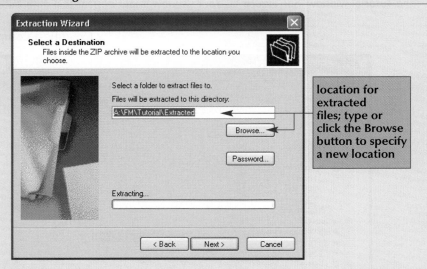

location for extracted files; type or click the Browse button to specify a new location

▶ **4.** Click the **Next** button. The Extraction Complete dialog box opens, indicating that your files have been successfully extracted to the specified folder.

▶ **5.** Make sure the **Show extracted files** check box is checked, and then click the **Finish** button. The Extracted folder opens, showing the Graphics, Job Hunt, and Playground folders.

▶ **6.** Open each folder to make sure it contains the files you worked with in this tutorial.

▶ **7.** Close all open windows.

Shannon says you have successfully completed basic Windows XP file management tasks, and are ready to use Windows XP to organize your files.

Review

Quick Check

1. What is the term for a collection of data that has a name and is stored on a disk or other storage medium?
2. If you have only one floppy disk drive on your computer, it is usually identified by the letter _____.
3. The letter C is typically used for the _____ drive of a computer.
4. What are the two tools that Windows XP provides for exploring the files and folders on your computer?
5. What is the notation you can use to indicate a file's location on your computer?
6. True or False: The advantage of moving a file or folder by dragging with the right mouse button is that you can efficiently complete your work with one action.
7. In a filename, the _____ identifies the file's type and indicates the program in which the file was created.
8. True or False: When you extract a file, the original file is deleted from the compressed folder.

Review

Tutorial Summary

In this tutorial, you examined Windows XP file organization, noting that you need to organize files and folders to work efficiently. You learned about typical file management strategies, whether you are working on a hard disk or a removable disk. Then you applied these strategies to organizing files and folders by creating folders, moving and copying files, and renaming and deleting files. You also learned how to copy files to a compressed (zipped) folder, and then extract files from a compressed folder.

Key Terms

backup	extract	move
compact disc (CD)	file	My Computer
compressed (zipped) folder	file path	My Documents folder
copy	file system	pane
disk	filename	Recycle Bin
document	floppy disk	root directory
drive	folder	subfolder
Explorer bar	Folders pane	Windows Explorer
extension	hard disk	Zip disk

Practice

Practice the skills you learned in the tutorial.

Review Assignments

Data Files needed for the Review Assignments: Commissions.xls, Contracts.xls, Customer Accounts.xls, Billing Worksheet.wk4, Car Savings Plan.xls, Personal Loan.doc, Speech.wav, Filenames.pps, Water lilies.jpg

Complete the following steps, recording your answers to any questions in the spaces provided:

1. Use My Computer or Windows Explorer as necessary to record the following information:
   - Where are you supposed to store the files you use in the Review Assignments for this tutorial? _____
   - Describe the method you will use to navigate to the location where you save your files for this book. _____

   - Do you need to follow any special guidelines or conventions when naming the files your save for this book? For example, should all the filenames start with your course number or tutorial number? If so, describe the conventions. _____

   - When you are instructed to open a file for this book, what location are you supposed to use? _____
   - Describe the method you will use to navigate to this location. _____

2. Use My Computer or Windows Explorer to navigate to and open the FM\Review folder provided with your Data Files.
3. Examine the nine files in the Review folder included with your Data Files, and then answer the following questions:
   - How will you organize these files? _____

   - What folders will you create? _____

- Which files will you store in these folders? _____

- Will you use any built-in Windows folders? If so, which ones? For which files?

   _____

4. In the Review folder, create three folders: Business, Personal Finances, and Project Media.
5. Move the **Commissions**, **Contracts**, **Customer Accounts**, and **Billing Worksheet** files from the Review folder to the Business folder.
6. Move the **Car Savings Plan** and **Personal Loan** files to the Personal Finances folder.
7. Copy the remaining files to the Project Media folder.
8. Delete the files in the Review folder (do *not* delete any folders).
9. Rename the **Speech** file in the Project Media folder to **Ask Not**.
10. Create a compressed (zipped) folder in the Review folder named **Final Review files** that contains all the files and folders in the Review folder.
11. Extract the contents of the Final Review files folder to a new folder named **Extracted**. (*Hint:* The file path will end with "\FM\Review\Extracted.")
12. Use Windows Explorer or My Computer to locate all copies of the **Personal Loan** file in the subfolders of the Review folder. In which locations did you find this file?

   _____

13. Close all open windows.

Case Problem 1

Apply

Use the skills you learned in the tutorial to manage files and folders for an arts organization.

Data Files needed for this Case Problem: Invoice Jan.xls, Invoice Feb.xls, Invoice March.xls, Painting Class – Agenda.doc, Painting Class – Questionnaire.doc, Painting Class – Teaching Manual.doc, Paris.jpg, Vegetables.jpg

Jefferson Street Fine Arts Center Rae Wysnewski owns the Jefferson Street Fine Arts Center (JSFAC) in Pittsburgh, and offers classes and gallery, studio, and practice space for aspiring and fledgling artists, musicians, and dancers. Rae opened JSFAC two years ago, and this year the center has a record enrollment in its classes. Knowing you are multitalented, she hires you to teach a painting class for three months and to show her how to manage her files on her new Windows XP computer. Complete the following steps:

1. In the FM\Cases folder provided with your Data Files, create two folders: Invoices and Painting Class.
2. Move the **Invoice Jan**, **Invoice Feb**, and **Invoice March** files from the Cases folder to the Invoices folder.
3. Rename the three files in the Invoices folder to remove "Invoice" from each name.
4. Move the three text documents from the Cases folder to the Painting Class folder. Rename the three documents, using shorter but still descriptive names.
5. Copy the remaining files to the Painting Class folder.

Explore

6. Using My Computer or Windows Explorer, switch to Details view and then answer the following questions:
   a. What is the largest file in the Painting Class folder? _____
   b. How many files (don't include folders) are in the Cases folder? _____
   c. How many word-processed documents are in the Cases folder and its subfolders? ___
   d. How many files in the Painting Class folder are JPEG images? (*Hint:* Look in the Type column to identify JPEG images.) _____
7. Delete the **Paris** and **Vegetables** files from the Painting Class folder.

8. Open the Recycle Bin folder by double-clicking the Recycle Bin icon on the desktop. Do the Paris and Vegetables files appear in the Recycle Bin folder? Explain why or why not. _____

9. Copy the Painting Class folder to the Cases folder. The name of the duplicate folder appears as "Copy of Painting Class." Rename the "Copy of Painting Class" folder as "Graphics."

10. Create a new folder in the Cases folder named "JSFAC." Move the Invoices, Painting Class, and Graphics folders to the JSFAC folder.

Challenge

Extend what you've learned to discover other methods of managing files for a social service organization.

Case Problem 2

There are no Data Files needed for this Case Problem.

First Call Outreach Victor Crillo is the director of a social service organization named First Call Outreach in Toledo, Ohio. Its mission is to connect people who need help from local and state agencies to the appropriate service. Victor has a dedicated staff, but they are all relatively new to Windows XP. In particular, they have trouble finding files that they have saved on their hard disks. He asks you to demonstrate how to find files in Windows XP. Complete the following:

Explore

1. Windows XP Help and Support includes topics that explain how to search for files on a disk without looking through all the folders. Click the Start button and then click Help and Support to start Windows Help and Support. Use one of the following methods to locate topics on searching for files.
   - On the Home page, click the Windows Basics link. On the Windows Basics page, click a link related to searching for files or information, and then click a topic related to searching for files or folders.
   - On the Index page, type "files" (no quotation marks) in the Type in the keyword to find text box. In the list of entries for "files," double-click "searching for." In the Topics found dialog box, double-click "Searching for files or folders."
   - In the Search box, type "searching for files," and then click Search. Click the Searching for files or folders link.

Explore

2. Read the topic and click the Related Topics link at the end of the topic, if necessary, to provide the following information:
   a. To display the Search dialog box, you must click the _____ button, point to _____ from the menu, and finally click _____ from the submenu.
   b. Do you need to type in the entire filename to find the file? _____
   c. Name three file characteristics you can use as search options. _____ _____ _____

Explore

3. Use the Index page in Windows XP Help and Support to locate topics related to managing files and folders. Write out two procedures for managing files and folders that were not covered in the tutorial. _____ _____ _____ _____

SAM Assessment and Training

If you have a SAM user profile, you may have access to hands-on instruction, practice, and assessment of the skills covered in this tutorial. Log in to your SAM account and go to your assignments page to see what your instructor has assigned.

Reinforce

Lab Assignments

The New Perspectives Labs are designed to help you master some of the key concepts and skills presented in this text. The steps for completing this Lab are located on the Course Technology Web site. Log on to the Internet and use your Web browser to go to the Student Online Companion for New Perspectives Office 2003 site at **www.course.com/np/office2003**. Click the Lab Assignments link, and then navigate to the assignments for this tutorial.

Review

Quick Check Answers

1. file
2. A
3. hard disk
4. Windows Explorer and My Computer
5. file path
6. true
7. extension
8. false

Read This Before You Begin

To the Student

Data Files

To complete the Using Common Features of Microsoft Office 2003 tutorial, you need the starting student Data Files. Your instructor will either provide you with these Data Files or ask you to obtain them yourself.

The Using Common Features of Microsoft Office 2003 tutorial requires the folder named "OFF" to complete the Tutorial, Review Assignments, and Case Problems. You will need to copy this folder from a file server, a stand-alone computer, or the Web to the drive and folder where you will be storing your Data Files. Your instructor will tell you which computer, drive letter, and folder(s) contain the files you need. You can also download the files by going to www.course.com; see the inside back or front cover for

more information on downloading the files, or ask your instructor or technical support person for assistance.

If you are storing your Data Files on floppy disks, you will need one blank, formatted, high-density disk for this tutorial. Label your disk as shown, and place on it the folder indicated.

▼Common Features of Office: Data Disk

   OFF folder

When you begin this tutorial, refer to the Student Data Files section at the bottom of the tutorial opener page, which indicates which folders and files you need for the tutorial. Each end-of-tutorial exercise also indicates the files you need to complete that exercise.

To the Instructor

The Data Files are available on the Instructor Resources CD for this title. Follow the instructions in the Help file on the CD to install the programs to your network or standalone computer. See the "To the Student" section above for information on how to set up the Data Files that accompany this text.

You are granted a license to copy the Data Files to any computer or computer network used by students who have purchased this book.

System Requirements

If you are going to work through this book using your own computer, you need:

- **Computer System** Microsoft Windows 2000 or Windows XP Professional or higher must be installed on your computer. This tutorial assumes a typical installation of Microsoft Office 2003. Additionally, to

complete the steps for accessing Microsoft's Online Help for Office, an Internet connection and a Web browser are required.

- **Data Files** You will not be able to complete the tutorals or exercises in this book using your own computer until you have the necessary starting Data Files.

www.course.com/NewPerspectives

Objectives

- Explore the programs that comprise Microsoft Office
- Start programs and switch between them
- Explore common window elements
- Minimize, maximize, and restore windows
- Use personalized menus and toolbars
- Work with task panes
- Create, save, close, and open a file
- Use the Help system
- Print a file
- Exit programs

Using Common Features of Microsoft Office 2003

Preparing Promotional Materials

Case

Delmar Office Supplies

Delmar Office Supplies, a company in Wisconsin founded by Jake Alexander in 1996, sells recycled office supplies to businesses and home-based offices around the world. The demand for quality recycled papers, reconditioned toner cartridges, and renovated office furniture has been growing each year. Jake and all his employees use Microsoft Office 2003, which provides everyone in the company the power and flexibility to store a variety of information, create consistent files, and share data. In this tutorial, you'll review how the company's employees use Microsoft Office 2003.

Student Data Files

▼**OFF folder**

▽ **Tutorial folder**

    (no starting Data Files)

▽ **Review folder**

    Finances.xls
    Letter.doc

Exploring Microsoft Office 2003

Microsoft Office 2003, or simply **Office**, is a collection of the most popular Microsoft programs: Word, Excel, PowerPoint, Access, and Outlook. Each Office program contains valuable tools to help you accomplish many tasks, such as composing reports, analyzing data, preparing presentations, compiling information, sending e-mail, and planning schedules.

Microsoft Word 2003, or simply **Word**, is a word-processing program you use to create text documents. The files you create in Word are called **documents**. Word offers many special features that help you compose and update all types of documents, ranging from letters and newsletters to reports, brochures, faxes, and even books—all in attractive and readable formats. You can also use Word to create, insert, and position figures, tables, and other graphics to enhance the look of your documents. The Delmar Office Supplies sales representatives create their business letters using Word.

Microsoft Excel 2003, or simply **Excel**, is a spreadsheet program you use to display, organize, and analyze numerical data. You can do some of this in Word with tables, but Excel provides many more tools for recording and formatting numbers as well as perform-ing calculations. The graphics capabilities in Excel also enable you to display data visually. You might, for example, generate a pie chart or a bar chart to help readers quickly see the significance of and the connections between information. The files you create in Excel are called **workbooks**. The Delmar Office Supplies operations department uses a line chart in an Excel workbook to visually track the company's financial performance.

Microsoft Access 2003, or simply **Access**, is a database program you use to enter, orga-nize, display, and retrieve related information. The files you create in Access are called **databases**. With Access you can create data entry forms to make data entry easier, and you can create professional reports to improve the readability of your data. The Delmar Office Supplies operations department tracks the company's inventory in a table in an Access database.

Microsoft PowerPoint 2003, or simply **PowerPoint**, is a presentation graphics program you use to create a collection of slides that can contain text, charts, pictures, and so on. The files you create in PowerPoint are called **presentations**. You can show these presenta-tions on your computer monitor, project them onto a screen as a slide show, print them, share them over the Internet, or display them on the World Wide Web. You can also use PowerPoint to generate presentation-related documents such as audience handouts, out-lines, and speakers' notes. The Delmar Office Supplies sales department has created an effective slide presentation with PowerPoint to promote the company's latest product line.

Microsoft Outlook 2003, or simply **Outlook**, is an information management program you use to send, receive, and organize e-mail; plan your schedule; arrange meetings; organize contacts; create a to-do list; and jot down notes. You can also use Outlook to print schedules, task lists, phone directories, and other documents. Jake Alexander uses Outlook to send and receive e-mail, plan his schedule, and create a to-do list.

Although each Office program individually is a strong tool, their potential is even greater when used together.

Integrating Office Programs

One of the main advantages of Office is **integration**, the ability to share information between programs. Integration ensures consistency and accuracy, and it saves time because you don't have to re-enter the same information in several Office programs. The staff at Delmar Office Supplies uses the integration features of Office daily, including the following examples:

- The accounting department created an Excel bar chart on the previous two years' fourth-quarter results, which they inserted into the quarterly financial report created in Word. They included a hyperlink in the Word report that employees can click to open the Excel workbook and view the original data.
- The operations department included an Excel pie chart of sales percentages by divisions of Delmar Office Supplies on a PowerPoint slide, which is part of a presentation to stockholders.
- The marketing department produced a mailing to promote the company's newest products by combining a form letter created in Word with an Access database that stores the names and addresses of customers.
- A sales representative wrote a letter in Word about a sales incentive program and merged the letter with an Outlook contact list containing the names and addresses of his customers.

These are just a few examples of how you can take information from one Office program and integrate it into another.

Starting Office Programs

You can start any Office program by clicking the Start button on the Windows taskbar, and then selecting the program you want from the All Programs menu. Once the program starts, you can immediately begin to create new files or work with existing ones. If you or another user has recently used one of the Office programs, then that program might appear on the most frequently used programs list on the left side of the Start menu. You can click the program name to start the program.

Starting Office Programs	Reference Window

- Click the Start button on the taskbar.
- Point to All Programs.
- Point to Microsoft Office.
- Click the name of the program you want to start.

or

- Click the name of the program you want to start on the most frequently used programs list on the left side of the Start menu.

You'll start Excel using the Start button.

To start Excel and open a new, blank workbook:

1. Make sure your computer is on and the Windows desktop appears on your screen.

   Trouble? If your screen varies slightly from those shown in the figures, then your computer might be set up differently. The figures in this book were created while running Windows XP in its default settings, but how your screen looks depends on a variety of things, including the version of Windows, background settings, and so forth.

2. Click the **Start** button on the taskbar, and then point to **All Programs** to display the All Programs menu.

3. Point to **Microsoft Office** on the All Programs menu, and then point to **Microsoft Office Excel 2003**. See Figure 1. Depending on how your computer is set up, your desktop and menu might contain different icons and commands.

Figure 1 ▶ Start menu with All Programs submenu displayed

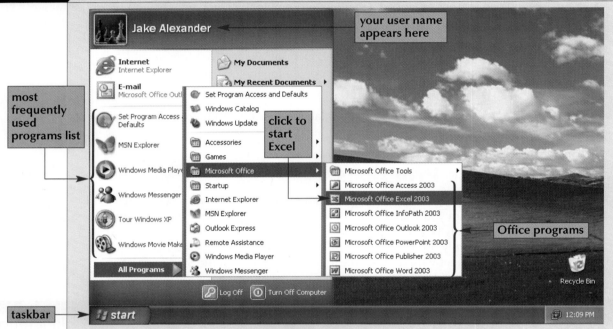

   Trouble? If you don't see Microsoft Office on the All Programs menu, point to Microsoft Office Excel 2003. If you still don't see Microsoft Office Excel 2003, ask your instructor or technical support person for help.

4. Click **Microsoft Office Excel 2003** to start Excel and open a new, blank workbook. See Figure 2.

New, blank Excel workbook | **Figure 2**

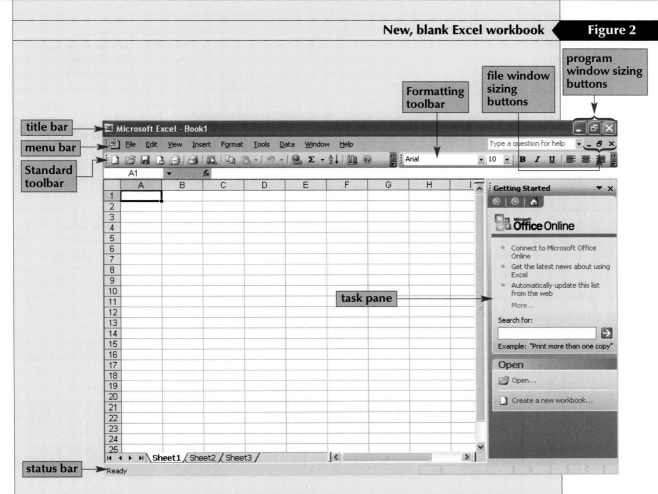

Trouble? If the Excel window doesn't fill your entire screen, the window is not maximized, or expanded to its full size. You'll maximize the window shortly.

You can have more than one Office program open at once. You'll use this same method to start Word and open a new, blank document.

To start Word and open a new, blank document:

▶ 1. Click the **Start** button on the taskbar.

▶ 2. Point to **All Programs** to display the All Programs menu.

▶ 3. Point to **Microsoft Office** on the All Programs menu.

   Trouble? If you don't see Microsoft Office on the All Programs menu, point to Microsoft Office Word 2003. If you still don't see Microsoft Office Word 2003, ask your instructor or technical support person for help.

▶ 4. Click **Microsoft Office Word 2003**. Word opens with a new, blank document. See Figure 3.

Figure 3 ▸ **New, blank document in Word**

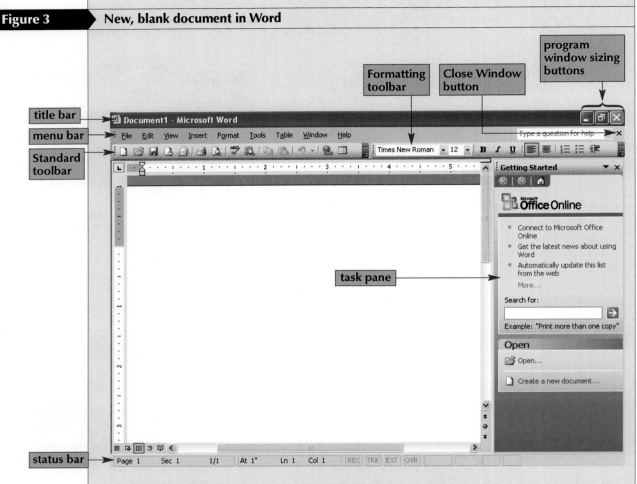

Trouble? If the Word window doesn't fill your entire screen, the window is not maximized. You'll maximize the window shortly.

When you have more than one program or file open at a time, you can switch between them.

Switching Between Open Programs and Files

Two programs are running at the same time—Excel and Word. The taskbar contains buttons for both programs. When you have two or more programs running, or two files within the same program open, you can use the taskbar buttons to switch from one program or file to another. The employees at Delmar Office Supplies often work in several programs at once.

To switch between Word and Excel:

► **1.** Click the **Microsoft Excel – Book1** button on the taskbar to switch from Word to Excel. See Figure 4.

Excel and Word programs opened simultaneously ◄ **Figure 4**

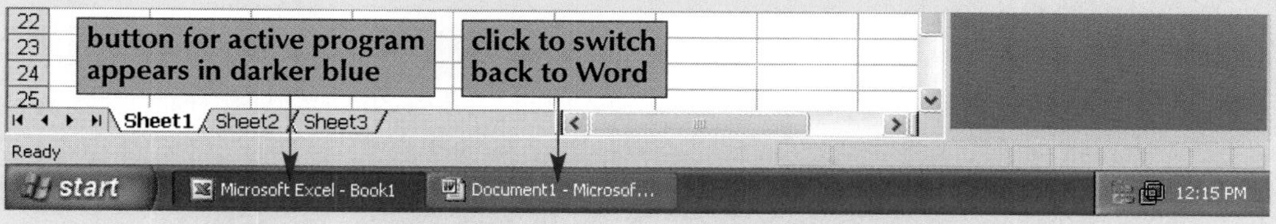

► **2.** Click the **Document1 – Microsoft Word** button on the taskbar to return to Word.

As you can see, you can start multiple programs and switch between them in seconds.

Exploring Common Window Elements

The Office programs consist of windows that have many similar features. As you can see in Figures 2 and 3, many of the elements you see in both the Excel program window and the Word program window are the same. In fact, all the Office programs have these same elements. Figure 5 describes some of the most common window elements.

Common window elements ◄ **Figure 5**

Element	Description
Title bar	A bar at the top of the window that contains the filename of the open file, the program name, and the program window sizing buttons
Menu bar	A collection of menus for commonly used commands
Toolbars	Collections of buttons that are shortcuts to commonly used menu commands
Sizing buttons	Buttons that resize and close the program window or the file window
Task pane	A window that provides access to commands for common tasks you'll perform in Office programs
Status bar	An area at the bottom of the program window that contains information about the open file or the current task on which you are working

Because these elements are the same in each program, once you've learned one program, it's easy to learn the others. The next sections explore the primary common features—the window sizing buttons, the menus and toolbars, and the task panes.

Using the Window Sizing Buttons

There are two sets of sizing buttons. The top set controls the program window and the bottom set controls the file window. There are three different sizing buttons. The Minimize button ▬, which is the left button, hides a window so that only its program button is visible on the taskbar. The middle button changes name and function depending on the status of the window—the Maximize button ▢ expands the window to the full screen size or to the program window size, and the Restore button ◱ returns the window to a predefined size. The right button, the Close button ✕, exits the program or closes the file.

Most often you'll want to maximize the program and file windows as you work to take advantage of the full screen size you have available. If you have several files open, you might want to restore the files so that you can see more than one window at a time or you might want to minimize the programs with which you are not working at the moment. You'll try minimizing, maximizing, and restoring windows now.

To resize windows:

▶ 1. Click the **Minimize** button 🗕 on the Word title bar to reduce the Word program window to a taskbar button. The Excel window is visible again.

▶ 2. If necessary, click the **Maximize** button 🗖 on the Excel title bar. The Excel program window expands to fill the screen.

▶ 3. Click the **Restore Window** button 🗗 on the Excel menu bar. The file window, referred to as the workbook window in Excel, resizes smaller than the full program window. See Figure 6.

| Figure 6 | Resized Excel windows |

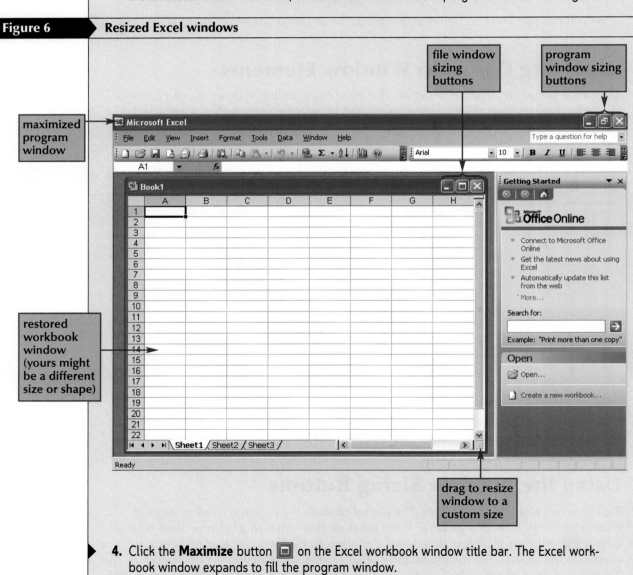

4. Click the **Maximize** button 🗖 on the Excel workbook window title bar. The Excel workbook window expands to fill the program window.

▶ **5.** Click the **Document1 - Microsoft Word** button on the taskbar. The Word program window returns to its previous size.

▶ **6.** If necessary, click the **Maximize** button 🔲 on the Word title bar. The Word program window expands to fill the screen.

The sizing buttons give you the flexibility to arrange the program and file windows on your screen to best fit your needs.

Using Menus and Toolbars

In each Office program, you can perform tasks using a menu command, a toolbar button, or a keyboard shortcut. A **menu command** is a word on a menu that you click to execute a task; a **menu** is a group of related commands. For example, the File menu contains commands for managing files, such as the Open command and the Save command. The File, Edit, View, Insert, Format, Tools, Window, and Help menus appear on the menu bar in all the Office programs, although some of the commands they include differ from program to program. Other menus are program specific, such as the Table menu in Word and the Data menu in Excel.

A **toolbar** is a collection of buttons that correspond to commonly used menu commands. For example, the Standard toolbar contains an Open button and a Save button. The Standard and Formatting toolbars (as well as other toolbars) appear in all the Office programs, although some of the buttons they include differ from program to program. The Standard toolbar has buttons related to working with files. The Formatting toolbar has buttons related to changing the appearance of content. Each program also has program-specific toolbars, such as the Tables and Borders toolbar in Word for working with tables and the Chart toolbar in Excel for working with graphs and charts.

A **keyboard shortcut** is a combination of keys you press to perform a command. For example, Ctrl+S is the keyboard shortcut for the Save command (you hold down the Ctrl key while you press the S key). Keyboard shortcuts appear to the right of many menu commands.

Viewing Personalized Menus and Toolbars

When you first use a newly installed Office program, the menus and toolbars display only the basic and most commonly used commands and buttons, streamlining the program window. The other commands and buttons are available, but you have to click an extra button to see them (the Expand button on a menu and the Toolbar Options button on a toolbar). As you select commands and click buttons, the ones you use often are put on the short, personalized menu and on the visible part of the toolbars. The ones you don't use remain available on the full menus and toolbars. This means that the Office menus and toolbars might display different commands and buttons on each person's computer.

To view a personalized and full menu:

▶ **1.** Click **Insert** on the Word menu bar to display the short, personalized menu. See Figure 7. The Bookmark command, for example, does not appear on the short menu.

Figure 7 | **Short, personalized menu**

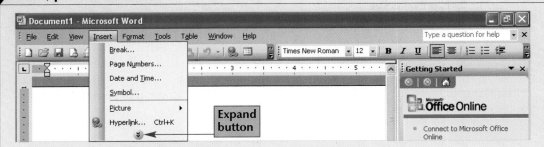

Trouble? If the Insert menu displays different commands than those shown in Figure 7, you need to reset the menus. Click Tools on the menu bar, click Customize (you might need to pause until the full menu appears to see the command), and then click the Options tab in the Customize dialog box. Click the Always show full menus check box to remove the check mark, if necessary, and then click the Show full menus after a short delay check box to insert a check mark, if necessary. Click the Reset menu and toolbar usage data button, and then click the Yes button to confirm that you want to reset the commands. Click the Close button. Repeat Step 1.

You can display the full menu in one of three ways: (1) pause until the full menu appears, which might happen as you read this; (2) click the Expand button at the bottom of the menu; or (3) double-click the menu name on the menu bar.

2. Pause until the full Insert menu appears, as shown in Figure 8. The Bookmark command and other commands are now visible.

Figure 8 | **Full, expanded menu**

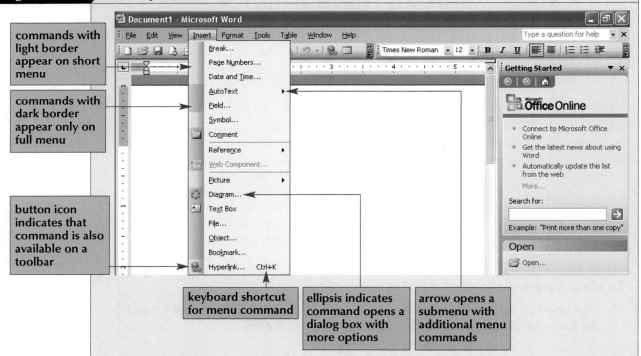

3. Click the **Bookmark** command. A dialog box opens when you click a command whose name is followed by an ellipsis (...). In this case, the Bookmark dialog box opens.

▶ **4.** Click the **Cancel** button to close the Bookmark dialog box.

▶ **5.** Click **Insert** on the menu bar again to display the short, personalized menu. The Bookmark command appears on the short, personalized menu because you have recently used it.

▶ **6.** Press the **Esc** key on the keyboard twice to close the menu.

As you can see, the menu changed based on your actions. Over time, only the commands you use frequently will appear on the personalized menu. The toolbars work similarly.

To use the personalized toolbars:

▶ **1.** Observe that the Standard and Formatting toolbars appear side by side below the menu bar.

Trouble? If the toolbars appear on two rows, you need to reset them to their default state. Click Tools on the menu bar, click Customize, and then click the Options tab in the Customize dialog box. Click the Show Standard and Formatting toolbars on two rows check box to remove the check mark. Click the Reset menu and toolbar usage data button, and then click the Yes button to confirm you want to reset the commands. Click the Close button. Repeat Step 1.

▶ **2.** Click the **Toolbar Options** button ⬚ on the Standard toolbar. See Figure 9.

Toolbar Options palette ◀ **Figure 9**

Trouble? If you see different buttons on the Toolbar Options palette, your side-by-side toolbars might be sized differently than the ones shown in Figure 9. Continue with Step 3.

▶ **3.** Click the **Show/Hide ¶** button ⬚ on the Toolbar Options palette to display the nonprinting screen characters. The Show/Hide ¶ button moves to the visible part of the Standard toolbar, and another button may be moved onto the Toolbar Options palette to make room for the new button.

Trouble? If the Show/Hide ¶ button already appears on the Standard toolbar, click another button on the Toolbar Options palette. Then click that same button again in Step 4 to turn off that formatting, if necessary.

Some buttons, like the Show/Hide ¶ button, act as a toggle switch—one click turns on the feature and a second click turns it off.

▶ **4.** Click the **Show/Hide ¶** button ⬚ on the Standard toolbar again to hide the nonprinting screen characters.

Some people like that the menus and toolbars change to meet their work habits. Others prefer to see all the menu commands or to display the default toolbars on two rows so that all the buttons are always visible. You'll change the toolbar setting now.

To turn off the personalized toolbars:

▶ **1.** Click the **Toolbar Options** button ▪ on the right side of the Standard toolbar.

▶ **2.** Click the **Show Buttons on Two Rows** command. The toolbars move to separate rows (the Standard toolbar on top) and you can see all the buttons on each toolbar.

You can easily access any button on the Standard and Formatting toolbars with one mouse click. The drawback is that when the toolbars are displayed on two rows, they take up more space in the program window, limiting the space you have to work.

Using Task Panes

A **task pane** is a window that provides access to commands for common tasks you'll perform in Office programs. For example, the Getting Started task pane, which opens when you first start any Office program, enables you to create new files and open existing ones. Task panes also help you navigate through more complex, multi-step procedures. All the Office programs include the task panes described in Figure 10. The other available task panes vary by program.

| Figure 10 | Common task panes |

Task pane	Description
Getting Started	The home task pane; allows you to create new files, open existing files, search the online and offline Help system by keyword, and access Office online
Help	Allows you to search the online and offline Help system by keyword or table of contents, and access Microsoft Office Online
Search Results	Displays available Help topics related to entered keyword and enables you to initiate a new search
New	Allows you to create new files; name changes to New Document in Word, New Workbook in Excel, New File in Access, and New Presentation in PowerPoint
Clip Art	Allows you to search for all types of media clips (pictures, sound, video) and insert clips from the results
Clipboard	Allows you to paste some or all of the items that have been cut or copied from any Office program during the current work session
Research	Allows you to search a variety of reference material and other resources from within a file

No matter what their purpose, you use the same processes to open, close, and navigate between the task panes.

Opening and Closing Task Panes

When you first start any Office program, the Getting Started task pane opens by default along the right edge of the program window. You can resize or move the task pane to suit your work habits. You can also close the task pane to display the open file in the full available program window. For example, you might want to close the task pane when you are typing the body of a letter in Word or entering a lot of data in Excel.

You will open and close the task pane.

To open and close the task pane:

▶ 1. If necessary, click **View** on the menu bar, and then click **Task Pane**. The most recently viewed task pane opens on the right side of the screen. See Figure 11.

Getting Started task pane | **Figure 11**

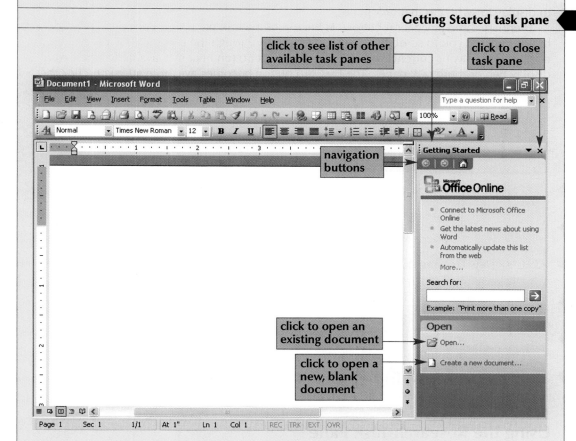

Trouble? If you do not see the task pane, you probably closed the open task pane in Step 1. Repeat Step 1 to reopen the task pane.

Trouble? If a different task pane than the Getting Started task pane opens, then another task pane was the most recently viewed task pane. You'll learn how to open different task panes in the next section; continue with Step 2.

▶ 2. Click the **Close** button ☒ on the task pane title bar. The task pane closes, leaving more room on the screen for the open file.

▶ 3. Click **View** on the menu bar, and then click **Task Pane**. The task pane reopens.

There are several ways to display different task panes.

Navigating Among Task Panes

Once the task pane is open, you can display different task panes to suit the task you are trying to complete. For example, you can display the New task pane when you want to create a new file from a template. The name of the New task pane varies, depending on the program you are using: Word has the New Document task pane, Excel has the New Workbook task pane, PowerPoint has the New Presentation task pane, and Access has the New File task pane.

One of the quickest ways to display a task pane is to use the Other Task Panes button. When you point to the name of the open task pane in the task pane title bar, it becomes the Other Task Panes button. When you click the Other Task Panes button, all the available task panes for that Office program are listed. Just click the name of the task pane you want to display to switch to that task pane.

There are three navigation buttons at the top of the task pane. The Back and Forward buttons enable you to scroll backward and forward through the task panes you have opened during your current work session. The Back button becomes available when you display two or more task panes. The Forward button becomes available after you click the Back button to return to a previously viewed task pane. The Home button returns you to the Getting Started task pane no matter which task pane is currently displayed.

You'll use each of these methods to navigate among the task panes.

To navigate among task panes:

1. Point to **Getting Started** in the task pane title bar. The title bar becomes the Other Task Panes button.

2. Click the **Other Task Panes** button. A list of the available task panes for Word is displayed. The check mark before Getting Started indicates that this is the currently displayed task pane.

3. Click **New Document**. The New Document task pane appears and the Back button is available.

4. Click the **Back** button in the task pane. The Getting Started task pane reappears and the Forward button is available.

5. Click the **Forward** button in the task pane. The New Document task pane reappears and the Back button is available.

6. Click the **Home** button in the task pane. The Getting Started task pane reappears.

Using the Research Task Pane

The Research task pane allows you to search a variety of reference materials and other resources to find specific information while you are working on a file. You can insert the information you find directly into your open file. The thesaurus and language translation tools are installed with Office and therefore are stored locally on your computer. If you are connected to the Internet, you can also use the Research task pane to access a dictionary, an encyclopedia, research sites, as well as business and financial sources. Some of the sites that appear in the search results are fee-based, meaning that you'll need to pay to access information on that site.

To use the Research task pane, you type a keyword or phrase into the Search for text box and then select whether you want to search all the books, sites, and sources; one category; or a specific source. The search results appear in the Research task pane. Some of the results appear as links, which you can click to open your browser window and display that information. If you are using Internet Explorer 5.01 or later as your Web browser, the Research task pane is tiled (appears side by side) with your document. If you are using another Web browser, you'll need to return to the task pane in your open file to click another link.

The Research task pane functions independently in each file. So you can open multiple files and perform a different search in each. In addition, each Research task pane stores the results of up to 10 searches, so you can quickly return to the results from any of your most recent searches. To move among the saved searches, click the Back and Forward buttons in the task pane.

Using the Research Task Pane

- Type a keyword or phrase into the Search for text box.
- Select a search category, individual source, or all references.
- If necessary, click a link in the search results to display more information.
- Copy and paste selected content from the task pane into your file.

Jake plans to send a copy of the next quarter's sales report to the office in France. You'll use the bilingual dictionaries in the Research task pane to begin entering labels in French into an Excel workbook for the sales report.

To use the bilingual dictionaries in the Research task pane:

1. Click the **Microsoft Excel – Book1** button on the taskbar to switch to the Excel window.

2. Click the **Other Task Panes** button on the Getting Started task pane, and then click **Research**. The Research task pane opens.

3. Click in the **Search for** text box, and then type **paper**.

4. Click the **Search for** list arrow and then click **Translation**. The bilingual dictionary opens in the Research task pane. You can choose from among 12 languages to translate to and from, including Japanese, Russian, Spanish, Dutch, German, and French.

   Trouble? If a dialog box opens stating the translation feature is not installed, click the Yes button to install it.

5. If necessary, click the **To** list arrow, and then click **French (France)**. See Figure 12.

Research task pane ◄ **Figure 12**

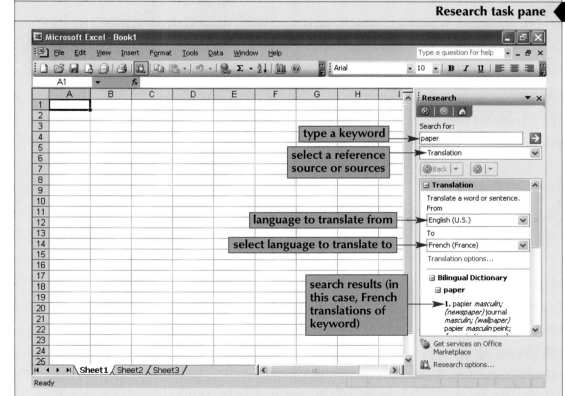

6. Scroll to read the different translations of "paper" in French.

After you locate specific information, you can quickly insert it into your open file. The information can be inserted by copying the selected content you want to insert, and then pasting it in the appropriate location in your file. In some instances, such as MSN Money Stock Quotes, a button appears enabling you to quickly insert the indicated information in your file at the location of the insertion point. Otherwise, you can use the standard Copy and Paste commands.

You'll copy the translation for "paper" into the Excel workbook.

To copy information from the Research task pane into a file:

▶ **1.** Select **papier** in the Research task pane. This is the word you want to copy to the workbook.

▶ **2.** Right-click the selected text, and then click **Copy** on the shortcut menu. The text is duplicated on the Office Clipboard.

▶ **3.** Right-click cell **A1**, and then click **Paste**. The word "papier" is entered into the cell. See Figure 13.

| Figure 13 | Translation copied into Excel |

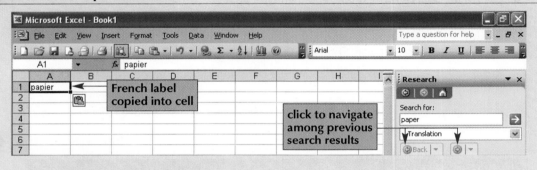

You'll repeat this process to look up the translation for "furniture" and copy it into cell A2.

To translate and copy another word into Excel:

▶ **1.** Double-click **paper** in the Search for text box to select the text, type **furniture**, and then click the **Start searching** button ➔ in the Research task pane.

▶ **2.** Verify that you're translating from English (U.S) to French (France).

▶ **3.** Select **meubles** in the translation results, right-click the selected text, and then click **Copy**.

▶ **4.** Right-click cell **A2**, and then click **Paste**. The second label appears in the cell.

The Research task pane works similarly in all the Office programs. You'll use other task panes later in this tutorial to perform specific tasks, including opening a file and getting assistance.

Working with Files

The most common tasks you'll perform in any Office program are to create, open, save, and close files. The processes for each of these tasks are the same in all the Office programs. In addition, there are several methods for performing most tasks in Office. This flexibility enables you to use Office in a way that fits how you like to work.

Creating a File

To begin working in a program, you need to create a new file or open an existing file. When you start Word, Excel, or PowerPoint, the program opens along with a blank file—ready for you to begin working on a new document, workbook, or presentation. When you start Access, the Getting Started task pane opens, displaying options for opening a new database or an existing one.

Jake has asked you to start working on the agenda for the stockholder meeting, which he suggests you create using Word. You enter text in a Word document by typing.

To enter text in a document:

▶ **1.** Click the **Document1 – Microsoft Word** button on the taskbar to activate the Word program window.

▶ **2.** Type **Delmar Office Supplies**, and then press the **Enter** key. The text you typed appears on one line in the Word document.

Trouble? If you make a typing error, press the Backspace key to delete the incorrect letters, and then retype the text.

▶ **3.** Type **Stockholder Meeting Agenda**, and then press the **Enter** key. The text you typed appears on the second line.

Next, you'll save the file.

Saving a File

As you create and modify Office files, your work is stored only in the computer's temporary memory, not on a hard disk. If you were to exit the programs, turn off your computer, or experience a power failure, your work would be lost. To prevent losing work, save your file to a disk frequently—at least every 10 minutes. You can save files to the hard disk located inside your computer or to portable storage disks, such as floppy disks, Zip disks, or read-write CD-ROMs.

The first time you save a file, you need to name it. This name is called a **filename**. When you choose a filename, select a descriptive one that accurately reflects the content of the document, workbook, presentation, or database, such as "Shipping Options Letter" or "Fourth Quarter Financial Analysis." Filenames can include a maximum of 255 letters, numbers, hyphens, and spaces in any combination. Office appends a **file extension** to the filename, which identifies the program in which that file was created. The file extensions are .doc for Word, .xls for Excel, .ppt for PowerPoint, and .mdb for Access. Whether you see file extensions depends on how Windows is set up on your computer.

You also need to decide where to save the file—on which disk and in what folder. A **folder** is a container for your files. Just as you organize paper documents within folders stored in a filing cabinet, you can organize your files within folders stored on your computer's hard disk or a removable disk. Store each file in a logical location that you will remember whenever you want to use the file again.

Reference Window | **Saving a File**

- Click the Save button on the Standard toolbar (*or* click File on the menu bar, and then click Save or Save As).
- In the Save As dialog box, click the Save in list arrow, and then navigate to the location where you want to save the file.
- Type a filename in the File name text box.
- Click the Save button.
- To resave the named file to the same location, click the Save button on the Standard toolbar (*or* click File on the menu bar, and then click Save).

The two lines of text you typed are not yet saved on disk. You'll do that now.

To save a file for the first time:

1. Click the **Save** button 🖫 on the Standard toolbar. The Save As dialog box opens. The first few words of the first line appear in the File name text box, as a suggested filename. You'll replace this with a more descriptive filename.

2. Click the **Save in** list arrow, and then click the location that contains your Data Files.

   Trouble? If you don't have the Common Office Features Data Files, you need to get them before you can proceed. Your instructor will either give you the Data Files or ask you to obtain them from a specified location (such as a network drive). In either case, be sure that you make a backup copy of your Data Files before you start using them, so that the original files will be available on your copied disk in case you need to start over because of an error or problem. If you have any questions about the Data Files, see your instructor or technical support person for assistance.

3. Double-click the **OFF** folder in the list box, and then double-click the **Tutorial** folder. This is the location where you want to save the document. See Figure 14.

4. Type **Stockholder Meeting Agenda** in the File name text box.

Figure 14 ▶ **Completed Save As dialog box**

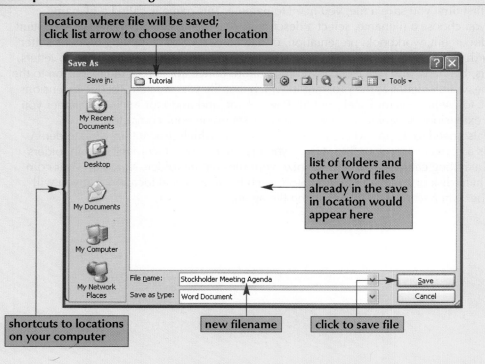

location where file will be saved; click list arrow to choose another location

list of folders and other Word files already in the save in location would appear here

shortcuts to locations on your computer

new filename

click to save file

Trouble? If the .doc file extension appears after the filename, then your computer is configured to show file extensions. Continue with Step 5.

▶ **5.** Click the **Save** button. The Save As dialog box closes, and the name of your file appears in the program window title bar.

The saved file includes everything in the document at the time you last saved it. Any edits or additions you then make to the document exist only in the computer's memory and are not saved in the file on the disk. As you work, remember to save frequently so that the file is updated to reflect the latest content of the document.

Because you already named the document and selected a storage location, the second and subsequent times you save, the Save As dialog box doesn't open. If you wanted to save a copy of the file with a different filename or to a different location, you would reopen the Save As dialog box by clicking File on the menu bar, and then clicking Save As. The previous version of the file remains on your disk as well.

You need to add your name to the agenda. Then you'll save your changes.

To modify and save a file:

▶ **1.** Type your name, and then press the **Enter** key. The text you typed appears on the next line.

▶ **2.** Click the **Save** button 🔲 on the Standard toolbar to save your changes.

When you're done with a file, you can close it.

Closing a File

Although you can keep multiple files open at one time, you should close any file you are no longer working on to conserve system resources as well as to ensure that you don't inadvertently make changes to the file. You can close a file by clicking the Close command on the File menu or by clicking the Close Window button in the upper-right corner of the menu bar.

As a standard practice, you should save your file before closing it. If you're unsure whether the file is saved, it cannot hurt to save it again. However, Office has an added safeguard: If you attempt to close a file or exit a program without saving your changes, a dialog box opens asking whether you want to save the file. Click the Yes button to save the changes to the file before closing the file and program. Click the No button to close the file and program without saving changes. Click the Cancel button to return to the program window without saving changes or closing the file and program. This feature helps to ensure that you always save the most current version of any file.

You'll add the date to the agenda. Then, you'll attempt to close the document without saving.

To modify and close a file:

▶ **1.** Type the date, and then press the **Enter** key. The text you typed appears under your name in the document.

▶ **2.** Click the **Close Window** button 🗙 on the Word menu bar to close the document. A dialog box opens, asking whether you want to save the changes you made to the document.

▶ **3.** Click the **Yes** button. The current version of the document is saved to the file, and then the document closes, and Word is still running.

Trouble? If Word is not running, then you closed the program in Step 2. Start Word, click the Close Window button on the menu bar to close the blank document.

Once you have a program open, you can create additional new files for the open program or you can open previously created and saved files.

Opening a File

When you want to open a blank document, workbook, presentation, or database, you create a new file. When you want to work on a previously created file, you must first open it. Opening a file transfers a copy of the file from the storage disk (either a hard disk or a portable disk) to the computer's memory and displays it on your screen. The file is then in your computer's memory and on the disk.

Reference Window | **Opening an Existing or a New File**

- Click the Open button on the Standard toolbar (*or* click File on the menu bar, and then click Open *or* click the More link in the Open section of the Getting Started task pane).
- In the Open dialog box, click the Look in list arrow, and then navigate to the storage location of the file you want to open.
- Click the filename of the file you want to open.
- Click the Open button.

or

- Click the New button on the Standard toolbar (*or* click File on the menu bar, click New, and then (depending on the program) click the Blank document, Blank workbook, Blank presentation, or Blank database link in the New task pane).

Jake asks you to print the agenda. To do that, you'll reopen the file. You'll use the Open button on the Standard toolbar.

To open an existing file:

▶ **1.** Click the **Open** button 📂 on the Standard toolbar. The Open dialog box, which works similarly to the Save As dialog box, opens.

▶ **2.** Click the **Look in** list arrow, and then navigate to the **OFF\Tutorial** folder included with your Data Files. This is the location where you saved the agenda document.

▶ **3.** Click **Stockholder Meeting Agenda** in the file list. See Figure 15.

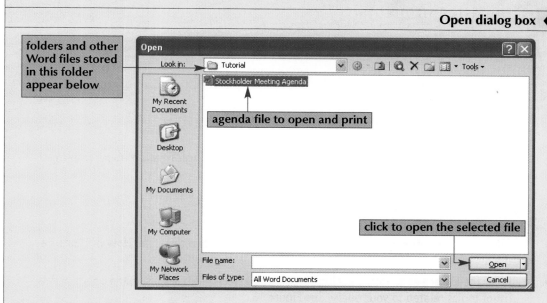

Open dialog box ◄ **Figure 15**

4. Click the **Open** button. The file containing the agenda opens in the Word program window.

Next, you'll get information about printing files in Word.

Getting Help

If you don't know how to perform a task or want more information about a feature, you can turn to Office itself for information on how to use it. This information, referred to simply as **Help**, is like a huge encyclopedia available from your desktop. You can access Help in a variety of ways, including ScreenTips, the Type a question for help box, the Help task pane, and Microsoft Office Online.

Using ScreenTips

ScreenTips are a fast and simple method you can use to get help about objects you see on the screen. A **ScreenTip** is a yellow box with the button's name. Just position the mouse pointer over a toolbar button to view its ScreenTip.

Using the Type a Question for Help Box

For answers to specific questions, you can use the **Type a question for help box**, located on the menu bar of every Office program, to find information in the Help system. You simply type a question using everyday language about a task you want to perform or a topic you need help with, and then press the Enter key to search the Help system. The Search Results task pane opens with a list of Help topics related to your query. You click a topic to open a Help window with step-by-step instructions that guide you through a specific procedure and explanations of difficult concepts in clear, easy-to-understand language. For example, you might ask how to format a cell in an Excel worksheet; a list of Help topics related to the words you typed will appear.

Reference Window | **Getting Help from the Type a Question for Help Box**

- Click the Type a question for help box on the menu bar.
- Type your question, and then press the Enter key.
- Click a Help topic in the Search Results task pane.
- Read the information in the Help window. For more information, click other topics or links.
- Click the Close button on the Help window title bar.

You'll use the Type a question for help box to obtain more information about printing a document in Word.

To use the Type a question for help box:

1. Click the **Type a question for help box** on the menu bar, and then type **How do I print a document?**

2. Press the **Enter** key to retrieve a list of topics. The Search Results task pane opens with a list of topics related to your query. See Figure 16.

Figure 16 | **Search Results task pane displaying Help topics**

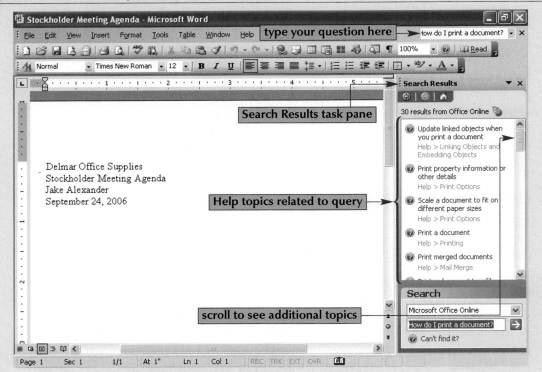

Trouble? If your search results list differs from the one shown in Figure 16, your computer is not connected to the Internet or Microsoft has updated the list of available Help topics since this book was published. Continue with Step 3.

3. Scroll through the list to review the Help topics.

4. Click **Print a document** to open the Help window and learn more about the various ways to print a document. See Figure 17.

Print a document Help window ◀ **Figure 17**

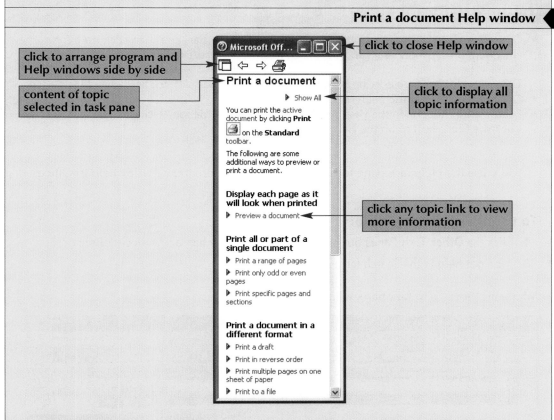

Trouble? If the Word program window and the Help window do not appear side by side, then you need to tile the windows. Click the Auto Tile button on the toolbar in the Help window.

5. Read the information, and then when you're done, click the **Close** button ☒ on the Help window title bar to close the Help window.

The Help task pane works similarly.

Using the Help Task Pane

For more in-depth help, you can use the **Help task pane**, a task pane that enables you to search the Help system using keywords or phrases. You type a specific word or phrase in the Search for text box, and then click the Start searching button. The Search Results task pane opens with a list of topics related to the keyword or phrase you entered. If your computer is connected to the Internet, you might see more search results because some Help topics are stored only online and not locally on your computer. The task pane also has a Table of Contents link that organizes the Help system by subjects and topics, like in a book. You click main subject links to display related topic links.

Reference Window   **Getting Help from the Help Task Pane**

- Click the Other Task Panes button on the task pane title bar, and then click Help (*or* click Help on the menu bar, and then click Microsoft Word/Excel/PowerPoint/Access/ Outlook Help).
- Type a keyword or phrase in the Search for text box, and then click the Start searching button.
- Click a Help topic in the Search Results task pane.
- Read the information in the Help window. For more information, click other topics or links.
- Click the Close button on the Help window title bar.

You'll use the Help task pane to obtain more information about getting help in Office.

To use the Help task pane:

1. Click the **Other Task Panes** button on the task pane title bar, and then click **Help**.
2. Type **get help** in the Search for text box. See Figure 18.

Figure 18   **Microsoft Word Help task pane with keyword**

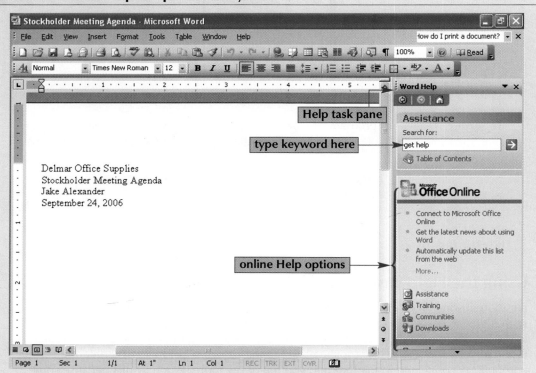

3. Click the **Start searching** button →. The Search Results task pane opens with a list of topics related to your keywords.
4. Scroll through the list to review the Help topics.
5. Click **About getting help while you work** to open the Microsoft Word Help window and learn more about the various ways to obtain help in Word. See Figure 19.

About getting help while you work Help window   Figure 19

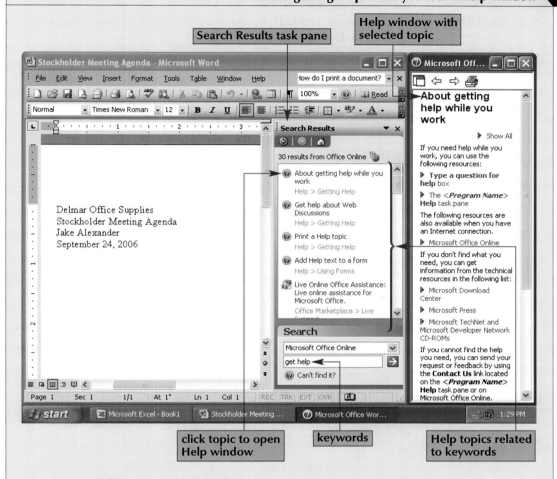

Trouble? If your search results list differs from the one shown in Figure 19, your computer is not connected to the Internet or Microsoft has updated the list of available Help topics since this book was published. Continue with Step 6.

Trouble? If the Word program window and the Help window do not appear side by side, then you need to tile the windows. Click the Auto Tile button on the toolbar in the Help window.

6. Click **Microsoft Office Online** in the right pane to display information about that topic. Read the information.

7. Click the other links about this feature and read the information.

8. When you're done, click the **Close** button ⊠ on the Help window title bar to close the Help window. The task pane remains open.

If your computer has a connection to the Internet, you can get more help information from Microsoft Office Online.

Using Microsoft Office Online

Microsoft Office Online is a Web site maintained by Microsoft that provides access to additional Help resources. For example, you can access current Help topics, read how-to articles, and find tips for using Office. You can search all or part of a site to find information about tasks you want to perform, features you want to use, or anything else you want more help with. You can connect to Microsoft Office Online from the Getting Started task pane, the Help task pane, or the Help menu.

To connect to Microsoft Office Online, you'll need Internet access and a Web browser such as Internet Explorer.

To connect to Microsoft Office Online:

▶ **1.** Click the **Back** button 🔄 in the Search Results task pane. The Word Help task pane reappears.

▶ **2.** Click the **Connect to Microsoft Office Online** link in the task pane. Internet Explorer starts and the Microsoft Office Online home page opens. See Figure 20. This Web page offers links to Web pages focusing on getting help and for accessing additional Office resources, such as additional galleries of clip art, software downloads, and training opportunities.

| Figure 20 | Microsoft Office Online home page |

Trouble? If the content you see on the Microsoft Office Online home page differs from the figure, the site has been updated since this book was published. Continue with Step 3.

▶ **3.** Click the **Assistance** link. The Assistance page opens. From this page, you browse for help in each of the different Office programs. You can also enter a keyword or phrase pertaining to a particular topic you wish to search for information on using the Search box in the upper-right corner of the window.

▶ **4.** Click the **Close** button ☒ on the Internet Explorer title bar to close the browser.

The Help features enable the staff at Delmar Office Supplies to get answers to questions they have about any task or procedure when they need it. The more you practice getting information from the Help system, the more effective you will be at using Office to its full potential.

Printing a File

At times, you'll want a paper copy of your Office file. The first time you print during each session at the computer, you should use the Print menu command to open the Print dialog box so you can verify or adjust the printing settings. You can select a printer, the number of copies to print, the portion of the file to print, and so forth; the printing settings vary slightly from program to program. For subsequent print jobs, you can use the Print button to print without opening the dialog box, if you want to use the same default settings.

Printing a File

- Click File on the menu bar, and then click Print.
- Verify the print settings in the Print dialog box.
- Click the OK button.

or

- Click the Print button on the Standard toolbar.

Now that you know how to print, you'll print the agenda for Jake.

To print a file:

1. Make sure your printer is turned on and contains paper.
2. Click **File** on the menu bar, and then click **Print**. The Print dialog box opens. See Figure 21.

Print dialog box ◄ **Figure 21**

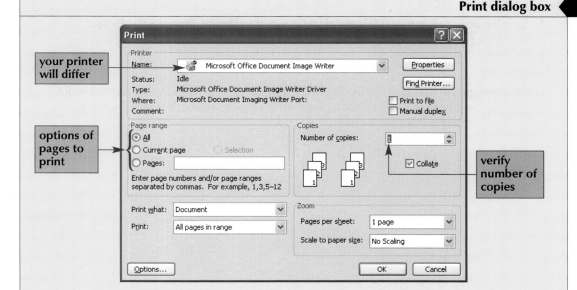

your printer will differ

options of pages to print

verify number of copies

▶ 3. Verify that the correct printer appears in the Name list box in the Printer area. If the wrong printer appears, click the **Name** list arrow, and then click the correct printer from the list of available printers.

▶ 4. Verify that **1** appears in the Number of copies text box.

▶ 5. Click the **OK** button to print the document.

Trouble? If the document does not print, see your instructor or technical support person for help.

Now that you have printed the agenda, you can close Word and Excel.

Exiting Programs

Whenever you finish working with a program, you should exit it. As with many other aspects of Office, you can exit programs with a button or from a menu. You'll use both methods to close Word and Excel. You can use the Exit command to exit a program and close an open file in one step. If you haven't saved the final version of the open file, a dialog box opens, asking whether you want to save your changes. Clicking the Yes button saves the open file, closes the file, and then exits the program.

To exit a program:

▶ 1. Click the **Close** button ⊠ on the Word title bar to exit Word. The Word document closes and the Word program exits. The Excel window is visible again on your screen.

Trouble? If a dialog box opens, asking whether you want to save the document, you may have inadvertently made a change to the document. Click the No button.

▶ 2. Click **File** on the Excel menu bar, and then click **Exit**. A dialog box opens asking whether you want to save the changes you made to the workbook.

▶ 3. Click the **Yes** button. The Save As dialog box opens.

▶ 4. Save the workbook in the **OFF\Tutorial** folder with the filename **French Sales Report**. The workbook closes, saving a copy to the location you specified, and the Excel program exits.

Exiting programs after you are done using them keeps your Windows desktop unclut-tered for the next person using the computer, frees up your system's resources, and pre-vents data from being lost accidentally.

Review

Quick Check

1. List the five programs included in Office.
2. How do you start an Office program?
3. Explain the difference between Save As and Save.
4. What is one method for opening an existing Office file?
5. What happens if you attempt to close a file or exit a program without saving the current version of the open file?
6. What are four ways to get help?

Review

Tutorial Summary

You have learned how to use features common to all the programs included in Microsoft Office 2003, including starting and exiting programs; resizing windows; using menus and toolbars; working with task panes; saving, opening, closing, and printing files; and getting help.

Key Terms

Access	menu	Outlook
database	menu bar	PowerPoint
document	menu command	presentation
Excel	Microsoft Access 2003	ScreenTip
file extension	Microsoft Excel 2003	task pane
filename	Microsoft Office 2003	toolbar
folder	Microsoft Office Online	Type a question for help box
Help	Microsoft Outlook 2003	Word
Help task pane	Microsoft PowerPoint 2003	workbook
integration	Microsoft Word 2003	
keyboard shortcut	Office	

Practice

Practice the skills you learned in the tutorial using the same case scenario.

Review Assignments

Data Files needed for the Review Assignments: Finances.xls, Letter.doc

Before the stockholders meeting at Delmar Office Supplies, you'll open and print documents for the upcoming presentation. Complete the following steps:

1. Start PowerPoint.
2. Use the Help task pane to learn how to change the toolbar buttons from small to large, and then do it. Use the same procedure to change the buttons back to regular size. Close the Help window when you're done.
3. Start Excel.
4. Switch to the PowerPoint window using the taskbar, and then close the presentation but leave open the PowerPoint program. (*Hint:* Click the Close Window button on the menu bar.)
5. Open a new, blank PowerPoint presentation from the Getting Started task pane. (*Hint:* Click Create a new presentation in the Open section of the Getting Started task pane.)
6. Close the PowerPoint presentation and program using the Close button on the PowerPoint title bar; do not save changes if asked.

7. Open the **Finances** workbook located in the **OFF\Review** folder included with your Data Files using the Open button on the Standard toolbar in Excel.
8. Use the Save As command to save the workbook as **Delmar Finances** in the **OFF\Review** folder.
9. Type your name, press the Enter key to insert your name at the top of the worksheet, and then save the workbook.
10. Print one copy of the worksheet using the Print command on the File menu.
11. Exit Excel using the File menu.
12. Start Word, and then use the Getting Started task pane to open the **Letter** document located in the **OFF\Review** folder included with your Data Files. (*Hint:* Click the More link in the Getting Started task pane to open the Open dialog box.)
13. Use the Save As command to save the document with the filename **Delmar Letter** in the **OFF\Review** folder.
14. Press and hold the Ctrl key, press the End key, and then release both keys to move the insertion point to the end of the letter, and then type your name.
15. Use the Save button on the Standard toolbar to save the change to the Delmar Letter document.
16. Print one copy of the document, and then close the document.
17. Exit the Word program using the Close button on the title bar.

Assess

SAM Assessment and Training

If you have a SAM user profile, you may have access to hands-on instruction, practice, and assessment of the skills covered in this tutorial. Log in to your SAM account and go to your assignments page to see what your instructor has assigned.

Review

Quick Check Answers

1. Word, Excel, PowerPoint, Access, Outlook
2. Click the Start button on the taskbar, point to All Programs, point to Microsoft Office, and then click the name of the program you want to open.
3. Save As enables you to change the filename and storage location of a file. Save updates a file to reflect its latest contents using its current filename and location.
4. Either click the Open button on the Standard toolbar or click the More link in the Getting Started task pane to open the Open dialog box.
5. A dialog box opens asking whether you want to save the changes to the file.
6. ScreenTips, Type a question for help box, Help task pane, Microsoft Office Online

New Perspectives on
Microsoft® Office PowerPoint® 2003

Tutorial 1   PPT 3
Creating a Presentation
Presenting Information About Humanitarian Projects

Tutorial 2   PPT 41
Applying and Modifying Text and Graphic Objects
Presenting and Preparing for an Expedition to Peru

Read This Before You Begin: Tutorials 1–2

To the Student

Data Files

To complete the Level I PowerPoint Tutorials (Tutorials 1 and 2), you need the starting student Data Files. Your instructor will either provide you with these Data Files or ask you to obtain them yourself.

The Level I PowerPoint Tutorials require the folders shown in the next column to complete the Tutorials, Review Assignments, and Case Problems. You will need to copy these folders from a file server, a standalone computer, or the Web to the drive and folder where you will be storing your Data Files. Your instructor will tell you which computer, drive letter, and folder(s) contain the files you need. You can also download the files by going to www.course.com; see the inside back or front cover for more information on downloading the files, or ask your instructor or technical support person for assistance.

If you are storing your Data Files on floppy disks, you will need **two** blank, formatted, high-density disks for these tutorials. Label your disks as shown, and place on them the folder(s) indicated.

▼ **PowerPoint 2003: Data Disk 1**
   Tutorial.01 folder
▼ **PowerPoint 2003: Data Disk 2**
   Tutorial.02 folder

When you begin a tutorial, refer to the Student Data Files section at the bottom of the tutorial opener page, which indicates which folders and files you need for the tutorial. Each end-of-tutorial exercise also indicates the files you need to complete that exercise.

To the Instructor

The Data Files are available on the Instructor Resources CD for this title. Follow the instructions in the Help file on the CD to install the programs to your network or standalone computer. See the "To the Student" section above for information on how to set up the Data Files that accompany this text.

You are granted a license to copy the Data Files to any computer or computer network used by students who have purchased this book.

System Requirements

If you are going to work through this book using your own computer, you need:

- **Computer System** Microsoft Windows 2000, Windows XP, or higher must be installed on your computer. These tutorials assume a complete installation of Microsoft Office PowerPoint 2003.

- **Data Files** You will not be able to complete the tutorials or exercises in this book using your own computer until you have the necessary starting Data Files.

www.course.com/NewPerspectives

Objectives

Session 1.1
- Open and view an existing PowerPoint presentation
- Switch views and navigate a presentation
- View a presentation in Slide Show view
- Create a presentation using the AutoContent Wizard

Session 1.2
- Add, move, and delete slides
- Promote and demote text in the Outline tab
- Create speaker notes for slides
- Check the spelling and style in a presentation
- Preview and print slides
- Print outlines, handouts, and speaker notes

Creating a Presentation

Presenting Information About Humanitarian Projects

Case

Global Humanitarian, Austin Office

In 1985, a group of Austin, Texas business leaders established a nonprofit organization called Global Humanitarian. Its goal was to alleviate abject poverty in the third world through public awareness and personal involvement in sustainable self-help initiatives in third-world villages. Today, Global Humanitarian is a large umbrella organization and clearinghouse for national and international humanitarian organizations. Its five major functions are to help provide the following: entrepreneurial support, service expeditions, inventory surplus exchange, funding and grant proposals, and student internships.

The president of Global Humanitarian is Norma Flores, who sits on the board of directors and carries out its policies and procedures. The managing director of the Austin office is Miriam Schwartz, and the managing director in Latin America is Pablo Fuentes, who lives and works in Lima, Peru. Miriam wants you to use PowerPoint to develop a presentation to provide information about Global Humanitarian's current projects to potential donors, expedition participants, and student interns.

In this tutorial, you'll examine a presentation that Miriam created to become familiar with **Microsoft Office PowerPoint 2003** (or simply **PowerPoint**). You'll then create a presentation based on content that PowerPoint suggests by using the AutoContent Wizard. You'll modify the text in the presentation, and you'll add and delete slides. You'll check the spelling and style of the presentation, and then you'll view the completed slide show. Finally, you'll save the slide show and print handouts.

Student Data Files

▼**Tutorial.01**

▽ **Tutorial folder**

Lorena.ppt

▽ **Review folder**

VillageOP.ppt

▽ **Cases folder**

LASIK.ppt
Seafoods.ppt

Session 1.1

What Is PowerPoint?

PowerPoint is a powerful presentation graphics program that provides everything you need to produce an effective presentation in the form of on-screen slides, a slide presentation on a Web site, black-and-white or color overheads, or 35-mm photographic slides. You may have already seen your instructors use PowerPoint presentations to enhance their classroom lectures.

Using PowerPoint, you can prepare each component of a presentation: individual slides, speaker notes, an outline, and audience handouts. The presentation you'll create for Miriam will include slides, notes, and handouts.

To start PowerPoint:

1. Click the **Start** button on the taskbar, point to **All Programs**, point to **Microsoft Office**, and then click **Microsoft Office PowerPoint 2003**. PowerPoint starts and the PowerPoint window opens. See Figure 1-1.

   Trouble? If you don't see the Microsoft Office PowerPoint 2003 option on the Microsoft Office submenu, look for it on a different submenu or as an option on the All Programs menu. If you still cannot find the Microsoft Office PowerPoint 2003 option, ask your instructor or technical support person for help.

Figure 1-1	**Blank PowerPoint window**

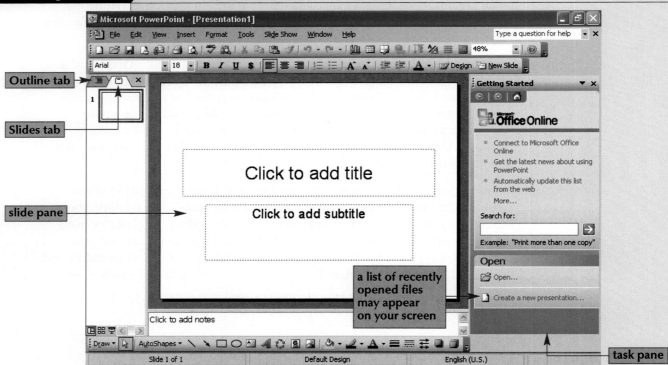

Trouble? If the PowerPoint program window is not maximized, click the Maximize 🔲 button on the program window title bar.

Trouble? If the Office Assistant (an animated icon, usually a paper clip with eyes) opens when you start PowerPoint, right-click the Office Assistant, and then click Hide to close it.

Opening an Existing PowerPoint Presentation

Before you prepare the presentation on Global Humanitarian, Miriam suggests that you view an existing presentation recently prepared under Norma's and Miriam's direction as an example of PowerPoint features. When you examine the presentation, you'll learn about some PowerPoint capabilities that can help make your presentations more interesting and effective. You'll open the presentation now.

To open the existing presentation:

1. Make sure you have access to the Data Files in the Tutorial.01 folder.

   Trouble? If you don't have the PowerPoint Data Files, you need to get them before you can proceed. Your instructor will either give you the Data Files or ask you to obtain them from a specified location (such as a network drive). In either case, be sure that you make a backup copy of your Data Files before you start using them, so that the original files will be available on your copied disk in case you need to start over because of an error or problem. If you have any questions about the Data Files, see your instructor or technical support person for assistance.

2. Click the **Open** link under Open in the Getting Started task pane. The Open dialog box appears on the screen.

   Trouble? If you don't see the Open link, either click More or point to the small triangle at the bottom of the task pane to view additional links.

3. Click the **Look in** list arrow to display the list of disk drives on your computer, and then navigate to the **Tutorial.01\Tutorial** folder included with your Data Files.

4. Click **Lorena** (if necessary), and then click the **Open** button to display Miriam's presentation. The presentation opens in Normal view. See Figure 1-2.

PowerPoint window with presentation open ◄ **Figure 1-2**

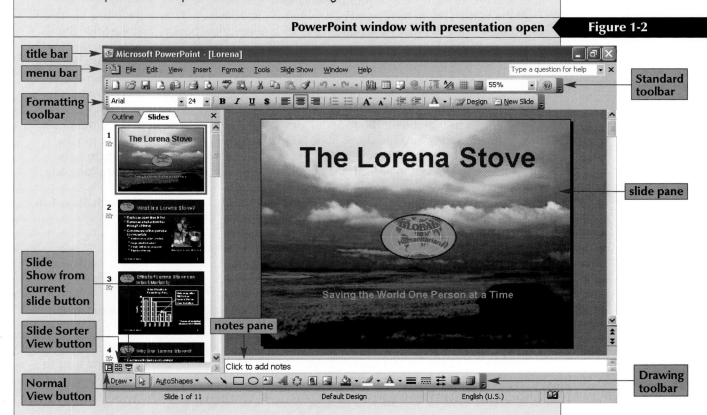

Trouble? If you see filename extensions on your screen (such as ".ppt" appended to "Lorena" in the filename), don't be concerned; they won't affect your work.

Trouble? If your screen doesn't show the Drawing toolbar, click View on the menu bar, point to Toolbars, and then click Drawing.

Trouble? If your screen shows the Standard toolbar and the Formatting toolbar on the same line, click Tools on the menu bar, click Customize, click the Options tab, click the Show Standard and Formatting toolbars on two rows check box to select it, and then click the Close button.

Switching Views and Navigating a Presentation

The PowerPoint window contains features common to all Windows programs, as well as features specific to PowerPoint. One obvious difference between the PowerPoint window and other Office programs is that the PowerPoint window is divided into sections. The section in the center of the screen, to the left of the task pane, is the slide pane. The **slide pane** shows the current slide as it will look during your slide show. Just below the slide pane is the notes pane. The **notes pane** contains notes (also called speaker notes) for the presenter; for example, the notes pane might contain specific points to cover or phrases to say during the presentation. During a slide show, the audience does not see the contents of the notes pane.

Along the left edge of the PowerPoint window, you can see two tabs, the Outline tab and the Slides tab. The **Slides tab** is on top when you first start PowerPoint. It shows a column of numbered slide **thumbnails** (miniature images) so you can see a visual representation of several slides at once. You can use the Slides tab to jump quickly to another slide in the slide pane by clicking the desired slide. The **Outline tab** shows an outline of the titles and text of each slide of your presentation.

At the bottom left of the PowerPoint window, just above the Drawing toolbar, are three view buttons: the Normal View button, the Slide Sorter View button, and the Slide Show from current slide button. These three buttons allow you to change the way you view a slide presentation. PowerPoint is currently in Normal view. Normal view is best for working with the content of the slides. You can see how the text and graphics look on each individual slide, and you can examine the outline of the entire presentation. When you switch to Slide Sorter view, the Slides and Outline tabs disappear from view and all of the slides appears as thumbnails. Slide Sorter view is an easy way to reorder the slides or set special features for your slide show. Slide Show view is the view in which you run the slide show presentation. When you click the Slide Show from current slide button, the presentation starts, beginning with the current slide (the slide currently in the slide pane in Normal view or the selected slide in Slide Sorter view).

Next you'll try switching views. PowerPoint is currently in Normal view with Slide 1 in the slide pane.

To switch views in PowerPoint:

1. Click the **Slide 2** thumbnail in the Slides tab. Slide 2 appears in the slide pane.

2. Click the **Next Slide** button ⬇ at the bottom of the vertical scroll bar in the slide pane. Slide 3 appears in the slide pane.

3. Drag the scroll box in the slide pane vertical scroll bar down to the bottom of the scroll bar. Notice the ScreenTip that appears as you drag. It identifies the slide number and the title of the slide at the current position.

4. Click the **Outline** tab. The text outline of the current slide appears in the Outline tab.

5. Drag the scroll box in the vertical scroll bar of the Outline tab up to the top of the scroll bar, and then click the **slide icon** ▣ next to Slide 3. Slide 3 again appears in the slide pane.

6. Click the **Slides** tab. The Outline tab disappears behind the Slides tab.

7. Click the **Slide Sorter View** button ▦. Slide Sorter view appears, and Slide 3 has a colored frame around it to indicate that it is the current slide.

8. Position the pointer over the **Slide 2** thumbnail. A thin, colored frame appears around Slide 2.

9. Click the **Slide 2** thumbnail to make it the current slide.

10. Double-click the **Slide 1** thumbnail. The window switches back to Normal view and Slide 1 appears in the slide pane. You could also have clicked the Normal View button to switch back to Normal view.

Now that you're familiar with the PowerPoint window, you're ready to view Miriam's presentation.

Viewing a Presentation in Slide Show View

Slide Show view is the view you use when you present an on-screen presentation to an audience. When you click the Slide Show from current slide button or click the Slide Show command on the View menu, the slide show starts. If you click the Slide Show from current slide button, the current slide fills the screen, and if you click the Slide Show command on the View menu, the first slide fills the screen. No toolbars or other Windows elements are visible on the screen.

In Slide Show view, you move from one slide to the next by pressing the spacebar, clicking the left mouse button, or pressing the → key. Additionally, PowerPoint provides a method for jumping from one slide to any other slide in the presentation during the slide show: you can right-click anywhere on the screen, point to Go to Slide on the shortcut menu, and then click one of the slide titles in the list that appears to jump to that slide.

When you prepare a slide show, you can add special effects to the show. For example, you can add **slide transitions**, the manner in which a new slide appears on the screen during a slide show. You can also add **animations** to the elements on the slide; that is, each text or graphic object on the slide can appear on the slide in a special way or have a sound effect associated with it. A special type of animation is **progressive disclosure**, a technique in which each element on a slide appears one at a time after the slide background appears. Animations draw the audience's attention to the particular item on the screen.

You can also add a footer on the slides. A **footer** is a word or phrase that appears at the bottom of each slide in the presentation.

You want to see how Miriam's presentation will appear when she shows it in Slide Show view at Global Humanitarian's executive meeting. You'll then have a better understanding of how Miriam used PowerPoint features to make her presentation informative and interesting.

To view the presentation in Slide Show view:

▶ **1.** With Slide 1 in the slide pane, click the **Slide Show from current slide** button 🖳. The slide show begins by filling the entire viewing area of the screen with Slide 1 of Miriam's presentation. Watch as the slide title moves down the slide from the top and the Global Humanitarian logo and motto gradually appear on the screen.

As you view this first slide, you can already see some of the types of elements that PowerPoint allows you to place on a slide: text in different styles, sizes, and colors; graphics; and a background picture. You also saw an example of an animation when you watched the slide title slide down the screen and the logo and motto gradually appear.

▶ **2.** Press the **spacebar**. The slide show goes from Slide 1 to Slide 2. See Figure 1-3. Notice that during the transition from Slide 1 to Slide 2, the presentation displayed Slide 2 by scrolling down from the top of the screen and covering up Slide 1.

| Figure 1-3 | Slide 2 in Slide Show view |

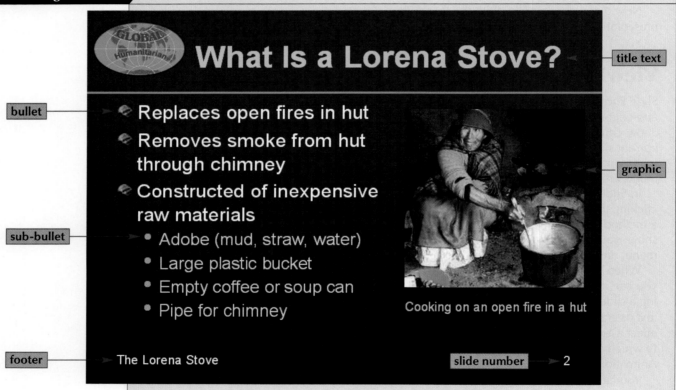

Trouble? If you missed the transition from Slide 1 to Slide 2, or if you want to see it again, press the ← key to redisplay Slide 1, and then press the spacebar to go to Slide 2 again.

Notice in Figure 1-3 that Slide 2 displays: (1) a colored background that varies in color across the slide, (2) Global Humanitarian's logo, (3) a title in large yellow text, (4) a bulleted list (with green textured bullets and white text, or solid cyan bullets with light yellow text), (5) a footer, (6) the slide number (in the lower-right corner of the slide), and (7) a photograph of a villager using an open fire.

▶ **3.** Click the left mouse button to proceed to Slide 3. During the transition from Slide 2 to Slide 3, you again see the slide scroll down onto the screen from the top. Once the slide appears on the screen, you see a chart slowly appear. PowerPoint supports features for creating and customizing this type of chart, as well as graphs, diagrams, tables, and organization charts.

▶ **4.** Press the **spacebar**. The title of Slide 4 appears on screen. What you don't see on the screen is a bulleted list. That's because this slide is designed for progressive disclosure. Additional slide elements will appear on screen after you press the spacebar or click on the screen.

▶ **5.** Press the **spacebar** to reveal the first bulleted item on Slide 4. The item is animated to fly onto the screen from the bottom.

▶ **6.** Press the **spacebar** again to reveal the next bulleted item. As this item appears, the previous item dims. Dimming the previous bulleted items helps focus the audience's attention on the current bulleted item.

▶ **7.** Press the **spacebar** again to cause the last bulleted item to dim.

So far, you've seen important PowerPoint features: slide transitions, progressive disclosure, animations, and graphics (photos and drawings). Now you'll finish the presentation and see custom animations and simple drawings.

To continue viewing the slide show:

▶ **1.** Press the **spacebar** to go to Slide 5, and then press the **spacebar** again. The label "Fuel chamber" and its accompanying arrow appear gradually on the screen. This is another example of an animation.

▶ **2.** Press the **spacebar** three more times, pausing between each to allow the label and arrow to appear gradually on the screen.

▶ **3.** Press the **spacebar** once more. A graphic labeled "smoke" comes into view, and you hear the sound of wind (or a breeze). The smoke object is an example of a user-drawn graphic.

▶ **4.** Press the **spacebar** again to animate the smoke graphic and repeat the sound effect. The smoke graphic travels from the fuel chamber up the stovepipe.

▶ **5.** Go to **Slide 6**. The graphic on this slide is a simple diagram drawn using drawing tools on the Drawing toolbar, which include not only shapes like circles, ovals, squares, and rectangles, but also arrows, boxes, stars, and banners.

▶ **6.** Continue moving through the slide show, looking at all the slides and pausing at each one to read the bulleted items and view the graphics, until you reach Slide 11, the last slide in the slide show.

▶ **7.** Press the **spacebar** to move from Slide 11. A black, nearly blank, screen appears. This signals that the slide show is over, as indicated by the line of text on the screen.

▶ **8.** Press the **spacebar** one more time to return to the view from which you started the slide show, in this case, Normal view.

▶ **9.** Close the current presentation by clicking the **Close Window** button ✕ on the menu bar, and then click the **No** button when asked if you want to save changes.

As you can see from this slide show, PowerPoint has many powerful features. You'll learn how to use many of these features in your own presentations as you work through these tutorials.

You're now ready to create Miriam's presentation on general information about Global Humanitarian's current projects. Before you begin, however, you need to plan the presentation.

Planning a Presentation

Planning a presentation before you create it improves the quality of your presentation, makes your presentation more effective and enjoyable, and, in the long run, saves you time and effort. As you plan your presentation, you should answer several questions: What is my purpose or objective for this presentation? What type of presentation is needed? Who is the audience? What information does that audience need? What is the physical location of my presentation? What is the best format for presenting the information contained in this presentation, given its location?

In planning your presentation, you should determine the following aspects:

- **Purpose of the presentation**: to provide general information about Global Humanitarian
- **Type of presentation**: training (how to become involved with Global Humanitarian)
- **Audience for the presentation**: potential donors, potential participants in humanitarian expeditions, and potential student interns
- **Audience needs**: to understand Global Humanitarian's mission and how to join the effort
- **Location of the presentation**: small conference rooms to large classrooms
- **Format**: oral presentation accompanied by an electronic slide show of 10 to 12 slides

You have carefully planned your presentation. Now you'll use the PowerPoint AutoContent Wizard to create it.

Using the AutoContent Wizard

PowerPoint helps you quickly create effective presentations by using a wizard, a special window that asks you a series of questions about your tasks, and then helps you perform them. The AutoContent Wizard lets you choose a presentation category, such as "Training," "Recommending a Strategy," "Brainstorming Session," or "Selling a Product or Service." After you select the type of presentation you want, the AutoContent Wizard creates a general outline for you to follow and formats the slides using a built-in design template and predesigned layouts. A **design template** is a file that contains the colors and format of the background and the font style of the titles, accents, and other text. Once you start creating a presentation with a given design template, you can change to any other PowerPoint design template or create a custom design template. A **layout** is a predetermined way of organizing the objects on a slide. You can change the layout applied to a slide or you can customize the layout of objects on a screen by moving the objects.

In this tutorial, you'll use the AutoContent Wizard to create a presentation with the goal of training employees, volunteers, and prospective donors on Global Humanitarian's mission. Because "Training" is predefined, you'll use the AutoContent Wizard, which will automatically create a title slide and standard outline that you can then edit to fit Miriam's needs.

To create the presentation with the AutoContent Wizard:

1. Click **File** on the menu bar, and then click **New**. The New Presentation task pane opens on the right side of the PowerPoint window.

2. Click the **From AutoContent wizard** link in the New Presentation task pane. The first dialog box of the AutoContent Wizard opens on top of the PowerPoint program window. The green square on the left side of the window indicates where you are in the wizard.

3. Read the information in the Start dialog box of the AutoContent Wizard, and then click the **Next** button. The next dialog box in the AutoContent Wizard appears. Note that the green square on the left side of the dialog box moved from Start to Presentation type. The Presentation type dialog box allows you to select the type of presentation you want.

▶ **4.** Click the **General** button, if necessary, and then click **Training**. See Figure 1-4.

Selecting the type of presentation in the AutoContent Wizard ◀ **Figure 1-4**

▶ **5.** Click the **Next** button. The Presentation style dialog box opens with the question, "What type of output will you use?" You could also change this option after you create the presentation. As noted in your plan, you want to create an on-screen presentation.

Trouble? If a dialog box opens telling you that PowerPoint can't display the template used in this document because the feature is not currently installed, you must install the Training template before continuing. If you are working on your own computer, click the Yes button. If you are working in a lab, ask your instructor or technical support person for help.

▶ **6.** Click the **On-screen presentation** option button to select it, if necessary, and then click the **Next** button. The Presentation options dialog box opens. In this dialog box, you specify the title and footer (if any) of the presentation.

▶ **7.** Click in the **Presentation title** text box, type **Global Humanitarian**, press the **Tab** key to move the insertion point to the **Footer** text box, and then type **Overview of Global Humanitarian**.

The title will appear on the title slide (the first slide) of the presentation. The footer will appear on every slide (except the title slide) in the presentation. If the other two options are checked, they will appear on either side of the footer on the presentation slides.

▶ **8.** Click the **Date last updated** check box to clear it, and leave the **Slide number** check box checked. You don't want to clutter the screen with information that is not pertinent for the audience. See Figure 1-5.

Selecting information in the AutoContent Wizard ◀ **Figure 1-5**

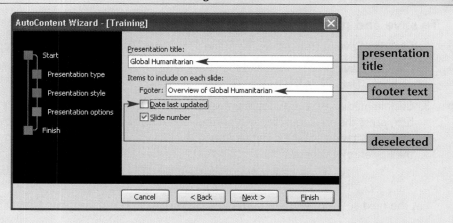

9. Click the **Next** button. The Finish dialog box opens, letting you know that you completed the questions for the AutoContent Wizard.

10. Click the **Finish** button. PowerPoint displays the AutoContent outline in the Outline tab and the title slide (Slide 1) in the slide pane. The filename in the title bar "Presentation" followed by a number is a temporary filename. See Figure 1-6.

Figure 1-6 | **Outline and slide after completing the AutoContent Wizard**

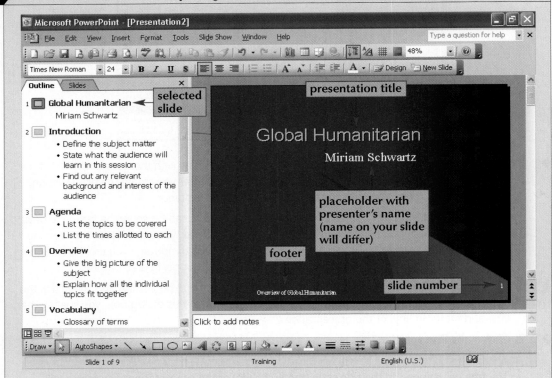

The AutoContent Wizard automatically displays the presenter's name (actually the name of the registered PowerPoint user) below the title in Slide 1. The name that appears on your screen will be different from the one shown in Figure 1-6.

Next, you'll save and name the presentation you created.

To save and name the presentation:

1. Click the **Save** button 🔲 on the Standard toolbar. The Save As dialog box opens.

2. Click the **Save in** list arrow, and then navigate to the **Tutorial.01\Tutorial** folder included with your Data Files, if necessary.

3. Click immediately after Global Humanitarian, the default filename, in the **File name** text box, press the **spacebar**, type **Overview**, and then click the **Save** button. PowerPoint saves the presentation as Global Humanitarian Overview and displays that name in the title bar of the PowerPoint window.

In the next session, you'll edit the text of Miriam's presentation, as well as create notes.

Session 1.1 Quick Check

1. Describe the components of a PowerPoint presentation.
2. Name and describe the two panes and two tabs in the PowerPoint window in Normal view.
3. Define or describe the following:
    a. progressive disclosure
    b. slide transition
    c. design template
    d. layout
4. What are some of the questions that you should answer when planning a presentation?
5. Describe the purpose of the AutoContent Wizard.
6. Describe Slide Show view.

Session 1.2

Modifying a Presentation

Now that you've used the AutoContent Wizard, you're ready to edit some of the words in the presentation to fit Miriam's specific needs. You'll keep the design template, which includes the blue background and the size and color of the text, used by the AutoContent Wizard.

The AutoContent Wizard automatically creates the title slide, as well as other slides, with suggested text located in placeholders. A **placeholder** is a region of a slide, or a location in an outline, reserved for inserting text or graphics. To edit the AutoContent outline to fit Miriam's needs, you must select the placeholders one at a time, and then replace them with other text. Text placeholders are a special kind of **text box**, which is a container for text. You can edit and format text in a text box, or you can manipulate the text box as a whole. When you manipulate the text box as a whole, the text box is treated as an **object**, something that can be manipulated or resized as a unit.

When text is selected, the text box is active and appears as hatched lines around the selected text with sizing handles (small circles) at each corner and on each side of the box. You drag **sizing handles** to make a text box or other object larger or smaller on the slide. When the entire text box is selected as a single object, the text box appears as a dotted outline with sizing handles.

Many of the slides that the AutoContent Wizard created in your presentation for Global Humanitarian contain bulleted lists. A **bulleted list** is a list of paragraphs with a special character (dot, circle, box, star, or other character) to the left of each paragraph. A **bulleted item** is one paragraph in a bulleted list. Bullets can appear at different outline levels. A **first-level bullet** is a main paragraph in a bulleted list; a **second-level bullet**—sometimes called a **sub-bullet**—is a bullet beneath (and indented from) a first-level bullet. Using bulleted lists reminds both the speaker and the audience of the main points of the presentation. In addition to bulleted lists, PowerPoint also supports numbered lists. A **numbered list** is a list of paragraphs that are numbered consecutively within the body text.

When you edit the text on the slides, keep in mind that the bulleted lists aren't meant to be the complete presentation; instead, they should emphasize the key points to the audience and remind the speaker of the points to emphasize. In all your presentations, you should follow the 6 × 6 rule as much as possible: Keep each bulleted item to no more than six words, and don't include more than six bulleted items on a slide.

Creating Effective Text Presentations

- Think of your text presentation as a visual map of your oral presentation. Show your organization by using overviews, making headings larger than subheadings, including bulleted lists to highlight key points, and numbering steps to show sequences.
- Follow the 6 × 6 rule: Use six or fewer items per screen, and use phrases of six or fewer words. Omit unnecessary articles, pronouns, and adjectives.
- Keep phrases parallel.
- Make sure your text is appropriate for your purpose and audience.

Miriam reviewed your plans for your presentation and she has several suggestions for improvement. First, she wants you to replace the text that the AutoContent Wizard inserted with information about Global Humanitarian. She also wants you to delete unnecessary slides, and change the order of the slides in the presentation. You'll start by editing the text on the slides.

Editing Slides

Most of the slides in the presentation contain two placeholder text boxes. The slide **title text** is a text box at the top of the slide that gives the title of the information on that slide; the slide **body text** (also called the **main text**) is a large text box in which you type a bulleted or numbered list. In this presentation, you'll modify or create title text and body text in all but the title slide (Slide 1).

To edit the AutoContent outline to fit Miriam's needs, you must select text in each of the placeholders, and then replace that text with other text. You'll now begin to edit and replace the text to fit Miriam's presentation. The first text you'll change is the presenter's name placeholder.

To edit and replace text in the first slide:

1. If you took a break after the previous session, make sure PowerPoint is running, and then open the presentation **Global Humanitarian Overview** located in the Tutorial.01\Tutorial folder included with your Data Files. Slide 1 appears in the slide pane and the Outline tab is on top.

2. Position the pointer over the presenter's name (currently the registered PowerPoint user's name) in the slide pane so that the pointer changes to I, and then drag it across the text of the presenter's name to select the text. The text box becomes active, as indicated by the hatched lines around the box and the sizing handles at each corner and on each side of the text box, and the text becomes highlighted.

3. Type your first and last name (so your instructor can identify you as the author of this presentation), and then click anywhere else on the slide. As soon as you start to type, the selected text disappears, and the typed text appears in its place. (The figures in this book will show the name Miriam Schwartz.)

   Trouble? If PowerPoint marks your name with a red wavy underline, this indicates that the word is not found in the PowerPoint dictionary. Ignore the wavy line for now, because spelling will be covered later.

You'll now edit Slides 2 through 9 by replacing the placeholder text and adding new text, and by deleting slides that don't apply to your presentation.

To edit the text in the slides:

▶ **1.** Click the **Next Slide** button 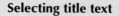 at the bottom of the vertical scroll bar in the slide pane. Slide 2 appears in the slide pane.

▶ **2.** Drag across the word **Introduction** (the title text) to select it. See Figure 1-7.

Selecting title text ◀ **Figure 1-7**

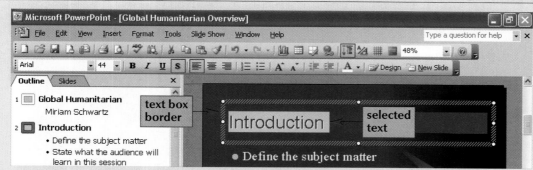

Now you're ready to type the desired title. As you perform the next step, notice not only that the words you type replace the selected text in the slide pane, but also that the slide title on the Outline tab changes.

▶ **3.** Type **Are You Rich?** and then click in a blank space in the slide pane, just outside the edge of the slide, to deselect the text box. The hatched lines and sizing handles disappear. Notice that the slide title changed on the Outline tab as well.

Trouble? If you clicked somewhere on the slide and selected another item, such as the bulleted list, click another place, preferably just outside the edge of the text box, to deselect all items.

Now you're going to edit the text from the Outline tab.

▶ **4.** In the Outline tab, select the text **Define the subject matter**. The text is highlighted by changing to white on black.

▶ **5.** Type **Home has non-dirt floor: top 50%**. Don't include a period at the end of the phrase. This bulleted item is an incomplete sentence, short for "If you live in a home with a non-dirt floor, you're in the top 50% of the wealthiest people on earth."

▶ **6.** Select the text of the second bulleted item in either the Outline tab or the slide pane, and then type **Home has more than one room: top 20%**. Again, don't include a period.

▶ **7.** Select the text of the third bulleted item in the slide pane, and then type **Own more than one pair of shoes: top 5%**.

With the insertion point at the end of the third bulleted item, you're ready to create additional bulleted items.

To create additional bulleted items:

▶ **1.** With the insertion point blinking at the end of the last bulleted item, press the **Enter** key. PowerPoint creates a new bullet and leaves the insertion point to the right of the indent after the bullet, waiting for you to type the text.

▶ **2.** Type **Own a refrigerator: top 3%** and then press the **Enter** key.

▶ **3.** Type **Own a car, computer, microwave, or VCR: top 1%**.

4. Click in a blank area of the slide pane to deselect the bulleted list text box. The completed Slide 2 should look like Figure 1-8.

| Figure 1-8 | Slide 2 after adding text |

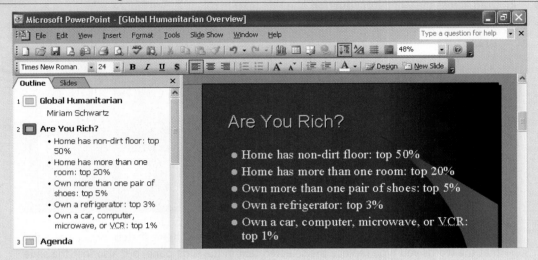

You're now ready to edit the text on another slide and create sub-bullets.

To create sub-bullets:

1. Click the **Next Slide** button ⬇ at the bottom of the vertical scroll bar four times to move to Slide 6. Slide 6 appears in the slide pane and on the Outline tab.

2. Select the title text **Topic One**, and then type **How You Can Help**.

3. Select all the text in the body text placeholder, not just the text of the first bulleted item.

4. Type **Become a member of Global Humanitarian**, press the **Enter** key, and then type **Contribute to humanitarian projects**. You've added two bulleted items to the body text.

Now you'll add some sub-bullets beneath the first-level bulleted item.

5. Press the **Enter** key to insert a new bullet, and then press the **Tab** key. The new bullet changes to a sub-bullet. In this design template, sub-bullets have a dash in front of them, which you won't be able to see until you start typing the text.

6. Type **Health and Education**, and then press the **Enter** key. The new bullet is a second-level bullet, the same level as the previous bullet.

7. Type **Water and Environment**, press the **Enter** key, type **Income Generation and Agriculture**, press the **Enter** key, and then type **Leadership and Cultural Enhancement**.

Now you want the next bullet to return to the first level.

8. Press the **Enter** key to create a new, second-level bullet, and then click the **Decrease Indent** button 🔾 on the Formatting toolbar. The bullet is converted to a first-level bullet. You can also press the Shift+Tab key combination to move a bullet up a level.

9. Type the remaining two first-level bulleted items: **Join a humanitarian expedition** and **Become a student intern**, and then click in a blank area of the slide to deselect the text box. See Figure 1-9.

Slide 6 after adding text | **Figure 1-9**

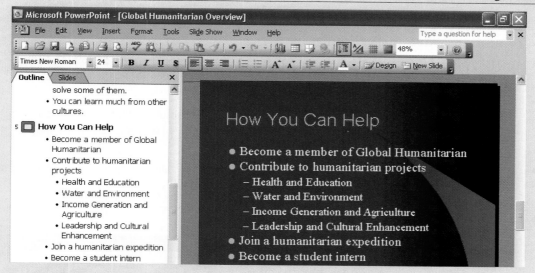

You have completed editing Slide 6. Miriam suggests that you delete the previous three slides, which are unnecessary for your presentation, before you edit the other slides.

Deleting Slides

When creating a presentation, you'll often delete slides. The AutoContent Wizard may create slides that you don't think are necessary, or you may create slides that you no longer want. You can delete slides in several ways: in Normal view, by clicking the slide thumbnail in the Slides tab or by clicking the slide icon in the Outline tab to select the slide, and then pressing the Delete key or using the Delete command on the shortcut or Edit menu; or in Slide Sorter view, by selecting the slide and then pressing the Delete key. Keep in mind that once you delete a slide, you can recover it by immediately clicking the Undo button on the Standard toolbar.

You need to delete Slide 3 ("Agenda"), Slide 4 ("Overview"), and Slide 5 ("Vocabulary").

To delete Slides 3 through 5:

1. With Slide 6 in the slide pane, click the **slide icon** ▢ next to Slide 3 ("Agenda") on the Outline tab. You might need to drag the Outline pane scroll box up to view Slide 3. This causes Slide 3 to appear in the slide pane. Now you're ready to delete the slide.

2. Right-click the Slide 3 ("Agenda") **slide icon** ▦ on the Outline tab, and then click **Delete Slide** on the shortcut menu. The entire slide is deleted from the presentation, and the rest of the slides are renumbered so that the slide that was Slide 4 becomes Slide 3, and so on. The renumbered Slide 3 ("Overview") appears in the slide pane.

3. Click the **Slides** tab. The Outline tab disappears and the Slides tab appears with thumbnails of all of the slides. With the Slides tab on top, notice that the labels identifying the Slides and Outline tabs change to icons.

4. With **Slide 3** ("Overview") selected in the Slides tab, press and hold the **Shift** key, and then click **Slide 4** on the Slides tab. Slides 3 and 4 are both selected on the Slides tab.

5. Click **Edit** on the menu bar, and then click **Delete Slide**. Both slides are deleted from the presentation. The new Slide 3, entitled "How You Can Help," now appears in the slide pane.

    Trouble? If the Delete Slide command is not on the Edit menu, click the double arrow at the bottom of the menu to display all of the commands on the menu.

Now you'll finish editing the presentation and save your work.

To edit and save the presentation:

1. Go to **Slide 4** ("Topic Two"), and then edit the title text to read **Benefits of Joining Global Humanitarian**. Notice that as you type the last word, PowerPoint automatically adjusts the size of the text to fit in the title text box.

   Trouble? If the font size of the text doesn't automatically adjust so that the text fits within the body text placeholder, click the AutoFit Options button 🔁 that appears in the slide pane, and then click the AutoFit Text to Placeholder option.

2. Select all the body text, not just the text of the first bulleted item, in the body text placeholder, and then type the bulleted items shown in Figure 1-10.

Figure 1-10 | Completed Slide 4

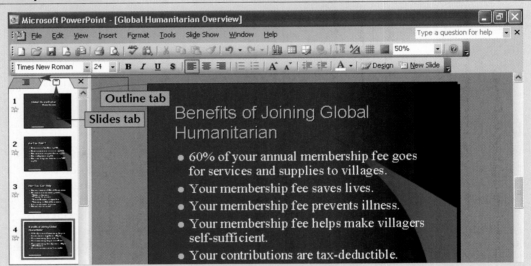

3. Go to **Slide 5**, and then modify the title and body text so that the slide looks like Figure 1-11.

Figure 1-11 | Completed Slide 5

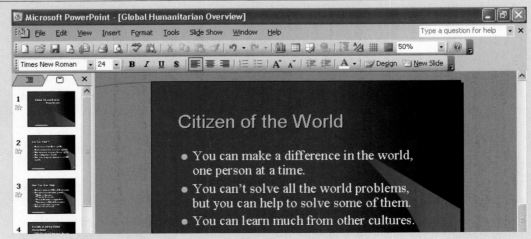

4. Delete **Slide 6** ("Where to Get More Information").

5. Click the **Save** button 🔲 on the Standard toolbar to save the presentation.

Miriam reviews your presentation and wants you to add a slide at the end of the presentation stating what action you want your readers to take as a result of your presentation.

Adding a New Slide and Choosing a Layout

Miriam suggests that you add a new slide at the end of the presentation explaining how individuals and families can join Global Humanitarian. When you add a new slide, PowerPoint formats the slide using a slide layout. PowerPoint supports four **text layouts**: Title Slide (placeholders for a title and a subtitle, usually used as the first slide in a presentation); Title Only (a title placeholder but not a body text placeholder); Title and Text (the default slide layout, with a title and a body text placeholder); and Title and 2-Column Text (same as Title and Text, but with two columns for text). PowerPoint also supports several **content layouts**—slide layouts that contain from zero to four charts, diagrams, images, tables, or movie clips. In addition, PowerPoint supports combination layouts, called **text and content layouts**, and several other types of layouts.

When you insert a new slide, it appears after the current one, and the Slide Layout task pane appears with a default layout already selected. This default layout is applied to the new slide. To use a different layout, you click it in the Slide Layout task pane.

To insert the new slide at the end of the presentation:

1. Because you want to add a slide after Slide 5, make sure Slide 5 is still in the slide pane.

2. Click the **New Slide** button on the Formatting toolbar. The Slide Layout task pane opens with the first layout in the second row under Text Layouts selected as the default, and a new Slide 6 appears in the slide pane with the default layout applied. See Figure 1-12.

New slide added ◀ **Figure 1-12**

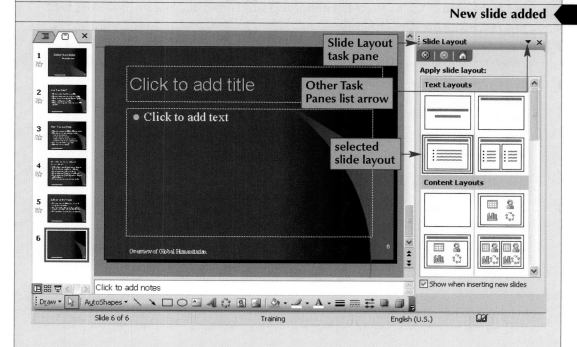

You'll accept the default layout for this slide. If you wanted a different layout, you would click the desired layout in the Slide Layout task pane.

Trouble? If the Slide Layout task pane does not appear, click View on the menu bar, click Task Pane, click the Other Task Panes list arrow at the top of the task pane, and then click Slide Layout. To make the Slide Layout task pane open automatically when you insert a new slide, click the Show when inserting new slides check box at the bottom of the task pane.

3. Position the pointer over the selected layout in the task pane. A ScreenTip appears, identifying this layout as the Title and Text layout.

Next you'll close the Slide Layout task pane to provide a larger view of the slide pane.

4. Click the **Close** button ✕ in the Slide Layout task pane title bar to close the task pane.

Trouble? If you accidentally click the Close button of the PowerPoint window or Presentation window, PowerPoint will ask you if you want to save the changes to your presentation. Click the Cancel button so that the presentation doesn't close, and then click the correct Close button on the task pane title bar.

The new slide contains text placeholders. On a new slide, you don't need to select the text on the slide to replace it with your text. You only need to click in the placeholder text box; the placeholder text will disappear and the insertion point will be placed in the text box, ready for you to type your text. Once you type your text, the dotted line outlining the edge of the text box will disappear. You'll add text to the new slide.

To add text to the new slide:

1. Click anywhere in the title text placeholder in the slide pane, where it says "Click to add title." The title placeholder text disappears and the insertion point blinks at the left of the title text box.

2. Type **Global Humanitarian Memmbership**. Make sure you type "Memmbership" with two *m*s in the middle. You'll correct this misspelling later. Again, the font size decreases to fit the text within the title placeholder.

3. Click anywhere in the body text placeholder. The placeholder text disappears and the insertion point appears just to the right of the first bullet.

4. Type **Individual membership: $75 per year**, press the **Enter** key, type **Family membership: $150 per year**, press the **Enter** key, type **Visit our Web site at www.globalhumanitarian.org**, and then press the **Enter** key.

When you press the Enter key after typing the Web site address, PowerPoint automatically changes the Web site address (the URL) to a link. It formats the link by changing its color and underlining it. When you run the slide show, you can click this link to jump to that Web site if you are connected to the Internet.

5. Type **Call Sam Matagi, Volunteer Coordinator, at 523–555–SERV**.

You have inserted a new slide at the end of the presentation and added text to the slide. Next you'll create a new slide by promoting text in the Outline tab.

Promoting, Demoting, and Moving Outline Text

You can modify the text of a slide in the Outline tab as well as in the slide pane. Working in the Outline tab gives you more flexibility because you can see the outline of the entire presentation, not only the single slide currently in the slide pane. Working in the Outline tab allows you to easily move text from one slide to another or to create a new slide by promoting bulleted items from a slide so that they become the title and body text on a new slide.

To **promote** an item means to increase the outline level of that item—for example, to change a bulleted item into a slide title or to change a second-level bullet into a first-level bullet. To **demote** an item means to decrease the outline level—for example, to change a slide title into a bulleted item on the previous slide or to change a first-level bullet into a second-level bullet. You'll begin by promoting a bulleted item to a slide title, thus creating a new slide.

To create a new slide by promoting outline text:

1. Click the **Outline** tab. The outline of the presentation appears.

2. Drag the scroll box in the slide pane up until the ScreenTip displays "Slide: 3 of 6" and the title "How You Can Help." Slide 3 appears in the slide pane and the text of that slide appears at the top of the Outline tab.

3. In the Outline tab, move the pointer over the bullet to the left of "Contribute to humanitarian projects" so that the pointer becomes ✛, and then click the bullet. The text for that bullet and all its sub-bullets are selected.

   Now you'll promote the selected text so that it becomes the title text and first-level bullets on a new slide.

4. Click the **Decrease Indent** button ▦ on the Formatting toolbar. PowerPoint promotes the selected text one level. Because the bullet you selected was a first-level bullet, the first-level bullet is promoted to a slide title on a new Slide 4, and the second-level bullets become first-level bullets on the new slide. See Figure 1-13.

Promoting a bulleted item to become a new slide ◄ **Figure 1-13**

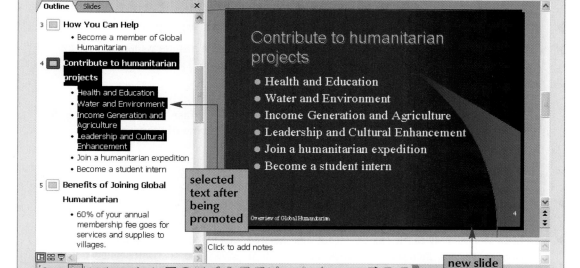

Now you'll edit this text, and then move some of the bulleted items to another slide.

▶ **5.** Click anywhere to deselect the text, select the Slide 4 title text in the Outline tab, and then type **Types of Humanitarian Projects in Third-World Villages**. Notice that the title changes in the slide pane as well.

Trouble? If all of the text on the slide becomes selected when you try to select the title text, make sure you position the pointer just to the left of the title text, and not over the slide icon, before you drag to select the text.

▶ **6.** Click the bullet to the left of "Join a humanitarian expedition" (the fifth bullet in Slide 4) in the Outline tab, and then, while holding down the left mouse button, drag the bullet and its text up until the horizontal line position marker is just under the bulleted item "Become a member of Global Humanitarian" in Slide 3, as shown in Figure 1-14.

Figure 1-14 **Moving text in the Outline tab**

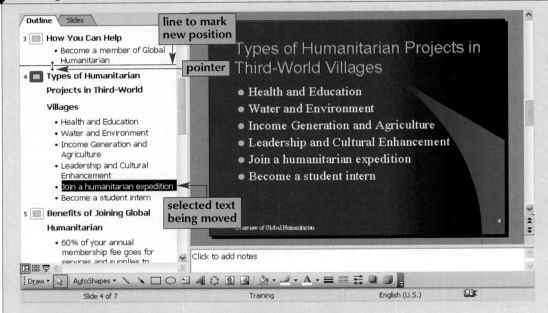

▶ **7.** Release the mouse button. The bulleted item moves to the new position.

▶ **8.** Using the same procedure, move the bulleted item "Become a student intern" from the end of Slide 4 to the end of Slide 3 in the Outline tab.

As you review your slides, you notice that in Slide 5, the phrase "Your membership fee" is repeated three times. You'll fix the problem by demoting some of the text.

To demote text on Slide 5:

▶ **1.** Click the **slide icon** ▤ next to Slide 5 ("Benefits of Joining Global Humanitarian") in the Outline tab.

▶ **2.** Click immediately to the right of "Your membership fee" in the second bulleted item in the Outline tab, and then press the **Enter** key. The item "saves lives" becomes a new bulleted item, but you want that item to appear indented at a lower outline level.

▶ **3.** Press the **Tab** key to indent "saves lives," and then press the **Delete** key, if necessary, to delete any blank spaces to the left of "saves lives."

4. Click the bullet to the left of "Your membership fee prevents illness" in the Outline tab, press and hold down the **Shift** key, and then click the bullet to the left of "Your membership fee helps make villagers self-sufficient." This selects both bulleted items at the same time.

5. Click the **Increase Indent** button ![icon] on the Formatting toolbar to demote the two bulleted items. Note this has the same effect as pressing the Tab key.

6. Delete the phrase "Your membership fee" and the space after it from the two items that you just demoted. Your slide should now look like Figure 1-15.

Slide 5 after demoting text to sub-bullets ◄ **Figure 1-15**

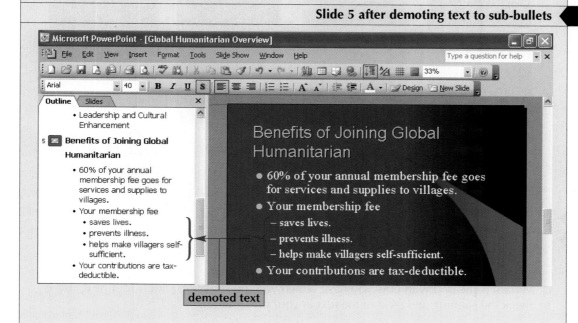

demoted text

Miriam looks at your presentation and suggests that you move the current Slide 4 ahead of Slide 3. You could make this change by clicking the slide icon and dragging it above the slide icon for Slide 3 in the Outline tab. Instead, you'll move the slide in Slide Sorter view.

Moving Slides in Slide Sorter View

In Slide Sorter view, PowerPoint displays all the slides as thumbnails, so that several slides can appear on the screen at once. This view not only provides you with a good overview of your presentation, but also allows you to easily change the order of the slides and modify the slides in other ways.

To move Slide 4:

1. Click the **Slide Sorter View** button ![icon] at the bottom of the Outline tab. You now see your presentation in Slide Sorter view.

2. Click **Slide 4**. A thick colored frame appears around the slide, indicating that the slide is selected.

3. Press and hold down the left mouse button, drag the slide to the left so that the vertical line position marker appears on the left side of Slide 3, as shown in Figure 1-16.

Figure 1-16 | **Moving a slide in Slide Sorter view**

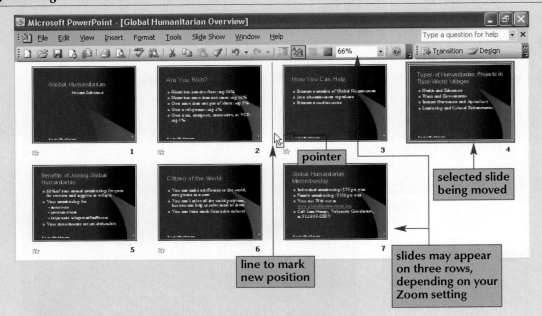

4. Release the mouse button. Slides 3 and 4 have switched places.

5. Click the **Normal View** button ⊞ to return to Normal view.

Miriam is pleased with how you have edited your presentation slides. Your next task is to check the spelling and style of the text in your presentation.

Checking the Spelling and Style in a Presentation

Before you print or present a slide show, you should always perform a final check of the spelling and style of all the slides in your presentation. This will help to ensure that your presentation is accurate and professional looking.

Checking the Spelling

If PowerPoint finds a word that's not in its dictionary, the word is underlined with a red wavy line in the slide pane. When you right-click the word, suggestions for alternate spellings appear on the shortcut menu, as well as commands for ignoring the misspelled word or opening the Spelling dialog box. You can also click the Spelling button on the Standard toolbar to check the spelling in the entire presentation.

You need to check the spelling in the Global Humanitarian presentation.

To check the spelling in the presentation:

1. Go to **Slide 7**. The spelling check always starts from the current slide.

2. Click the **Spelling** button 🏷️ on the Standard toolbar. The Spelling dialog box opens. The word you purposely mistyped earlier, "Memmbership," is highlighted in the Outline tab and listed in the Not in Dictionary text box in the Spelling dialog box. Two suggested spellings appear in the Suggestions list box, and the selected word in the Suggestions list box appears in the Change to text box.

3. With "Membership" selected in the Suggestions list box and in the Change to text box, click the **Change** button. If you knew that you misspelled that word throughout your presentation, you could click the Change All button to change all of the instances of the misspelling in the presentation to the corrected spelling.

The word is corrected, and the next word in the presentation that is not in the PowerPoint dictionary, Matagi, is flagged. This word is not misspelled; it is a surname.

4. Click the **Ignore** button. The word is not changed on the slide. If you wanted to ignore all the instances of that word in the presentation, you could click the Ignore All button. A dialog box opens telling you that the spelling check is complete.

Trouble? If another word in the presentation is flagged as misspelled, select the correct spelling in the Suggestions list, and then click the Change button. If your name on Slide 1 is flagged, click the Ignore button.

5. Click the **OK** button. The dialog box closes.

Next, you need to check the style in the presentation.

Using the Style Checker

The **Style Checker** checks your presentation for consistency in punctuation, capitalization, and visual elements and marks problems on a slide with a light bulb. For this feature to be active, you need to turn on the Style Checker.

To turn on the Style Checker:

1. Click **Tools** on the menu bar, click **Options** to open the Options dialog box, and then click the **Spelling and Style** tab.

2. Click the **Check style** check box to select it, if necessary. Now you'll check to make sure the necessary Style Checker options are selected.

Trouble? If a message appears telling you that the Style Checker needs to use the Office Assistant, click the Enable Assistant button. If another message appears telling you that PowerPoint can't display the Office Assistant because the feature is not installed, click the Yes button only if you are working on your own computer. If you are in a lab, ask your instructor or technical support person for assistance.

3. Click the **Style Options** button in the Options dialog box, click the **Slide title style** check box to select it, if necessary, click the list arrow to the right of this option, and then click **UPPERCASE**. When you run the Style Checker, it will suggest changing all of the titles to all uppercase.

4. Click the **Body text style** check box to select it, if necessary, click the list arrow to the right of this option, and then click **Sentence case**, if necessary. When you run the Style Checker, it will check to make sure that the text in each bullet in the body text has an uppercase letter as the first letter, and that the rest of the words in the body text start with a lowercase letter.

5. Click the bottom two check boxes under End punctuation to clear them, if necessary. Some of the bulleted lists in this presentation are complete sentences and some are not, so you want PowerPoint to allow variation in the end punctuation. See Figure 1-17.

| Figure 1-17 | Style Options dialog box |

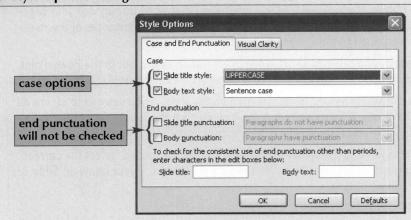

case options

end punctuation
will not be checked

6. Click the **OK** button to close the Style Options dialog box, and then click the **OK** button to close the Options dialog box.

From now on, PowerPoint will check the style in your presentation as you display each slide in the slide pane. Now you'll go through your presentation and check for style problems.

To fix problems marked by the Style Checker:

1. Go to **Slide 1**. A light bulb appears next to the title. This indicates that the Style Checker found a problem with the slide title. Since you did not type any of the titles in all uppercase letters, a light bulb will appear on every slide marking the titles as not matching the style.

2. Click the **light bulb**. The Office Assistant appears and displays a dialog box with a description of the problem and three options from which you can choose. See Figure 1-18.

| Figure 1-18 | Using the Style Checker |

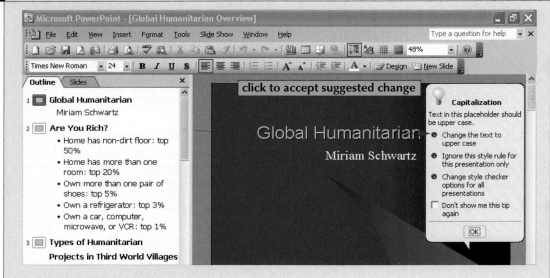

Trouble? If a message appears telling you that PowerPoint can't display the Office Assistant because the feature is not installed, click the Yes button only if you are working on your own computer. If you are in a lab, ask your instructor or technical support person for assistance.

▶ 3. Click the **Change the text to upper case** option button in the Office Assistant dialog box. All of the title text is now changed to uppercase.

▶ 4. Go to **Slide 2**.

▶ 5. Use the Style Checker to change the title text to uppercase.

▶ 6. Go to **Slide 3**, and then change the title text to uppercase. Another light bulb appears on Slide 3 next to the body text.

   Trouble? If, in this or subsequent steps, the light bulb doesn't appear by the body text, go to the next or the previous slide, and then return to the current slide as a way of telling the Style Checker to recheck the slide.

▶ 7. Click the **light bulb** to see that the error in the body text is another capitalization error, and then click the **Change the text to sentence case** option button in the Office Assistant dialog box. All the words in the bulleted items are converted to lowercase (except the first word in each bulleted item); that is, all the bulleted items are converted to sentence case.

▶ 8. Go to **Slide 4**, change the title text to uppercase, and then click the **light bulb** next to the body text. The Style Checker detects that the first bulleted item is in mixed case (the words "Global Humanitarian" are capitalized), but the organization's name should remain capitalized, so you don't need to make any changes here.

▶ 9. Click the **OK** button in the Office Assistant dialog box. PowerPoint ignores the style for that slide, and the light bulb no longer appears.

▶ 10. Correct the title and body text on Slide 5, and the title text on Slide 6, and then go to Slide 7.

▶ 11. Correct the title text on Slide 7, but do not correct the capitalization in the body text on Slide 7. The words that start with an uppercase letter in the body text on this slide are proper nouns or are part of the phone number. Now you need to turn off the Style Checker.

▶ 12. Click **Tools** on the menu bar, click **Options**, click the **Check style** check box on the Spelling and Style tab to clear it, and then click the **OK** button. The Style Checker is turned off.

As you create your own presentations, watch for the problems marked by the Style Checker. Of course, in some cases, you might want a certain capitalization that the Style Checker detects as an error. In these cases, just ignore the light bulb, or click it, and then click the OK button. The light bulb never appears on the screen during a slide show or when you print a presentation.

Using the Research Task Pane

PowerPoint enables you to use the Research task pane to search online services or Internet sites for additional help in creating a presentation. Using these resources helps you make your presentations more professional. For example, you could look up specific words in a thesaurus. A **thesaurus** contains a list of words and their synonyms, antonyms, and other related words. Using a thesaurus is a good way to add variety to the words you use or to choose more precise words. You could also look up information in online encyclopedias, news services, libraries, and business sites.

Miriam thinks the word "rich" in Slide 2 may be too informal. She asks you to find an appropriate replacement word. You'll now look for synonyms in the Office thesaurus.

To do research using the thesaurus:

▶ 1. Go to **Slide 2**, and then highlight the word **RICH** in either the Outline tab or the slide pane. Be careful not to highlight the question mark at the end of the phrase.

▶ 2. Click the **Research** button on the Standard toolbar. The Research task pane opens with the word "RICH" in the Search for text box.

▶ 3. Click the list arrow next to All Reference Books in the task pane, and then click **Thesaurus: English (U.S.)**.

▶ 4. Click the **green arrow** button next to the Search for text box to begin a search for synonyms for the word "rich," if necessary. The thesaurus provides several suggestions in a list organized so that the most relevant words are in bold, and additional synonyms are indented under the bold terms.

▶ 5. Scroll down, if necessary, to see the word "full" in boldface, and then click the **minus sign** button next to "full (adj.)." The minus sign changes to a plus sign, and the list of words under "full" collapses.

After looking over the list, Miriam decides that "full" and "opulent" do not convey the correct meaning. She decides that "wealthy" is the most appropriate synonym.

▶ 6. Position the pointer over the word **wealthy**, indented under the bold term **wealthy (adj.)**. A box appears around the term and a list arrow appears at the right side of the box.

▶ 7. Click the list arrow on the side of the box, as shown in Figure 1-19.

Figure 1-19 ▶ **Using the Thesaurus in the Research task pane**

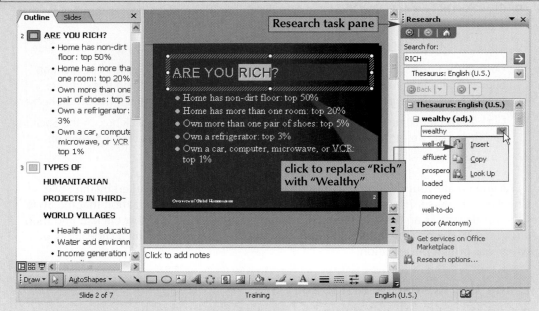

▶ 8. Click **Insert**. "WEALTHY" replaces "RICH" in the slide.

▶ 9. Close the task pane.

Creating Speaker Notes

When you show the presentation to Miriam, she is satisfied. Now you're ready to prepare the other parts of Miriam's presentation: the notes (also called speaker notes) and audience handouts (a printout of the slides). **Notes** are printed pages that contain a picture of and notes about each slide. They help the speaker remember what to say when a particular slide appears during the presentation. **Handouts** are printouts of the slides; these can be arranged with several slides printed on a page.

You'll create notes for only a few of the slides in the presentation. For example, Miriam wants to remember to acknowledge special guests or Global Humanitarian executives at any meeting where she might use this presentation. You'll create a note reminding her to do that.

To create notes:

1. Click the **Slides** tab, and then click **Slide 1** in the Slides tab. Slide 1 appears in the slide pane. The notes pane currently contains placeholder text.

2. Click in the notes pane, and then type **Acknowledge special guests and Global Humanitarian executives.** See Figure 1-20.

Notes on Slide 1 | **Figure 1-20**

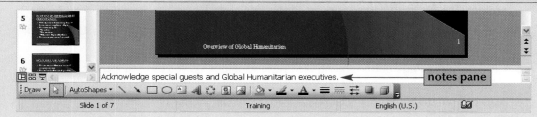

3. Click **Slide 2** in the Slides tab, click in the notes pane, and then type **Everyone in this room is in the top one percent of wealthy people who have ever lived on earth.**

4. Go to **Slide 3**, click in the notes pane, and then type **Give an example of each of these project types.** These are all the notes that Miriam wants.

5. Click the **Save** button 🔲 on the Standard toolbar to save the changes to the presentation.

Before Miriam gives her presentation, she'll print the notes of the presentation so she'll have them available during her presentations. You can now view the completed presentation to make sure that it is accurate, informative, and visually pleasing.

To view the slide show:

1. Go to **Slide 1**, and then click the **Slide Show from current slide** button 🖵 at the bottom of the Slides tab.

2. Proceed through the slide show as you did earlier, clicking the left mouse button or pressing the spacebar to advance from one slide to the next.

3. If you see a problem on one of your slides, press the **Esc** key to leave the slide show and display the current slide on the screen in Normal view, fix the problem on the slide, save your changes, and then click the **Slide Show from current slide** button 🖵 to resume the slide show from the current slide.

4. When you reach the end of your slide show, press the **spacebar** to move to the blank screen, and then press the **spacebar** again to return to Normal view.

Now you're ready to preview and print your presentation.

Previewing and Printing a Presentation

Before you give your presentation, you may want to print it. PowerPoint provides several printing options. For example, you can print the slides in color using a color printer; print in grayscale or pure black and white using a black-and-white printer; print handouts with 2, 3, 4, 6, or 9 slides per page; or print the notes pages (the speaker notes printed below a picture of the corresponding slide). You can also format and then print the presentation onto overhead transparency film (available in most office supply stores).

Usually you'll want to open the Print dialog box by clicking File on the menu bar, and then clicking Print, rather than clicking the Print button on the Standard toolbar. If you click the Print button, the presentation prints with the options chosen last in the Print dialog box. If you're going to print your presentation on a black-and-white printer, you should first preview the presentation to make sure the text will be legible. You'll use Print Preview to see the slides as they will appear when they are printed.

To preview the presentation:

▶ **1.** Go to **Slide 1**, if necessary, and then click the **Print Preview** button 🔍 on the Standard toolbar. The Preview window appears, displaying Slide 1.

▶ **2.** Click the **Options** button on the Preview toolbar, point to **Color/Grayscale**, and then click **Grayscale**. The slide is displayed in grayscale.

▶ **3.** Click the **Next Page** button 🔽 on the Preview toolbar. As you can see, part of the background graphic covers the text on Slide 2. See Figure 1-21. You'll need to remove the background from the slides so you can read them after you have printed them.

Figure 1-21	Slide 2 in Preview window

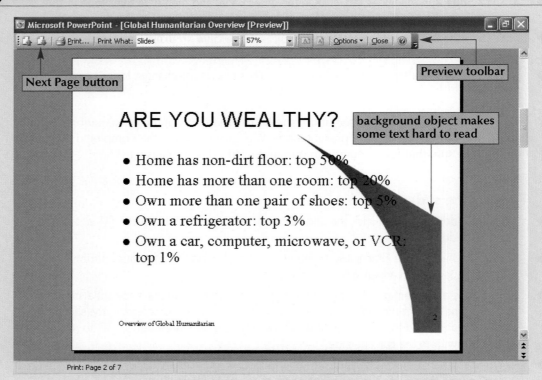

4. Click the **Close** button on the Preview toolbar to return to Normal view.

5. Click **Format** on the menu bar, click **Background** to display the Background dialog box, click the **Omit background graphics from master** check box, and then click the **Apply to All** button. The slide appears as before, but without the background graphic.

6. Click the **Print Preview** button 🔍 on the Standard toolbar, and then click the **Next Page** button 🔽 on the Preview toolbar. You can now easily read the text on Slide 2.

7. Click the **Print What** list arrow on the Preview toolbar, and then click **Handouts (4 slides per page)**. The preview changes to display four slides on a page.

8. Click the **Print** button on the Preview toolbar. The Print dialog box opens. See Figure 1-22.

Print dialog box ◄ **Figure 1-22**

9. Compare your dialog box to the one shown in Figure 1-22, make any necessary changes, and then click the **OK** button to print the handouts on two pages. Now you're ready to print the notes.

10. Click the **Print What** list arrow on the Preview toolbar, and then click **Notes Pages**. The current slide is displayed as a notes page, with the slide on the top and the notes on the bottom.

11. Click the **Print** button on the Print Preview toolbar, click the **Slides** option button in the Print range section of the Print dialog box, and then type **1-3**. These are the only slides with notes on them, so you do not need to print all seven slides as notes pages.

12. Click the **OK** button to print the notes. Slides 1-3 print on three pieces of paper as notes pages.

13. Click the **Close** button on the Preview toolbar. The view returns to Normal view.

Your last task is to view the completed presentation in Slide Sorter view to see how all the slides look together. First, however, you'll restore the background graphics.

To restore the background graphics and view the completed presentation in Slide Sorter view:

1. Click **Format** on the menu bar, click **Background**, click the **Omit background graphics from master** check box to clear it, and then click the **Apply to All** button. The background graphics are restored to the slides.

2. Click the **Slide Sorter View** button 🔡 at the bottom of the Slides tab. The slides appear on the screen in several rows, depending on the current zoom percentage shown in the Zoom box on the Standard toolbar and on the size of your monitor. You need to see the content on the slides better.

3. Click the **Zoom** list arrow on the Standard toolbar, and then click **75%**. See Figure 1-23.

Figure 1-23	Completed presentation in Slide Sorter view

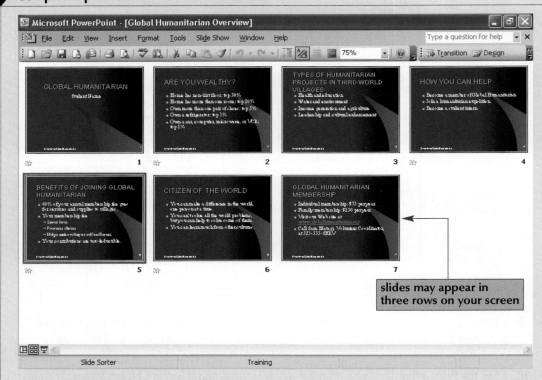

slides may appear in three rows on your screen

4. Compare your handouts with the slides shown in Slide Sorter view.

5. Click the **Close window** button ✖. A dialog box appears asking if you want to save your changes.

6. Click the **Yes** button to save the changes and close the presentation.

You have created a presentation using the AutoContent Wizard, edited it according to Miriam's wishes, and created and printed notes and handouts. Miriam thanks you for your help; she believes that your work will enable her to make an effective presentation.

Session 1.2 Quick Check

1. Explain how to do the following in the Outline tab:
   a. move text up
   b. delete a slide
   c. change a first-level bullet to a second-level bullet
2. What does it mean to promote a bulleted item in the Outline tab? To demote a bulleted item?
3. Explain a benefit of using the Outline tab rather than the slide pane.
4. What is the Style Checker? What is an example of a consistency or style problem that it might mark?
5. What are notes? How do you create them?
6. Why is it beneficial to preview a presentation before printing it?

Tutorial Summary

In this tutorial, you learned how to plan and create a PowerPoint presentation by modifying AutoContent slides. You learned how to edit the text in both the Outline tab and the slide pane; add a new slide and choose a slide layout; delete slides; and promote, demote and move text in your outline. You also learned how to check your presentation for consistency, create speaker notes, and preview and print your presentation.

Key Terms

animation	note	slide pane
body text	notes pane	slide transitions
bulleted item	numbered list	Slides tab
bulleted list	object	Style Checker
content layout	Outline tab	sub-bullet
demote	placeholder	text and content layout
design template	PowerPoint	text box
first-level bullet	progressive disclosure	text layout
footer	promote	thesaurus
handout	second-level bullet	thumbnail
layout	sizing handle	title text
main text		

Review Assignments

Data File needed for the Review Assignments: VillageOP.ppt

Miriam Schwartz, the managing director of the Austin, Texas headquarters of Global Humanitarian, asks you to prepare a PowerPoint presentation explaining the Village Outreach Program to potential donors and volunteers. She gives you a rough draft of a PowerPoint presentation. Your job is to edit the presentation. Complete the following:

1. Open the presentation **VillageOP** in the Tutorial.01\Review folder included with your Data Files.
2. Save the file as **Village Outreach Program** in the same folder.
3. In Slide 1, change the subtitle placeholder ("Global Humanitarian") to your name.

4. In Slide 2, use the Outline tab to demote the bulleted items "Health," "Education," "Clean water," and "Environment," so that they become second-level bulleted items.

5. Below the sub-bulleted item "Clean water," insert another second-level bulleted item: "Agriculture and Income-producing Projects."

6. In Slide 3, delete all occurrences of the word "the" to reduce the number of words in each bulleted item and thus approach the 6×6 rule.

7. Move the last bulleted item in Slide 3 ("Assist villagers in organizing health committees") in the Outline tab so it becomes the second bulleted item in the body text of Slide 3.

8. Go to Slide 5, and then promote the bulleted item "Agriculture and Income-producing Opportunities" in the Outline tab so it becomes the title of a new slide (Slide 6).

9. Return to Slide 5 and promote the last three second-level bulleted items so they become bullets on the same level as "Help villagers build."

10. In Slide 7, move the second bulleted item ("Mobilize resources") so it becomes the fourth bulleted item.

11. Add a new Slide 8 with the default Title and Text layout.

12. In Slide 8, type the slide title "Village Projects."

13. Type the following as first-level bulleted items in Slide 8: "Wells," "Water Pumps," "Greenhouses," "Lorena Stoves," "First aid supplies," and "School supplies."

14. In Slide 2, add the following speaker note: "Relate personal experiences for each topic."

15. In Slide 3, add the following speaker note: "Explain that we need volunteers, especially physicians, dentists, optometrists, and nurses."

16. Switch to Slide Sorter view, and then drag Slide 5 to the left of Slide 4.

17. Use the Research task pane to replace "Agriculture" on Slide 6 with another word, and then make this same change on Slide 2.

18. Check the spelling in the presentation and change or ignore each flagged word as appropriate.

19. Turn on the Style Checker, set the Case options so that the slide title style is uppercase and the body text style is sentence case, and then examine the slides for elements that the Style Checker flags, correcting slides as appropriate. Turn off the Style Checker when you are finished.

20. View the presentation in Slide Show view. Look carefully at each slide and check the content. If you see any errors, press the Esc key to end the slide show, fix the error, and then start the slide show again.

21. Go to Slide 6. When you viewed the presentation, did you notice the typographical error "load" in the final bulleted item? (It should be "loan.") If you did not fix this error already, fix it now.

22. Save the changes to the presentation, preview the presentation in grayscale, and then print the presentation in grayscale as handouts, four slides per page.

23. Print Slides 2 and 3 as notes pages in grayscale, and then close the file.

Case Problem 1

There are no Data Files needed for this Case Problem.

e-Commerce Consultants   Kendall Koester founded e-Commerce Consultants, a consulting company that helps local businesses with their e-commerce needs, including Web page design, order fulfillment, and security. Kendall hired you to prepare a presentation to businesses to sell the services of e-Commerce Consultants. Complete the following:

1. Start PowerPoint, and then start the AutoContent Wizard.

2. In the Presentation type window, select the Sales/Marketing category, and then select Selling a Product or Service.

3. In the Presentation style window, select On-screen presentation.

4. In the Presentation options window, type "Developing Strategies for Your Future" as the presentation title, and type "e-Commerce Consultants" as the footer.

5. Omit the date last updated from the presentation, but include the slide number.

6. In Slide 1, change the subtitle placeholder to your name, if necessary.

7. In Slide 2 ("Objective"), replace the slide title with "What We Offer," and replace the body text with the following first-level bulleted items: "Overcoming barriers to e-commerce," "Surviving today's shaky market," "Setting up your Web site," and "Managing your orders."

8. In Slide 3 ("Customer Requirements"), leave the title text as is, and then replace the body text with the following bulleted items: "Web site design and development," "Order taking and fulfillment," "Security," and "Other." Don't modify or delete the radial diagram on the slide.

9. In Slide 4, change the slide title to "Meeting Your Needs," and then replace the body text with the following first-level bulleted items: "Promoting your product," "Securing startup funds," "Arranging for credit card accounts," and "Answering all your questions." Don't modify or delete the three pyramid diagrams.

10. Delete Slides 5 ("Cost Analysis") and 6 ("Our Strengths").

11. In the new Slide 5 ("Key Benefits"), leave the title text as is, and then replace the body text with the following first-level bulleted items: "You can focus on your products, your services, and your bottom line."; and "We'll help you sell your product on the Internet."

12. In Slide 6 ("Next Steps"), leave the title text as is, and then replace the body text with the following first-level bulleted items: "List what you want us to do," "Draw up an agreement," "Determine a timeline," "Establish the order-fulfillment process," and "Launch the Web-based e-commerce system."

13. Save the presentation as **e-Commerce Consultants** in the Tutorial.01\Cases folder included with your Data Files.

14. In Slide 2, indent (demote) "Managing your orders" so it is a sub-bullet under "Setting up your Web site," and then add another sub-bullet, "Handling online credit."

15. In Slide 3, add the following sub-bulleted items under "Web site design and development": "know-how," "graphic design," "software," and "programming."

16. In Slide 4, insert a new first bullet "We can help by," and then make all the other phrases the sub-bullets.

17. Move the last bulleted item "Answering all your questions" up to become the first sub-bullet.

18. In Slide 6 ("Next Steps"), delete excess words like "a," "an," and "the" to achieve the 6 × 6 rule as closely as possible.

19. Add a new slide after Slide 6 with the Title and Text layout, type "Your Account Representative" as the title text, and then type the following information in five bullets: Kendall Koester, e-Commerce Consultants, 1666 Winnebago St., Pecatonica, IL 61063, 555-WEB-PAGE. The city, state, and Zip code should all be part of the same bulleted item. (Note that the first letter of "e-Commerce" changes to an uppercase letter as soon as you press the spacebar. This is PowerPoint's AutoFormat.)

20. Click to the right of the first letter "E" in "E-Commerce," press the Backspace key, and then type "e."

21. Turn on the Style Checker, set the Case options so that the slide title style is title case and the body text style is sentence case, and then go through each slide of the presentation to see if the Style Checker marks any potential problems. (Don't forget to double-check each slide by moving to the next or previous slide and then back to the current slide to recheck it.) When you see the light bulb, click it, and then assess whether you want to accept or reject the suggested change. You'll want to accept

most of the suggested changes, but make sure you leave words like "Web" and "Internet" capitalized, and don't change the capitalization of the address and phone number you typed on Slide 7. Turn off the Style Checker when you are finished.

22. Check the spelling in the presentation. Correct any misspellings, and ignore any words that are spelled correctly.

23. View the presentation in Slide Show view.

24. Save the presentation, preview it in grayscale, print the presentation in grayscale as handouts with four slides per page, and then close the file.

Apply

Apply the skills you learned to modify an existing presentation for a seafood distributor.

Case Problem 2

Data File needed for this Case Problem: Seafoods.ppt

Northwest Seafoods Paul Neibaur is president of Northwest Seafoods, a seafood distribution company with headquarters in Vancouver, British Columbia. He buys fish and other seafood from suppliers and sells to restaurant and grocery store chains. Although his company has been in business and profitable for 27 years, Paul wants to sell the company and retire. He wants you to help him create a PowerPoint presentation to prospective buyers. Complete the following:

1. Open the file **Seafoods** located in the Tutorial.01\Cases folder included with your Data Files, and then save it as **Northwest Seafoods** in the same folder.

2. In Slide 1, replace the subtitle placeholder ("Paul Neibaur") with your name.

3. In Slide 2, add the speaker's note "Mention that regular customers are large grocery stores and fast-food franchises."

4. Add a sixth bulleted item to Slide 2: "Contracts with 13 distributors."

5. Move the second bulleted item ("Low debt") so that it becomes the last bulleted item.

6. In Slide 3, edit the third bulleted item so that "walk-in freezers," "cutting devices," and "other equipment" are second-level bulleted items below the main bullet.

7. Promote the bulleted item "Experienced employees" and its sub-bullets so that they become a new, separate slide.

8. Use the Slides tab to move Slide 5 ("Profitability") to become Slide 4.

9. Add a new slide after Slide 7 with the Title and Text layout, and then replace the title placeholder text with "British Columbia Business Brokers."

10. Create three new bulleted items with the address on the first line ("107-5901 Granville Street"), the city, province, and postal code on the second line ("Coquitlam, BC V6M 4J7"), and the phone number on the third line ("604.555.SELL").

11. Check the spelling in the presentation. Correct any spelling errors and ignore any words that are spelled correctly.

12. Turn on the Style Checker, change the options so that the slide title style is uppercase and the body text style is sentence case, and then go through all the slides correcting any flagged style problems. Be sure not to let the Style Checker change the case for "Small Business Administration" or modify the address you typed on Slide 8; otherwise, accept the Style Checker's suggested case changes. Turn off the Style Checker when you are finished.

13. View the presentation in Slide Show view.

14. Go to Slide 4. When you viewed the presentation, did you notice the two typographical errors on this page? If you did not fix these errors, fix them now.

15. Save the presentation, preview the presentation in grayscale, print the presentation in grayscale as handouts with four slides per page, and then print Slide 2 as a notes page, and then close the file.

Challenge

Explore more advanced features of PowerPoint by formatting text, paragraphs, and lists, and by changing slide layouts and adding a design template.

Case Problem 3

Data File needed for this Case Problem: LASIK.ppt

Camellia Gardens Eye Center Dr. Carol Wang, head ophthalmologist at the Camellia Gardens Eye Center in Charleston, South Carolina, performs over 20 surgeries per week using laser-assisted in situ keratomileusis (LASIK) to correct vision problems of myopia (nearsightedness), hyperopia (farsightedness), and astigmatism. She asks you to help prepare a PowerPoint presentation to those interested in learning more about LASIK. Complete the following:

1. Open the file **LASIK** located in the Tutorial.01\Cases folder included with your Data Files, and then save it as **Camellia LASIK** in the same folder.
2. In Slide 1, replace the subtitle placeholder ("Camellia Gardens Eye Center") with your name.
3. In Slide 2, move the first bulleted item down to become the third bulleted item.
4. Edit the sub-bullets "Myopia," "Hyperopia," and "Astigmatism" in the first item so they're part of the first-level bullet and there are no sub-bullets. Be sure to add commas after the first two words, and add the word "and" before the last word.
5. Add a fourth bulleted item with the text "Patients no longer need corrective lenses."

Explore

6. Still in Slide 2, center the text in the title text box. (*Hint*: Click anywhere in the title text, and then position the pointer over the buttons on the Formatting toolbar to see the ScreenTips to find a button that will center the text.)

Explore

7. In Slide 3, change the bulleted list to a numbered list. (*Hint*: Select all of the body text, and then look for a button on the Formatting toolbar that will number the list.)

Explore

8. Have PowerPoint automatically split Slide 3 into two slides. (*Hint*: First, click the AutoFit Options button in the slide pane and click the Stop Fitting Text to This Placeholder option button. Then, with the insertion point in the body text box, click the AutoFit Options button again, and then click the appropriate option.)

Explore

9. On the new Slide 4, change the numbering so it continues the numbering from Slide 3 rather than starting over at number 1. (*Hint*: Right-click anywhere in the first item in the numbered list, click Bullets and Numbering on the shortcut menu, click the Numbered tab, and then change the Start at value.)
10. At the end of the title in Slide 4, add a space and "(cont.)," the abbreviation for continued.
11. In Slide 5, demote the two bullets under "With low to moderate myopia," so they become sub-bullets.

Explore

12. Still in Slide 5, tell the PowerPoint Spell Checker to ignore all occurrences of the word "hyperopia," which is not found in PowerPoint's dictionary. (*Hint*: Right-click the word to see a shortcut menu with spelling commands.)

Explore

13. If any of the bulleted text doesn't fit on the slide, but drops below the body text box, set the text box to AutoFit. (*Hint*: Click anywhere in the text box, click the AutoFit Options button that appears, and then click the desired option.)
14. In Slide 6, join the final two bullets to become one bullet. Be sure to add a semicolon between the two bullets and change the word "Other" to lowercase.
15. In Slide 8, move the second bullet "Schedule eye exam to determine" (along with its sub-bullets) up to become the first bullet.
16. In Slide 8, edit the bulleted item ("Analysis of . . .") so that "eye pressure," "shape of cornea," and "thickness of cornea" are sub-bullets below "Analysis of."

Explore

17. Change the layout of Slide 8 so that the body text appears in two columns. (*Hint*: Click the AutoFit Options button in the slide pane, and then click Change to Two-Column Layout.) Drag the last two bullets over to the second column in the body text. (*Hint*: After you select the bulleted item, position the pointer over the selected

text instead of over the bullet, and then drag the pointer to immediately after the new bullet in the second column, using the vertical line indicator that appears to help guide you.)

18. Add a new Slide 9, and then apply the Title Only layout in the Text Layout section of the Slide Layout task pane.

Explore

19. In Slide 9, add the title "Camellia Gardens Eye Center," create a new text box near the center of the slide, and then add the address "8184 Camellia Drive" on the first line, "Charleston, SC 29406" on the second line, and the phone number "(843) 555-EYES" on the third line. (*Hint*: Click the Text Box button on the Drawing toolbar, and then click on the slide at the desired location.)

Explore

20. Change the size of the text in the new text box on Slide 9 so that it's 32 points. (*Hint*: Click the edge of the text box to select the entire text box and all of its contents, and then click the Font Size list arrow on the Formatting toolbar.)

Explore

21. Turn on the Style Checker, and then set the style options for end punctuation so that the Style Checker checks to make sure that slide titles do not have end punctuation, and that paragraphs in the body text have punctuation. Set the slide title style to title case and the body text style to sentence case. Also, set the Visual Clarity options so that the maximum number of bullets should not exceed six, the number of lines per title should not exceed two, and the number of lines per bulleted item should not exceed two. (*Hint*: Use the End punctuation section of the Case and End Punctuation tab and the Legibility section of the Visual Clarity tab in the Style Options dialog box.)

Explore

22. Go through all the slides, correcting problems of case (capitalization) and punctuation. Be sure not to let the Style Checker change the case for proper nouns. Let the Style Checker correct end punctuation for complete sentences, but you shouldn't allow (or you should remove) punctuation for words or phrases that don't form complete sentences. Do not accept the Style Checker's suggestions to remove question marks in the slide titles.

Explore

23. Change the Style Options back so that the next time the Style Checker is run, only the Slide title style and Body text style options on the Case and End Punctuation tab and the Fonts options on the Visual Clarity tab are selected, and then turn off the Style Checker.

24. Check the spelling in the presentation.

Explore

25. Apply the design template called "Watermark," which has a white background with violet circles. (*Hint*: Click the Design button on the Formatting toolbar, and then use the ScreenTips in the Slide Design task pane to find the Watermark design template.) If you can't find the Watermark design template, choose a different design template.

26. View the presentation in Slide Show view.

27. Save the presentation, preview it in grayscale, print the presentation in grayscale as handouts with four slides per page, and then close the file.

Research

Use the Internet to research bestsellers and use PowerPoint's Help system to find out how to format text.

Case Problem 4

There are no Data Files needed for this Case Problem.

Book Review   Your English teacher asks you to prepare a book review for presentation to the class. The teacher asks you to review any book from a bestseller list, past or present, such as the Barnes & Noble Top 100 Books or Amazon's Top 100 Bestsellers. To help you give your class presentation, you want to use PowerPoint slides. Your task is to prepare a presentation of at least six PowerPoint slides. Complete the following:

1. Go to **www.bn.com**, **www.amazon.com**, or any other bestseller list, and find the title of a book you have read. If you can't find a book from among these lists, get approval from your instructor to report on another book.

2. Use the AutoContent Wizard to begin developing slides based on "Generic" from the General category of presentation types.

   a. Title the presentation "Review of" followed by your book title, and then add "Review of" followed by the book subject as the footer. For example, the title might be "Review of Harry Potter and the Order of the Phoenix," along with the footer "Review of a Recent Bestseller."

   b. Include both the date and the slide number.

Explore ➤ 3. Use PowerPoint's Help system to find out how to italicize text. Close the Help window and the task pane, and then edit Slide 1 so that the book title is italicized.

4. In Slide 1, change the subtitle to your name, if necessary.

5. In Slide 2 ("Introduction"), include the following information in the bulleted list: title, author(s), publisher, publication year, and the number of pages in the book.

6. In Slide 3 ("Topics of Discussion"), include the categories used in reviewing the book, for example, "Plot," "Action," "Characterization," "Description," "Humor," and "Comparison with Other Books in the Series."

7. Delete Slides 4 through 9.

8. Create at least one slide for each of the topics you listed on Slide 3, and then include bulleted lists explaining that topic.

Explore ➤ 9. Connect to the Internet, and then use the Research task pane to find additional information about the topic of the book you've chosen or about the author. (*Hint*: In the Research task pane, type the topic or author name into the Search for text box, make sure your computer is connected to the Internet, select a research site such as Encarta Encyclopedia, and then click the green arrow button, if necessary, to start searching.) You might want to create one or more new slides, cut and paste information into the new slides, and then edit the information into one or more appropriate bulleted lists.

10. Create a slide titled "Summary and Recommendations" as the last slide in your presentation, giving your overall impression of the book and your recommendation for whether the book is worth reading.

11. View the presentation on the Outline tab. If necessary, change the order of the bulleted items on the slides, or change the order of the slides.

Explore ➤ 12. If you see any slides with more than six bulleted items, split the slide in two. (*Hint*: With the insertion point in the body text box, click the AutoFit Options button that appears near the lower-left corner of the text box, and then click the appropriate option.)

13. Turn on the Style Checker, and then go through all the slides, correcting problems of case (capitalization), punctuation, number of bulleted items per slide, and number of lines per bulleted item. Be sure not to let the Style Checker change the case for proper nouns. Let the Style Checker correct end punctuation for complete sentences, but you shouldn't allow (or you should remove) punctuation for words or phrases that don't form complete sentences.

14. Check the spelling of your presentation.

15. View the presentation in Slide Show view. If you see any typographical errors or other problems, stop the slide show, correct the problems, and then continue the slide show. If you find slides that aren't necessary, delete them.

16. Save the presentation as **Book Review** in the Tutorial.01\Cases folder included with your Data Files.

17. Preview the presentation in grayscale, and then print the presentation in grayscale as handouts with four slides per page. Print speaker notes if you created any, and then close the file.

Research

Go to the Web to find information you can use to create presentations.

Internet Assignments

The purpose of the Internet Assignments is to challenge you to find information on the Internet that you can use to work effectively with this software. The actual assignments are updated and maintained on the Course Technology Web site. Log on to the Internet and use your Web browser to go to the Student Online Companion for New Perspectives Office 2003 at **www.course.com/np/office2003**. Click the Internet Assignments link, and then navigate to the assignments for this tutorial.

Assess

SAM Assessment and Training

If you have a SAM user profile, you may have access to hands-on instruction, practice, and assessment of the skills covered in this tutorial. Log in to your SAM account and go to your assignments page to see what your instructor has assigned.

Review

Quick Check Answers

Session 1.1

1. A presentation's components can consist of individual slides, speaker notes, an outline, and audience handouts.
2. The slide pane shows the slide as it will look during your slide show. The notes pane contains speaker notes. The Outline tab shows an outline of your presentation. The Slides tab displays thumbnails of each slide.
3. a. a feature that causes each element on a slide to appear one at a time
   b. the manner in which a new slide appears on the screen during a slide show
   c. a file that contains the colors and format of the background and the font style of the titles, accents, and other text
   d. a predetermined way of organizing the objects on a slide
4. What is my purpose or objective? What type of presentation is needed? What is the physical location of my presentation? What is the best format my presentation?
5. The AutoContent Wizard lets you choose a presentation category and then creates a general outline of the presentation.
6. The view you use to present an on-screen presentation to an audience.

Session 1.2

1. a. Click a slide or bullet icon, and then drag the selected item up.
   b. Right-click the slide icon of the slide to be deleted in the Outline tab, and then click Delete Slide on the shortcut menu; or, move to the slide you want to delete in the slide pane, click Edit on the menu bar, and then click Delete Slide.
   c. Click the slide or bullet icon in the Outline tab, and then click the Decrease Indent button on the Formatting toolbar.
2. Promote means to decrease the level (for example, from level two to level one) of an outline item; demote means to increase the level of an outline item.
3. In the Outline tab, you can see the text of several slides at once, which makes it easier to work with text. In the slide pane, you can see the design and layout of the slide.
4. The Style Checker automatically checks your presentation for consistency and style. For example, it will check for consistency in punctuation.
5. Notes are notes for the presenter. They appear in the notes pane in Normal view or you can print notes pages, which contain a picture of and notes about each slide.
6. By previewing your presentation, you make sure that the slides are satisfactory, and that the presentation is legible in grayscale if you use a monochrome printer.

Objectives

Session 2.1
- Create a presentation from a template
- Apply a new template
- Insert, resize, and recolor a clip-art image
- Modify the design using the slide master
- Insert a bitmap image on a slide
- Reformat text and resize text boxes
- Apply a second design template
- Insert tab stops to align text
- Change the layouts of existing slides
- Reposition text boxes

Session 2.2
- Create and modify a table
- Create a diagram using the Diagram Gallery
- Draw a simple graphic using AutoShapes
- Modify and rotate an AutoShape graphic
- Insert and rotate text boxes
- Create a summary slide

Applying and Modifying Text and Graphic Objects

Presenting and Preparing for an Expedition to Peru

Case

Global Humanitarian, Lima Office

The objectives of Global Humanitarian's expeditions are to help villagers build homes, schools, greenhouses, wells, culinary water systems, and Lorena adobe stoves; to provide medical and dental services; and to teach basic hygiene, literacy, and gardening skills. The village council of Paqarimuy, a small village in the puna (also called the altiplano, or high-altitude plains of the Andes Mountains), requested help in accomplishing some of these objectives. Therefore, Pablo Fuentes, the managing director of Global Humanitarian in Lima, Peru, is organizing a service expedition to that village. He plans the expedition as a two-week trip. To complete everything he hopes to accomplish, he needs approximately 25 volunteers. He thinks that the best way to recruit volunteers is to present a PowerPoint slide show to interested students at local colleges and universities. During the presentation, he can give an overview to the audience members so that they will have enough information to consider the trip. He can answer questions that the audience might have during and after the presentation. He asks you to help prepare a PowerPoint presentation to prospective expedition participants.

In this tutorial, you'll create a new presentation based on a design template, modify the design template, apply a design template to an existing presentation, and then enhance the presentation by adding graphics to the slides. You will also add a slide summarizing the content of the presentation.

Student Data Files

▼ **Tutorial.02**

▽ **Tutorial folder**
- GHLogo.jpg
- MntTop.jpg
- PeruExp2.ppt

▽ **Review folder**
- Boots.jpg
- Camera.jpg
- Food.jpg
- GHLogo.jpg
- PackList.ppt
- Personal.jpg
- PrMeds.jpg
- SlpBag.jpg
- Vitamins.jpg

▽ **Cases folder**
- Excycle.jpg
- MyBody.ppt
- Payroll.ppt
- PESLogo.jpg
- PKPBadg.jpg
- PKPKey.jpg
- SBcam.jpg
- SBfile.jpg
- SBpages.jpg
- SBpaper.jpg
- SBpens.jpg
- SBphoto.jpg
- SBsciss.jpg
- StrMach.jpg
- Treadmil.jpg
- Vitamins.jpg
- Weights.jpg

Session 2.1

Planning a Presentation

Before creating his text presentation, Pablo and his staff planned the presentation as follows:

- **Purpose of the presentation**: to convince potential volunteers to apply for a position in the Peru expedition
- **Type of presentation**: an onscreen (electronic) information presentation
- **Audience**: students, health professionals, and other people interested in serving villages in a third-world country
- **Location of the presentation**: a conference room at the offices of Global Humanitarian, as well as classrooms and business offices
- **Audience needs**: to recognize the services they can provide and the adventure they can enjoy as expedition volunteers
- **Format**: one speaker presenting an onscreen slide show consisting of seven to 10 slides

After planning the presentation, Pablo and his staff discuss how they want the slides to look.

Creating a New Presentation from a Design Template

Plain white slides with normal text (such as black Times New Roman or Arial) often fail to hold an audience's attention. In today's information age, audiences expect more interesting color schemes, fonts, graphics, and other effects.

To make it easy to add color and style to your presentations, PowerPoint comes with design templates. A **design template** is a file that contains the color scheme, text formats, background colors and objects, and graphics in the presentation. The **color scheme** is the eight colors used in a design template. A **graphic** is a picture, clip art, photograph, shape, design, graph, chart, or diagram that you can add to a slide. A graphic, like a text box, is an object. Pablo asks you to create a new presentation with the Teamwork design template so that he can see what it looks like.

Reference Window	Creating a New Presentation from a Design Template

- Click File on the menu bar, and then click New.
- Click the From design template link in the New Presentation task pane.
- Click the design template you want to use.

You'll begin enhancing Pablo's presentation by changing the design template.

To create a new presentation from a design template:

1. Start PowerPoint, and then click the **Create a new presentation** link at the bottom of the Getting Started task pane. The New Presentation task pane opens.

   Trouble? If you don't see the Create a new presentation link in the Getting Started task pane, point to the small, downward-pointing triangle at the bottom of the task pane to scroll the task pane automatically so that you can see the commands at the bottom of the task pane.

Trouble? If PowerPoint is already running and the task pane is not open, click File on the menu bar, and then click New to open the New Presentation task pane.

2. Click the **From design template** link in the New Presentation task pane. Slide 1 (the title slide) of a new blank presentation opens in Normal view and the Slide Design task pane opens. Notice that Default Design appears in the status bar below the slide pane to indicate that this is the current design template. A thumbnail showing the Default Design template also appears in the Slide Design task pane under Used in This Presentation. In the Default Design template, the slides have black text on a plain white background.

3. Move the pointer over the **Default Design template** thumbnail under Used in This Presentation in the task pane. A ScreenTip appears, identifying the template. See Figure 2-1.

Blank presentation with Default Design template applied ◀ **Figure 2-1**

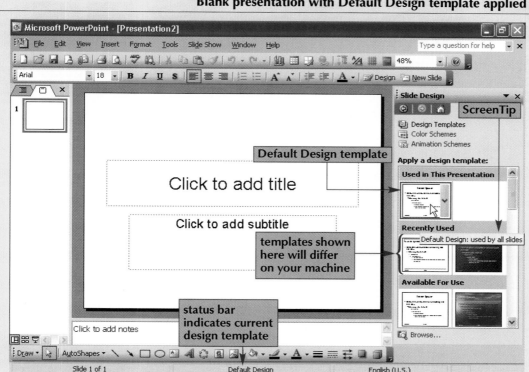

4. Scroll down through the thumbnail views of the design templates, and move the pointer over the thumbnails under **Available For Use** until you find **Teamwork**, a dark green thumbnail.

Trouble? If the Teamwork template is not in the task pane, you must install it. If you are working in a lab, ask your instructor or technical support person for help. If you are working on your own computer, click the Additional Design Templates thumbnail to install additional templates.

5. Click the **Teamwork** design template. The design template of the new presentation changes from Default Design to Teamwork. See Figure 2-2.

Figure 2-2 ▶ Teamwork design template applied

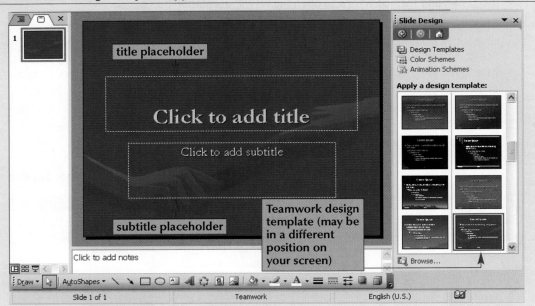

▶ **6.** Click in the **title** placeholder in the slide pane, and then type **Peru Expedition 2006**.

▶ **7.** Click in the **subtitle** placeholder and then type your own name.

▶ **8.** Click the **Close** button ✕ in the Slide Design task pane.

▶ **9.** Save the presentation as **PeruExp** in the Tutorial.02\Tutorial folder included with your Data Files.

▶ **10.** Click **File** on the menu bar, and then click **Print** to open the Print dialog box.

▶ **11.** Click the **Color/grayscale** list arrow, click **Grayscale**, click the **Print what** list arrow, and then click **Slides**, if necessary.

▶ **12.** Click the **OK** button. The one-page presentation prints in full slide format (one slide fits the entire page).

▶ **13.** Close the presentation (but leave PowerPoint running).

Pablo takes the new presentation you created, adds more slides to the presentation, and saves the file as PeruExp2. After considering the Teamwork design template, he decides that he doesn't like it because the hands in the background are hard to see. You'll change the design template now.

Applying a Design Template

The design template you choose for your presentation should reflect the content and the intended audience. For example, if you are presenting a new curriculum to a group of elementary school teachers, you might choose a template that uses bright, primary colors. Likewise, if you are presenting a new marketing plan to a mutual fund company, you might choose a plain-looking template that uses dark colors formatted in a way that appears sophisticated.

Although Pablo's presentation is serious, he wants to make the trip seem attractive to prospective participants. He decides that he wants to use a color scheme that includes a dark blue background with a color gradient and some graphics representing the Peruvian Andes Mountains. He thinks such a design would give his presentation more interest.

Reference Window

Applying a Different Design Template

- Display the Slide Design templates in the task pane by clicking the Design button on the Formatting toolbar.
- Scroll through the design template thumbnails until you see one you'd like to apply, and then click the design template thumbnail.

To change the design template:

▶ **1.** Open the presentation file **PeruExp2** located in the Tutorial.02\Tutorial folder included with your Data Files.

▶ **2.** Save the file in the same folder using the filename **Peru Expedition**. The presentation title slide appears in the slide pane.

▶ **3.** Click the **Design** button on the Formatting toolbar to open the Slide Design task pane.

▶ **4.** Scroll down through the thumbnail views of the design templates in the task pane under Available For Use, and then click the **Mountain Top** template. Don't forget to move the pointer over the templates to see their names. The design template of Peru Expedition changes from Teamwork to Mountain Top. See Figure 2-3.

Presentation with Mountain Top design template applied ◀ **Figure 2-3**

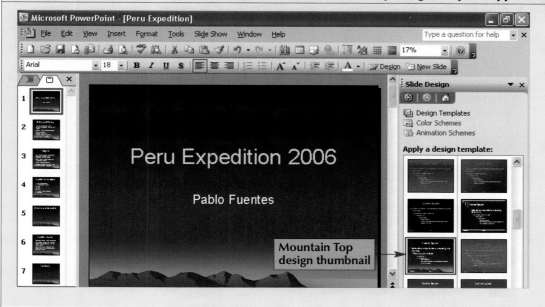

As you can see, the title slide has a dark blue background with varying color, and a background graphic of a mountain top along the bottom of the slide. Next, you'll modify this template to make it more appropriate for this presentation.

Understanding Graphics

Graphics add information, clarification, emphasis, variety, and even pizzazz to a PowerPoint presentation. PowerPoint enables you to include many types of graphics in your presentation: graphics created using another Windows program; scanned photographs, drawings, or cartoons; and other picture files or clip art located on a CD or other disk. You can also create graphics using the drawing tools in PowerPoint. In addition, you can add graphical bullets to a bulleted list.

Inserting Clip Art

Slide 6, "Expedition Information," has six bulleted items of text. Pablo wants to include some clip art to add interest to this slide. In PowerPoint, **clip art** refers specifically to images in the Media Gallery that accompanies Office 2003, or images that are available from the Clip Art and Media section of Microsoft Office Online. Pablo decides that an image of a globe would help emphasize the global aspects of the expedition.

To add clip art to a slide, you can use a slide layout that has a place for clip art, or you can insert the clip art as you would a picture. If you insert clip art using the Insert Clip Art button on the Drawing toolbar, the Clip Art task pane opens and you can search for clips that match keywords you type, and then browse the results. If you insert clip art by clicking a button on a layout that includes a placeholder for clip art, you can browse through all of the clips stored on your machine as well as search for clips that match keywords you type. You'll change the existing slide layout before adding clip art.

To change the layout of a slide and add clip art:

▶ **1.** Go to **Slide 6** ("Expedition Information").

▶ **2.** Click **Format** on the menu bar, and then click **Slide Layout** to display the Slide Layout task pane.

▶ **3.** Scroll down the task pane until you see Text and Content Layouts, and then click the **Title, Text, and Content** layout (the first layout under Text and Content Layouts). The bulleted list moves to the left side of the slide and the content placeholder appears on the right of the slide. See Figure 2-4. Notice that PowerPoint automatically reduces the size of the text in the bulleted list so that it will fit properly within the reduced text box.

| Figure 2-4 | Slide 6 after changing slide layout to Title, Text, and Content |

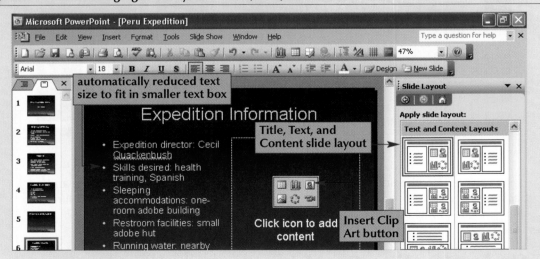

Trouble? If the text size doesn't automatically change or if it doesn't change to a small enough size, click anywhere in the body text, click the AutoFit Options button that appears near the lower-left corner of the body text, and then click the AutoFit Text to Placeholder option button.

▶ **4.** Click the **Close** button ☒ in the task pane title bar to close the task pane.

▶ **5.** Click the **Insert Clip Art** button 🖼 in the content placeholder. The Select Picture dialog box opens. If necessary, drag the box by its title bar so you can see all of it. Now you'll search for a piece of clip art that relates to a globe.

▶ **6.** Type **globe** in the Search text box at the top of the dialog box, and then click the **Go** button. Depending upon how Office was installed on your computer, PowerPoint displays from just a few to over 250 pieces of clip art that contain a representation of a globe.

▶ **7.** If necessary, drag the scroll button up to the top of the scroll bar in the Select Picture dialog box, and then double-click the image of a globe in the center of a red circular background. The Select Picture dialog box closes, the content placeholder disappears from the slide, and the clip art you selected appears in its place. See Figure 2-5.

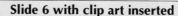 **Slide 6 with clip art inserted** ◀ **Figure 2-5**

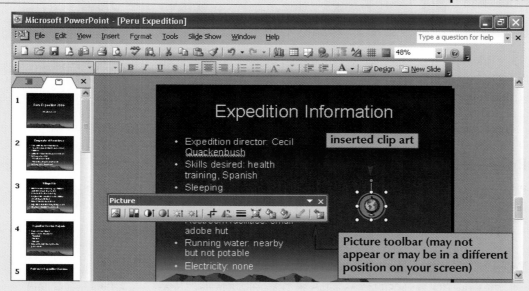

Now you'll modify this clip art image by changing its size and some of its colors.

Resizing Clip Art

The clip art is too small, and so is the body text box, making the autofit text in the bulleted list too small. You will increase the size of the clip art and the text box.

To resize the clip art image:

▶ **1.** Drag the upper-right corner sizing handle of the globe clip art toward the upper-right corner of the slide until the image is approximately tripled in size.

▶ **2.** Position the pointer over the selected clip art image so that it changes to ⬆, and then drag the entire clip art image so that it's centered between the top and bottom of the slide, and near the right edge of the slide. Compare your screen to Figure 2-6 and adjust the size or position of the graphic as necessary.

Figure 2-6 | Slide 6 with repositioned clip art

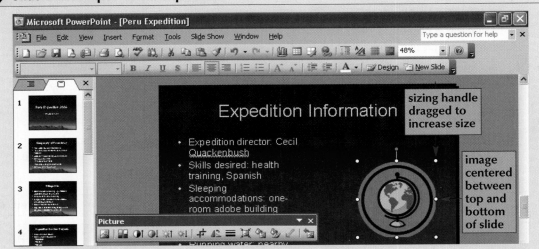

3. Click anywhere in the body text to display the text box and its sizing handles, and then drag the right-center sizing handle to the right until it just touches the left edge of the clip art.

With the clip art inserted and resized, you're ready to change some of the colors.

Recoloring Clip Art

Pablo thinks the red colors on the clip art don't match the blue hues of the design template, so he asks you to change the red to dark blue. You can recolor clip art, but you may not always be able to change the color on other types of pictures.

To recolor a clip art image:

1. Click the **clip art** in Slide 6 to select it. The sizing handles appear around the image, and the Picture toolbar appears.

   Trouble? If the Picture toolbar doesn't appear automatically, click View on the menu bar, point to Toolbars, and then click Picture.

2. Click the **Recolor Picture** button on the Picture toolbar to display the Recolor Picture dialog box. The colored rectangular tiles under Original are all of the colors used in this piece of clip art.

3. Drag the scroll box down to the bottom of the scroll bar in the dialog box so you can see the red and off-red tiles. See Figure 2-7.

Recolor Picture dialog box ◄ **Figure 2-7**

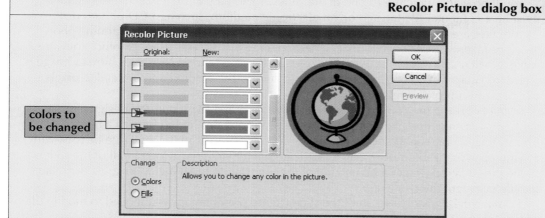

4. Click the **off-red color tile** list arrow in the New column, and then click the **light violet tile** on the palette of default colors. The **default colors** are those colors associated with the overall color scheme of the design template. The globe's shadow in the Preview box changes from off-red to light violet.

5. Change the **red tile** in the New column to the **royal blue tile** (not the dark blue tile) on the palette of default colors.

6. Click the **Preview** button in the Recolor Picture dialog box, and then drag the dialog box by its title bar so that you can see the colors applied to the clip art on the slide. The recolored clip art looks much better than the red colors did.

7. Click the **OK** button, and then click outside the selected object to deselect it. See Figure 2-8.

Recolored clip art and resized body text box ◄ **Figure 2-8**

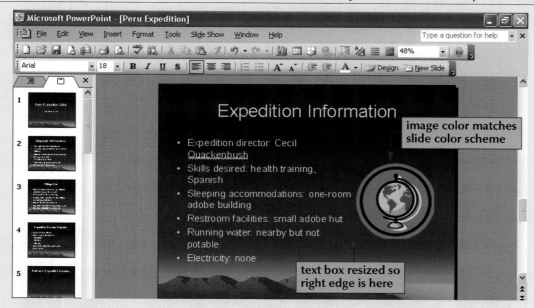

8. Click the **Save** button on the Standard toolbar to save your changes.

You'll now add a picture to one of the slides. To add a picture to a slide, the picture must be a computer file located on an electronic medium, such as a CD or hard disk. Picture files are generated by taking photographs with a digital camera, scanning photographs taken with a conventional camera, or drawing pictures using graphics software (such as Microsoft Paint). These types of picture files are bitmap images. A **bitmap image** is a grid (or "map") of colored dots that form a picture. The colored dots are called **pixels**, which stands for picture elements.

Instead of using the current background graphic of the Mountain Top design template, Pablo prefers an actual photograph of the Andes Mountains, in the form of a bitmap image. To get a bitmap file of the Andes Mountains, Pablo scanned a picture he took with a 35mm camera. Pablo also wants to add Global Humanitarian's logo to all of the slides in the presentation. To get a bitmap file of the logo, Pablo hired a graphic artist to create the file using graphics software.

To make these changes to all of the slides in the presentation, you'll need to modify the design template in Slide Master view.

Modifying the Design Template in the Slide Master

A **master** is a slide that contains the elements and styles of the design template, including the text and other objects that appear on all the slides of the same type. Masters never appear when you show or print a presentation. PowerPoint presentations have four types of masters: the **title master**, which contains the objects that appear on the title slide (most presentations have only one title slide, but some have more than one); the **slide master**, which contains the objects that appear on all the slides except the title slide; the **handout master**, which contains the objects that appear on all the printed handouts; and the **notes master**, which contains the objects that appear on the notes pages.

You use slide and title masters so that all the slides in the presentation have a similar design and appearance. This ensures that your presentation is consistent. To make changes to the masters, you need to switch to Slide Master view. You'll do this now.

To switch to Slide Master view:

1. Click **View** on the menu bar, point to **Master**, and then click **Slide Master**. The view changes to Slide Master view, and the Slide Master View toolbar appears. See Figure 2-9.

| Figure 2-9 | Slide Master view |

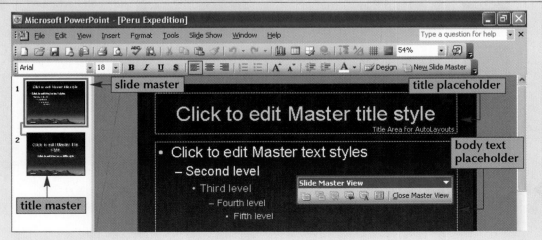

As you can see from the thumbnail slides in the Slides tab, Slide Master view includes two slides: the slide master (as Slide 1) and the title master (as Slide 2). The slide master is currently selected and appears in the slide pane. In Slide Master view, you always see both the slide master and the title master. They appear in Slide Master view as a set, and this is referred to as a **slide-title master pair**.

▶ 2. Click the **title master** (Slide 2) in the Slides tab. The slide pane now displays the master for the title slide.

▶ 3. Click **View** on the menu bar, point to **Master**, and then click **Handout Master**. The layout of handouts appears in the slide pane, and the Handout Master View toolbar appears. You can click the buttons on this toolbar to change the layout of the handout master.

▶ 4. Click **View** on the menu bar, point to **Master**, and then click **Notes Master**. The layout of the notes pages appears in the slide pane, and the Notes Master View toolbar opens.

▶ 5. Click the **Close Master View** button on the Notes Master View floating toolbar. PowerPoint returns to Normal view.

You can modify the slide and title master in Slide Master view by changing the size and design of the title and body text, adding or deleting graphics, and changing the background. You cannot delete or add objects to the background unless you are in Slide Master view.

Modifying Slide and Title Masters

Reference Window

- Click View on the menu bar, point to Master, and then click Slide Master; *or* press and hold the Shift key and then click the Normal View button at the bottom of the Slides or Outline tab to switch to Slide Master view.
- Click the thumbnail of the master slide type that you'd like to modify, either the slide master (Slide 1) or the title master (Slide 2).
- Make any changes to the slide or title master such as changing the background color; modifying the text size, color, font, or alignment; inserting clip art, bitmap images, or other graphics; and changing the size or location of text placeholders.
- Click the Normal View button or click the Close Master View button on the Slide Master View toolbar to return to Normal view.

Before you can insert Pablo's photograph of the Andes Mountains, you must delete the graphic of the mountains currently in the design template.

To modify the slide master:

▶ 1. Switch again to Slide Master view. The slide master appears.

You're going to delete the background image containing the mountain tops. The image is made up of three bitmaps that need to be deleted individually: the sky, the brown mountains, and the dark shading on the mountains.

▶ 2. Position the pointer over the bitmap image so that it changes to ⬚, and then click the teal-green area at the lower-right side of the slide as shown in Figure 2-10. Be careful not to click inside the placeholder titled Object Area for AutoLayouts or inside the placeholder for the Number Area. Sizing handles appear around the selected bitmap.

Figure 2-10 **First bitmap in background image selected**

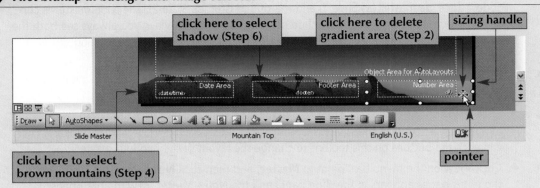

3. Press the **Delete** key. The selected bitmap is deleted.

   Trouble? If you accidentally deleted the Number Area placeholder, click the Undo button on the Standard toolbar, and then repeat Steps 2 and 3.

4. Click the brown mountain at the lower-left side of the slide as indicated in Figure 2-10. Be careful not to click inside the Date Area placeholder.

5. Press the **Delete** key. The bitmap of the mountains is deleted.

   Trouble? If you accidentally deleted the Date Area placeholder, click the Undo button on the Standard toolbar, and then repeat Steps 4 and 5.

6. Click the dark brown shadow in the area just above and to the left of the Footer Area placeholder, as indicated in Figure 2-10. Be careful not to click inside the Footer Area placeholder.

7. Press the **Delete** key. The last bitmap is deleted. The bottom of the slide no longer contains any graphics.

   Trouble? If you have difficulty selecting the shadow, click the Footer Area placeholder, press the ↓ key three times, and then repeat Steps 6 and 7. After you delete the shadow, click the Footer Area placeholder again, and then press the ↑ key three times to return the Footer Area placeholder to its original position.

8. Click the **Save** button on the Standard toolbar to save your changes.

Because you deleted the mountain graphic in Slide Master view, it will be deleted from every slide in the presentation, except the title slide. Now you'll insert the new photo of the Andes Mountains on all of the slides.

Inserting and Modifying a Bitmap Image on a Slide

To add the new bitmap image to all of the slides, you will insert it on the slide master in Slide Master view. To insert a bitmap image on just one slide, you use the same procedure in Normal view.

Inserting a Graphic on a Slide

- If necessary, switch to Normal view, and then open the Slide Layout task pane by clicking Format on the menu bar and clicking Slide Layout.
- Click one of the Content layouts or one of the Text and Content layouts to change the layout of the current slide.
- Click the Insert Clip Art or Insert Picture button in the content placeholder, and then find the desired clip art or navigate to the folder containing the desired picture file.
- Double-click the graphic that you want to insert into the slide.
  or
- Click the Insert Picture button on the Drawing toolbar, navigate to and click the picture file you want to insert, and then click the Insert button.

To insert a graphic into a slide:

1. Click the **Insert Picture** button on the Drawing toolbar. The Insert Picture dialog box opens.

2. Navigate to the Tutorial.02\Tutorial folder included with your Data Files.

3. Click **MntTop**, the bitmap image file of the photograph, and click the **Insert** button. The picture is inserted into your slide master in the middle of the slide, and the Picture toolbar appears.

   Trouble? If the Picture toolbar doesn't appear, click View on the menu bar, point to Toolbars, and then click Picture.

You need to move and resize the image to fit along the bottom of the slide master.

To reposition and resize a picture on a slide:

1. Position the pointer over the bitmap image so that it changes to ⬚, and then drag the photo to the lower-left corner of the slide. See Figure 2-11.

Slide master with bitmap image | **Figure 2-11**

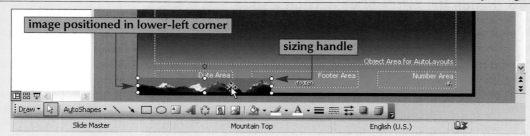

Trouble? If the Picture or Slide Master View toolbar covers the lower-left corner, drag the toolbar by its title bar to another location on the screen.

As you can see, the selected bitmap image has sizing handles in each corner and on each side of the picture. You'll drag a sizing handle to resize the image to the width of the slide.

2. Drag the upper-right sizing handle up and to the right until the width of the bitmap image is the same as the width of the slide, and approximately double its original height. See Figure 2-12. Because you are dragging a corner sizing handle, the height and width of the image resizes proportionally.

Figure 2-12 ▶ **Resized picture of Andes Mountains**

You have two tasks left to perform on the bitmap image. First, the blue sky in the background of the photo interrupts the gradient colors in the background. You'll set a transparent color, which is a color on the bitmap image that becomes transparent (invisible). Second, you'll change the order of objects so that the bitmap image is behind the placeholders at the foot of the slide.

To set a color to transparent in a bitmap image:

▶ **1.** Make sure the image is still selected, and then click the **Set Transparent Color** button on the Picture toolbar. The pointer changes to .

▶ **2.** Click anywhere in the blue sky above the mountain tops in the bitmap image. The sky color becomes transparent so that the slide background color appears.

Now you want to make sure the mountain top picture is behind the three text placeholders at the bottom of the slide. To do this, you will change the order of the objects on the slide. Imagine each object is on a piece of paper and you lay each piece of paper down on the slide as you add objects. Objects you add last will be on top of the other objects on the slide.

To change the order of objects on a slide:

▶ **1.** Make sure the image is still selected, click the **Draw** button on the Drawing toolbar, point to **Order**, and then click **Send to Back**. The bitmap image is sent to the back of all the objects on the slide master, including the slide background, so you can no longer see the mountains. Therefore, you need to move the mountains one object forward.

▶ **2.** Make sure you can still see the sizing handles of the selected image, click the **Draw** button on the Drawing toolbar, point to **Order**, and then click **Bring Forward**. The mountains now properly appear in the slide master, in front of the background but behind the text placeholders.

Trouble? If you accidentally deselected the mountain image before you brought it forward again, click the Undo button on the Standard toolbar to bring the image to the front again, and then repeat Steps 1 and 2.

As you can see, changing the drawing of mountaintops to a digital photograph of Andean mountaintops makes the background graphic more realistic. Now you'll make the same changes on the title master that you just made on the slide master.

To change the background graphic on the title master:

1. Make sure the resized bitmap image that you just added to the slide master is still selected, and then click the **Copy** button 🗐 on the Standard toolbar. The image is copied to the Clipboard.

2. Click the **title master** thumbnail (Slide 2) in the Slides tab. The title master appears in the slide pane. The original drawing of the mountain top appears at the bottom of the slide.

3. Delete all three components of the original mountain top drawing, as you did before.

4. Click the **Paste** button 🗐 on the Formatting toolbar to paste the bitmap image on the slide.

5. Send the image to the back, so that it's behind all the other objects on the title master, and then bring it forward one object to place it in front of the background. Now both the title master and the slide master have the bitmap image of Andean mountaintops as a background picture in the design template.

6. Click the **Save** button 🖫 on the Standard toolbar to save your changes.

Next, Pablo wants you to change the font of the body text on the slide master, and to modify the color of the title text on the slide master.

Modifying Text on a Slide

In PowerPoint, text is described in terms of the font, font size, and font style. A **font** is the design of a set of characters. Some names of fonts include Arial, Times New Roman, Helvetica, and Garamond. Font size is measured in **points**. Text in a book is typically printed in 10- or 12-point type. **Font style** refers to special attributes applied to the characters; for example, bold and italics are font styles.

Pablo wants you to replace the current subtitle and body text font (Arial) with a different font (Times New Roman), and to change the color of the title text from light violet to light blue. He also wants you to add the Global Humanitarian logo on the slides by placing it next to the title text on each slide.

Modifying the Format of Text on a Slide

To change the format of all the text in a text box, you first need to select the text box. To do this, you click the edge of it. This changes the text box border to a thick line composed of little dots. On the other hand, when you click *inside* a text box, you make the box active—that is, ready to accept text that you type or paste—but this doesn't select the text box, as indicated by the borders composed of slanted lines. When you select a text box (with a border of a thick line composed of little dots), any formatting changes you make are global formatting changes and are applied to all of the text in the text box. (This is different than if you select specific text within the text box and make a local formatting change to the selected text.)

You'll now select text boxes in the slide and title to change the font on all the slides.

To modify the fonts in text boxes on a slide:

▶ **1.** Click the **slide master** thumbnail (Slide 1) in the Slides tab.

▶ **2.** Click the dotted-line edge of the body text placeholder on the slide master in the slide pane. The entire placeholder text box is selected, as indicated by the border, which is now a thick line composed of little dots and sizing handles.

   Trouble? If the box surrounding the placeholder is composed of slanted lines, the text box is active, not selected. Click the edge of the text box to change it to a thick line composed of dots.

▶ **3.** Click the **Font** list arrow Arial ▾ on the Formatting toolbar, scroll down, if necessary, and then click **Times New Roman** to change the body text font from Arial to Times New Roman.

▶ **4.** Click the dotted-line edge of the title placeholder to select the entire text box, click the **Font Color** list arrow **A ▾** on the Drawing or Formatting toolbar, click **More Colors** to open the Colors dialog box, and then click the **Standard** tab. You can now see a honeycomb of color cells from which to select a new font color. See Figure 2-13.

Figure 2-13 ▶ Standard tab in the Colors dialog box

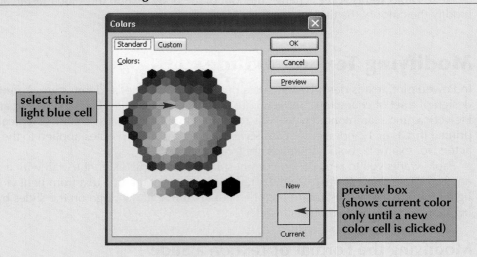

> **select this light blue cell**

> **preview box (shows current color only until a new color cell is clicked)**

▶ **5.** Click the light blue cell, as indicated in Figure 2-13. The light blue color appears under New in the preview box in the lower-right corner of the dialog box.

▶ **6.** Click the **OK** button. The font color of the title on the slide master changes from light violet to light blue. Now you'll change the text alignment so that the title text on the slide master is left-aligned rather than centered.

▶ **7.** With the title text box still selected, click the **Align Left** button ≡ on the Formatting toolbar. The title text is now left-aligned.

▶ **8.** Click the **title master** thumbnail (Slide 2) in the Slides tab. Note that the changes you made to the text boxes on the slide master have also been applied to the text boxes on the title master. Any changes you make to the format of the text on the slide master are also applied to the text on the title master. This does not, however, work in reverse; in other words, text-formatting changes that you make to the title master do not affect the text on the slide master.

   You don't want the title text on the title master left-aligned.

9. Select the **title** text box on the title master, and then click the **Center** button 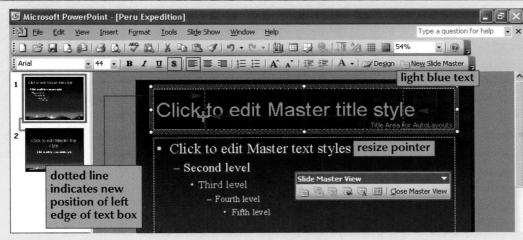 on the Formatting toolbar. The text is center-aligned, while the title text on the slide master stays left-aligned.

Next, you need to resize the title text box on the slide so you can insert the Global Humanitarian logo next to the title.

Resizing a Text Box on a Slide

To resize a text box, you need to select it, and then drag a sizing handle. You'll resize the title text box on the slide master by dragging the left-center sizing handle. As with the formatting changes you made to the text, you would follow this same procedure to resize text boxes in Normal view.

To resize a text box:

1. Click the **slide master** thumbnail in the Slides tab, and then select the title text box. The sizing handles appear.

2. Drag the left-center sizing handle to the right approximately one inch, as shown in Figure 2-14, and then release the mouse button. This leaves room for the logo, which will go in the upper-left corner of the slide master, to the left of the title text box.

Resizing the title text placeholder ◀ **Figure 2-14**

3. Insert the picture file **GHLogo**, located in the Tutorial.02\Tutorial folder included with your Data Files, into the slide master.

4. Drag the logo up near the upper-left corner of the slide, so that the top of the logo is aligned with the top of the title text box.

5. Drag the lower-right sizing handle up and to the left until the logo just fits in the space to the left of the title placeholder.

6. Set the black area surrounding the globe to transparent, and then click a blank area of the slide to deselect the logo. See Figure 2-15.

Figure 2-15 | **Slide master after adding and reformatting logo**

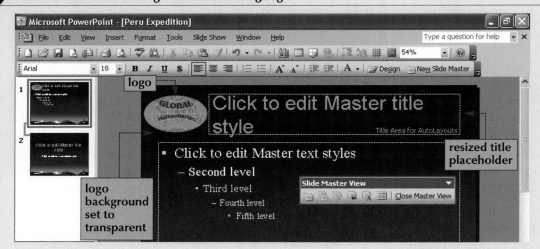

Trouble? If your slide master does not look like the one shown in Figure 2-15, make any necessary adjustments now.

▶ **7.** Click the **Close Master View** button on the Slide Master View toolbar. The presentation returns to Normal view.

▶ **8.** Save the presentation.

Applying a Second Design Template

Normally all your slides in one presentation will have the same design template. On occasion, however, you might want to apply a second design template to only one, or a few, of the slides in your presentation. Pablo wants you to change the design template for Slide 8, "Expedition Costs (Per Person)" from the modified Mountain Top design template to the Globe design template. All of the other slides present points about the expedition itself. He wants this slide to stand out from the others because it lists the costs of the trip for each participant.

To apply a second design template to a presentation:

▶ **1.** Go to **Slide 8** ("Expedition Costs (Per Person)"). When you want to apply a design template to only one slide, you'll usually want that slide to appear in the slide pane.

▶ **2.** Click the **Design** button on the Formatting toolbar to open the Slide Design task pane.

▶ **3.** Scroll the task pane until you locate the Globe design template, but do not click it. If you just click the Globe design template, it will appear on all the slides rather than just the selected slide.

▶ **4.** Position the pointer over the **Globe** design template, and then click the **Design Template** list arrow. See Figure 2-16.

Applying a new design template to this slide only | Figure 2-16

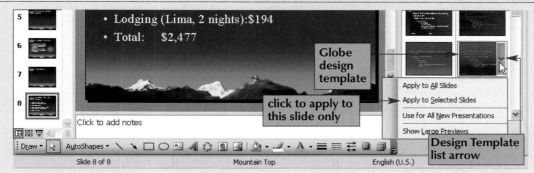

Trouble? If you clicked the design thumbnail instead of the Design Template list arrow, click the Undo button [↺] on the Standard toolbar, and then repeat Step 4.

5. Click **Apply to Selected Slides**. Because Slide 8 is the only selected slide in the Slides tab, it's the only one to which the design template is applied.

6. Click the **Close** button [✕] in the Slide Design task pane, select the title text box in the slide pane, and then adjust the size and alignment of the title text box so that it's similar to the title text box on the other slides and so that the text doesn't overlap the Global Humanitarian logo. You need to change the body text font to match the other slide.

7. Select the body text box, change the font to Times New Roman, change the font size to 36, and then click a blank area of the slide. See Figure 2-17.

Slide 8 with Globe design template | Figure 2-17

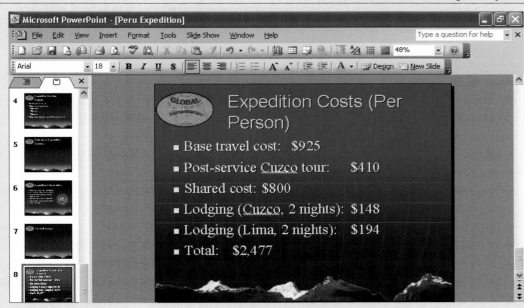

8. Save your changes.

You applied the Globe design template to only one slide in the presentation. The modified Mountain Top design remains on the other slides. The next time you switch to Slide Master view, you will see a second slide-title master pair for the Globe design template below the customized Mountain Top slide-title master pair. Now you need to modify the tab stops on Slide 8 to align the dollar amounts.

Adding and Modifying Tab Stops

A **tab** adds space between the left margin and the beginning of the text on a particular line, or between the text in one column and the text in another column. (When you create several long columns of data, however, you probably want to use a table instead of tabs.) For example, in Slide 8 ("Expedition Costs"), Pablo typed the cost description and a colon, pressed the Tab key to add space, and then typed the dollar amounts for each expense. A **tab stop** is the location where the insertion point moves (including any text to the right of it) when you press the Tab key. The default tab stops on a slide are set at one-inch intervals. You can add your own tab stops to override the default tab stops to align text on a slide. You can set tab stops so that the text left-aligns, right-aligns, center-aligns, or aligns on a decimal point.

The default tab stops on the ruler are left tabs, which position the left edge of text at the tab stop and extend the text to the right. However, you want to align the right sides of the dollar amounts in Slide 8, so you want to use a right tab stop, which positions the right edge of text at the tab stop and extends the text to the left. You'll change the tab stops on Slide 8 now.

To change the tab stops:

1. Click **View** on the menu bar, and then click **Ruler**. Horizontal and vertical rulers appear on the screen.

    Trouble? If rulers were already visible on your screen, then clicking Ruler on the View menu hid them. Click View on the menu bar, and then click Ruler again to redisplay the rulers.

2. Click anywhere in the body text box. The default tab stops for the body text appear as light gray rectangles, or hash marks, under the ruler, and the Left Tab button appears to the left of the horizontal ruler. When Pablo typed the text on this slide, he pressed the Tab key after typing the colon in each line, so the dollar amounts on each line are aligned at the next available tab stop. See Figure 2-18.

Tabs for body text box on ruler ◄ **Figure 2-18**

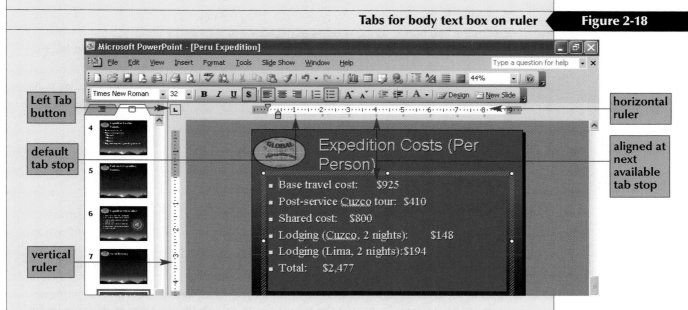

Trouble? If a button other than the Left Tab button appears to the left of the ruler, click the Tab button as many times as necessary until the Left Tab button appears.

3. Click the **Left Tab** button ⌊ to the left of the horizontal ruler so that the button changes to the Center Tab button ⌊, and then click the **Center Tab** button ⌊ to change it to the Right Tab button ⌊. If you were to click the Tab button again, the Decimal Tab button ⌊ would appear, and if you were to click once more, the Left Tab button would appear again.

4. Position the pointer immediately before the word "Base" in the first bulleted item, and then click and drag to the bottom of the body text to select all of the bulleted items. The selected text is highlighted.

5. Click just below the 8-inch mark in the white area of the horizontal ruler, and then click anywhere within the selected text. A new, right tab stop appears at the location you clicked, the default tab stops to the left of the new tab stop disappear, and the dollar amounts in the body text box become right-aligned at the new tab stop. See Figure 2-19.

Slide 8 after inserting new tab stop in body text paragraphs ◄ **Figure 2-19**

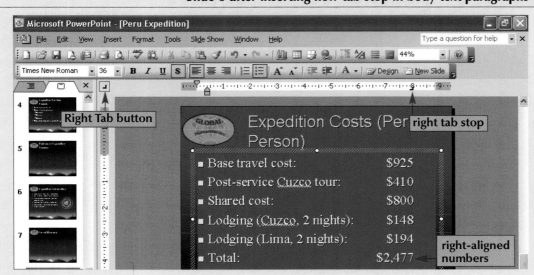

Trouble? If you used the wrong type of tab, drag the new tab stop off the ruler to delete it, click the Tab button as many times as necessary to display the Right Tab button, and then repeat Steps 4 and 5. If you clicked in the wrong place on the ruler, drag the tab stop character to the right or left until it's positioned where you want it.

▶ 6. Click **View** on the menu bar, and then click **Ruler**. The rulers disappear from the slide pane.

▶ 7. Click a blank area of the slide pane to deselect the text box, and then save your changes.

Next, you'll insert footers and slide numbers.

Inserting Footers and Slide Numbers

When you used the AutoContent wizard, you typed footer text to be displayed at the bottom of each slide. A **header** is text that appears at the top of each page. PowerPoint already provides a footer placeholder on the slide master, and both header and footer placeholders on the notes and handout masters.

As part of the overall slide design, Pablo wants you to include footers and the current slide number on each slide, except the title slide. You'll use the footer placeholders to add the footer and the slide number to each of the slides (except the title slide).

To insert a footer into your presentation:

▶ 1. Click **View** on the menu bar, click **Header and Footer** to open the Header and Footer dialog box, and then click the **Slide** tab, if necessary, to display the slide footer information. In the Preview box in the lower-right corner of the dialog box, two of the rectangles at the bottom of the preview slide are black. These black rectangles correspond to the selected check boxes on the Slides tab, in this case, the Date and time and the Footer check boxes.

▶ 2. Click the **Date and time** check box to clear it. The left rectangle in the Preview box turns white.

▶ 3. Click the **Slide number** check box to select it. The right rectangle in the Preview box turns black. Now the slide number will appear on each slide.

▶ 4. Make sure the Footer check box is selected, and then click in the **Footer** text box.

▶ 5. Type **Peru Expedition 2006**, and then click the **Don't show on title slide** check box to select it. See Figure 2-20. The slide number and the text you typed in the Footer text box will appear on every slide except the title slide.

Figure 2-20

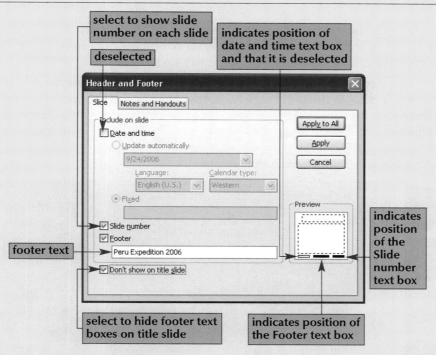

select to show slide number on each slide

deselected

indicates position of date and time text box and that it is deselected

indicates position of the Slide number text box

footer text

select to hide footer text boxes on title slide

indicates position of the Footer text box

▶ **6.** Click the **Apply to All** button in the Header and Footer dialog box. All the slides (except the title slide) now contain a footer.

The footer has several problems. First, after you applied the new design template to Slide 8, the mountains at the bottom of the slide appear in front of the footer. Second, the footer text isn't legible because the font is too small and its white color makes it unreadable against the white peak of an Andean mountaintop. You can solve these problems by modifying the slide master of the Globe design template, moving the footer on the slide master so that it appears on the left side of the slide, and increasing the font size of the text in the footer. Before you can reposition the footer placeholder text box, you need to delete the date and time placeholder text box.

To delete and reposition text boxes:

▶ **1.** Display the slide master, make sure the slide master of the Globe design (Slide 3 in the Slides tab) is selected, and send the mountain bitmap image to the back and bring it forward in front of the background, as before.

▶ **2.** On the same slide master, click the edge of the **date and time** placeholder (labeled Date Area) in the lower-left corner of the slide, and press the **Delete** key. The placeholder text box is deleted.

▶ **3.** Select the **footer** placeholder (labeled Footer Area), currently located in the bottom middle of the slide, and then press the ← key until the placeholder is aligned on the left with the body text placeholder. By using the ← key rather than dragging and dropping, you ensure that you move the placeholder horizontally but not vertically.

▶ **4.** With the footer placeholder still selected, click the **Align Left** button ![] on the Formatting toolbar so the text in the footer placeholder is left-aligned rather than centered in the text box.

▶ **5.** With the footer placeholder still selected, press and hold the **Shift** key, and then click the **slide number** placeholder (labeled Number Area) in the lower-right corner of the slide. Both the footer and the slide number placeholders are selected.

▶ **6.** Press the ↓ key two or three times until the bottoms of the two placeholders are on the bottom of the slide, as shown in Figure 2-21. Make sure that you position the bottom of the placeholders at the bottom of the slide and not at the bottom of the drop shadow behind the slide.

Figure 2-21	Reformatted Globe design template slide master

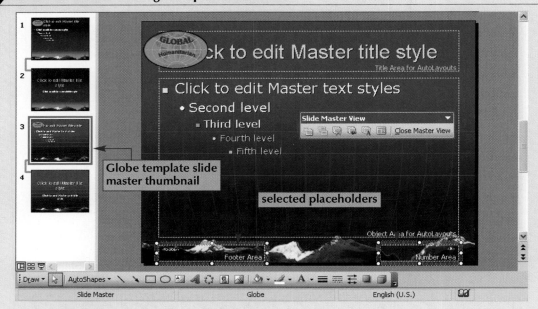

Trouble? If you can't position the text boxes where you want to, press and hold the Ctrl key while you press the ↓ key to nudge the placeholders in smaller increments than pressing the ↓ key alone.

▶ **7.** With the footer and slide number placeholders still selected, click the **Font Size** list arrow ![10] on the Formatting toolbar, and then click **24** to change the font size to 24 points.

▶ **8.** Click the **Mountain Top slide master** (Slide 1) in the Slides tab and then repeat Steps 2 through 7 to make the same changes on the slide master of the Mountain Top design template.

▶ **9.** Click the **Close Master View** button on the Slide Master View toolbar. Now you can read the footer text and the slide number, but the footer text wraps to a second line because the footer placeholder is too small to contain all the footer text on one line.

▶ **10.** Switch back to Slide Master view, select the footer placeholder, and then drag the right-center sizing handle of the footer placeholder to the right until the right edge of the text box is near the center of the slide.

▶ **11.** Repeat Step 10 on the Mountain Top slide master, and then click the **Normal View** button ![] at the bottom of the Slides tab.

12. Go to **Slide 4** to make sure that you can read the footer and the slide number on a slide with the Mountain Top design template. See Figure 2-22.

Slide 4 with adjusted footer and slide number ◄ **Figure 2-22**

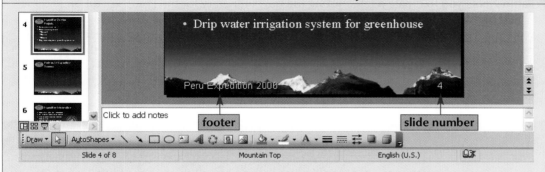

Trouble? If your footer and slide number aren't the same font size and color and in the same position as shown in Figure 2-22, return to Slide Master view and make any necessary adjustments.

13. Save the presentation.

Pablo is pleased with how the footer and page number appear at the bottom of each slide. You've completed most of Pablo's presentation. In Session 2.2, you'll finalize the slides by creating a table, diagram, and simple drawing.

Session 2.1 Quick Check

Review

1. List at least three reasons to add graphics to your presentation.
2. Explain the meaning of the following terms:
   a. design template
   b. bitmap image
   c. graphic
   d. Default Design template
3. Describe how to do the following:
   a. make a text box active
   b. select a text box
   c. scale a graphic to change its size
   d. move an object on a slide
   e. apply a second design template to selected slides
   f. recolor clip art
4. What is the difference between the title master and the slide master?
5. What are tabs? What are tab stops? Describe how to insert a right tab stop on the ruler.
6. What are the three objects included in a footer on a slide as part of the master?

Session 2.2

Creating a Table in a Slide

Pablo wants you to create a table listing the travel itinerary for the Peru expedition in Slide 7. A **table** is information arranged in horizontal rows and vertical columns. The area where a row and column intersect is called a **cell**. Each cell contains one piece of information and is identified by a column and row label; for example, the cell in the upper-left corner of a table is cell A1 (column A, row 1), the cell to the right of that is B1, the cell below A1 is A2, and so forth. A table's structure is indicated by borders, which are lines that outline the rows and columns.

Reference Window | **Inserting a Table on a Slide**

- Click Format on the menu bar, and then click Slide Layout to open the Slide Layout task pane.
- Change the slide layout of the desired slide to one of the Content layouts.
- Click the Insert Table button.
- Specify the desired table size—the numbers of columns and rows—and then click the OK button.
- Add information to the cells. Use the Tab key to move from one cell to the next, and the Shift+Tab keys to move to previous cells.
- Modify the borders as desired.
- Click in a blank area of the slide to deselect the table.

The itinerary table you'll create needs to have four columns: one for the date of travel, one for the departure or arrival city, one for the time of departure or arrival, and one for the flight number. The table needs to have nine rows: one row for column labels, and eight rows for the data. Now you'll create the travel itinerary table.

To create a table:

1. If you took a break after the previous session, make sure PowerPoint is running, and then open the presentation **Peru Expedition** located in the Tutorial.02\Tutorial folder included with your Data Files.

2. Go to **Slide 7** ("Travel Itinerary"), click **Format** on the menu bar, and then click **Slide Layout** to open the Slide Layout task pane.

3. Click the **Title and Content** layout. The layout of the current slide changes.

4. Click the **Insert Table** button 🖽 in the content placeholder in the slide pane. The Insert Table dialog box opens.

5. Type **4** in the Number of columns text box, press the **Tab** key to move the insertion point to the Number of rows text box, type **9**, and then click the **OK** button. A table made up of four columns and nine rows is inserted in the slide with the insertion point blinking in the first cell (cell A1), and the Tables and Borders toolbar opens.

   Trouble? If the table doesn't have four columns and nine rows, click the Undo button 🔄 on the Standard toolbar to undo your creation of the table, and then repeat Steps 4 and 5.

Trouble? If the Tables and Borders toolbar doesn't appear, click View on the main menu bar, point to Toolbars, and then click Tables and Borders.

▶ **6.** Close the task pane.

Now you're ready to fill the blank cells with information. To enter data in a table, you click in the cell in which you want to enter data. Once you start typing in a cell, you can use the Tab and arrow keys to move from one cell to another. If you want to add a new row at the bottom of the table, move the insertion point to the last cell in the table, and then press the Tab key. A new row will be inserted automatically.

To add information to the table:

▶ **1.** With the insertion point blinking in the first cell, type **Date**, press the **Tab** key to move to cell B1, type **City**, press the **Tab** key to move to cell C1, type **Time**, press the **Tab** key to move to cell D1 (the last cell in the first row), and then type **Flight**. This completes the column labels.

Trouble? You might have to drag the Tables and Borders toolbar by its title bar to see the table cells.

▶ **2.** Press the **Tab** key. The insertion point moves to cell A2.

▶ **3.** Type **Dec. 25**, and then press the **Tab** key to move to cell B2.

▶ **4.** Type **Lv Dallas** (short for "Leave Dallas") in cell B2, type **4:22 PM** in cell C2, and then type **AA 982** (short for American Airlines flight 982) in cell D2. This completes the first row of data.

▶ **5.** Complete the information in the rest of the cells, as shown in Figure 2-23, and then click a blank area of the slide to deselect the table.

Slide 7 with completed table ◀ **Figure 2-23**

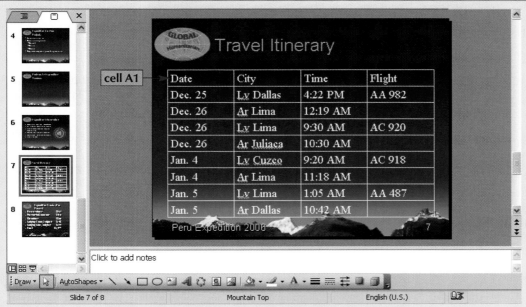

Trouble? If you pressed the Tab key after typing the last entry, you added a new row to the table. Click the Undo button 🔄 on the Standard toolbar to remove the extra row.

To make the column labels appear visually separated from the data, you'll change the border below the top row so that it is more visible.

To draw a border:

► **1.** Click anywhere in the table to make it active and display the Tables and Borders toolbar.

► **2.** Click the **Draw Table** button 🖾 on the Tables and Borders toolbar, and then move the pointer off of the toolbar. The pointer changes to ⌀.

► **3.** Click the **Border Width** list arrow `1 pt ▾` on the Tables and Borders toolbar, and then click **3 pt** to change the border line width to three points.

► **4.** Click the **Border Color** button 🖉 on the Tables and Borders toolbar, and then click the light blue tile (the custom color *below* the main row of tiles). Now when you draw a border, it will be a 3-point, light blue line.

► **5.** Drag ⌀ along the border between the first and second rows in the table. As you draw the border, a dotted line appears to indicate the border as it is drawn. When you release the mouse button, the light blue line appears.

► **6.** Click the **Draw Table** button 🖾 on the Table and Borders toolbar to deselect it.

In addition to changing the border lines in a table, you can add and change diagonal lines within cells of a table. First, click the Table button on the Tables and Borders toolbar, click Borders and Fill, click the Borders tab, and then click one or both of the Diagonal Line buttons.

Although the colored border visually separates the column labels from the data in the table, the labels would stand out more if they were formatted differently from the data. You will format the text in the top row to be a light blue, bold, Arial font.

To modify the font in a table:

► **1.** Drag I across all the text in the top row to select it.

► **2.** Change the font to **Arial**, as you would any other type of text.

► **3.** Click the **Bold** button B on the Formatting toolbar to make the selected text bold.

► **4.** Click the **Font Color** list arrow A ▾ on the Drawing or Formatting toolbar, and then click the light blue tile (the custom color *below* the main row of tiles).

► **5.** Click a blank area of the slide pane to deselect the table. See Figure 2-24.

Table after modifying border and column headings ◄ **Figure 2-24**

6. Save your changes.

You have completed the table that shows the flight itinerary for the Peru expedition. The Tables and Borders toolbar also lets you remove rows, add and remove columns, combine cells, split cells, and perform other modifications to the table. If you want to do any of these tasks, use PowerPoint's Help system. In addition, try right-clicking anywhere on the table to see a shortcut menu containing commands specific to working with tables.

Your next task is to create a diagram on Slide 5 to show the relationship between the four major parties involved in a humanitarian service project.

Creating a Diagram on a Slide

PowerPoint allows you to create the following types of diagrams on slides:

- **Cycle diagrams**—show a process that has a continuous cycle
- **Organizational charts**—show the relationship between individuals or units within an organization
- **Radial diagrams**—show the relationships of a core element
- **Pyramid diagrams**—show foundation-based relationships
- **Venn diagrams**—show areas of overlap between elements
- **Target diagrams**—show steps toward a goal

In the Peru Expedition presentation, Pablo wants you to add a Venn diagram on Slide 5 ("Partners in Expedition Success") to show the relationship between the four major parties involved in a humanitarian service project: the village for which the service is being performed, the volunteers who perform the service, the humanitarian organization that sponsors the service, and the donors who contribute money to support the service. You'll create the Venn diagram now.

To create a Venn diagram:

1. Go to **Slide 5**, and then change the layout to the **Title and Content** layout in the Content Layouts section.

2. Close the task pane, and then click the **Insert Diagram or Organization Chart** button ⌖ in the content placeholder in the slide pane. The Diagram Gallery dialog box opens.

3. Click the **Venn Diagram** icon (the middle icon in the second row), and then click the **OK** button. A diagram with three intersecting circles and text box placeholders is added to the slide, and the Diagram toolbar opens. The text box placeholders are hard to see on the dark blue part of the background. Selection handles—gray circles with small *X*s in them— appear around the top circle in the diagram. When you see selection handles instead of sizing handles on a slide, it means that the selected object is part of a larger object, and although you can modify the selected object by changing its color or other attributes, you can't resize the individual object.

   Next, you'll edit the diagram by adding another circle, adding text, and modifying the circle colors.

4. Click the **Insert Shape** button on the Diagram toolbar. A fourth circle is added to the diagram. The new circle is the same color as the bottom circle. You'll change the color of the bottom circle.

5. Right-click the bottom circle, click **Format AutoShape** on the shortcut menu to open the Format AutoShape dialog box, and then click the **Colors and Lines** tab, if necessary.

6. Click the **Color** list arrow in the Fill section at the top of the dialog box, and then click the light blue tile (the custom color) located on its own row just above the More Colors command.

7. Click the **OK** button. The bottom circle is recolored light blue. See Figure 2-25.

| Figure 2-25 | **Venn diagram with new shape added** |

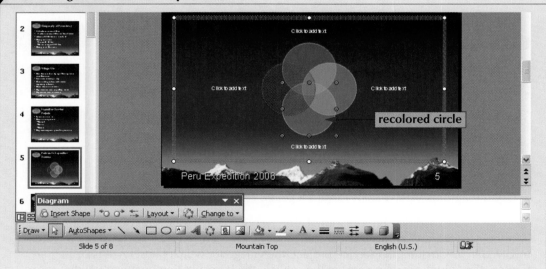

Now you'll label each circle in the Venn diagram.

To add and modify text in the Venn diagram:

▶ **1.** Click in the text box placeholder (labeled "Click to add text") above the top circle, and then type **Village**.

▶ **2.** Type **Volunteers** in the text box placeholder to the right of the right circle.

▶ **3.** Click in the text box placeholder to the left of the left circle, type **Global**, press the **Enter** key, and then type **Humanitarian**.

▶ **4.** Type **Donors** in the text box placeholder below the bottom circle.

Because the font of the text around the Venn diagram is small, the text is hard to read. You'll increase the font size now.

▶ **5.** Shift-click the four text boxes (press and hold the Shift key, and then click each of the text boxes) to select them all, and then change the font size to **24** points.

▶ **6.** Click a blank area of the slide pane to deselect everything in the slide. See Figure 2-26.

Slide 5 with completed Venn diagram ◀ **Figure 2-26**

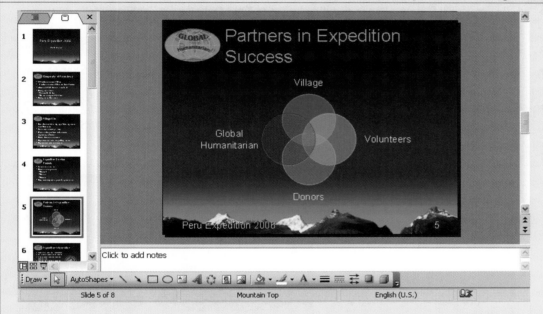

▶ **7.** Save your changes.

This completes the diagram on Slide 5. When Pablo uses this slide show to give a presentation, he'll discuss how the roles of the village, volunteers, donors, and Global Humanitarian overlap to make a successful project.

Pablo now asks you to insert a new Slide 6, and create a shape in the slide.

Creating and Manipulating a Shape

For the last graphic to be included in his presentation, Pablo asks you to add an inverted triangle with labels along each side to a new Slide 6. The labels on each side of the triangle will list the three components of the Global Humanitarian strategy—village outreach projects, expeditions, and internships. Pablo wants you to use an equilateral triangle to point out that each of the three strategies is equally important. This graphic will be a strong visual reminder to potential Global Humanitarian contributors and volunteers of this threefold strategy.

To create the triangle, you'll use the triangle AutoShape. When you click the AutoShapes button on the Drawing toolbar, you are presented with the following categories of shapes from which to choose: lines, connectors, basic shapes (for example, rectangles and triangles), block arrows, flowchart shapes, stars and banners, callouts, and action buttons.

To insert a shape in a slide using AutoShapes:

1. Insert a new Slide 6, change the slide layout to **Title Only** (under Text Layouts), and then close the Slide Layout task pane.

2. Type **Global Humanitarian Strategy** in the title placeholder.

3. Click the **AutoShapes** button on the Drawing toolbar, and then point to **Basic Shapes**. The Basic Shapes palette opens.

4. Click the **Isosceles Triangle** button on the Basic Shapes palette, as indicated in Figure 2-27, and then position the pointer over the slide in the slide pane. The pointer changes to ┼.

Figure 2-27 ▶ **Selecting an AutoShape**

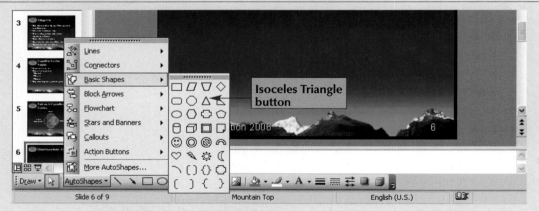

5. Position ┼ approximately one inch below the "o" in "Global" (in the title of the slide), press and hold down the **Shift** key, and then click and and drag the pointer down and to the right. The outline of a triangle appears as you drag. Pressing the Shift key while you drag makes the triangle equilateral—the three sides are of equal length. (Similarly, if you click the Oval button, you can press and hold the Shift key while you drag to draw a circle, and if you click the Rectangle button, you can press and hold the Shift key while you drag to draw a square.)

6. Release the mouse button and the Shift key when your triangle is approximately the same size and shape as the one shown in Figure 2-28.

Slide 6 with isosceles triangle shape ◀ **Figure 2-28**

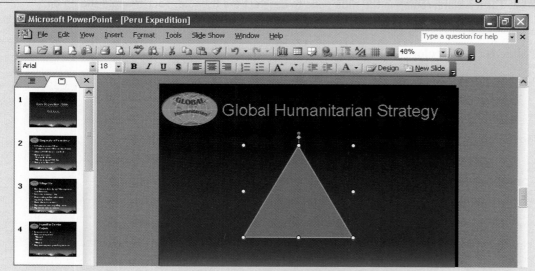

Trouble? If your triangle doesn't look like the one in Figure 2-28, you can move it by dragging it to a new location, resize or change its shape by dragging one or more of the sizing handles, or delete it by pressing the Delete key, and then repeating Steps 3 through 6 to redraw it.

In addition to the sizing handles, the selected triangle has a yellow diamond and a green circle at its top. The yellow diamond is an **adjustment handle**; if you drag it, the shape of the tip of the triangle changes without changing the overall size of the object. The green circle is the **rotate handle**, which you can drag to rotate the shape.

The default color of the drawn object is the blue color from the set of default colors, but Pablo prefers the same color of blue as the title text.

To change the fill color of an AutoShape:

1. With the triangle still selected, click the **Fill Color** list arrow ⬛ on the Drawing toolbar. The color palette appears on the screen.

2. Click the light blue tile (the custom color located below the row of default tiles). The color of the triangle changes to light blue.

The triangle is the desired size and color, but Pablo wants you to flip (invert) the triangle so that it points down instead of up. You can use commands on the Draw menu on the Drawing toolbar to rotate and flip objects.

To flip an object:

▶ 1. With the triangle still selected, click the **Draw** button on the Drawing toolbar, point to **Rotate or Flip**, and then click **Flip Vertical**.

▶ 2. Click a blank region in the slide pane to deselect the triangle. Your triangle should be sized, positioned, colored, and oriented like the one shown in Figure 2-29.

Figure 2-29 | **Slide 6 after recoloring and flipping triangle**

▶ 3. Save the presentation.

Now you'll add the text labels along the sides of the triangle.

Inserting Text Boxes

Sometimes you need to add a text box in a different location than any of the text box placeholders on the layouts. You need to add text boxes on each of the three sides of the triangle in Slide 6.

Adding Text to the Diagram

You're ready to add the text naming the three strategies of Global Humanitarian on each side of the triangle. You'll now add three text boxes around the AutoShape triangle you just created.

To add a text box to the slide:

▶ 1. Click the **Text Box** button 🔲 on the Drawing toolbar, and then position the pointer over the slide. The pointer changes to ↓.

▶ 2. Position ↓ so it is just above and centered on the top side of the triangle, and then click. A small text box appears above the triangle with the insertion point blinking in it. The position doesn't have to be exact.

Trouble? If the insertion point is blinking in the middle of the triangle instead of in a new text box above the triangle, you clicked the edge of the triangle. Click the Undo button on the Standard toolbar, and then repeat Steps 1 and 2.

3. Click the **Center** button on the Formatting toolbar, and then type **Village Outreach Projects**.

4. Click the **Text Box** button on the Drawing toolbar, click ↓ to the right of the triangle, and then type **Expeditions**.

5. Create a third text box to the left of the triangle, click the **Align Right** button on the Formatting toolbar, and then type **Internships**.

6. Click the **Text Box** button again, and then drag to draw a text box *inside* the triangle.

7. Type **Global Humanitarian**.

   Trouble? If the text you type appears upside down, you did not drag to create the text box inside the triangle, you simply clicked. Click the Undo button on the Standard toolbar twice, and then repeat Steps 6 and 7.

8. If the text inside the triangle does not fit on one line, drag a sizing handle on the text box to increase the size of the text box.

9. Select the three text boxes that you created outside the triangle by Shift-clicking them, and then change the font size to **24** points.

10. Click in a blank area of the slide to deselect the text boxes. Your slide should now look similar to Figure 2-30.

Text boxes added in and around triangle ◀ **Figure 2-30**

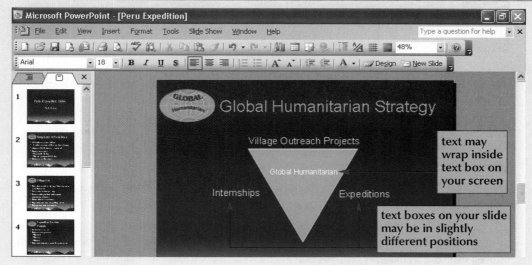

Next you'll rotate the text boxes to make them parallel to the sides of the triangle.

Rotating and Moving Text Boxes

The method for rotating text is similar to the one for rotating graphics (or rotating any other object). You use the Rotate or Flip commands on the Draw menu on the Drawing toolbar, or you drag the rotate handle on the object. You will rotate the text boxes on the left and right sides of the triangle.

To rotate and move the text boxes:

▶ 1. Click anywhere within the "Expeditions" text box. The sizing handles and the rotate handle appear around the text box.

▶ 2. Position the pointer over the rotate handle. The pointer becomes 🜪.

▶ 3. Press and hold the **Shift** key, and then drag the rotate handle counterclockwise until the top edge of the box is parallel to the lower-right edge of the triangle. Holding down the Shift key causes the rotation to occur in 15-degree increments.

▶ 4. Drag the "Expeditions" text box to position it against and centered on the lower-right edge of the triangle. See Figure 2-31.

| Figure 2-31 | Slide 6 with rotated and repositioned text box |

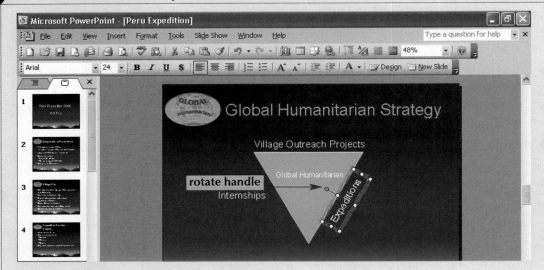

Trouble? If the edge of the text box isn't parallel to the edge of the triangle, you can repeat Steps 2 and 3 to fix the rotation. If necessary, try it without pressing the Shift key.

Trouble? If the text box jumps from one location to another as you drag it, and you can't position it exactly where you want it, hold down the Alt key as you drag the box. (The Alt key temporarily disables a feature that forces objects to snap to invisible gridlines on the slide.)

▶ 5. Rotate the "Internships" text box clockwise so that the top edge of the text is parallel to the lower-left edge of the triangle, and then position the text box so it's against and centered on the left edge of the triangle.

▶ 6. Adjust the position of (but don't rotate) the "Village Outreach Projects" text box so it's centered over the triangle.

▶ 7. Reposition the text box inside the triangle so that it is centered in the triangle.

▶ 8. Click a blank area of the slide pane to deselect the text box. Your slide should look like Figure 2-32.

Slide 6 with completed diagram ◄ | **Figure 2-32**

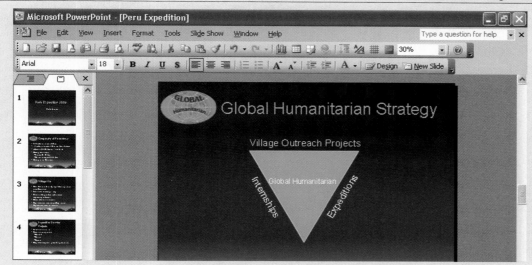

9. Save the presentation.

Pablo asks you to perform one final task before the presentation is finished. He wants you to add a summary at the end of the presentation.

Adding a Summary Slide

A **summary slide** is a slide containing the slide titles of selected slides in the presentation. PowerPoint helps you create a summary slide automatically. You'll do this now.

To create a summary slide:

▶ **1.** Click the **Slide Sorter View** button ▦ at the bottom of the Slides tab. The presentation appears in Slide Sorter view.

▶ **2.** Click **Slide 2**, press and hold down the **Shift** key, and then click **Slide 9**. All of the slides except Slide 1 are selected. (If you wanted to select nonsequential slides, you would press and hold the Ctrl key while you clicked the desired slides.)

▶ **3.** Click the **Summary Slide** button ▦ on the Slide Sorter toolbar. PowerPoint creates a new slide in front of the first selected slide with the title "Summary Slide" and body text consisting of a list of the titles of the selected slides.

Trouble? If you don't see the Summary Slide button on the Slide Sorter toolbar, click the Toolbar Options button ▦ on the Slide Sorter toolbar.

▶ **4.** Drag **Slide 2** (the new summary slide) to the right of Slide 10. Slide 2 becomes Slide 10, and the other slides are renumbered automatically.

▶ **5.** Double-click **Slide 10** to return to Normal view with Slide 10 in the slide pane.

▶ **6.** Double-click **Slide** in the title text to select the entire word, press the **Delete** key, and then deselect the text box. The selected text is deleted and the title becomes "Summary." See Figure 2-33.

Figure 2-33 | New summary slide

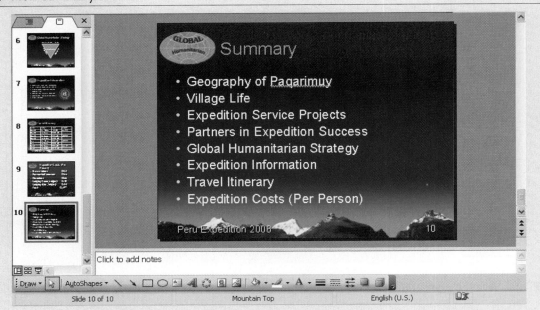

You have completed the entire presentation, so you should save the final version to the disk.

▶ **7.** Save the file.

As usual, you should finish up your presentation by checking the spelling, viewing it in Slide Show view, and printing it.

To check, view, and print the presentation:

▶ **1.** Click the **Spelling** button ![spelling icon] on the Standard toolbar to start checking the spelling of your presentation. Decide how to handle each word that is flagged because it was not found in the PowerPoint dictionary. (In most cases, you should click the Ignore All button because the words are proper nouns, such as "Paqarimuy" and "Cuzco.")

▶ **2.** Go to **Slide 1**, and then click the **Slide Show from current slide** button ![slide show icon] at the bottom of the Slides tab. The slide show starts.

▶ **3.** Press the **spacebar** or click the mouse button to advance through the slide show.

▶ **4.** If you see any problems while you are watching the slide show, press the **Esc** key to exit the slide show and return to Normal view, make the necessary corrections, and then return to Slide Show view.

▶ **5.** Go to **Slide 1**, and then replace Pablo's name with your own name.

▶ **6.** Print the presentation in grayscale as handouts, with six slides per page. Don't worry that the footers and one of the graphics are illegible in grayscale.

▶ **7.** Save the presentation, and then close the presentation.

Pablo is pleased with the additions and modifications you made to the presentation. He is anxious to use it to recruit volunteers for the next Peru expedition.

Review

Session 2.2 Quick Check

1. How do you add a table to a slide?
2. Where is cell A1 in a table?
3. What is a Venn diagram?
4. How do you add a text box to a slide?
5. How do you draw a shape, such as a rectangle or a circle, on a slide?
6. How do you rotate or flip an object using menu commands?
7. How do you rotate an object without using menu commands?
8. Describe the Summary Slide command in PowerPoint.

Review

Tutorial Summary

In this tutorial, you learned how to create a new presentation using a design template, and how to apply a new design template to selected (or all) the slides in the presentation. You learned how to insert, format, and resize graphics, including clip art and photographs. You also learned how to modify the design template in the slide master and the title master. You learned how to add tab stops to align text on a slide. You learned how to insert footer information on slides. You also learned how to insert a table, a diagram, a shape, and a text box on slides. And finally, you learned how to add a summary slide to a presentation.

Key Terms

adjustment handle	font style	rotate handle
bitmap image	graphic	slide master
cell	handout master	slide-title master pair
clip art	header	summary slide
color scheme	master	tab
default colors	notes master	tab stop
design template	pixel	table
font	point	title master

Practice

Review Assignments

Practice the skills you learned in the tutorial using the same case scenario.

Data Files needed for the Review Assignments: PackList.jpg, GHLogo.jpg, SlpBag.jpg, Boots.ppt, Camera.jpg, Food.jpg, Personal.jpg, PrMeds.jpg, Vitamins.jpg

One of the common questions from volunteers who sign up for a service expedition is, "What items will I need for the trip?" In other words, they want to see a packing list to give them an idea of what they'll have to purchase and pack if they decide to go on the trip. Pablo decides to give a presentation to all volunteers to explain what they must take on the service expedition. He asks you to create a PowerPoint presentation on the Peru expedition packing list. Complete the following:

1. Open the file **PackList** located in the Tutorial.02\Review folder included with your Data Files, and then save it as **Peru Packing List** in the same folder.
2. Apply the design template titled "Teamwork," and then replace the subtitle in Slide 1 with your name.

3. Add the footer "Packing List" and slide numbers to all the slides except Slide 1.
4. In the title master, insert the logo file **GHLogo**, also located in the Tutorial.02\Review folder, position the graphic near the lower-right corner of the slide, just above the Number Area (the slide number placeholder text box), and then make the background of the logo transparent.
5. On both the title master and the slide master, change the title font color from light blue to the light yellow-green color found among the scheme colors. Switch back to Normal view when you are finished.
6. On Slide 2, change the slide layout so you can place clip art to the right of the bulleted list, search for clip art that deals with money, and then insert the piece of clip art that shows a dollar sign in an orange circle.
7. Recolor the clip art so that it is green (the third color from the right in the color palette).
8. Resize the clip art so it fits properly on the slide, and then resize the bulleted-list text box as needed so the text is as large as possible without overlapping the clip art. If the font size does not increase automatically when you increase the size of the text box, then use the Font Size button on the Formatting toolbar.
9. In Slide 3, insert the bitmap image file **SlpBag** ("sleeping bag") located in the Tutorial.02\Review folder.
10. Resize the sleeping bag image to increase its size so it fills more of the space on the right side of the slide, and then make the background of the image transparent.
11. In Slides 4 through 9, insert appropriate bitmap images located in the Tutorial.02\Review folder, resize the images as large as possible, and make the backgrounds transparent. Modify the layouts or resize the body text boxes as needed.
12. Add a new Slide 10 using the Title Only layout (under Text Layouts), type "Areas of Personal Preparation" as the title, draw a square in the middle of the blank area of the slide below the title, and change the fill color to the light blue color in the default color palette.
13. Add text just outside of the square on each of its four sides, using the words "Physical," "Mental," "Social," and "Spiritual." It doesn't matter which word you place on which side.
14. Rotate the text on the sides of the box so the bottom edges of the text boxes face toward the square. Adjust the text boxes so that each word is centered along the edge of the square and almost resting on the box. Resize the font to a readable size.
15. Add a new Slide 11 with the Title and Content layout, type "Discount Items" as the title, insert a table with three columns and five rows, and then add the text as follows:

Item	Regular Price	Discount Price
Boots	$198	$118
Sleeping bag	$162	$98
Water filter	$51	$32
Flashlight	$26	$16

16. Select the text and numbers in columns 2 and 3, and then right-align it.
17. Draw a light yellow-green, 4½ point border below the top row, and then modify the format of the text in the top row so it is 32 points and light yellow-green.
18. Drag the bottom-center sizing handle of the table up so that the table stays the same width but decreases in height so the text fits better in the cells of the table.

19. To Slide 11 only, apply the design template titled "Glass Layers," and then change the font and alignment of the title text on the slide master for this slide so that it matches the rest of the slides.

20. Add a new Slide 12 with the Title and Content layout, type "Thank You" as the title, and then insert a Pyramid diagram. Apply the teamwork design template to this slide.

21. Click the bottom placeholder in the diagram, type "You," click the middle placeholder, type "Global Humanitarian," click the top placeholder, type "The World," and then reformat all three labels to 28-point bold Arial.

22. Create a summary slide that includes titles from all the slides except Slides 1 and 12, and change the title to "Summary." Notice that PowerPoint creates two summary slides, because all of the slide titles will not fit on a single slide.

23. Check the spelling in the presentation, view the slide show, fix any problems you see, save the presentation, print it in grayscale as handouts with six slides per page, and then close the file.

Apply

Apply the skills you learned in this tutorial to modify a presentation for a health and fitness company.

Case Problem 1

Data Files needed for this Case Problem: MyBody.ppt, Weights.jpg, StrMach.jpg, Excycle.jpg, Treadmil.jpg, Vitamins.jpg

MyBodyTrainer.com   Several years ago, Jerry Wursten received an M.S. degree in exercise physiology and became a board-certified strength and conditioning specialist (CSCS). Recently, he started a new e-commerce company called MyBodyTrainer.com, which provides services and products for health, fitness, weight loss, and sports conditioning. The services include personalized training and weight-loss programs, and the products include fitness equipment and dietary supplements. Jerry's business is expanding rapidly, and he needs additional capital. He needs to hire three more CSCS employees and several other employees to process orders, and he needs to purchase additional inventory and rent additional warehouse and office space. He asks you to help him prepare a PowerPoint presentation giving an overview of his business. He will give the presentation to bankers and investors to help him raise money for his company. Complete the following:

1. Open the file **MyBody** located in the Tutorial.02\Cases folder included with your Data Files, and then save it as **MyBodyTrainer** in the same folder.

2. Apply the design template titled "Shimmer," and then replace the subtitle in Slide 1 with your name.

3. In the slide master, change the title text box so it is center-aligned, rather than left-aligned.

4. Using the AutoShapes, draw a heart in the upper-left corner of the slide master, to the left of the title text box.

5. Change the fill color of the heart to red.

6. In Slides 7 and 8, change the slide layout to Title, Text, and 2 Content, and then add two bitmap images to each slide. In Slide 7, use the **Weights** and **StrMach** (strength machines) files, and in Slide 8 use the **Excycle** (exercise cycle) and **Treadmil** (treadmill) files; these bitmap images are located in the Tutorial.02\Cases folder.

7. In Slide 8, adjust the two images so they are side-by-side and fill the area to the right of the text. Similarly, in Slide 7, adjust the size and position of the images so they are visible and attractive.

8. In Slide 9, change the layout to Title, Text, and Content, and then add the bitmap image **Vitamins**, located in the Tutorial.02\Cases folder.

9. In Slide 3, change the layout to Title, Text, and Content, insert appropriate clip art, and then, if necessary, recolor the clip art so it matches the design template color scheme. (Note that if the image you choose is a bitmap image, you will not be able to recolor it.)

10. In Slide 4, draw a large equilateral Regular Pentagon in the middle of the blank area of the slide below the title.

11. Invert the pentagon so it's pointed down.

12. Add white, 18-point Arial text just outside the pentagon on each of its five sides, using the phrases (starting at the top of the pentagon and going clockwise): "Motivation," "Strength Training," "Cardio Exercise," "Nutrition," and "Flexibility."

13. Rotate the text boxes so they are parallel to their respective sides of the pentagon. Adjust the size of the pentagon and the position of the text so that each phrase is centered along an edge, and almost resting on the shape.

14. In Slide 11, insert a table with two columns and five rows, and then add the text as follows:

Expense Item	Amount Needed
CSCS Employees	$230,000
Other Employees	$312,000
Inventory	$186,000
Rent	$21,000

Explore

15. Add a new row with "Total" in the left column and "$749,000" in the right column. (*Hint*: To add a row to an existing table, click in the last cell, in this case cell B5, and then press the Tab key.)

16. Drag the bottom-center sizing handle of the table up so that the table stays the same width but decreases in height so the text fits better in the cells of the table.

17. Right-align the text and numbers in column 2.

Explore

18. Change the fill color of the top row of the table to dark amber. (*Hint*: Use the Fill Color button on the Tables and Borders toolbar.)

19. Create a summary slide that includes titles from Slides 5 through 10, and change the slide title to "Products and Services." Leave the slide as the new Slide 5 in the presentation.

20. Check the spelling, view the slide show, fix any problems you see, and then save the presentation.

21. Print the presentation in grayscale as handouts with six slides per page, and then close the file.

Challenge

Apply the skills you learned in this tutorial, and explore some new ones, to modify a presentation for an accountancy firm.

Case Problem 2

Data File needed for this Case Problem: Payroll.ppt

Payroll Partners Payroll Partners, founded by Sara Ostergaard, is a Wichita, Kansas-based accountancy office that helps small businesses process payroll and perform other financial tasks. Recently, Sara was approached by lawyers of a national chain of payroll-processing offices who expressed interest in buying her business. Sara is interested in exploring the idea, and asks you to prepare a presentation that she can use to present to the board of directors of the national chain in hopes of getting the best deal possible. Complete the following:

1. Open the file **Payroll** located in the Tutorial.02\Cases folder included with your Data Files, and then save it as **Payroll Partners** in the same folder.
2. Apply the design template titled "Textured," and then replace the subtitle in Slide 1 with your name.
3. In the title master and slide master, change the title text so it's the same color (sky blue) as the square bullets in the main text of the slide master.

Explore

4. In the slide master, add a yellow-gold, 3-point border around the title text box. (*Hint*: Use the Line Color and Line Style buttons on the Drawing toolbar. Note that yellow-gold is one of the default colors.)
5. Add the footer "Payroll Partners" and slide numbers to all the slides except Slide 1.
6. Change the layout of Slide 3 to Title and Content, and then insert a Venn diagram consisting of three circles.
7. Add text labels next to each of the circles (in the designated placeholders): "Software Development," "Accounting," and "Small Business Payroll."
8. Near the bottom of the slide and centered below the Venn diagram, insert a text box with the phrase "Niche Region." Change the text to 32-point, yellow-gold text.

Explore

9. Add a yellow-gold line border around the "Niche Region" text box. (*Hint*: Select the box and then click the Line Color button on the Drawing toolbar.)

Explore

10. Draw a black, 3-point arrow from this text box to the center of the Venn diagram where the three circles overlap. (*Hint*: Use the Arrow and Line Style buttons on the Drawing toolbar.)
11. In Slide 5, change the layout to Title, Text, and Content, and then insert clip art that deals with money. If necessary, recolor the clip art to match the slide color scheme. If necessary, use the AutoFit option to fit the text in the placeholder.
12. In Slide 6, change the font color of the asking price to yellow-gold.
13. In Slide 7, insert a table with three columns and five rows, and then add the text as follows:

Year	Gross Revenues	Earnings
2002	$180,000	$70,000
2003	$270,000	$122,000
2004	$350,000	$188,000
2005	$510,000	$238,000

14. Drag the bottom-center sizing handle of the table up so that the table stays the same width but decreases in height so the text fits better in the cells of the table.

Explore

15. Select the top row of text, and change the vertical alignment so the text appears at the bottom of each cell in the row. (*Hint*: Use the Align Bottom button on the Tables and Borders toolbar.)

16. Right-align the text and numbers in columns 2 and 3.
17. Create a summary slide that includes titles from Slides 3 through 8, move the slide to the end of the presentation so it becomes Slide 9, and then change the title to "Summary."
18. Check the spelling, view the slide show, fix any problems you see, and then save the presentation.
19. Print the presentation in grayscale as handouts with six slides per page, and then close the file.

Create

Create a new presentation about scrapbooking by using and expanding on the skills you learned in this tutorial.

Case Problem 3

Data Files needed for this Case Problem: SBcam.jpg, SBfile.jpg, SBpages.jpg, SBpaper.jpg, SBpens.jpg, SBphoto.jpg, SBsciss.jpg

Sally's Scrapbooking   Four years ago, Brian and Sally DiQuattro started a business called Sally's Scrapbooking Supplies, which distributes wholesale scrapbooking supplies to retail stores in the Atlanta area. More recently, Brian and Sally opened their own specialty retail store (called Sally's Scrapbooking) and stocked it with scrapbooking supplies, which include binders, paper and plastic sheets and protectors, colored pens and markers, stickers and die cuts, stencils, scissors and cutting boards, glues and adhesives, and other miscellaneous items. As part of their marketing, Brian and Sally give presentations to scrapbooking clubs, women's clubs, crafts clubs, church groups, genealogical societies, and others interested in preserving their family histories through picture scrapbooks. The DiQuattros asked you to prepare a presentation for members of these organizations. The seven slides in your completed presentation should look like the slides shown in Figure 2-34.

Figure 2-34

The following information will help you in creating the slide show. Read all the steps before you start creating your presentation.

1. The design template is called "Crayons."
2. The font is Comic Sans MS, the default font for the Crayons design template, but if your system doesn't support Comic Sans MS, you could use Eras Medium BT, Futura Bk BT, Kids, Microsoft Sans Serif, Technical, or some other font of your choosing.
3. In Slide 1, add your name in the subtitle placeholder.
4. Slides 2 through 7 contain one or more bitmap images. You'll find all these images in the Tutorial.02\Cases folder. You should use each image once.
5. The text at the bottom of the slides is a footer and an automatic slide number.
6. Modify the slide master so that the footer on your slides is in the same place as shown in the figure.
7. The content on Slides 2 through 7 reviews the following points:
   a. Quality supplies are critical in scrapbooking.
   b. Scrapbookers need acid-free and lignin-free paper to protect their photos from damage. (Lignin is a substance in paper that yellows over time.)
   c. Scrapbookers need archival-quality pens with ink that won't bleed through the paper.
   d. Page layout is easy with the right die cuts and stickers.
   e. Buy quality cutting tools and keep them sharpened.
   f. File photos in groups to prepare to lay out pages.
8. Remember to check the spelling in the final presentation, and to view the slide show.
9. Print the final presentation in grayscale as handouts with four slides per page.
10. Save the file as **Sally's Scrapbooking** to the Tutorial.02\Cases folder.

Case Problem 4

Research

Use the Internet to collect information about a collegiate honor society and create a new presentation based on this information.

Data Files you might use in this Case Problem: PESLogo.jpg, PKPBadge.jpg, PKPKey.jpg,

College Honor Society Honor societies recognize students who distinguish themselves in academics and leadership. Your assignment is to prepare a PowerPoint presentation on an honor society at your college or university. Complete the following:

1. Gather information on an honor society from honor society advisors, college advisement centers, or the office of the Dean of Students. For the names, locations, and phone numbers, call information at your college, or consult your student directory or catalog. You can also gather information from the Internet. For general information about members of the Association of College Honor Societies, including a list of most honor societies in the United States and Canada, consult **www.achsnatl.org**. For information on a specific national, nondiscipline-specific honor society, Phi Kappa Phi, consult **www.phikappaphi.org**. For a national freshman honor society, Phi Eta Sigma, consult **www.phietasigma.org**.
2. Create a new PowerPoint presentation based on an appropriate design template. Type the name of the society on the title slide, and type your name as the subtitle.
3. Create at least eight slides with information about the society. Information on your slides might include local and national names and addresses of advisors and officers, purposes, eligibility, activities, scholarships, recognition programs, famous members, history, meetings, local and national conventions, merchandise, and publications.
4. Modify the slide master by adding a text box or graphics object, changing the font attributes, or making some other desired change that will appear on all the slides.

5. Include the slide number and an appropriate footer on each slide, except the title slide. In the slide master, change the font style, size, and color, and change the position of the footer and slide number text.

6. Include in your presentation at least one piece of clip art.

Explore

7. Click Insert on the menu bar, point to Picture, and then click Clip Art to open the Clip Art task pane. Click the Clip Art on Office Online link in the task pane to go to Microsoft's Design Gallery Live, where you can search through hundreds of pieces of clip art. Find and insert at least one image connected specifically to the honor society you are describing. If you can't find the image on the Design Gallery Live site, look elsewhere on the Web, or request an image from the local chapter of the honor society. If you choose to describe Phi Kappa Phi or Phi Eta Sigma, bitmap images of their logos are located in the Tutorial.02\Cases folder.

8. Recolor the clip art you inserted to match the presentation color scheme or the colors of the other graphics in your presentation.

9. Include a table or an organizational chart in your presentation. (For information on organizational charts, use the PowerPoint Help system.) You might include a table with the name, description, location, and dates of chapter activities; a table listing the chapter merchandise and prices; or a table with names, addresses, phone numbers, and e-mail addresses of chapter officers. You might include an organizational chart showing the structure of officers in the honor society.

10. Include a drawing that you create from lines, arrows, AutoShapes, or text boxes. For example, you might create a diagram showing the procedure for becoming a member of the honor society, using text boxes and arrows.

11. Apply a second design template to one of the slides.

12. Create a summary slide, and change its title to "Summary of Phi Kappa Phi" (but use the name of your selected honor society).

13. Check the spelling in your presentation, view the slide show, and then save the presentation to the Tutorial.02\Cases folder using the filename **Honor Society**.

14. Print the presentation in grayscale as handouts with four slides per page, and then close the file.

Research

Go to the Web to find information you can use to create presentations.

Internet Assignments

The purpose of the Internet Assignments is to challenge you to find information on the Internet that you can use to work effectively with this software. The actual assignments are updated and maintained on the Course Technology Web site. Log on to the Internet and use your Web browser to go to the Student Online Companion for New Perspectives Office 2003 at **www.course.com/np/office2003**. Click the Internet Assignments link, and then navigate to the assignments for this tutorial.

Assess

SAM Assessment and Training

If you have a SAM user profile, you may have access to hands-on instruction, practice, and assessment of the skills covered in this tutorial. Log in to your SAM account and go to your assignments page to see what your instructor has assigned.

Quick Check Answers

Session 2.1

1. Graphics add information, clarification, emphasis, variety, and pizzazz.
2. a. a file that contains the color scheme, graphics, text formats, and background colors and objects in the presentation
   b. a grid (or "map") of colored dots that form a picture
   c. a picture, clip art, photograph, shape, design, graph, chart, or diagram
   d. the design template applied to a presentation if no other template is chosen (black text on a white background)
3. a. Click anywhere in the text box.
   b. Click the edge of the text box.
   c. Drag a sizing handle.
   d. Drag the object (or in the case of a text box, the edge of the box).
   e. Display the slide in the slide pane, click the list arrow of the desired design template in the Design Template task pane, and then click Apply to Selected Slides.
   f. Select the clip-art image, click the Recolor Picture button on the Picture toolbar, and modify the original colors to new colors.
4. The title master is a slide that contains the objects that appear on the title slide of the presentation. The slide master is a slide that contains the objects that appear on all the slides except the title slide.
5. Tabs add space between the left margin and the beginning of the text on a particular line, or between the text in one column and the text in another column. Tab stops are the locations where text moves when you press the Tab key. Click the Tab button until the Right Tab button appears, and then click the desired location on the ruler.
6. date and time, footer, and slide number

Session 2.2

1. Change the slide layout to a Content layout, click the Insert Table button, set the desired number of columns and rows, insert information into the cells, and modify the table format as desired.
2. upper-left corner
3. a diagram used to show overlap between different elements
4. Click the Text Box button on the Drawing toolbar, and click or drag at the desired location in the slide.
5. Click the AutoShapes list arrow on the Drawing toolbar, point to the appropriate category (such as Basic Shapes), click the desired shape button, move the pointer into the slide pane, and then drag the pointer to draw the figure.
6. Select the triangle, click the Draw button on the Drawing toolbar, point to Rotate or Flip, and then click the appropriate command.
7. Drag the rotate handle of the object in the slide pane.
8. a method for automatically creating a slide with the titles of the slides selected in Slide Sorter view

New Perspectives on

Microsoft® Office PowerPoint® 2003

Tutorial 3   PPT 91
Presenting a Slide Show
Customizing and Preparing a Presentation

Tutorial 4   PPT 148
Integrating PowerPoint with Other Programs and Collaborating with Workgroups
Presenting Information About an Annual Banquet

Read This Before You Begin: Tutorials 3–4

To the Student

Data Files

To complete the Level II PowerPoint Tutorials (Tutorials 3 and 4), you need the starting student Data Files. Your instructor will either provide you with these Data Files or ask you to obtain them yourself.

The Level II PowerPoint tutorials require the folders indicated to complete the Tutorials, Review Assignments, and Case Problems. You will need to copy these folders from a file server, a standalone computer, or the Web to the drive and folder where you will be storing your Data Files. Your instructor will tell you which computer, drive letter, and folder(s) contain the files you need. You can also download the files by going to www.course.com; see the inside back or front cover for more information on downloading the files, or ask your instructor or technical support person for assistance.

If you are storing your Data Files on floppy disks, you will need **five** blank, formatted, high-density disks for these tutorials. Label your disks as shown, and place on them the folder(s) indicated.

▼**PowerPoint 2003 Level II: Data Disk 1**
  Tutorial.03\Tutorial folder

▼**PowerPoint 2003 Level II: Data Disk 2**
  Tutorial.03\Review folder

▼**PowerPoint 2003 Level II: Data Disk 3**
  Tutorial.03\Cases folder

▼**PowerPoint 2003 Level II: Data Disk 4**
  Tutorial.04\Tutorial folder
  Tutorial.04\Review folder

▼**PowerPoint 2003 Level II: Data Disk 5**
  Tutorial.04\Cases folder

When you begin a tutorial, refer to the Student Data Files section at the bottom of the tutorial opener page, which indicates which folders and files you need for the tutorial. Each end-of-tutorial exercise also indicates the files you need to complete that exercise. For Tutorials 3 and 4, you should save all your work to a high-capacity disk, such as a Zip disk or the hard disk on your computer. Because of the file sizes generated, you will not be able to save all the files back to your Data Disks if you are working from floppy disks. If you don't have access to a hard disk or some other high-capacity disk, in Tutorial 3, skip those steps in which you're asked to insert a digital image or movie into the presentation; and in Tutorial 4, skip those steps in which you're asked to create a Web page. If you have any questions about the Data Files, see your instructor or technical support person for assistance.

To the Instructor

The Data Files are available on the Instructor Resources CD for this title. Follow the instructions in the Help file on the CD to install the programs to your network or standalone computer. See the "To the Student" section above for information on how to set up the Data Files that accompany this text.

You are granted a license to copy the Data Files to any computer or computer network used by students who have purchased this book.

System Requirements

If you are going to work through this book using your own computer, you need:

- **Computer System** Microsoft Windows 2000, Windows XP, or higher must be installed on your computer. These tutorials assume a complete installation of Microsoft PowerPoint 2003.

- **Data Files** You will not be able to complete the tutorials or exercises in this book using your own computer until you have the necessary starting Data Files.

www.course.com/NewPerspectives

Objectives

Session 3.1
- Insert slides from another presentation
- Create and apply a custom design template
- Apply graphics and sounds
- Add a textured background

Session 3.2
- Create a chart (graph)
- Create an organization chart
- Apply slide transitions and animations
- Use the pointer pen during a slide show
- Hide slides in a presentation
- Prepare a presentation to run on another computer

Labs

Multimedia

Student Data Files

Presenting a Slide Show

Customizing and Preparing a Presentation

Case

Global Humanitarian, Peru Expedition

Pablo Fuentes, the managing director of Global Humanitarian in Lima, Peru, recently led a humanitarian expedition to Paqarimuy, a village in the Peruvian altiplano. The board of directors of Global Humanitarian asked Pablo to give a report on the expedition. He decided that he wants to present the report using a PowerPoint presentation, and he now asks you to help him prepare the presentation. He emphasizes the importance of preparing a high-quality presentation that includes a custom design template, graphics, sound effects, animations, charts, graphs, and other elements to maximize the visual effects of the presentation.

To help you get started, Pablo prepared a presentation with most of the text and some of the graphics of the expedition report. He also gave you access to other PowerPoint presentations from which you can extract slides.

In this tutorial, you'll insert slides from one presentation into another presentation; create a custom design template; add a digital image, movie, and sound clips to a presentation; create a graph and organization chart; apply special visual effects to your slides; and save the presentation ro a CD so it can be run on another computer.

▼**Tutorial.03**

▽ **Tutorial folder**

MPLogo.jpg
Paq.wav
PaqaPic.jpg
PaqMovie.avi
PeruPlan.ppt
PeruRep.ppt
Taq.wav

▽ **Review folder**

Cuzco.wav
CuzcTour.ppt
HuaynaP.wav
MachPicc.wav
PeruExp.ppt
PeruLogo.jpg
SacsMov.avi
SacsSnd.wav

▽ **Cases folder**

ACWBus.ppt   GeNetics.ppt
Alaskan.ppt   kitchen.jpg
Applause.wav   livingrm.jpg
Atorv.jpg   Totem.jpg
bedrm1.jpg
bedrm2.jpg
Bonnie.jpg
Bowls.jpg.
cabinfnt.jpg
Drugs.jpg
fireplac.jpg
fitness.jpg

Session 3.1

Planning the Presentation

Before you begin to create Pablo's slide show, he discusses with you the purpose of, and the audience for, his presentation:

- **Purpose of the presentation**: to present details of the recent humanitarian expedition to Paqarimuy
- **Type of presentation**: report
- **Audience**: Global Humanitarian's board of directors
- **Audience needs**: an overview of the expedition with pictures and data
- **Location of the presentation**: small boardroom for the Board of Directors; office or classroom for other interested parties
- **Format**: on-screen slide show

With this general plan for the presentation, Pablo prepares the text and some of the pictures for the report.

Inserting Slides from Another Presentation

After Pablo discusses his presentation plan with you, he gives you two presentation files: PeruRep, which contains the text and some pictures to include with his report; and PeruPlan, a presentation used to show expedition plans to prospective volunteers. First, you'll open PeruRep and look through it to see what information Pablo has already included. Then, you'll add slides to it from the PeruPlan presentation.

To insert slides from another presentation, you first need to open the presentation to which you want to add the slides. Then you use the Slides from File command on the Insert menu to insert specific slides from any other presentation. If the inserted slides have a different design than the current presentation, the design of the current presentation will override the design of the inserted slides.

Reference Window	**Inserting Slides from Another Presentation**

- Go to the slide after which you want to insert slides from another presentation.
- Click Insert on the menu bar, and then click Slides from File to open the Slide Finder dialog box.
- Click the Browse button, and then open the presentation file in the Slide Finder dialog box from which you want to get the slides.
- Click the slides that you want inserted into your presentation to select them.
- Click the Insert button, and then click the Close button in the Slide Finder dialog box.

To open the PeruRep presentation and save it with a new name:

1. Open the file **PeruRep**, located in the Tutorial.03\Tutorial folder included with your Data Files.
2. Maximize the PowerPoint window, if necessary.
3. Save the presentation file as **Peru Expedition Report**. See Figure 3-1.

Slide 1 of Peru Expedition Report ◄ **Figure 3-1**

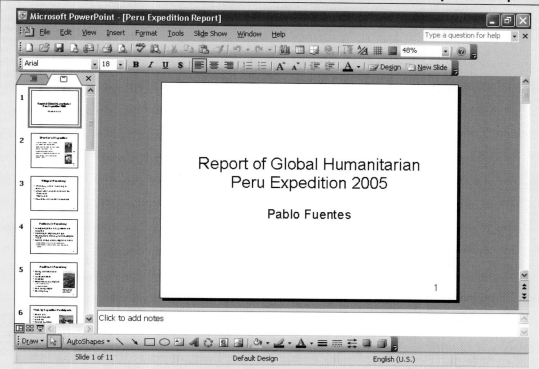

Trouble? If you're using a floppy disk for your Data Files, you won't have enough space to save the file you create in this tutorial. If you don't have access to a hard disk or some other high-capacity disk, skip those steps in which you're asked to insert a digital image or a movie into the presentation. Then you'll have enough room to save the results to a floppy disk.

4. Scroll through all 11 slides of the presentation so you have an idea of its current content. Notice that there is no design template applied to this presentation because you are going to create your own design template later in this tutorial.

Your first task is to insert slides from the presentation file PeruPlan. Pablo told you that he wants you to insert Slides 2 and 3 from PeruPlan.

To insert slides from one presentation into another:

1. Go to **Slide 2** of Peru Expedition Report. When you insert slides from another presentation, they are inserted after the current slide.

2. Click **Insert** on the menu bar, and then click **Slides from Files**. The Slide Finder dialog box opens.

3. Click the **Browse** button, navigate to the **Tutorial.03\Tutorial** folder included with your Data Files, and then double-click **PeruPlan**. The slides in PeruPlan are listed horizontally in the Slide Finder dialog box. Notice that the slides have a shaded red background and that the slide titles are yellow. See Figure 3-2.

Figure 3-2 Slide Finder dialog box

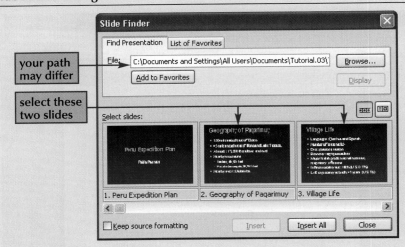

4. Click the **Slide 2** thumbnail ("Geography of Paqarimuy"), and then click the **Slide 3** thumbnail ("Village Life") to select them. The two selected slides have a dark-blue frame around them.

5. Click the **Insert** button, and then click the **Close** button in the Slide Finder dialog box. The two new slides are inserted into the current presentation after the current slide. See Figure 3-3.

Figure 3-3 New Slide 4 after inserting two slides from other presentation

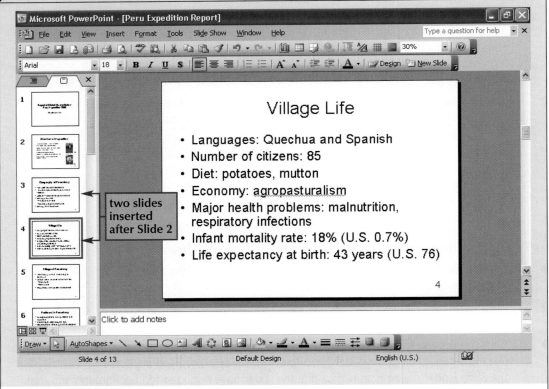

Slides 2 and 3 from PeruPlan are now Slides 3 and 4 in Peru Expedition Report. The two new slides contain detailed information about the village that was helped during the Peru expedition. The Peru Expedition Report presentation now has 13 slides.

With most of the slides now created for the presentation, you're ready to create a custom design template.

Creating a Custom Design Template

As you recall, a design template is a file that contains the color scheme, attributes, and format for the titles, main text, other text, and background for the presentation. You have used several of the design templates that come with PowerPoint. Sometimes, however, you'll want to design your own, custom template. When you create a design template, you need to make sure that the colors go well together, that the text remains clear and legible, and that the color scheme meets the needs of your presentation.

Reference Window

Creating a Custom Design Template

- Using an existing or new presentation, create the desired color scheme, bullets, fonts, background color, and background graphics.
- If you don't want any existing slides, text, or other objects in your custom design template, delete all but the first slide, and delete any text or foreground objects from the slide.
- Click File, click Save As, click the Save as type list arrow, and then click Design Template.
- Navigate to the desired location in the Save in list box, type a filename, and then click the Save button.

For the report on the Peru expedition, Pablo doesn't want you to use any of the built-in design templates; instead, he wants you to create a completely original design that better matches the subject and the colors of the pictures.

Creating a Custom Color Scheme

A **color scheme** is a set of matching colors that makes up the background, fonts, and other elements of a presentation. Each of the design templates included with PowerPoint, including the Default Design template, has several color schemes associated with it. It is easy to select colors that don't match or make text illegible; for example, red text on a blue background might seem like a good combination, but it's actually difficult to read at a distance from the screen. It's usually safer, therefore, to select one of the built-in color schemes and stick to it, or make only minor modifications.

A PowerPoint color scheme includes eight items to which you can assign a color:

- **Background**—the default color of the area on which you add text and other objects.
- **Text and lines**—the default color of the body text and of lines drawn on the slide.
- **Shadows**—the default color of the shadow applied to an object (e.g., a shape or a text box). This does not, however, specify the color of the text shadow that you apply using the Font dialog box.
- **Title text**—the default color of the title (but not the subtitle) text on the title slide and of the title text on other slide layouts.
- **Fills**—the default color that fills shapes (e.g., the color of a square or circle).
- **Accent**—a color that might appear automatically in a PowerPoint chart or graph or one that you can use, if you choose, for bullets, fills, and accented text. Accent colors appear by default only in multicolored charts, but not automatically in text, AutoShapes, lines, and other objects.

- **Accent and hyperlink**—the default color for hyperlink text and another color that might appear by default in multicolored charts.
- **Accent and followed hyperlink**—the default color for hyperlinks that have been followed; in other words, if you click a hyperlink and thereby jump to another location, when you return to the original slide, the color of the hyperlink text will be changed to indicate that you have followed that hyperlink. This color also appears by default in some multicolored charts.

Once you have specified a coordinated set of eight colors, they will appear by default in text and objects, but you can use any of the eight to change the default color of text, fills, shadows, and so forth.

As you look at the pictures of Paqarimuy, you can see that the colors are mostly earth tones—browns and yellows—so you'll create a color scheme now using those colors.

To create a custom color scheme:

1. Click the **Design** button on the Formatting toolbar to display the Slide Design task pane, and then click the **Color Schemes** link in the task pane. The task pane changes to show the color schemes associated with the current design. You can create the color scheme with any slide in the slide pane.

2. If necessary, scroll down so you can see the last color scheme in the task pane, the one with the dark-brown background. See Figure 3-4.

Figure 3-4	Slide Design task pane open

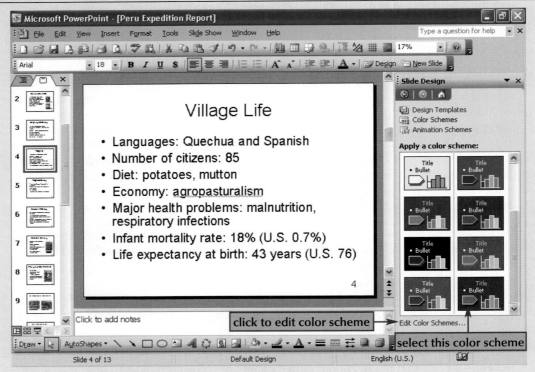

3. Click the color scheme thumbnail with the dark-brown background and tan title text, located in the bottom-right corner of the task pane. PowerPoint applies the color scheme to all the slides in your presentation.

You think the title text could stand out a little more, so next, you'll modify the color of the title text.

4. Click the **Edit Color Schemes** link at the bottom of the task pane. The Edit Color Scheme dialog box opens with the Custom tab on top. Here you can see color tiles of each of the major elements of the slide—the background, the text and lines, the shadows, and so forth.

5. Click the **Title text** tile, click the **Change Color** button to open the Title Text Color dialog box, and then click the **Standard** tab. See Figure 3-5.

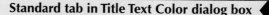
Standard tab in Title Text Color dialog box ◄ Figure 3-5

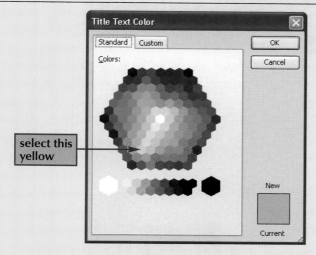

6. Click the bright-yellow tile indicated in Figure 3-5, and then click the **OK** button. The Title Text Color dialog box closes. The Title text color tile changes from tan to yellow, and the title text in the preview pane on the right side of the dialog box changes to yellow also.

7. Click the **Apply** button. The Edit Color Scheme dialog box closes and the new color scheme is applied to your presentation. As you can see in the slide pane, the title is now bright yellow. If you look at the other slides on the Slides tab on the left, you see that the titles on those slides are also bright yellow.

8. Click the **Close** button ⊠ on the task pane title bar.

You'll now change the background of the slides. You could have used the Edit Color Scheme dialog box to change to a solid color for the background (by clicking the Background tile), but if you want special effects, such as shading, you must use the Background dialog box.

Creating a Custom Background

The color scheme of your presentation has a brown background, but Pablo asks you to add shading to the background to add interest and a professional touch to the presentation. You decide to use a **gradient fill**, which is a type of shading in which one color blends into another or varies from one shade to another.

When you use a gradient fill, you also choose a shading style and a variant. The **shading style** identifies the direction in which the shading will be applied—horizontally, vertically, diagonally up, diagonally down, from a corner, or from the title. A **variant** is a variation of a particular shading style; there are four variants of each shading style.

You'll change the background of your presentation to a two-color gradient fill.

To create a custom background with a two-color gradient fill:

1. Click **Format** on the menu bar, and then click **Background**. The Background dialog box opens.

2. Click the **Background fill** list arrow (underneath the preview box), and then click **Fill Effects**. The Fill Effects dialog box opens.

3. Click the **Gradient** tab, if necessary, and then click the **Two colors** option button in the Colors section. Two shades of the background color appear on the right side of the Colors section. See Figure 3-6.

Figure 3-6	Gradient tab in Fill Effects dialog box

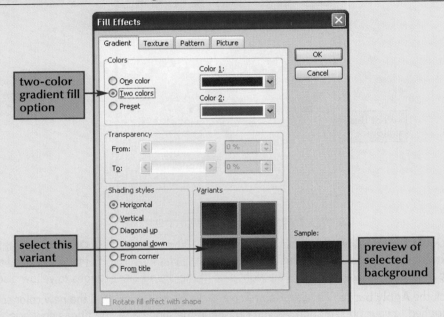

PowerPoint automatically sets the two colors to dark brown and medium brown. You can change one or both of these colors by clicking the Color 1 or Color 2 list arrows and then selecting the desired color, but a dark gradient fill works well with light text colors, so you choose to keep the two colors as they are. The horizontal shading style is selected by default, and this style works well for most presentations. The default variant is the variant in the upper-left corner of the Variants section of the dialog box in which the color varies from dark to light. You'll use the default shading style, but you'll select a different variant.

4. Click the variant in the lower-left corner of the Variants section, as indicated in Figure 3-6. This variant places the dark brown at the top and bottom of the slide, and the lighter brown in the middle.

5. Click the **OK** button. The Fill Effects dialog box closes.

6. Click the **Apply to All** button in the Background dialog box. The Background dialog box closes, and the background gradient fill and variant you selected are applied to all the slides.

7. Save the presentation.

As you can see from the slide pane and the Slides tab, all of the slides now have a background with a gradient fill. You'll now modify the fonts used on the slides.

Modifying Fonts and Bullets

All the current text in your presentation is in a sans serif font called Arial. This is a good general-purpose font, but Pablo wants something with a bit more pizzazz. In this case, he wants you to change the title font from Arial to Impact, a thicker sans serif font, and change the body text font from Arial to Book Antiqua, an attractive serif font. Rather than change the fonts on each of the individual slides, you can make these changes for all the slides at once by changing the fonts on the slide master and title master. As you might recall, the title master contains the objects that appear on the title slide, and the slide master contains the objects that appear on all the slides except the title slide. Now you'll modify the fonts on these two masters.

To modify the fonts on the slide master:

▶ 1. Shift-click the **Normal View** button ▣. (If you position the mouse pointer over the Normal button while you hold down the Shift key, you'll see that the ScreenTip becomes Slide Master View.)

▶ 2. Click the border of the title placeholder text box to select the entire box, click the **Font** list arrow [Arial ▾] on the Formatting toolbar, scroll down until you see **Impact**, and then click that font name. The title font changes from Arial to Impact.

 Trouble? If your computer doesn't have the Impact font installed, keep Arial as the font, but make it bold by clicking the Bold button [B] on the Formatting toolbar.

▶ 3. Select the placeholder text box for the bulleted list text (the body text), and change the font to **Book Antiqua**. See Figure 3-7.

 Trouble? If your computer doesn't have the Book Antiqua font installed, select Times New Roman instead.

Slide master with new fonts ◀ **Figure 3-7**

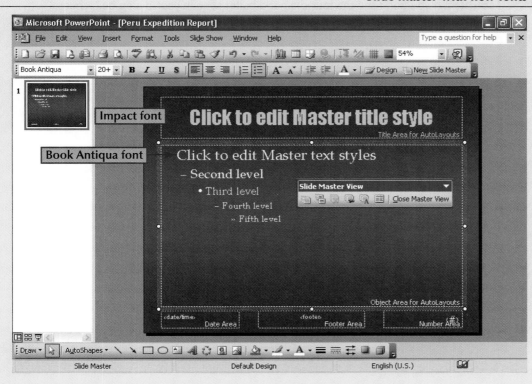

You have made the fonts more interesting. Now you're ready to change the bullets.

To change the bullets style on the slide master:

▶ **1.** Right-click the line that reads "Click to edit Master text styles," and then click **Bullets and Numbering** on the shortcut menu. The Bullets and Numbering dialog box opens with the Bulleted tab on top. See Figure 3-8.

| Figure 3-8 | Bullet tab in Bullets and Numbering dialog box |

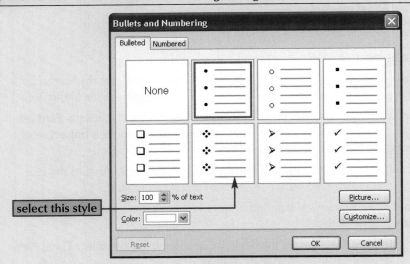

select this style

▶ **2.** Click the four-diamond bullet style, as indicated in Figure 3-8.

Trouble? If you don't see the four-diamond bullet style in your dialog box, choose another style.

▶ **3.** Click the **Color** list arrow, and then click the bright-yellow tile. The new bullets will be bright yellow.

▶ **4.** Click the **OK** button to accept the changes to the top-level bullets. You now see a yellow four-diamond bullet on the first-level bulleted item.

▶ **5.** Using the same procedure, change the bullet in the second line ("Second level") to a solid, blue-gray, small square. (The blue-gray color is the right-most tile on the color palette.)

▶ **6.** Click the **Normal View** button ⊞ to return to Normal view, and then click the **Slide 3** thumbnail in the Slides tab to see the effect of the changes you made. See Figure 3-9.

Slide 3 with new fonts and bullets ◄ **Figure 3-9**

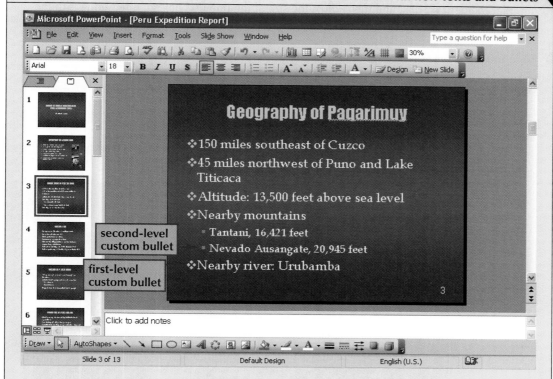

Trouble? If your bullet characters or colors are different from those shown in Figure 3-9, return to the slide master and make any necessary changes.

7. Save the presentation.

You've almost completed the custom design template. Your final task is to add a digital image to the title and slide masters.

Adding a Background Image

Pablo realizes that the best-known image of Peru is Machu Picchu, the ancient Incan ruins located on the edge of the Peruvian jungle. He wants you to add a photo of Machu Picchu to the background of all the slides in the presentation.

Because Pablo wants this image to be on all the slides in the presentation, you'll add it to the title and slide masters. (You'll recall that you added an image to the background when you worked with the title and slide masters in Tutorial 2.)

To add a background image to the slide master:

1. Shift-click the **Normal View** button ▣ to return to Slide Master view.

2. Click the **Insert Picture** button 🖼 on the Drawing toolbar. The Insert Picture dialog box opens.

3. Click the **Look in** list arrow and navigate to the **Tutorial.03\Tutorial** folder included with your Data Files, click **MPLogo**, if necessary, and then click the **Insert** button. A small picture of Machu Picchu appears in the middle of the slide master.

▶ **4.** Drag the picture so it's positioned with its left edge flush with the left edge of the title placeholder text box, and then adjust the size of the title text box so its left edge is to the right of the picture. See Figure 3-10.

Figure 3-10 | **Slide master after adding logo and adjusting title placeholder**

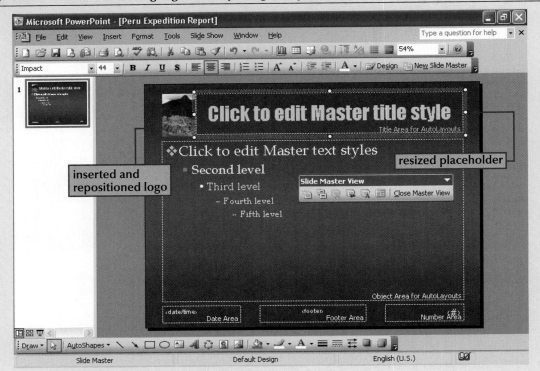

Trouble? If the Slide Master View toolbar is in the way, drag it out of the way by its title bar.

Recall that the title text on the title slide is in a different position than the title text on the rest of the slides. But notice that PowerPoint doesn't automatically include a title master with the Default Design template. You'll need to add a title master, and then modify it to reposition the background graphic to an appropriate spot.

▶ **5.** Click the **Insert New Title Master** button 🖼 on the Slide Master View toolbar. A title master is added and the view switches to Title Master view.

Next, you'll change the size of the Machu Picchu picture. In the past, when you changed a picture size, you dragged the sizing handles. However, if you want to change the picture to a specific, predetermined size (in this case, two inches in height), you should use the Size tab in the Format Picture dialog box. You'll do that now.

▶ **6.** Click the **Machu Picchu** image to select it, and then click the **Format Picture** button 🖾 on the Picture toolbar. The Format Picture dialog box opens.

Trouble? If the Picture toolbar does not appear on your screen, click View on the menu bar, point to Toolbars, and then click Picture.

▶ **7.** Click the **Size** tab, drag to select the value in the Height text box in the Size and rotate section, type **2**, make sure that the **Lock aspect ratio** check box is checked, and then click the **OK** button. The image is resized so that the height is two inches and the width is proportional to the original width.

▶ **8.** Drag the **Machu Picchu** picture into the title master so it's centered just above the title placeholder text box, as shown in Figure 3-11.

Title master after moving logo ◄ **Figure 3-11**

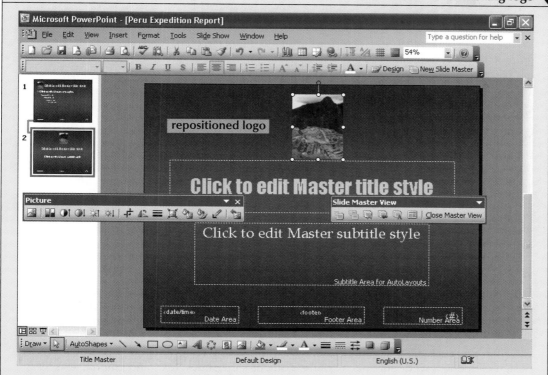

9. Resize the two title placeholders to a little larger than half their original height by selecting each one and dragging a sizing handle, and then drag the picture and the two title placeholders down so they are better centered vertically in the slide, as shown in Figure 3-12.

Title master after moving objects ◄ **Figure 3-12**

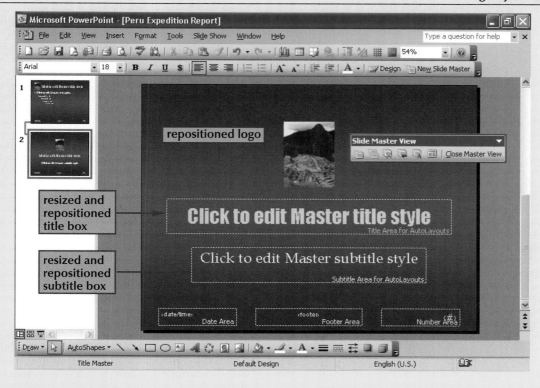

▶ **10.** Click the **Normal View** button ⊞ to return to Normal view, and then save the presentation.

The design template is now complete, with a customized color scheme, gradient background, new fonts, and the picture of Machu Picchu in the background of all the slides. Pablo now asks you to save the custom design template so he can apply it to other presentations.

Saving a Custom Design Template

You used several built-in design templates in earlier tutorials by clicking the Design button on the Formatting toolbar to display the Slide Design task pane, and then clicking the desired design template. What if you want to use a custom design template? That's exactly what Pablo wants. When he creates another expedition plan, report, or some other presentation that would look good using the custom design of the Peru Expedition Report presentation, he wants to be able to select that design from the task pane, just as he would any other design template. Fortunately, PowerPoint allows you to save the design from any PowerPoint presentation as a design template.

The default location for a PowerPoint presentation saved as a design template is the Templates folder. If you save a design template to that folder, then the next time you start PowerPoint, your custom template will appear as one of the templates in the Slide Design task pane. No matter where a template is stored, however, you can create a new presentation based on the template by clicking the Browse link at the bottom of the Slide Design task pane.

When you save a PowerPoint presentation as a design template, not only are all the design elements saved, but also all of the content—the slides, text, and graphics—is saved. Therefore, you usually want to delete all the slides but the title slide, and you even want to delete the text and foreground graphic (if any) from that slide, leaving only the objects on the title master and slide master. This will reduce the file size and conform to the standard of built-in templates. You'll delete the content and then save the custom design template now.

To save a presentation as a design template:

▶ **1.** Click the **Slide Sorter View** button ⊞ to switch to Slide Sorter view, click **Edit** on the menu bar, click **Select All** to select all the slides, press and hold the **Ctrl** key, click **Slide 1** to deselect just that slide, and then release the **Ctrl** key. All the slides except Slide 1 are now selected, as indicated by the thick border around them.

▶ **2.** Press the **Delete** key to delete all the selected slides. Only Slide 1 remains.

▶ **3.** Return to Normal view, and then delete all of the text (but not the placeholder text boxes) on the slide. Only the design and title master graphics and placeholders remain on the slide. See Figure 3-13.

Slide with only background colors, background object and placeholders ◀ **Figure 3-13**

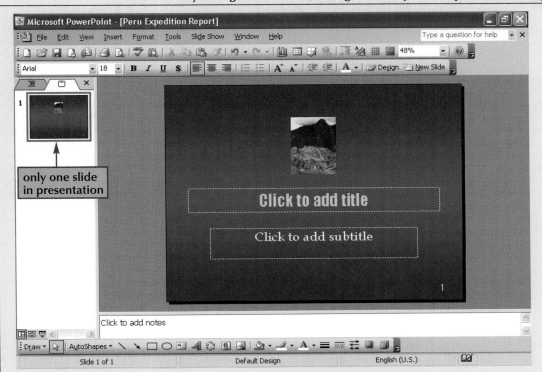

4. Click **File**, click **Save As**, click the **Save as type** list arrow, and then click **Design Template**. The Save in folder changes to Templates. Normally, you would save a design template file in this folder. For the purposes of this tutorial, however, you need to save your template file to the same location where you saved Peru Expedition Report (in the Tutorial.03\Tutorial folder).

5. Click the **Save in** list arrow, and then navigate to the **Tutorial.03\Tutorial** folder included with your Data Files (or to the location where you saved Peru Expedition Report).

6. Replace the text in the File name text box with **Peru Template**, and then click the **Save** button. PowerPoint saves the file as a design template.

7. Click the **Close Window** button ✕ on the right side of the menu bar. PowerPoint should still be running, but with no file in the presentation window.

You have now created a custom design template that Pablo and others can use with any new presentation.

Using a Custom Design Template

You decide to test your new custom design template on a new presentation.

To apply a custom design template:

1. Click the **New** button 🗋 on the Standard toolbar to open a new presentation.

2. Click the **Design** button on the Formatting toolbar to open the Slide Design task pane. Because you saved your design template in the Tutorial.03\Tutorial folder rather than in the default design template folder, your new template doesn't appear in the task pane, so you need to direct PowerPoint to your folder by clicking the Browse link.

3. Click the **Browse** link at the bottom of the Slide Design task pane, and then change the Look in folder to the **Tutorial.03\Tutorial** folder included with your Data Files (or the location where you saved Peru Template).

4. Double-click **Peru Template** in the list of files in the Tutorial.03\Tutorial folder. As you can see, the new presentation has the design of your custom design template.

5. Click the **New Slide** button on the Formatting toolbar to create a Title and Text slide. Again, you can see the design of your custom design template, with the yellow title text, the picture of Machu Picchu in the upper-left corner, and the yellow diamond bullet in the main text placeholder. If you were actually creating a presentation, you would add text and other objects to the title slide and to the other slides.

6. Click the **Close Window** button ☒ on the right side of the menu bar, and then click the **No** button in the dialog box that asks if you want to save changes.

You can now report to Pablo that your custom design template works as planned.

Multimedia

Applying Graphics and Sounds to Your Presentation

PowerPoint allows you to add various types of graphics and sounds to your presentation. You're already familiar with adding clip art, drawn images, and digital photos to a slide. In fact, the original PeruPlan file came with images of Paqarimuy and other places and people of Peru. Moreover, you have already inserted the image of Machu Picchu into the slide background, and in Tutorial 2, you inserted a photo, clip art, and drawings you created using the tools on the Drawing toolbar. In addition to still photos and other graphics, you can insert movies and sounds into a presentation.

Reference Window | Adding Movies and Sounds to a Presentation

- On the slide to which you want to add a movie or sound, click Insert on the menu bar, point to Movies and Sounds, and then click the desired source (the Clip Organizer or a user-specified file) for the movie or sound.
- Select the movie or sound file from a specified folder and click the OK button, or click the desired movie or sound in the Clip Art task pane.
- When asked whether you want the movie or sound to start automatically or when clicked, click either the Automatically or When Clicked button.

For the presentation on the Peru expedition, you'll use photos, movies, and sound files that are included with your Data Files. In other presentations, you might have to acquire the graphics and sounds in other ways. For example, you can do the following:

- Use a digital camera to take digital photographs.
- Scan prints of photos or slides to create digital images.
- Create images or movies using graphics software.
- Record sound files with a microphone attached to your computer and appropriate software.
- Download images or sound clips from the Internet.
- Insert images or sounds from the PowerPoint Clip Art Organizer.
- Use built-in PowerPoint sound effects (you'll learn about these later in this tutorial).

Pablo asks you to insert a digital image of the village of Paqarimuy into Slide 3, a video clip of the Peruvian altiplano into Slide 5, and sound clips into Slides 2 and 6. All of these files were created by Pablo or other members of the humanitarian expedition.

Adding a Digital Photo to a Slide

In Tutorial 2, you added a photo to the slide master. In a similar way, you can add any photo to a slide as long as it is in, or converted to, a digital format. The procedure for adding a photo to a slide is the same as the procedure for adding a photo to the slide master. You'll begin by adding the digital image to Slide 3.

To add an image to a slide:

▶ **1.** Open **Peru Expedition Report** and go to **Slide 3** ("Geography of Paqarimuy").

▶ **2.** Make sure the Slide Layout task pane appears on the right side of your screen, and then click the thumbnail for the **Title, Text, and Content** layout (the top-left thumbnail under Text and Content Layouts). The slide layout now includes a title, a placeholder for bulleted text, and a content placeholder on the right side of the slide.

▶ **3.** If the bulleted text extends below the bottom of the slide, click anywhere in the body text box, click the **AutoFit Options** button ⬍ located in the slide pane adjacent to the selected text box, and then click the **AutoFit Text to Placeholder** option button. The font size automatically decreases so that all the text fits on the slide. See Figure 3-14.

Slide 3 after changing slide layout ◀ **Figure 3-14**

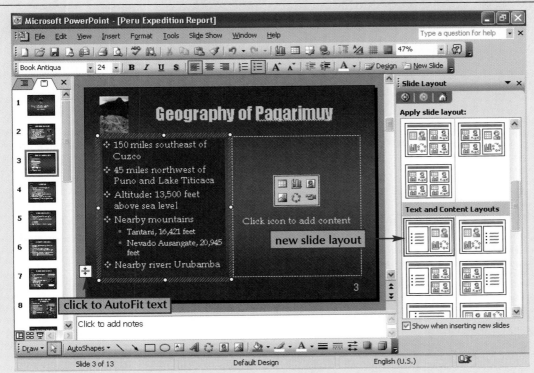

▶ **4.** Click the **Insert Picture** button 🖾 in the content placeholder. The Insert Picture dialog box opens.

5. If necessary, click the **Look in** list arrow and switch to the **Tutorial.03\Tutorial** folder included with your Data Files, click **PaqaPic** (a digital photograph of the village of Paqarimuy), and then click the **Insert** button. The picture of Paqarimuy is inserted into the slide. See Figure 3-15.

Figure 3-15 | **Slide 3 after adding picture**

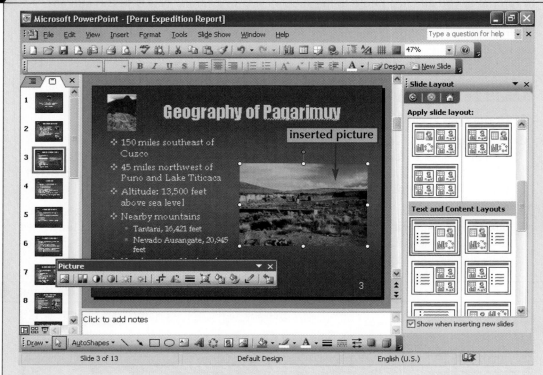

6. Click a blank area of the slide to deselect the picture.

You could have moved or resized the picture of Paqarimuy, but its position and size are adequate.

Adding a Movie

A **video clip**, or **digital movie**, is an animated picture file. Files with the filename extension .avi are video clips. Another common video format is an animated GIF. An **animated GIF** file is actually a series of images that are quickly displayed one after another. These files are identified with the file extension .gif.

Pablo wants to give his audience an idea of how barren and desolate the Peruvian altiplano can be, so he asks you to add a video clip to one of the slides. Pablo's video clip shows a 180-degree pan of the land around Paqarimuy. He prepared a simple, low-resolution video clip for this purpose. He made it low resolution to keep the file size smaller so it would load faster into the PowerPoint presentation and take up less disk space.

You can insert a video clip in two ways. You can change the layout to a Content layout, click the Insert Media Clip button, and then use the dialog box that opens, or you can use commands on the menu bar. You'll add the movie now using the Insert Media Clip button in a Content layout.

To add a movie to a slide and view it:

1. Go to **Slide 5**, click the **Title, Text and Content** layout, and then close the task pane.

2. Click the **Insert Media Clip** button in the content placeholder. The Media Clip dialog box opens, displaying thumbnails of all available media clips, both video and sound, that have been categorized in the Microsoft Clip Organizer. The Clip Organizer lets you add clips to or delete clips from the Clip Art task pane. Video clips are identified by an animation star in the lower-right corner of the thumbnail.

   You need to import the video clip that Pablo recorded into the Clip Organizer.

3. Click the **Import** button in the Media Clip dialog box, click the **Look in** list arrow, navigate to the **Tutorial.03\Tutorial** folder included with your Data Files, click **PaqMovie**, and then click the **Add** button. The clip appears as the first clip in the Media Clip dialog box.

   Trouble? If the clip is already in the Media Clip dialog box, you don't need to add it again, although doing so is not a problem.

4. Double-click the **PaqMovie** thumbnail in the Media Clip dialog box. PowerPoint displays a message asking you how you want your movie to start—automatically, or when clicked during the slide show. In other words, do you want the movie to begin automatically as soon as the slide appears during the slide show, or do you want the viewer or presenter to click the movie to play it?

5. Click the **Automatically** button to indicate that you want the movie to play automatically. The first frame of the movie appears in the right side of the slide. Now you'll increase the size of the movie picture, but you don't want to make it too big or its low resolution will become a distraction.

6. Drag the upper-right sizing handle of the picture until the height is about two inches, move the picture to the right-center of the slide, and then resize the text box so its right edge is near the left edge of the movie picture. Compare your screen to Figure 3-16 and make any necessary adjustments.

Slide 5 after inserting movie ◀ **Figure 3-16**

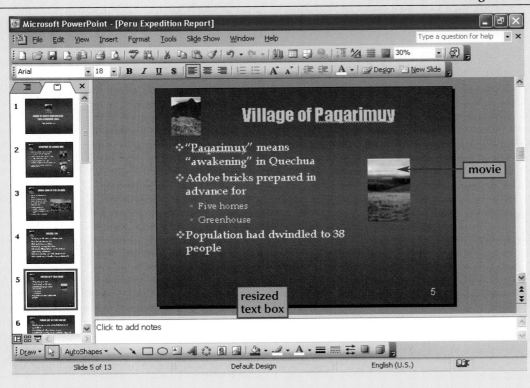

Having inserted the digital movie, you are now ready to view it.

▶ 7. Double-click the **movie** object. As you can see, the movie shows the rolling hills of the puna grassland and high Andes Mountains, along with alpaca grazing in the foreground. In fact, the video is an animated, wider-angled view of the picture shown in Slide 7.

Because you clicked the Automatically button, the movie will play when Slide 5 appears during the slide show. But Pablo wants the movie to play continuously while Slide 5 is on the screen during the slide show. You'll set the movie so that it loops continuously.

To edit the movie object:

▶ 1. Right-click the **movie** object, and then click **Edit Movie Object** on the shortcut menu. The Movie Options dialog box opens. This dialog box includes several options for playing and displaying the clip while the slide show is running. See Figure 3-17.

Figure 3-17	Movie Options dialog box

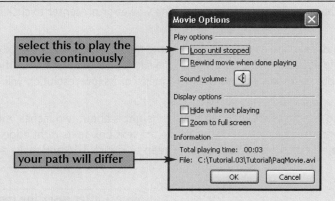

select this to play the movie continuously

your path will differ

▶ 2. Click the **Loop until stopped** check box to select it, and then click the **OK** button.

Now you'll test it to see how it works.

▶ 3. Click the **Slide Show from current slide** button ⬚ to start the slide show from the current slide. Slide 5 appears in Slide Show view and the movie plays continuously.

▶ 4. Right-click anywhere on the slide, and then click **End Show** on the shortcut menu to return to Normal view.

▶ 5. Save the presentation.

Next, you'll add sound to your presentation.

Adding Sound Clips

Now that you've added the movie, Pablo wants you to add sound clips of the spoken names of the two villages mentioned in the presentation: Paqarimuy and Taquile. If someone views the presentation without his assistance, the pronunciation of these two names will be available. Pablo's recordings are in .wav files, which is the most common file format for short sound clips.

As with video clips, there are a couple of ways you can add a sound clip to a slide. You can use the Insert Media Clip button in a Content layout, as you did when you inserted the video clip, or you can use menu commands. You'll add the sound files now using menu commands.

To add sound clips to the presentation:

1. Go to **Slide 2**, where the word "Paqarimuy" first appears in the presentation.

2. Click **Insert** on the menu bar, point to **Movies and Sounds**, and then click **Sound from File**. The Insert Sound dialog box opens.

3. Click the **Paq** sound file, located in the **Tutorial.03\Tutorial** folder included with your Data Files, click the **OK** button, and then click the **When Clicked** button to indicate that you don't want the sound to play automatically. PowerPoint inserts a sound icon in the middle of the slide to indicate that a sound clip is available on that slide.

4. Drag the **sound** icon immediately to the right of "Paqarimuy, Peru," and then click a blank area of the slide to deselect the icon. See Figure 3-18.

Slide 2 after inserting sound clip 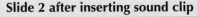 **Figure 3-18**

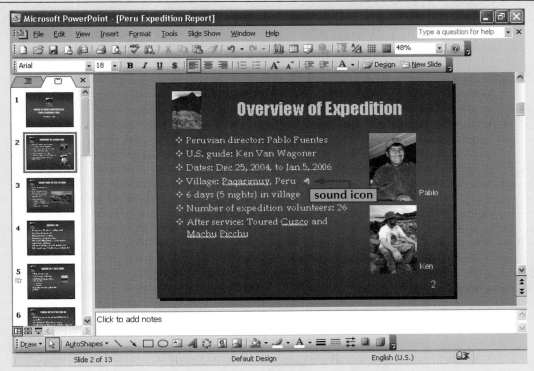

5. Double-click the **sound** icon to play the sound clip.

6. Go to **Slide 6**, where the name of another Peruvian village (Taquile) appears.

7. Using the same method as before, insert the sound clip **Taq** (located in the **Tutorial.03\Tutorial** folder included with your Data Files) into Slide 6, and then drag its **sound** icon to the right of the word "Taquile." Make sure you indicate that you want the sound clip to play when clicked.

8. Double-click the **sound** icon in Slide 6 to hear the pronunciation of "Taquile."

9. Click the **Slide Show from current slide** button 🖵. Slide 6 appears in Slide Show view.

10. Click the **sound** icon on the slide, listen to the sound being played, and then press the **Esc** key to end the slide show and return to Normal view.

11. Save the presentation.

Now, anyone who wants to know how to pronounce the names of the villages can click the sound icons during the slide show.

Adding a Textured Background

Pablo was so pleased with the work of the expedition volunteers that he wants a way to highlight Slide 12, which shows a group photograph of the volunteers. He decides that he wants you to add an appropriate textured background to the slide. You'll do that now.

Reference Window	**Applying a Textured Background**

- Click Format on the menu bar, and then click Background to display the Background dialog box.
- Click the Background fill list arrow, and then click Fill Effects to display the Fill Effects dialog box.
- Click the Texture tab, click the desired texture tile, click the OK button, and then click the Apply or Apply to All button.

To add a textured background:

1. Go to **Slide 12**, click **Format** on the menu bar, click **Background** to display the Background dialog box, click the **Background fill** list arrow, click **Fill Effects** to display the Fill Effects dialog box, and then click the **Texture** tab. As you can see, PowerPoint provides various textures that you can use as slide backgrounds, including green, white, and brown marble. See Figure 3-19.

Figure 3-19	**Texture tab in Fill Effects dialog box**

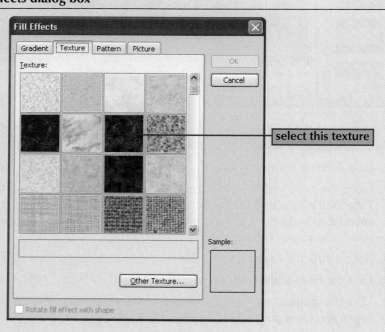

You'll select the brown marble for the background of Slide 12.

▶ **2.** Click the **Brown marble** tile (as indicated in Figure 3-19), click the **OK** button to return to the Background dialog box, and then click the **Apply** button. The brown marble background appears in Slide 12. If you had clicked the Apply to All button, the textured background would have appeared on all the slides. See Figure 3-20.

Slide 12 with textured background ◀ **Figure 3-20**

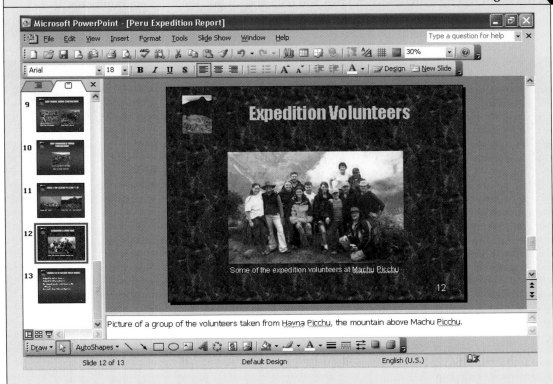

▶ **3.** Save the presentation.

Pablo is pleased with how Slide 12 stands out from the others, and he is happy with the progress you're making on the presentation.

Session 3.1 Quick Check

Review

1. Describe how to insert slides from one presentation into another.
2. What is a color scheme?
3. In creating a custom design template, what are four (or more) elements in your presentation that you might want to change?
4. Define variant as it applies to a gradient fill background.
5. Describe how to save a PowerPoint presentation as a design template.
6. What is a video clip?

Session 3.2

Creating a Chart (Graph)

A **chart**, or **graph**, is a visual depiction of data in a datasheet. The **datasheet** is a grid of cells, similar to a Microsoft Excel worksheet. **Cells** are the boxes that are organized in rows and columns, in which you can add data and labels. The rows are numbered 1, 2, 3, etc., and the columns are labeled A, B, C, etc. You can use a chart to show an audience data trends or to visually compare data.

Reference Window	Creating a Chart (Graph)

- Change the slide layout to a Content layout.
- Click the Chart button in the content placeholder.
- Edit the information in the datasheet for the data that you want to plot.
- Modify the chart type, if necessary.
- Modify the chart options, adding titles, modifying the font, and so forth, as desired.
- Click outside the chart area to make the chart inactive.

Pablo feels that the presentation should stress the importance of a village greenhouse by showing the average daytime high and nighttime low temperatures during each month of the year. He asks you, therefore, to add a new slide with a chart showing this relationship. You'll create the chart now.

To insert a chart:

1. If you took a break after the previous session, open the presentation **Peru Expedition Report** located in the **Tutorial.03\Tutorial** folder included with your Data Files.

2. Go to **Slide 10**, the slide before which you want to insert the new slide with a graph.

3. Click the **New Slide** button on the Formatting toolbar to insert a new Slide 11, and then click the **Title and Content** layout in the Slide Layout task pane.

4. Click the title placeholder, and then type **Climate of Paqarimuy**.

5. Close the task pane to provide more space for the slide pane, and then click the **Insert Chart** button 📖 in the content placeholder. PowerPoint inserts a sample chart and datasheet. See Figure 3-21.

New Slide 11 for creating chart | Figure 3-21

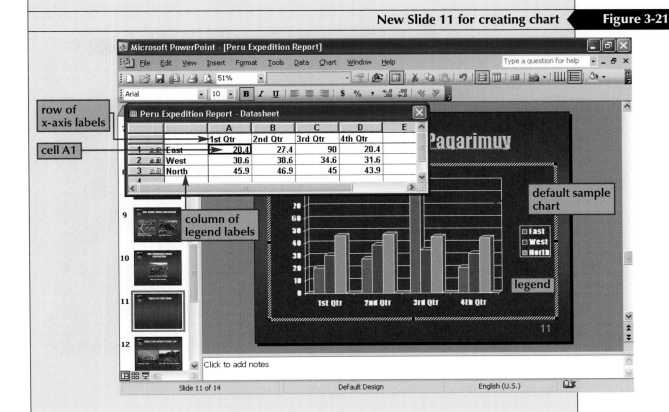

To create the chart for Pablo's presentation, you simply edit the information in the sample datasheet on the screen. When you work with a datasheet, the cell in which you are entering data is the **active cell**. The active cell has a thick border around it. In this chart, you want only two rows: one for the daytime high temperature, and the other for the daytime low temperature. You'll begin by deleting the third row of data on the datasheet.

To modify the chart:

1. Click the row **3** heading on the left side of the datasheet. The entire row is selected.

2. Press the **Delete** key to clear the entire row.

3. Click the first cell in row 1 with the label "East," just to the left of cell A1, type **High** (to indicate the high temperature), and then press the **Enter** key. The label is changed and the active cell moves down to the first cell in row 2. Notice that the legend in the chart also changed to reflect the new row label.

4. Replace the label "West" with **Low**.

5. Click the cell with the label "1st Qtr," just above cell A1 in column A, type **J** (for January), and then press the **Tab** key to move to the label for column B.

6. Type **F** (for February), press the **Tab** key to move to the label for column C, type **M** (for March), press the **Tab** key, type **A** (for April), and then press the **Tab** key. The active cell moves to the top cell in column E and the datasheet scrolls left.

7. Continue labeling the rest of the columns **M, J, J, A, S, O, N,** and **D** to label columns E through L. Notice that empty columns are added to the chart as you add column labels to the datasheet. See Figure 3-22.

Figure 3-22 | **Datasheet for creating a chart**

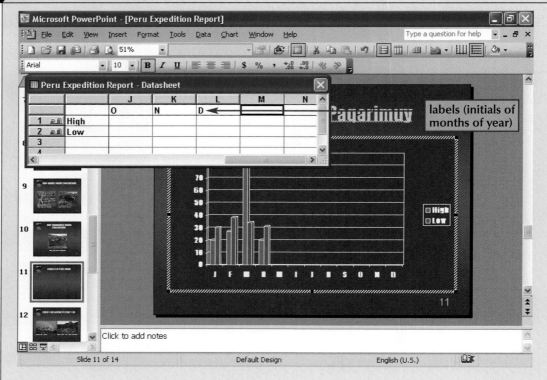

So far, you've created the labels for your chart. Now you'll type the data—the high and low average temperatures for each month in Paqarimuy.

To insert the data into the datasheet:

▶ **1.** Drag the horizontal scroll button on the bottom of the datasheet all the way to the left so that you can see cell A1.

▶ **2.** Click cell **A1** (which currently contains the number 20.4), type **48** (the average high temperature in degrees Fahrenheit during the month of January), press the **Tab** key to go to cell B1, type **50** (the average high during February), press the **Tab** key to go to cell C1, type **49** (the average high during March), and continue in the same way typing the temperatures **45**, **42**, **38**, **36**, **37**, **40**, **43**, **45**, and **48** in cells D1 through L1 for the months of April through December.

▶ **3.** Scroll back to the left to see cell A2, click cell **A2** (which currently contains the number 30.6), and type the following 12 numbers, pressing the **Tab** key between each one, to fill cells A2 through L2 with the nighttime low temperatures for January through December: **25**, **27**, **26**, **23**, **22**, **21**, **21**, **21**, **22**, **23**, **25**, and **26**. Your datasheet is now complete and the chart contains columns to reflect all of the data you entered.

The chart now contains all of the data, but you need to modify the chart to make it more useful to your audience. The chart type is a column chart, but you want to change it to a line chart. You also want to include some additional labels on the chart, and to change the font to make the labels more legible. First, you'll change the chart type.

To change the chart type:

1. Click **Chart** on the menu bar, click **Chart Type** to open the Chart Type dialog box, click the **Standard Types** tab, if necessary, and then click **Line** in the Chart type list box. See Figure 3-23.

Chart Type dialog box ◀ **Figure 3-23**

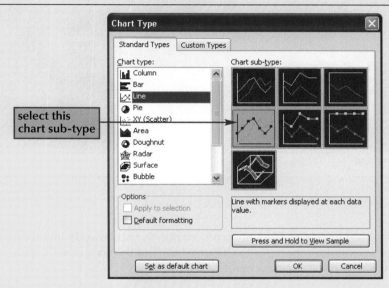

2. If necessary, click the first chart thumbnail in the second row in the Chart sub-type section, as indicated in Figure 3-23, and then click the **OK** button. The chart changes to a line chart. Now that you have entered the desired chart type, you'll add a chart title and an axis label.

3. Click **Chart** on the menu bar, click **Chart Options** to open the Chart Options dialog box, and then click the **Titles** tab, if necessary.

4. Click in the **Chart title** text box, and then type **Average Monthly Temperatures**. After a moment, the chart title you typed appears above the preview of the chart on the right.

5. Click in the **Value (Y) axis** text box, type **Temperature (degrees F)** to indicate that the temperatures are in Fahrenheit, and then click the **OK** button. Your chart should now look like the one shown in Figure 3-24.

Figure 3-24 | **Datasheet and chart after adding data**

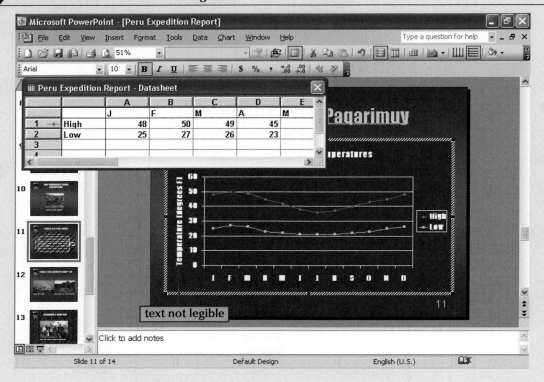

You've almost completed the chart. The only problem now is that PowerPoint automatically uses the title text font, bold Impact, for the chart labels, but this font is not legible in the chart. You'll change all the text in your chart to Arial.

To change the font of the chart labels:

1. Click in the chart area, and then click the **chart title** ("Average Monthly Temperatures") to select the chart title text box.

   Trouble? If you can't see the chart title because the datasheet is in the way, drag the datasheet out of the way by its title bar.

2. Click the **Font** list arrow on the Formatting toolbar, click **Arial**, and then click the **Bold** button **B** on the Formatting toolbarto turn off the bold formatting.

3. Double click the **legend** (which shows the line color and symbols for High and Low) to open the Format Legend dialog box, click the **Font** tab, click **Arial** in the Font list box, click **Regular** in the Font style list box, and then click the **OK** button.

4. Change the font of the **Value axis title** (the title written vertically along the y-axis) to **Arial Regular**.

5. Double-click one of the **Category axis labels** (the labels along the x-axis) to open the Format Axis dialog box. Notice that you can't select this axis as a text box because it's part of the data in the datasheet, not a separate text box.

   Trouble? If the Format Chart Area dialog box opens instead of the Format Axis dialog box, you did not double-click the Category axis. Click the Cancel button, position the pointer over one of the labels on the Category axis so that you see a ScreenTip identifying the Category axis, and then double-click.

6. Click the **Font** tab, if necessary, change the font to **Arial** and the font style to **Regular**, and then click the **OK** button.

7. Double-click one of the **Value axis labels** (the temperature values along the left edge of the graph), change the font to **Arial Regular**, and then click the **OK** button.

8. Click anywhere on the slide outside the chart area to close the datasheet and make the chart inactive, and then click outside the chart again to deselect the chart object. Your completed Slide 11 should look like Figure 3-25.

Slide 11 with completed chart ◀ Figure 3-25

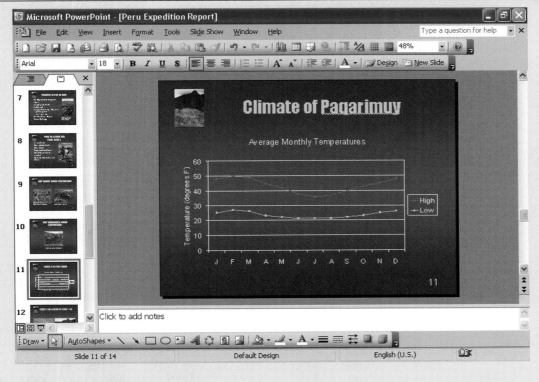

9. Save the presentation.

Pablo is pleased with your chart, which graphically shows how cold the climate is in Paqarimuy, and hence the need for a greenhouse to grow certain vegetables.

Building and Modifying an Organization Chart

Because the members of the board of directors and prospective volunteers for future projects like to know how each expedition is organized, Pablo wants you to create an organization chart showing the people involved in the Peru expedition. An **organization chart** is a diagram of boxes connected with lines, showing the hierarchy of positions within an organization. Fortunately, PowerPoint provides a feature for easily creating and modifying an organization chart.

Reference Window

Creating an Organization Chart

- Change the slide layout to one of the Content layouts, click the Insert Diagram or Organization Chart button in the content placeholder, click the Organization Chart button, and then click the OK button.
- Type the personnel names, positions, and other information, as desired, into the boxes of the organization chart.
- To add new boxes, click the Insert Shape list arrow on the Organization Chart toolbar, and then click the desired box.
- Select the organization chart boxes and modify the font and fill color if desired.
- Click anywhere outside the organization chart area.

Now you'll insert a new Slide 14 and create an organization chart.

To create an organization chart:

1. Go to **Slide 13** ("Expedition Volunteers"), insert a new Slide 14, give the slide the title **Expedition Organization**, change the slide layout to **Title and Content**, and then close the task pane.

2. Click the **Insert Diagram or Organization Chart** button 🔄 in the content placeholder to open the Diagram Gallery dialog box, click the **Organization Chart** icon (the first icon in the first row), and then click the **OK** button. PowerPoint creates a skeleton of a basic organization chart and displays the Organization Chart toolbar, as shown in Figure 3-26. Now you'll add text to the boxes in the organization chart, delete some boxes, and add new boxes to create the desired chart.

Figure 3-26 | New Slide 14 with organization chart

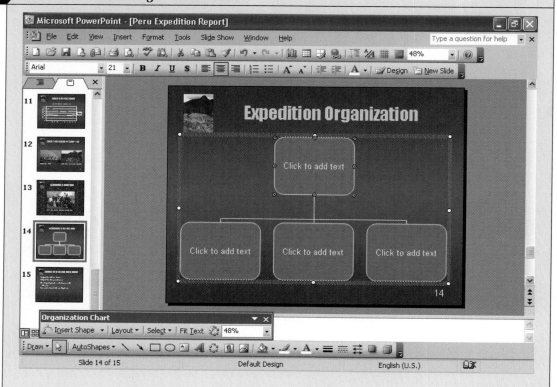

3. Click the **top (level 1)** box of the organization chart. A light-blue insertion point, which might be hard to see, blinks in the center of the box.

4. Type **Pablo Fuentes**, press the **Enter** key, and then type **Expedition Coordinator**. The text you typed replaces the placeholder text in the box. The text overlaps the edges of the box. You'll fix this later.

5. Click outside of the level 1 box, but inside the organization chart area, to deselect the level 1 box but keep the organization chart active.

Now you'll delete all but one of the three boxes on level 2 because only one person, Ken Van Wagoner, is on the level below Pablo in the organization chart.

To modify an organization chart:

1. Click the edge of the first box in level 2. The gray selection handles at the corners of the box indicate that it's been selected. See Figure 3-27.

Preparing to delete an organization chart box   Figure 3-27

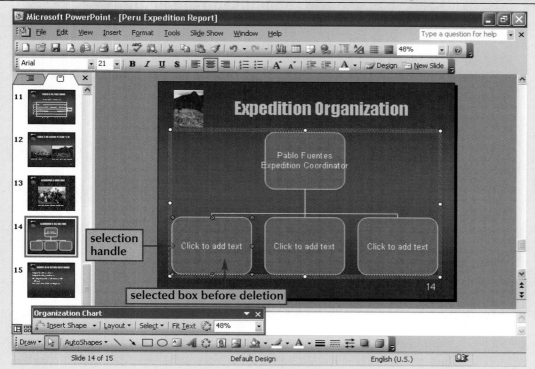

Trouble? If the box has a hatched line around it and no selection handles, click the edge of the box again.

2. Press the **Delete** key to delete the selected box, and when the next box in that row automatically becomes selected, press the **Delete** key again to delete it. Now you should have only one box in level 2.

3. Click in the **level 2** box, type **Ken Van Wagoner**, press the **Enter** key, and then type **Expedition Leader**. Now you're ready to add level 3 boxes below Ken Van Wagoner.

4. Click the **Insert Shape** list arrow on the Organization Chart toolbar, click **Subordinate**, click in the new **level 3** box, and then type **Cultural Team Leader**. You won't type a name associated with the various team leaders because Pablo's audience doesn't know the expedition volunteers, and is interested only in the organization. Now you'll insert a box for another team leader, a co-worker of the cultural team leader.

5. Click the **Insert Shape** list arrow on the Organization Chart toolbar, click **Coworker**, click in the new level 3 box, and then type **Medical Team Leader**.

6. Insert another level 3 co-worker box with the text **Educational Team Leader**, and then click anywhere on the slide outside the organization chart. Compare your Slide 14 to Figure 3-28.

| Figure 3-28 | Organization chart with first three levels completed |

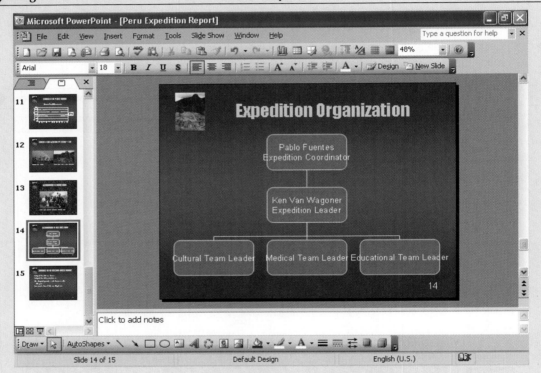

You've made good progress on the organization chart and have to add only three more boxes, subordinates to the Medical Team Leader box.

7. Click anywhere in the organization chart to activate it, and then click the edge of the **Medical Team Leader** box to select it.

8. Click the **Insert Shape** button on the Organization Chart toolbar. You don't have to use the list arrow because the default is to insert a subordinate box. Your chart now has a level 4 box. PowerPoint draws a bent line from the bottom of the Medical Team Leader box to the side of the new subordinate box, but you want a line straight down from the Medical Team Leader box.

9. With the Medical Team Leader box still selected, click **Layout** on the Organization Chart toolbar, and then click **Standard**. Now the subordinate is connected with a straight line to the Medical Team Leader box.

10. Click in the **level 4** box, and then type **Health Team**.

11. Insert two more level 4 boxes to the right of the Health Team box, one with the text **Hygiene Team** and the other with the text **Dental Team**, and then click outside the chart area to deselect the organization chart. Your chart should look like Figure 3-29.

Slide 14 with all boxes of organization chart ◄ **Figure 3-29**

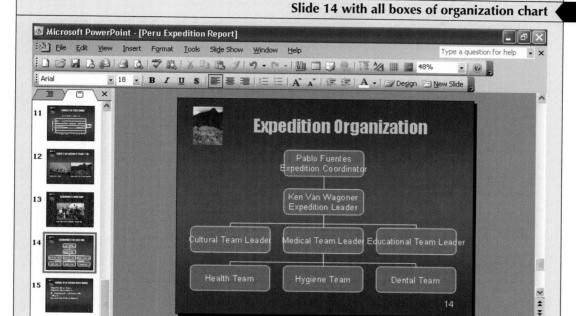

You completed all the organization chart boxes. Pablo looks over this slide and tells you that he thinks yellow text on a dark-brown background would be better for this chart than the default colors of white text on a light-brown background. He also wants you to increase the font size to make the text more legible. Now you'll modify the chart accordingly.

To change font size and color, change the fill color, and make other adjustments:

1. Click anywhere in the organization chart to make it active, press and hold the mouse button, drag from the far upper-left corner of the organization chart area to the lower-right corner to select all elements of the chart (so that a dotted-line border surrounds all of the organization chart boxes), and then release the mouse button. Selection handles appear on all the selected boxes of the chart. Make sure all of the boxes are selected.

Trouble? If some of the boxes aren't selected, press and hold the Ctrl key, and then click them.

You'll start by changing the font size and color.

2. Click the **Font Size** list arrow on the Formatting toolbar, and then click **16**. The font size of the selected boxes changes to 16 points.

3. Click the **Font Color** list arrow ▲ ▾ on the Formatting toolbar, and then click the yellow tile in the color palette. The font color of all the organization chart text changes to yellow.

4. Click the **Fill Color** list arrow on the Drawing toolbar, and then click the dark-brown tile located on the far left of the color palette. The box fill color changes to dark brown.

5. Click a blank area of the slide to deselect the chart. See Figure 3-30.

Figure 3-30 **Slide 14 with completed organization chart**

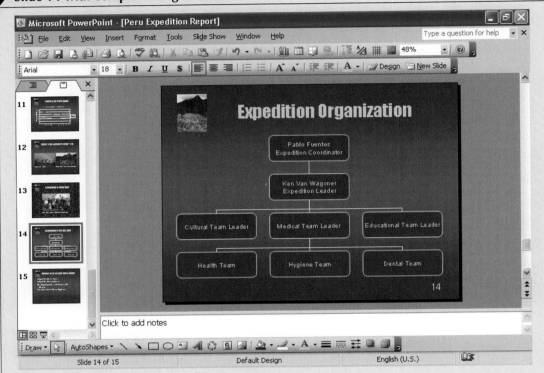

Trouble? If the text doesn't fit inside any of the boxes, click the edge of the box to display the selection handles, drag the left-center or right-center selection handle until the box is large enough to contain the text, and then drag the entire box to position it so it doesn't overlap with other boxes.

6. Save the presentation.

This completes Slide 14 with its organization chart, and completes the text and content of all the slides in the Peru Expedition Report presentation. The only thing left to do is add some special effects and animations.

Applying Special Effects

Special effects—such as causing one slide to fade out as another slide appears, animated (moving) text, and sound effects—can liven up your presentation, help hold your audience's attention, and emphasize key points. On the other hand, special effects can also distract or even annoy your audience. Your goal is to apply special effects conservatively and tastefully so that, rather than making your presentation look gawky and amateurish, they add a professional look and feel to your slide show.

Reference Window

Using Special Effects

- Don't feel that you must include special effects in your slides. Special effects can distract your audience from the message of the presentation. When in doubt, leave them out.
- If you include transitions, use only one type of transition for all the slides. This will keep your audience from trying to guess what the next transition will be and, instead, will help them stay focused on your message.
- If you include animation, use only one type of animation for all the bulleted lists in the slides. This will keep your presentation consistent and conservative.
- Use sound effects sparingly, just enough to provide emphasis, but not enough to distract the audience from your message.

Pablo wants you to add a few special effects to your presentation. The first special effect that you will add is a slide transition.

Adding Slide Transitions

A slide **transition** is a method of moving one slide off the screen and bringing another slide onto the screen during a slide show. Although applying transitions is usually easier in Slide Sorter view because you can easily select several (or all) slides at once, you can also apply a transition in Normal view.

Reference Window

Adding Slide Transitions

- Switch to Slide Sorter view, and then select the slide(s) to which you want to add a transition.
- Click the Transition button on the Slide Sorter toolbar to display the Slide Transition task pane.
- Click the desired transition effect in the Slide Transition task pane.
- Set the speed, if desired.

You'll add a transition to all the slides in the presentation.

To add a transition effect:

1. Click the **Slide Sorter View** button ⊞ to switch to Slide Sorter view, click the **Zoom** list arrow on the Standard toolbar, and then click a percentage that enables you to see all 15 slides at once. On some screens, no change is needed; on others, the zoom might need to be changed to 50% to make all the slides fit in the window.

2. Click **Edit** on the menu bar, and then click **Select All** (or press the **Ctrl+A** key combination) to select all the slides. Now when you apply a slide transition, all the slides will have that transition.

3. Click the **Transition** button on the Slide Sorter toolbar. The Slide Transition task pane opens.

   Trouble? If the Transition button is not visible on the Slide Sorter toolbar, click the Toolbar Options button ⊠ on the Slide Sorter toolbar to see the rest of the buttons on the Slide Sorter toolbar.

4. Scroll down the **Apply to selected slides** list box in the task pane, and then click **Dissolve**. PowerPoint demonstrates the dissolve transition in the slide thumbnails in the slide sorter pane, and a transition icon appears below the lower-left corner of each slide. See Figure 3-31.

Figure 3-31	**Completed presentation with Dissolve transition applied to all slides**

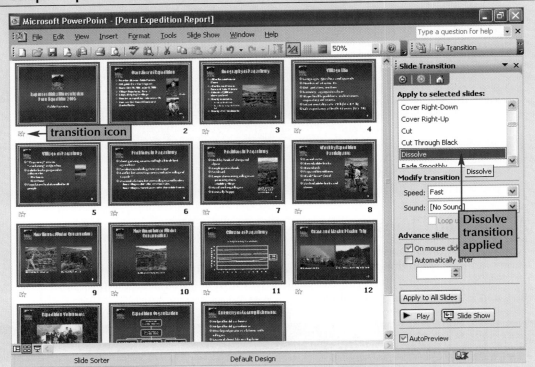

You can change the speed of the dissolve using the Modify transition section of the Slide Transition task pane.

▶ **5.** Click the **Speed** list arrow in the task pane, and then click **Medium**. The transition speed is now set to medium.

▶ **6.** Make sure that the **On mouse click** check box in the task pane is checked, and that the **Automatically after** check box is not.

▶ **7.** Click a blank area of the slide sorter pane to deselect the slides. You'll test the transition by clicking a transition icon.

▶ **8.** Click the **transition** icon below Slide 2. PowerPoint momentarily displays the Slide 1 image at that location, and then performs the dissolve transition to Slide 2. Click any of the transition icons to see how the transition looks for that slide.

When Pablo advances the slide show from one slide to another, each slide will dissolve onto the screen. Now that you've added transitions to the slides, you're ready to add animation.

Applying a Built-In Animation Scheme

An **animation scheme** is a special visual or audio effect applied to an object, such as a graphic or a bulleted list, on a slide. For example, you can add an animation effect to display bulleted items on a slide one item at a time. This process is called **progressive disclosure**. When a slide with a bulleted list has a progressive disclosure animation effect added, only the slide title appears when you first display the slide in your slide show.

Then, when you click the left mouse button (or press the spacebar), the first bulleted item appears. When you click the left mouse button again, the second bulleted item appears, and so on. The advantage of this type of animation effect is that you can focus your audience's attention on one item at a time, without the distractions of items that you haven't discussed yet.

Applying an Animation Scheme

- In Slide Sorter view, select the slide(s) to which you want to add an animation effect.
- Click the Design button on the Slide Sorter toolbar, and then click the Animation Schemes link in the Slide Design task pane.
- Click the desired animation effect displayed in the task pane.

PowerPoint supports three general types of animations: Subtle (the simplest and most conservative animations), Moderate (moderately simple and moderately conservative animations), and Exciting (more complex and less conservative animations). For academic or business presentations, you should generally stick with Subtle or maybe Moderate animations. If you're giving a casual or informal presentation, such as one describing a group game or explaining an exciting travel vacation, you might want to use Exciting animations. For this presentation, you will apply a Moderate animation.

Note that if you apply an animation effect after applying a slide transition, the animation effect will override the transition previously applied. On the other hand, if you apply a transition effect after applying an animation effect, both effects will be applied.

Now you'll add an animation effect to the bulleted lists in Pablo's presentation. For some presentations, you might include only one or two animation effects, but Pablo wants to try various animation effects before he completes his final presentation.

To add an animation scheme:

1. In Slide Sorter view, click **Slide 2**, press and hold the **Shift** key, and then click **Slide 8** to select the first seven slides that have bulleted lists.

2. Click the **Design** button on the Slide Sorter toolbar to display the Slide Design task pane, and then click the **Animation Schemes** link in the task pane. A list of the PowerPoint built-in animations appears in the task pane.

   Trouble? If the Design button is not visible on the Slide Sorter toolbar, click the Toolbar options button 🔳 on the Slide Sorter toolbar to see the rest of the buttons on the Slide Sorter toolbar.

3. Scroll down the **Apply to selected slides** list box until you see the **Moderate** animations, and then click **Ascend**. PowerPoint demonstrates the Ascend animation on each of the selected slides.

   Trouble? If the animation doesn't show automatically, click the AutoPreview check box at the bottom of the task pane to select it.

4. Click **Slide 15**, the only other slide with a bulleted list, to select it, and then apply the **Ascend** animation to it.

5. Close the task pane.

You'll test the transitions and animation effects you applied to the presentation.

To run a slide show with transitions and animation effects:

► **1.** Click **Slide 1**, and then click the **Slide Show from current slide** button 🖵. Slide 1 appears in Slide Show view by dissolving onto the screen.

► **2.** Click the left mouse button. The title of Slide 2 appears on the screen.

► **3.** Click the left mouse button again. The first bulleted item on Slide 2 appears and ascends up the screen to its final location.

► **4.** Continue clicking the left mouse button to progress through the slide show, and then return to Slide Sorter view.

► **5.** Save the presentation.

Next, you'll apply a custom animation effect to Slide 2.

Applying Custom Animation

The built-in animation schemes offer you many ways to display titles and bulleted items on the screen, but they don't allow you to change the color of previously viewed bulleted items, animate other types of objects (user-added text boxes, sound icons, pictures, and so forth), add sound effects to animations, or change the order of animations. To do these types of things, you have to apply custom animations.

For example, in Slide 2, Pablo wants you to modify the presentation to do the following:

• Add a sound effect to each bulleted item so that it makes a "whooshing" sound when the item appears on the screen during the slide show.
• Dim (change color) each bulleted item after the next bulleted item appears on the screen.
• Animate the sound icon to appear on screen after the bulleted item that contains the word "Paqarimuy."
• Animate the two pictures, along with their captions, so that they appear after the bulleted list.

You'll apply these custom animations to Slide 2 now.

To apply custom animations:

► **1.** Double-click **Slide 2** to switch to Normal view with Slide 2 in the slide pane.

► **2.** Click **Slide Show** on the menu bar, and then click **Custom Animation**. The Custom Animation task pane opens, and a number appears next to each bulleted item in the slide pane. PowerPoint automatically assigns a number to each animated item in the slide. If you animate additional objects on a slide, PowerPoint will assign them new numbers. You use the numbers to help you customize the animation. These numbers do not appear in Slide Show view. The sound icon has a pointing finger next to it. This indicates that you chose to have the sound played when the mouse is clicked instead of playing automatically when the slide appears during a slide show. See Figure 3-32.

Slide 2 with animated text ◀ **Figure 3-32**

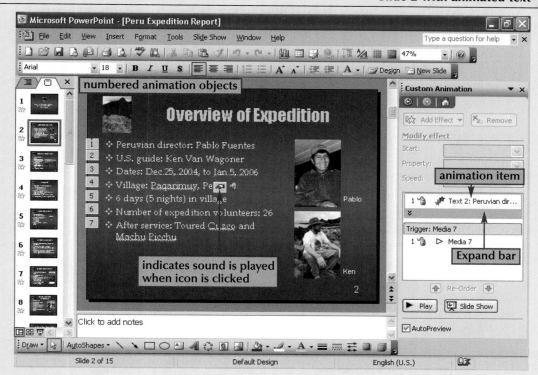

3. Click anywhere within the **bulleted list** text box to select it. This box contains animation items 1 through 7, but only item 1 (called Text 2) appears in the Custom Animation task pane. Because the other items are part of the same text box, PowerPoint doesn't usually display them.

4. In the task pane, click the animation item **1, Text 2: Peruvia...** list arrow, and then click **Effect Options** to display the Ascend dialog box.

5. Click the **Sound** list arrow, drag the scroll bar down to the bottom, and then click **Whoosh** to add this sound effect to the progressive disclosure.

   Trouble? If a message appears telling you that sound effects are not installed, check with your instructor or technical support person if you are working in a lab. If you are working on your own computer, click the Yes button to install the feature now.

6. Click the **After animation** list arrow, and then click the gray tile (the right-most tile in the color palette).

7. Click the **OK** button. The slide automatically animates the progressive disclosure.

   Trouble? If you don't hear anything, you may not have a sound card in your computer system, or you may need to turn up the volume.

You applied custom animation effects to the bulleted list in Slide 2. Next, you'll animate the sound icon so that it appears on the screen along with bulleted item number 4 ("Village: Paqarimuy, Peru") because the sound clip gives the pronunciation of "Paqarimuy."

To animate the sound icon:

1. Click a blank area of the slide to deselect the text box, and then click the **sound** icon to select it. Sizing handles appear at each corner of the object, and the animation item Media 7 is selected in the task pane.

2. Click the **Add Effect** button at the top of the task pane, point to **Entrance**, and then click **Fly In**. The sound icon animates by flying in from the bottom, and the icon that indicated the sound is played on a mouse click changes to animation number 8. You'll change the animation so that the icon flies in from the right.

   Trouble? If you don't see Fly In on the Entrance list, click More Effects to open the Add Entrance Effect dialog box, and then click Fly In.

3. With the sound icon still selected, click the **Direction** list arrow in the task pane, and then click **From Right**. You decide to leave the speed at Very Fast. Now you'll change the animation order by moving the sound icon up just below animation object.

4. Click the **Expand bar** in the task pane just below animation item 1, Text 2 Peruvian dir... to display all the bulleted items, 1 through 7.

5. Click animation item **8, Media 7** in the task pane, if necessary, and then click the **Re-Order Up Arrow** button near the bottom of the task pane three times so that animation item Media 7 is just below animation item 4, Village: Paqarim.... See Figure 3-33.

Figure 3-33	Slide 2 with sound icon set to animate after animation item 4

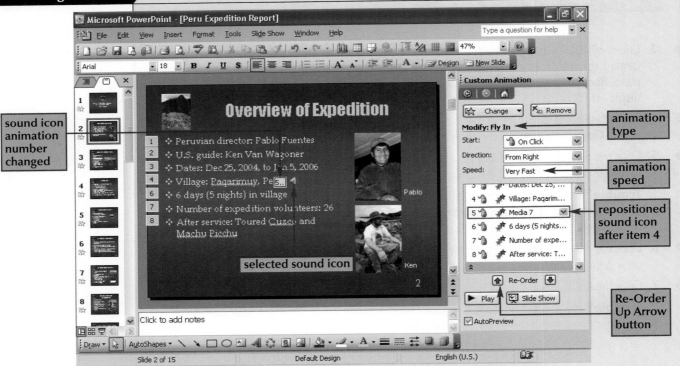

6. Click the **Play** button at the bottom of the task pane to see and hear the animations in Slide 2.

Your final task in Slide 2 is to animate the two pictures and their captions so they appear on the slide after the bulleted list.

To animate the pictures and their captions:

▶ **1.** Click the picture of Pablo, animate it with the **Entrance** effect to **Fly In**, and then set the Direction to **From Right**.

▶ **2.** Animate the text box "Pablo" with the same animation effect as the photo.

▶ **3.** Animate the picture of Ken and the text box "Ken" so that they also fly in from the right. After you animate these objects, each one will be listed on the task pane. See Figure 3-34.

Slide 2 with picture and caption animation | **Figure 3-34**

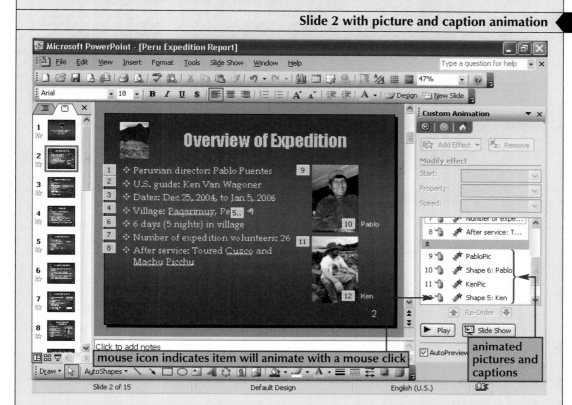

Notice that each animated object listed in the Custom Animation task pane has a mouse icon next to it, as indicated in Figure 3-34. The mouse icon indicates that during the slide show, the animation for that item occurs when someone clicks the left mouse button (or presses the spacebar). Pablo wants the sound icon, the pictures, and the captions to animate automatically, without the presenter clicking the mouse button. You'll set these objects to animate automatically now.

To change how animation occurs during a slide show:

▶ **1.** In the slide pane, click the **sound** icon, press and hold the **Ctrl** key, and then click each of the two pictures and their captions so that animation items 5 and 9 through 12 are selected.

▶ **2.** Click the **Start** list arrow near the top of the task pane, and then click **With Previous**. This means that during the slide show, the animation of these items will start at the same time as the animation of the previous object. In other words, it will animate automatically, without a mouse click. Now all these objects animate automatically. See Figure 3-35.

Figure 3-35 **Slide 2 after completing custom animation**

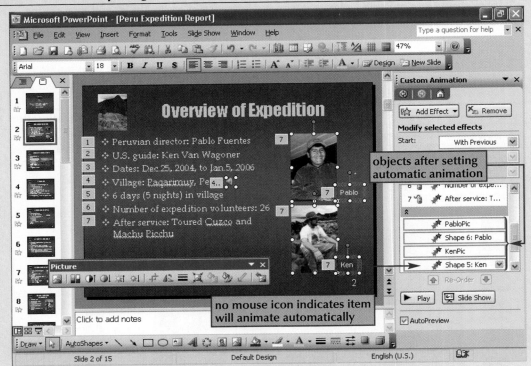

3. Click the **Slide Show from current slide** button 🖵 at the bottom of the task pane to begin the slide show with Slide 2, and then press the **spacebar** seven times to display each of the seven bulleted items.

4. Press the **spacebar** once more to dim the seventh bulleted item, and then click the **sound** icon to hear the pronunciation of "Paqarimuy."

5. Press the **Esc** key to return to Normal view rather than going on to the other slides.

6. Go to **Slide 6** and animate the sound icon so that it has the same custom effect as the sound icon in Slide 2 (fly in from the right), and then set it to appear at the same time as the third bulleted item by repositioning it in the animation items list in the task pane so that it is listed immediately after the third bulleted item, and then setting its Start option to With Previous.

7. Start the slide show from Slide 6 and test the animation to make sure that the sound icon flies automatically from the right at the same time as the third bulleted item, and then end the slide show.

8. Close the task pane, and then save the presentation.

This completes the presentation. You could edit each slide, one at a time, with custom animations to focus on key information or to add interest and excitement to the slide. But Pablo feels that the presentation has enough animation.

Now you'll run through the entire slide show to see how all the animation effects, transitions, the video clip, and so on will appear.

To run through the entire slide show:

1. Go to **Slide 1**, and then click the **Slide Show from current slide** button 🖵. The slide show starts with Slide 1 dissolving onto the screen. This is the transition effect you added.

2. Click the left mouse button or press the **spacebar** to move to Slide 2, advance through the animation of the bulleted list, and then click the **sound** icon on the slide after you dim the seventh bulleted item.

3. Continue through the slide show until the title of Slide 5 ("Village of Paqarimuy") appears on the screen, click the left mouse button or press the **spacebar** three more times to display the three bulleted items. The movie starts after the last bulleted item appears on screen, and plays continuously.

4. Advance to **Slide 6** ("Problems in Paqarimuy"), click the **sound** icon on this slide at the appropriate time, and then continue advancing through the slide show.

5. When you have finished viewing the slide show, go to **Slide 1**, replace Pablo's name in the subtitle with your name, and then save the presentation.

6. Print the presentation in grayscale as handouts, with six slides per page.

Pablo now wants to practice his presentation, including marking slides with the pointer pen.

Using the Pointer Pen to Mark Slides During a Slide Show

The **pointer pen** is a PowerPoint mouse pointer icon that allows you to draw lines on the screen during a slide show. For example, you might use it to underline a word or phrase that you want to emphasize, or to circle a graphic that you want to point out. After you go through a presentation and mark it, PowerPoint gives you the choice of keeping the markings or discarding them. Now you'll show Pablo how to use the pointer pen.

To use the pointer pen during a slide show:

1. Go to **Slide 3** and start the slide show.

2. Press the **spacebar** five times to display the last bulleted item ("Nearby river: Urubamba") in Slide 3. You want to underline the phrase "13,500 feet" to emphasize that Paqarimuy is a very high-altitude village.

3. Move the mouse until you see the mouse pointer, and then click the **Pen** icon ✎, located in the lower-left corner of the screen to open a menu. The Pen icon and others appear only when you move the mouse, and they appear as transparent until you position the pointer over them.

4. Click **Felt Tip Pen**, which changes the mouse pointer to a red-filled circle. By clicking and dragging the pen on the screen, you can draw lines.

5. Move the pointer below the "1" in "13,500," press and hold the left mouse button, and then drag the pointer from left to right to draw a line below "13,500 feet." See Figure 3-36.

Figure 3-36 ▶ Slide 3 with ink mark

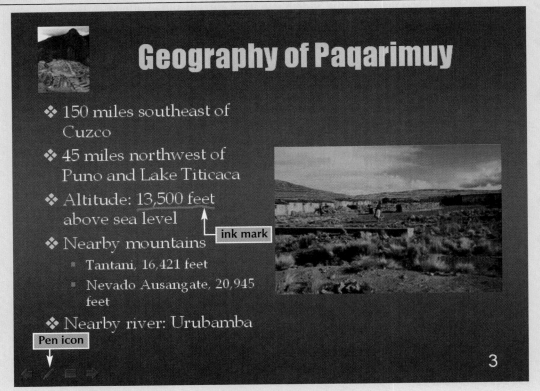

6. Press the **spacebar** to move to the next slide. Note that you cannot click the left mouse button to proceed through the slide show while a pointer pen is selected.

7. Click the **Pen** icon in the lower-left corner, and then click **Arrow**. The mouse pointer changes back to the ordinary arrow pointer.

8. Press the **Esc** key to terminate the slide show. A dialog box appears asking if you want to keep your annotations.

9. Click the **Discard** button. Slide 4 appears in the slide pane in Normal view.

As you can see, the pointer pen is a powerful tool for highlighting and pointing out information during a slide show.

Hiding Slides

Pablo decides that he can also use most of the slides in this presentation for prospective expedition volunteers; however, all of the slides are not appropriate for the volunteers. For example, he doesn't feel that Slide 11 ("Climate of Paqarimuy") with its temperature chart, will be of interest to most potential expedition volunteers. One solution is to temporarily hide that slide so it won't show up during the presentation.

You'll demonstrate how to hide and unhide a slide.

To hide and unhide a slide:

▶ **1.** Go to **Slide 11**, click **Slide Show** on the menu bar, and then click **Hide Slide**. The slide remains in the slide pane in Normal view, but PowerPoint marks the slide number in the Slides tab so that you know the slide will be hidden during the slide show. See Figure 3-37. Now you'll see your slides in Slide Show view.

Slide 11 after hiding slide ◀ **Figure 3-37**

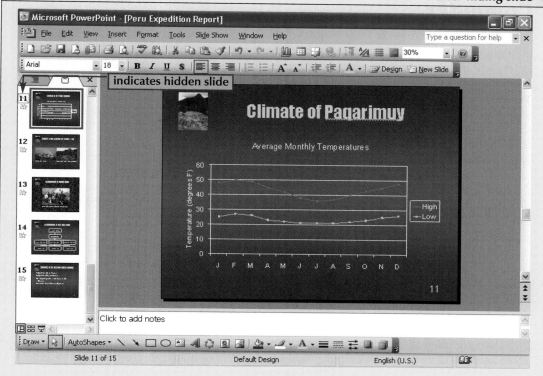

▶ **2.** Go to **Slide 10**, and then click the **Slide Show from current slide** button ▣.

▶ **3.** Press the **spacebar** or click the left mouse button. Slide 12 ("Cuzco and Machu Picchu Trip") appears on the screen. The slide show skips Slide 11 ("Climate of Paqarimuy") as you intended.

▶ **4.** Press the **Esc** key to end the slide show. Slide 12 appears in the slide pane in Normal view.

Now that you've seen how to hide a slide, you should go back and "unhide" it so it will be available for Pablo's presentation to the board of directors.

To unhide a slide:

▶ **1.** Go to **Slide 11**, click **Slide Show** on the menu bar, and then click **Hide Slide**. This toggles the Hide Slide effect off for Slide 11. The hidden slide icon disappears from the Slides tab.

▶ **2.** Go to **Slide 10**, switch to Slide Show view, and then press the **spacebar** to view Slide 11, verifying that it does indeed show up in the slide show now.

▶ **3.** Return to Normal view, and then save the presentation.

Pablo is now confident that his presentation will go smoothly, providing the needed information to his audiences in an engaging manner. Your final tasks are to help him prepare the materials to run not only on his computer, but also on the computers in the rooms where he'll give his presentations.

Preparing the Presentation to Run on Another Computer

Pablo will present the electronic (on-screen) slide show to the board of directors in a suitably equipped conference room at Global Humanitarian; however, he might be using computers without PowerPoint to give presentations to potential volunteers. He knows that he doesn't need PowerPoint installed because he can use PowerPoint Viewer. **PowerPoint Viewer** is a separate program that you can use to give your slide show on any Windows 95/98/2000/NT/XP computer. The Microsoft PowerPoint license allows you to create a Viewer disk and install the Viewer program on other computers without additional charge. Pablo asks you to use the Package for CD feature to create a CD that contains the PowerPoint Viewer files and a copy of his presentation. **Package for CD** places the entire presentation on a CD so you can take the presentation and show it on any computer with the Viewer program. Pablo can then use this CD to install PowerPoint Viewer and run the presentation file on any computer. Although Pablo can't modify any of the slides using PowerPoint Viewer, he can review the entire slide show, including special effects, and he can use the pen pointer during the slide show.

Pablo wants to make sure that whatever computer he uses, the fonts (Impact and Book Antiqua) are available, so he'll save the presentation with embedded fonts. With embedded fonts, the presentation will always have the desired fonts, regardless of whether they are installed on the computer where you give the slide show. Be aware, however, that embedding fonts increases the size of the presentation file, so you want to embed fonts only if necessary.

Before completing the following steps, consult with your instructor. You'll need a computer with a CD writer (often called a "CD burner") and a blank, unused, writable CD.

To save a file with embedded fonts, and use Package for CD:

1. Click **File** on the menu bar, and then click **Save As** to display the Save As dialog box.

2. Click **Tools** on the dialog box toolbar, and then click **Save Options**. The Save Options dialog box opens.

3. Click the **Embed TrueType fonts** check box to select it, and then click the **OK** button. (In some cases, you might want to select the Embed characters in use only check box to save disk space, but the risk in this is that if you need to add text to your presentation, you might not find the needed characters.)

4. Click the **Save** button in the dialog box, and then click the **Yes** button when you're asked if you want to replace the existing file. The **Peru Expedition Report** file is now saved with the fonts embedded so it will have the same appearance on computers that might not have those fonts.

5. Click **File** on the menu bar, and then click **Package for CD**. The Package for CD dialog box opens.

   Trouble? If the Package for CD feature isn't installed, PowerPoint will ask you if you want to install it now. If you are working in a lab, ask your instructor or technical support person for assistance; if you are working on your own computer, click the Yes button.

6. Type **Peru Expedition** in the Name the CD text box. See Figure 3-38.

Package for CD dialog box ◄ **Figure 3-38**

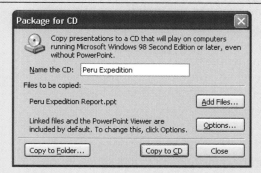

▶ **7.** Click the **Copy to CD** button. The CD drive drawer on your computer automatically opens, and a message appears asking you to insert a blank CD into the drive.

▶ **8.** Place a blank, writable CD in the CD drive and close the drawer, and then click the **Retry** button. PowerPoint copies the presentation files and PowerPoint Viewer to the CD. This might take a minute or so. When the copying is complete, the CD drawer opens again, and PowerPoint asks if you want to make another copy.

▶ **9.** Click the **No** button in the dialog box, and then click the **Close** button in the Package for CD dialog box.

▶ **10.** Close the PowerPoint program window without saving any changes to the presentation.

▶ **11.** Remove the CD from the CD drive.

You can now test the CD with your PowerPoint presentation.

To run the PowerPoint presentation from a CD:

▶ **1.** Insert the CD that you just created into the CD drive and close the drawer. A dialog box appears containing the PowerPoint Viewer license agreement.

▶ **2.** Click the **Accept** button. The dialog box closes and the slide show starts automatically.

▶ **3.** Go through the slide show.

Trouble? If the movie does not play automatically on Slide 5, click it to play it, and then click it again to stop it. Sometimes, media clips do not play automatically when you use the Viewer.

Trouble? If the presentation doesn't work exactly as you prepared it, don't worry. Some features don't translate to the CD exactly.

▶ **4.** After the blank screen appears at the end of the presentation, click the left mouse button or press the **spacebar** to end the presentation.

You give the CD to Pablo so he can show his presentation on any computer that has a CD drive.

You've completed Pablo's presentation. He believes that the graphics, sound, and special effects for the on-screen slide show will help his audience stay focused on his presentation. He thanks you for your help.

Session 3.2 Quick Check

1. Describe how to insert a chart into a slide.
2. What is an organization chart?
3. How do you insert an organization chart into a slide?
4. Define the following terms:
   a. transition effect
   b. animation effect
   c. progressive disclosure
   d. sound effect
   e. pointer pen
5. Describe how to add a transition effect to a slide.
6. What is PowerPoint Viewer?

Tutorial Summary

In this tutorial, you learned how to insert slides from another presentation and create a design template by creating a custom color scheme and background and by changing the typeface and color of the font. You also learned how to add a background image, apply graphics and sound in the form of digital images, video clips, and audio clips, and add a textured background. You learned how to create a chart (graph) and an organization chart, and how to apply special effects such as slide transitions and animations. Finally, you learned how to use the pointer pen to mark slides during a slide show, hide a slide, and prepare a presentation to run on another computer.

Key Terms

active cell	digital movie	progressive disclosure
animated GIF	gradient fill	shading style
animation scheme	graph	special effect
cell	organization chart	transition
chart	Package for CD	variant
color scheme	pointer pen	video clip
datasheet	PowerPoint Viewer	

Review Assignments

Data Files needed for the Review Assignments: CuzcTour.ppt, PeruLogo.jpg, PeruExp.ppt, Cuzco.wav, SacsSnd.avi, MachPicc.wav, HuaynaP.wav, SacsMov.wav

A key attraction to potential volunteers of the humanitarian expeditions is the tour of Peru after the service project. Pablo wants to create a PowerPoint presentation that focuses on the tourism part of the Peru expedition. He wants to provide prices, dates, pictures, and other details about the tour of the Cuzco and Machu Picchu areas of Peru. He asks you to help him create the presentation.

1. Open the presentation file **CuzcTour** from the Tutorial.03\Review folder included with your Data Files, change the name on Slide 1 from Pablo Fuentes to your name, and then save the presentation as **Cuzco Machu Picchu Tour** to your high-capacity disk (your hard disk or a Zip disk).
2. Apply the built-in color scheme for the Default Design template that has a black background and white text.

3. Change the background of all the slides to a two-color gradient fill using the default colors (Color 1 set to black and Color 2 set to green), with the Horizontal shading style and the variant with black on top and green on the bottom.

4. In the slide master, change the title text to left-aligned yellow and bold, leaving the title font at 44-point Arial. Change the main text (bulleted list text) to Times New Roman and leave it white.

5. In the slide master, change the first-level bullets to yellow squares, and the second-level bullets to medium-blue circles.

6. Also in the slide master, resize the width of the title text box about an inch smaller so that you can insert a logo to the left of the title, and then insert the graphic file **PeruLogo** (in the Tutorial.03\Review folder) and position it to the left of the title text box. Adjust the graphic size and the title text box so they look good together at the top of the slide.

7. Add a title master, and then reposition the logo on the title master so it's centered above the title text box.

8. In Normal view, change the background texture of Slide 1 (only) to Medium Wood.

9. Save the current version of the presentation as a normal presentation file, and then save it as a custom design template to the Tutorial.03\Review folder using the filename **Cuzco Machu Picchu Template**. Make sure you delete any unnecessary slides and text from the template file.

10. Close the design template file, reopen the **Cuzco Machu Picchu Tour** file, and then insert Slide 8, "Expedition Costs (Per Person)," from the presentation file **PeruExp** located in the Tutorial.03\Review folder at the end of the presentation, after Slide 8 ("Organization of Tour Company").

11. In Slide 2, insert the sound file **Cuzco**, located in the Tutorial.03\Review folder, set the sound to play automatically during the slide show, and position the sound icon to the right of the title.

12. Repeat the procedure of the previous step, except insert the sound file **SacsSnd** into Slide 4, the sound file **MachPicc** into Slide 6, and the sound file **HuaynaP** into Slide 7.

13. In Slide 4, insert the movie file **SacsMov**, located in the Tutorial.03\Review folder, and set it to play automatically during the slide show. Resize the movie object to make it easier to see, and set it to loop continuously. (*Hint*: If the sound icon moves, drag it back to its position next to the slide title. If the Title, Text, and Content layout does not apply to the slide, click Insert on the menu bar, point to Movies and Sounds, and then click Movie from File.)

14. In Slide 3, create a chart of the monthly rainfall in Cuzco. Use the following data (month, rainfall in inches): J, 6.0; F, 4.2; M, 4.0; A, 1.8; M, 0.5; J, 0.2; J, 0.1; A, 0.1; S, 0.7; O, 2.2; N, 2.8; D, 4.5. Make sure the Chart type is Column, and set the Chart sub-type to Clustered Column (the first chart sub-type in the first row). Add the Value (Y) axis label "Rainfall (inches)." Don't include a title or a label for the months.

15. Click the legend that PowerPoint automatically inserts to the right of the bar graph to select it, and then press the Delete key. (*Hint*: If the chart is no longer active, double-click it.)

16. In the graph, change the font size of the labels on the Value (Y) axis and the Category (X) axis to 24 points.

17. In Slide 8, create an organization chart. Make a single box at level 1 with the text "U.S. Expedition Head," a single box at level 2 with the text "Local Leader," and three boxes at level 3 with the text "Cuzco Tour Director," "Machu Picchu Tour Director," and "Lima Tour Director." Decrease the font size to 18 points to fit the text in the boxes.

18. Add the Push Up slide transition to all the slides, change the speed to Medium, and add the Camera sound effect to the slide transition.

19. Apply the Moderate animation scheme called Elegant to Slides 2, 4, 6, and 9 (those with bulleted lists). (*Hint*: Press and hold the Ctrl key while you click the slides to select them.)

20. In all the slides with photographs and captions (but not in the slide with the movie), set the pictures to have the Entrance animation called Zoom, set the captions to have the Entrance animation called Appear, and set the photographs to enter after the bulleted list (if any) on a mouse click, and set the caption to appear immediately, without a mouse click, after the picture is on the screen (After Previous).

21. In Slide 6, set the bulleted items to dim after animation. Set the dim color to black.

22. Hide Slide 3, and then go through the slide show. Use the pointer pen to mark words, phrases, pictures, or other objects in the slides. At the end of the show, keep the pen marks.

23. Save the presentation. (Don't unhide Slide 3.)

24. Package the presentation for a CD, and embed the fonts. Name the CD **Cuz-MP Tour**.

25. Print the presentation in grayscale as handouts with six slides per page.

Case Problem 1

Data Files needed for this Case Problem: GeNetics.ppt, Bonnie.jpg, Atorv.jpg, Drugs.jpg, Applause.wav

GeNetics Research Labs Dr. Bonnie Ornatowski, who received her Ph.D. in biochemistry from Bryn Mawr College, is a chief scientist for GeNetics Research Labs, a company based in Cambridge, Massachusetts. GeNetics takes drug formulations developed at university laboratories, tests the drugs, develops the delivery systems, gets approval for sale of the drugs from the Federal Drug Administration (FDA), sells the drugs, and then pays the university and its discoverers a royalty from the profits. Over the past six years, Bonnie has supervised the clinical testing, FDA approval, production, and marketing of a new statin drug, which lowers blood cholesterol, triglycerides (fats), and low-density lipoproteins (LDLs). Recently, Bonnie was selected as Honored Alumni from the College of Science at her alma mater, and was invited to give a presentation on some aspect of her career. She wants you to help her prepare a presentation that explains her career and her work with the new statin drug. Remember to change the slide layouts as needed when you complete the following:

1. Open the presentation file **GeNetics** from the Tutorial.03\Cases folder included with your Data Files, change the name on Slide 1 from Bonnie Ornatowski to your name, and save the presentation to a high-capacity disk using the filename **GeNetics Research Labs**.

2. Apply the design template called Digital Dots, which has a light-blue background and white text.

3. In the slide master, change the title text to light yellow, which is not one of the color scheme colors, but which you can find on the Standard tab of the Colors dialog box.

4. Change the second-level bullet to the same yellow color as you did the title text. Leave it the same character.

5. In the slide master and title master, change the slide number text box to 20-point Arial, switch to Normal view, open the Header and Footer dialog box, and display only the slide number on all of the slides (except the title slide).

6. In Slide 2, change the layout, and then add the digital image of Bonnie, which is the file **Bonnie** in the Tutorial.03\Cases folder. Position the picture to the right side of the slide, and then increase the size of the bulleted list text box so that the first two bulleted paragraphs fit on two lines each. The third one will then fit on three lines. Change the white background of the image to transparent.

7. In Slide 4, add an organization chart. In each box, include a person's name, and below the name, his or her position in the company. Don't include any punctuation in the boxes. In the top-level box, add "Karen Lamb, R&D Vice President." In the second-level boxes, add "Bonnie Ornatowski, Senior Scientist" on the left and "Alberto Thurston, Senior Scientist" on the right. Keep only two boxes on the second level. Below Bonnie, add three boxes: "James Jordan, Team 1A Leader," "Daniel Kelsch, Team 2A Leader," and "Kennedy Guisman, Team 3A Leader."

8. In Slide 7, change the slide layout to Title and Content over Text, and in the content placeholder, add the chemical structure of atorvastatin, located in the file **Atorv**. Make the size of the structure as large as possible while still fitting between the title text and the bulleted list.

9. In Slide 8, add a bar chart based on the data in the following table:

	Tot Chol	LDL-C	HDL-C	Trigly
Placebo	3	4	-2	9
Zocor	-43	-33	8	-24

10. Change the chart type to clustered column (no 3-D effect), and then add a Value (Y) axis label of "Percent Change."

Explore

11. Change the slide background of Slide 8 to only one color, bright blue (one of the color scheme colors).

12. In Slide 10, add the digital image **Drugs**, located in the Tutorial.03\Cases folder. Change the white background of the image to transparent, and then resize and reposition it to make the slide look attractive.

13. In Slide 11, add the sound clip **Applause**. Set it to play automatically in the slide show. Position the sound icon to the right of "Career" in the title.

14. Set the slide transition for all the slides to Cover Left-Down. Set its speed to Slow. Set its sound to Click.

15. In Slides 3, 9, and 10, set the text to enter by fading in one by one.

16. In Slide 9, set the bulleted items to dim to bright blue after the next item appears on the screen.

17. In Slide 10, set the image to enter using Center Revolve (under Moderate).

18. Hide Slide 4, and then go through the slide show. Use the pointer pen to make marks on some of the slides as you go through. Keep the pen marks once you're done.

19. Unhide the slide, and save the presentation.

20. Print the presentation in grayscale as handouts with six slides per page.

Challenge

Explore additional PowerPoint features that are associated with the skills you learned in this tutorial to complete a presentation for a small business.

Case Problem 2

Data Files needed for this Case Problem: Alaskan.ppt, ACWBus.ppt, Totem.jpg, Bowls.jpg

Alaskan Creative Woodworks Bobette Perkins of Anchorage, Alaska, has what she thinks is a winning business idea, but she needs money to start a company that will lead from ideas to profits. She has an appointment with the Alaska State Economic Development Agency (ASEDA), which provides small-business loans for promising new businesses and allocates grants for new businesses in economically depressed areas of Alaska. Bobette asks you to help her prepare the presentation of her business plan to the ASEDA. She has supplied information for two short presentations, but now wants you to combine the information and create an attractive, interesting slide show. Complete the following:

1. Open the presentation file **Alaskan**, located in the Tutorial.03\Cases folder included with your Data Files, change the name in Slide 1 from Bobette Perkins to your name, and save the presentation to a high-capacity disk as **Alaskan Creative Woodworks**.

2. Go to Slide 4. After Slide 4 in the current presentation, insert Slides 2, 3, and 4 from the beginning of Bobette's business plan presentation for Alaskan Creative Woodworks, located in the file **ACWBus** in the Tutorial.03\Cases folder.

3. Edit the color scheme according to the following directions: change the Background to a dark brown, Text and lines to white, Shadows to a dark green, Title text to yellow, Fills to a light brown, Accent to a light green, Accent and hyperlink to black, and Accent and followed hyperlink to medium green. Apply the new color scheme to all the slides.

4. Change the background to a two-color gradient fill, with the dark brown Background color in the upper-left corner of the slide, and the light brown Fills color in the bottom-right corner.

5. Change the title text font to 44-point bold Tahoma, if necessary. If your system doesn't have the Tahoma font, select any other TrueType sans serif font except Arial.

6. Change the body text font to Garamond, leaving other font attributes unchanged. If your computer doesn't have the Garamond font, select any other TrueType serif font except Times New Roman or any other Times font.

7. Change the first-level bullets to a yellow square.

8. Change the second-level bullets to a light green filled circle.

9. Save the presentation, and then save it as a design template with only necessary slides and content. Name the template file **Alaskan Creative Woodworks Template** and save it to the same location as your presentation. Close the template file and then reopen the presentation file.

Explore

10. In Slide 3, add an organization chart. In the top box, type "Bobette Perkins" on the first line, "President" on the second line, and "12 Years' Experience" on the third line. Add two second-level boxes, each with three lines; for the one on the left, type the text "Jianyin Shao," "V.P. Marketing," and "8 Years' Experience"; for the one on the right, type the text "Miwako Turley," "V.P. Operations," and "14 Years' Experience." Add two third-level boxes below Jianyin Shao, each with only two lines of text; for the one on the left, type "Karl Jorgensen" and "Advertising Director," and for the one on the right, type "Melissa Platt" and "Marketing Director." Add three subordinates below Miwako Turley, each box with only two lines of text; for the one on the left, type "Paulette Torre" and "Human Resources Director," for the one in the middle, type "Seymour Cleveland" and "Manufacturing Director," and for the one on the right, type "Paul Robertson" and "Executive Secretary."

Explore

11. Change the organization chart style to Bookend Fills. Click the AutoFormat button on the Organization Chart toolbar, click Bookend Fills, and then click the OK button. Insert hard returns, if necessary, in the text lines that don't fit within their boxes so that the text spans two lines.

12. In Slide 6, add a picture of a wooden totem pole, using the file **Totem**. Adjust, as desired, the slide layout, the size and position of the image, and the size of the bulleted list text box to maximize the readability and appearance of the slide. Set the picture to animate onto the screen (immediately, without a mouse click) using the Entrance effect Center Revolve.

13. In Slide 10, add a picture of wooden bowls, using the file **Bowls**. Adjust, as desired, the slide layout, the size and position of the image, and the size of the bulleted list text box to maximize the readability and appearance of the slide. Set the picture to animate in the same way as the one in Slide 6.

14. In Slide 5, add a line chart showing the trend in tourism in Alaska. Set the Chart type to Line with markers displayed at each data value (the first sub-type in the second row). In the datasheet, use the following labels in the top row: "2002," "2003," "2004," and "2005." Use the label "Tourists" in the cell to the left of cell A1. For the number of tourists in each of the above years, type (respectively) "1.25," "1.47," "1.28," and "1.42."

15. Add the Value (Y) axis label "Number of Tourists (in millions)."

Explore

16. In the chart, click the legend to select it, and then press the Delete key to delete the legend.

Explore

17. Change the thickness of the line and the size and color of the markers on the line in the chart. Click the line to select it, right-click it, click Format Data Series on the shortcut menu, and then click the Patterns tab. In the Line section, click the Weight list arrow, and then click the thickest line in the list. In the Marker section, change the size to 15 points, and then change the foreground and background colors of the marker to yellow.

18. Add the Moderate Entrance effect Zoom to the chart. Have the chart appear automatically.

Explore

19. Add the Wipe Left slide transition to Slides 4 through 9. Set the speed to Medium and the sound to Click for that transition effect.

20. Set all the slides with multiple bullets, except those with picture images, to progressive disclosure using the Moderate effect Descend with a dimming color set to a light brown-orange.

21. Go through the presentation in Slide Show view. Use the pointer pen to underline keywords. Keep the marks when you are finished.

22. Save the presentation, and then print the presentation in grayscale as handouts with six slides per page.

23. Package the presentation for a CD.

Case Problem 3

Create

Create slides for a presentation about a rental property company by using the skills you learned in this tutorial.

Data Files needed for this Case Problem: bedrm1.jpg, bedrm2.jpg, cabinfnt.jpg, fireplac.jpg, fitness.jpg, kitchen.jpg, livingrm.jpg

Recreation Rentals, Inc. Linda Halgren is a property agent for Recreation Rentals, Inc. (RRI) of Las Vegas, Nevada. RRI specializes in renting cabins and condos on behalf of their owners. She contacts owners who rent their properties, encourages them to list their properties with her, and then rents the properties to interested vacationers. Recently, Linda signed an agreement with an owner of a cabin located near one of the ski resorts at Lake Tahoe, Nevada. She wrote the text of a PowerPoint presentation and took digital photographs of the property, but she needs your help in creating an exciting presentation to show to potential renters. Create a presentation that looks like Figure 3-39. Select colors, fonts, bullets, and other elements as close to those in Figure 3-39 as you can.

Figure 3-39

Lake Tahoe Rental Cabin

Linda Halgren
Recreation Rentals, Inc
Las Vegas, Nevada
www.recreation-rentals.com
702-555-FENT(702 555-7368)

Bed and Bath

- 3 bedrooms
- 2 full bathrooms
- Walkout decks
- Jetted tub in master bedroom
- Linens and towels provided

2

Living Room

- Fireplace
- All-leather furniture
- Entertainment center
  - 27" color TV
  - Digital cable (HBO, Showtime, ESPN, etc.)
  - 200-watt stereo with 50 CDs
  - VHS and DVD player
- Reading library

3

Kitchen/Dining

- Farm table seats for 8
- Refrigerator
- Dishwasher
- Microwave oven
- Conventional oven
- "Flat-top" range
- Blender and mixer
- Coffee maker
- Telephone

4

Beech Mountain Club

- Free guest membership
- Golf
- Tennis
- Swimming
- Fitness room
- Recreation areas

5

Nearby Activities

- Biking (mountain)
- Bird Watching
- Bowling
- Canoeing
- Golf
- Hiking
- Historic Sites
- Ice Waking
- Miniature golf
- Movies
- Museums
- Rafting
- Rock Climbing
- Site Seeing
- Skiing
- Sledding
- Swimming
- Tennis
- Theatre
- Water sports

6

Average Snow Depth

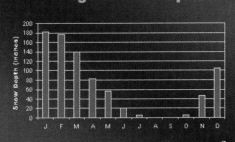

7

Cabin Rates

- Peak seasons (Winter and Summer)
  - $250 per night
  - $800 per week
- Off season (Spring and Fall)
  - $175 per night
  - $650 per week
- Deposit and cleaning fee required
- No smoking, no pets

8

To help you complete the presentation, do the following:

1. Use a color scheme of mostly earth tones—browns, tans, black, white, and grays.
2. Change the background to a two-color gradient fill.
3. Add the digital images provided in the Tutorial.03\Cases folder included with your Data Files to the appropriate slides. Resize the images and the text boxes to maximize readability and appearance. (*Hint*: For slides with two pictures, change the slide layout to Title, Text, and 2 Content.)
4. In the slide on average snow depth, for the average depth from January through December, respectively, use these values: 182, 176, 140, 82, 56, 20, 5, 0, 0, 5, 47, 105.
5. In Slide 1 (only), add the textured background as shown.
6. Add the Newsflash slide transition to all the slides.
7. Customize the animation so that the images animate onto the screen. Once you pick an animation effect, apply the same effect to all the images.
8. Use an animation scheme to set all the slides with multiple bullets to progressive disclosure, with dimming color set to a yellowish color in the color palette.
9. Replace Linda Halgren's name on Slide 1 with your name, save the presentation with the filename **RRI Tahoe Cabin**, and then print the presentation in grayscale as handouts with four slides per page.

Research

Use the Internet to research restaurants in your area and compile the data in a presentation.

Case Problem 4

There are no Data Files needed for this Case Problem.

Comparison of Local Restaurants Students spend a lot of money on food, and new students are always interested in which local restaurants provide the best food and service at a reasonable price. Your task is to conduct a study and compare the prices of at least three restaurants in your area, and then create a PowerPoint presentation to present your results. Do the following:

1. Connect to the Internet and then go to the Web sites of at least three local restaurants of the same general type that have menus posted. Note the prices of similar menu items. Include at least three categories (appetizers, salads, entrees, desserts, breads or baked goods, drinks, and so forth), and in each category, include at least three items.
2. Open a new PowerPoint presentation titled "Comparison of . . ." and list the names of the restaurants that you studied. Add your name as the presenter. Save it using the filename **Local Restaurant Comparison**.
3. Include at least one slide explaining your methodology—how you conducted your study.
4. Include at least one table or chart comparing the relative costs of the restaurants. You'll probably want to organize the presentation with one category per slide.
5. In your presentation, include at least three pictures or clip-art images. You can acquire the pictures from the Internet, scan pictures from magazines, or take your own digital photographs.
6. Include a slide with an organization chart of a typical or representative management structure of a restaurant. Show that organization with positions (but not necessarily names). You might want to send an e-mail to one of the restaurants in your comparison asking how the store's management is set up.
7. Apply an appropriate built-in design template.
8. Apply appropriate slide transitions and custom animations to make your presentation interesting and attractive.

9. Search for sound clips on the Internet and add one or more to your presentation. Try searching for clips of money being counted or a cash register being opened.

10. Select one of the slides that you think your audience might be least interested in, and hide that slide.

11. Save the presentation using the default filename, and then print it as handouts with four or six slides per page.

Internet Assignments

Research

Go to the Web to find information you can use to create presentations.

The purpose of the Internet Assignments is to challenge you to find information on the Internet that you can use to work effectively with this software. The actual assignments are updated and maintained on the Course Technology Web site. Log on to the Internet and use your Web browser to go to the Student Online Companion for New Perspectives Office 2003 at **www.course.com/np/office2003**. Click the Internet Assignments link, and then navigate to the assignments for this tutorial.

Lab Assignments

Reinforce

Multimedia

The New Perspectives Labs are designed to help you master some of the key concepts and skills presented in this text. The steps for completing this Lab are located on the Course Technology Web site. Log on to the Internet and use your Web browser to go to the Student Online Companion for New Perspectives Office 2003 at **www.course.com/np/office2003**. Click the Lab Assignments link, and then navigate to the assignments for this tutorial.

SAM Assessment and Training

Assess

If you have a SAM user profile, you may have access to hands-on instruction, practice, and assessment of the skills covered in this tutorial. Log in to your SAM account and go to your assignments page to see what your instructor has assigned.

Quick Check Answers

Review

Session 3.1

1. Click Insert on the menu bar, click Slides from File to open the Slide Finder dialog box, select the desired PowerPoint file, click the desired slides, and then click the Insert button.

2. the set of matching colors that makes up the background, fonts, and other elements of the presentation

3. background, fonts, font sizes, font colors, bullets, and background graphics

4. a variation of a particular shading style

5. Delete all the slides but one, delete the text and graphics from that slide, click File, click Save As, change the file type to Design Template, and then select the desired filename and folder location.

6. an animated picture file, usually with the filename extension .avi

Session 3.2

1. Change the slide layout to one of the Content layouts, click the Chart button in the content placeholder, edit the datasheet, and then change other chart options as desired.
2. a diagram of boxes, connected with lines, showing the hierarchy of positions within an organization
3. Change the slide layout to one of the Content layouts, click the Diagram button in the content placeholder, select the organization chart, click the OK button, type text into the boxes, and then add and remove organization chart boxes as desired.
4. Definitions:
   a. transition effect: a method of moving one slide off the screen and bringing another slide onto the screen during a slide show
   b. animation effect: a special visual or audio effect applied to an object (such as graphics or bulleted text)
   c. sound effect: a sound that takes place during a slide show
   d. pointer pen: a PowerPoint mouse pointer that allows you to draw lines on the screen during a slide show
5. Select the slide in Slide Sorter view, click the Slide Transition button, and then select a slide transition.
6. PowerPoint Viewer is a separate program that you can use to present your slide show on any Windows 95/98/2000/NT computer.

Objectives

Session 4.1
- Apply a template from another presentation
- Import, modify, and export a Word outline
- Import graphics into a presentation
- Embed and modify a table from Word
- Link and modify an Excel chart

Session 4.2
- Add links to slides within a presentation and to other presentations
- Add action buttons to a presentation
- View a slide show with embedded or linked objects
- Publish a presentation as a Web page
- Learn how to collaborate with workgroups

Labs

The Internet: World Wide Web

Student Data Files

Integrating PowerPoint with Other Programs and Collaborating with Workgroups

Presenting Information About an Annual Banquet

Case

Global Humanitarian, Fundraising

Fundraising is a major activity of Global Humanitarian. Funds are needed to help finance the following: service expeditions; village development projects (build water catchment systems, wells, irrigation systems, culinary water systems, Lorena stoves, greenhouses, schoolhouses, and clinics); student internships; and business mentoring projects. In addition, funds are needed to pay for the necessary administration costs of running this large organization.

▼**Tutorial.04**

▽ **Tutorial folder**

Gala.ppt
GalaOutl.doc
GalaTabl.doc
Gala03.jpg
Gala06.jpg
Gala08.jpg
Gala09.jpg
Gala11.jpg
Gala12.jpg
GHChart.xls
GHMission.ppt

▽ **Review folder**

Chicken.jpg
Crafts.jpg
Dolls.jpg
Guide.jpg
Herd.jpg
Loan.ppt
LoanOtln.doc
Loans.xls
Mentor.jpg
ProjTabl.doc
Taxi.jpg
Weave.jpg

▽ **Cases folder**

GCChat.jpg
GCDes.ppt
GCGroup.jpg
GCOtln.doc
HAOHikes.doc
HAOServ.ppt
HAOTempl.ppt

HeadQ.jpg
Music.ppt
PPCData.xls
PPCDes.ppt
PPCOtln.doc
PPCTbl.doc
Temp.jpg

Global Humanitarian raises funds in the following ways:

- **Direct appeal to individuals and companies.** Development officers meet personally with potential benefactors and follow up with mailings and telephone calls.
- **Web presence.** Global Humanitarian maintains a Web site, and they include a link on the site for people to use to make a donation.
- **Annual Global Humanitarian gala.** The gala is an annual dinner, and it is the biggest fundraising event of the year.

The Global Humanitarian administrators who oversee the annual gala are the top administrators—Norma Flores, president of Global Humanitarian; Miriam Schwartz, managing director of the Austin office; and Pablo Fuentes, managing director of the Lima office. One of their first tasks for organizing the gala is to prepare a presentation for the other administrators and volunteers who will help with the event. Norma asks you to bring together several pieces of previously prepared materials to create an effective PowerPoint presentation about the gala.

In this tutorial, you'll import, modify, and export a Microsoft Word outline to and from your presentation, and you'll import a digital photograph. You will embed and modify a Word table in your presentation and link and modify an Excel chart. You will also create and edit hyperlinks, add action buttons, create and customize a toolbar, and publish a presentation on the World Wide Web.

Session 4.1

Planning the Presentation

Before you begin to create Norma's slide show, she discusses with you her plans for the presentation.

- **Purpose of the presentation**: to present an overview of the fundraising gala and assign responsibilities
- **Type of presentation**: training
- **Audience for the presentation**: Global Humanitarian's employees and volunteers
- **Audience needs**: an overview of the gala and specific task assignments
- **Location of the presentation**: meeting rooms at Global Humanitarian headquarters
- **Format**: on-screen slide show

With the above general plan for the presentation, Norma, Miriam, and Pablo prepare the outline of the presentation, as well as some of the key information about the gala.

Applying a Template from Another Presentation

You already know how to apply a design template from a design template file. You can use a similar method to apply a design from any other presentation file.

For the gala presentation, Norma wants you to use the design template from a presentation she recently prepared about Global Humanitarian's mission and purpose. You'll apply that design template now.

To apply a design template from another presentation:

▶ **1.** Open the file **Gala** from the **Tutorial.04\Tutorial** folder included with your Data Files, and then save the file with the new filename **Gala Planning** to the same folder. The title slide appears on the screen with the name of the two principal presenters, Norma Flores and Miriam Schwartz, listed. The presentation has the Curtain Call design template applied. Notice that this presentation includes only this one slide. See Figure 4-1. You'll add additional slides later.

Title page of new presentation with the Curtain Call design template applied ◀ **Figure 4-1**

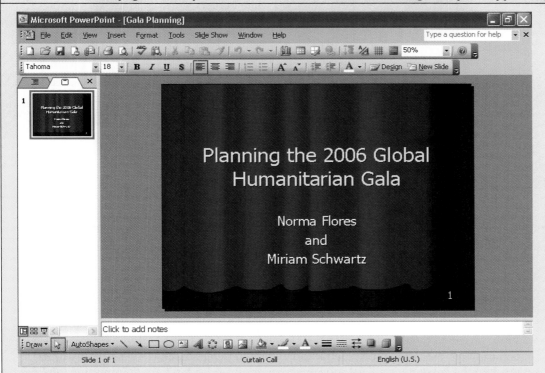

Trouble? If you're using a floppy disk for your Data Files, you won't have enough space to save all of the files you create in this tutorial. If you don't have access to a hard disk or some other high-capacity disk, skip those steps in which you're asked to create a Web page (in the "Publishing Presentations on the World Wide Web" section).

▶ **2.** Click the **Design** button on the Formatting toolbar to display the Slide Design task pane. You won't use one of these built-in template files or a custom slide design, but rather a slide design already created in another presentation file.

▶ **3.** Click the **Browse** link at the bottom of the task pane. The Apply Design Template dialog box opens.

▶ **4.** Click the **Look in** list arrow, navigate to the **Tutorial.04\Tutorial** folder included with your Data Files, and then, if necessary, change the **Files of type** list box to **All PowerPoint Files**. The dialog box displays all the presentation files within the folder. Now you'll select the presentation Norma prepared earlier.

► **5.** Click **GHMission**, and then click the **Apply** button. The design template from the presentation GHMission is applied to the Gala Planning presentation. See Figure 4-2.

Figure 4-2 **Presentation with new design template**

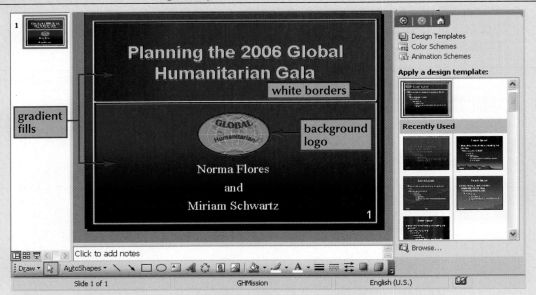

► **6.** Close the task pane, and then save the file with its new design using the default filename.

In Figure 4-2, you can see some of the design elements that Norma created in her original presentation, including the color scheme with a blue-to-black gradient background, yellow title text, white body text, a background graphic of white borders, and the Global Humanitarian logo.

Now you're ready to add additional slides to your presentation. All the slides you will add exist in some format already; your job will be to integrate files created in other programs into the presentation. First, however, you must understand about importing, embedding, and linking objects.

Using Integration Techniques: Importing, Embedding, and Linking

As you learned in Tutorial 1, an **object** is anything in a presentation that you can manipulate as a whole. This includes clip art, photos, and text boxes, as well as other graphics, diagrams, and charts that you've already worked with. In addition, you can insert objects, such as a word-processing document or a spreadsheet chart, that were created in other Office programs. The program in which the objects are created is the **source file**; the program into which the objects are inserted is the **destination file**.

When you insert objects, you either import, embed, or link them. Refer to Figure 4-3 as you read the definitions of each of these following terms.

Integration techniques | **Figure 4-3**

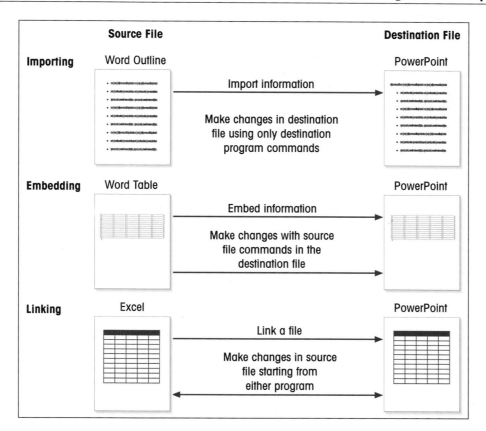

Importing an object means simply copying a file that was created using one program into another program's file. For example, when you insert graphics and sounds into a presentation, you actually import them. Imported objects become part of the PowerPoint presentation. When you import a file, the source program and the destination program don't communicate with each other in any way, as illustrated in Figure 4-3. For example, if you want to modify a graphic (such as change its size or colors) after importing it into PowerPoint, you make these changes in PowerPoint rather than in the graphics program. If you want to access the source program's commands to modify the object, you need to start the source program and then open and modify the file in the source program. To see the changes you made to the object in the destination program, you need to import the object again.

Embedding is similar to importing but allows a one-way connection to be maintained with the source program, not the source file. For example, if you embed a Word table in a PowerPoint presentation and then double-click the table, you will be able to access and use Word commands to edit the table while still in PowerPoint. When you finish editing the embedded table and return to PowerPoint, the changes you made to the table will appear in the object in PowerPoint only; the changes do not appear in the original Word file that you used to create the table. This is because the embedded object is a copy of the original Word file, not the Word file itself. Therefore, if you make subsequent changes to the original Word file using Word, the changes will not be reflected in the embedded Word table in PowerPoint. In other words, an embedded object has no relationship to the original source file, but it does maintain a connection to the source program.

When you **link** an object, you create a connection between the source file and the linked object. You do not place a copy of the source file in the destination file; instead, you place a representation of the actual source file in the destination file. When an object is linked, you can make changes to the source file, and those changes are reflected in the representation of the linked object in the destination program. When you link, for example, an Excel spreadsheet to a PowerPoint slide, the spreadsheet file must be available to the PowerPoint presentation file if you want to edit the file; otherwise, PowerPoint treats the spreadsheet as an embedded file.

You should be aware that not all software allows you to embed or link objects. Only those programs that support **object linking and embedding** (or **OLE**, pronounced oh-LAY) let you embed or link objects from one program to another. Fortunately, sophisticated programs, such as PowerPoint, Word, and Excel, are all OLE-enabled programs and fully support object linking and embedding.

Norma has created an outline in Word listing the text of many of the slides she wants to include in her presentation. Your next task is to import the Word outline into the presentation.

Importing and Exporting a Word Outline

If your presentation contains quite a bit of text, it might be easier to create the outline of your presentation in Word, so that you can take advantage of the extensive text-editing features available in that program. Fortunately, if you create an outline in a Word document, you don't need to retype it in PowerPoint. You can import it directly into your presentation.

Although you can create handouts in PowerPoint, if you want to enhance the handouts using Word's formatting commands to make it easier to read, or use the presentation of the outline as the outline for a more detailed document, you can export the outline to a Word document.

First, you'll import an outline into your presentation.

Importing the Word Outline

As you know, when you work in the Outline tab in PowerPoint, each level-one heading (also called Heading 1 or A head) automatically becomes a slide title; each level-two heading (also called Heading 2 or B head) automatically becomes a level-one bulleted paragraph; each level-three heading (also called Heading 3 or C head) automatically becomes a level-two bulleted paragraph, and so forth. Similarly, Word has an outline mode in which you can create outline text that automatically becomes level-one text, level-two text, and so forth, in the Word document. The level-one text becomes a built-in Heading 1 style; level-two text becomes a built-in Heading 2 style, and so forth. So Norma created a Word document using the outline mode (alternatively, she could have simply applied the built-in headings to the outline text). Your next task, then, is to import her outline into PowerPoint.

To import a Word outline:

1. Click **Insert** on the menu bar, and then click **Slides from Outline**. The Insert Outline dialog box opens.

2. Change the Look in folder to the **Tutorial.04\Tutorial** folder included with your Data Files, click **GalaOutl**, and then click the **Insert** button. The Word outline is inserted as new slides after the current slide in the PowerPoint presentation, with all the level-one text becoming new slide titles. See Figure 4-4. No matter what the font and font sizes of the text in the Word document were, the text is formatted with the default font and sizes of the PowerPoint presentation.

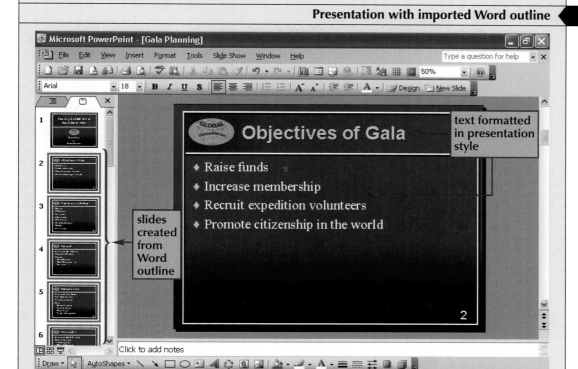

Because you imported the outline, the text is now part of PowerPoint and has no relationship with the Word file GalaOutl. Any changes you make to the PowerPoint text will have no effect on the GalaOutl file.

Exporting the Outline to Word

After looking over the presentation, Norma wants you to move the information on fundraising sources so that it appears earlier in the presentation, and then export the revised text as a Word outline so that she can create assignment sheets based on the revised outline. You'll do this now.

To modify the outline:

1. Switch to Slide Sorter view. Norma wants you to move Slide 12 ("Fundraising Sources") so that it appears earlier in the presentation.

2. Drag **Slide 12** to the left of Slide 3. The Fundraising Sources slide becomes the new Slide 3. The old Slide 3 ("Events and Activities") becomes the new Slide 4, and all the other slides similarly change their slide numbers.

3. Double-click **Slide 3** to return to Normal view, and then click the **Outline** tab so you can see the text of the outline. By changing the order of the slides, you changed the outline. See Figure 4-5.

Figure 4-5 Presentation with modified outline

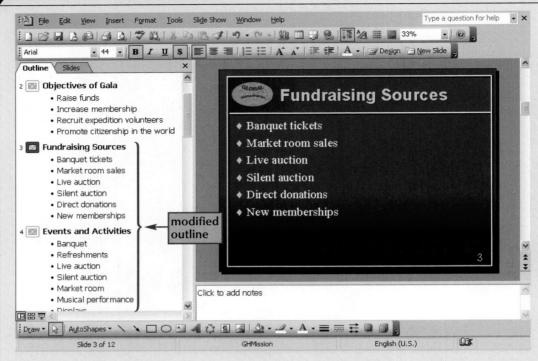

Now you'll export the revised outline to a Word file.

To export the outline to Word:

1. Click **File** on the menu bar, point to **Send to**, and then click **Microsoft Office Word**. The Send To Microsoft Office Word dialog box opens. See Figure 4-6.

Figure 4-6 Send To Microsoft Office Word dialog box

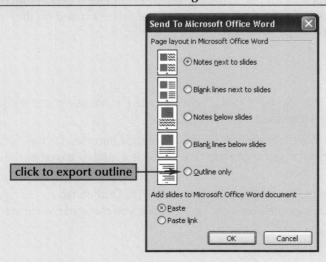

You could export the presentation in a variety of ways, but for this presentation, you'll choose to export only the outline.

2. Click the **Outline only** option button, and then click the **OK** button. Word automatically starts and opens a new Word document containing the PowerPoint text. See Figure 4-7. Notice that the process of exporting the outline preserves the font, font styles, and bullets of the PowerPoint presentation. Also notice that the text on the PowerPoint title slide becomes the title and subtitle in the Word document.

Exported outline in Microsoft Word | **Figure 4-7**

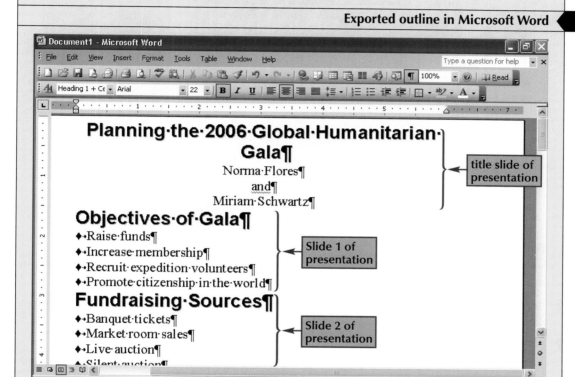

3. Save the Word document to the **Tutorial.04\Tutorial** folder using the filename **Gala Outline**, and then exit Word.

Now, Norma wants you to add digital photographs to the presentation. You'll do this next.

Importing Graphics

You already know how to import graphics, as you have inserted digital images and clip art into earlier presentations. Now, to make the Gala Planning presentation more attractive, you'll import digital photographs of last year's gala to give the Global Humanitarian personnel a better idea of some of the events.

To import (insert) graphics into the presentation:

1. Click the **Slides** tab so you don't see the outline, but rather the slide thumbnails.

2. With Slide 3 ("Fundraising Sources") in the slide pane, use the **Insert Picture** button on the Drawing toolbar to insert the file **Gala03**, located in the **Tutorial.04\Tutorial** folder. A photo of people preparing for last year's gala appears in Slide 3.

▶ **3.** Reposition the picture so that it's centered between the top and bottom of the slide and aligned to the right of the bulleted text. See Figure 4-8.

| Figure 4-8 | Slide 3 after importing graphic |

▶ **4.** Repeat the above step for Slides 6, 8, 9 (put this picture below the bulleted list), 11, and 12 using the picture files **Gala06**, **Gala08**, **Gala09**, **Gala11**, and **Gala12**.

▶ **5.** Save the presentation file using the default filename.

The Gala Planning presentation now has the desired design template, text slides, and graphics. Your next task will be to embed a table into one of the slides in the presentation.

Embedding and Modifying a Word Table

You know how to use PowerPoint commands to create a table in a slide, but what if you've already created a table using Word? You don't have to re-create it in PowerPoint; instead, you can copy the table and place it in a slide. If you embed the table instead of importing it, you can then edit it using Word's table commands.

| Reference Window | **Embedding a Word Table** |

- In Normal view, click Insert on the menu bar, and then click Object to open the Insert Object dialog box.
- Click the Create from file option button to select it, click the Browse button, navigate to the location of the file you want to insert, click it, and then click the OK button.
- Make sure the Link check box is not selected.
- Click the OK button.

Now you're ready to embed the Word table. Keep in mind that Norma created the table with a black font on a white background, so it is legible in a Word document. But as you'll see, it's not legible in the PowerPoint presentation, with its dark background.

To embed a Word file in a presentation:

1. Insert a new Slide 13 into the presentation, change its slide layout to **Title Only**, close the task pane, and then type the text **Gala Personnel** in the title placeholder.

2. Click **Insert** on the menu bar, and then click **Object**. The Insert Object dialog box opens. You can now create a new embedded file or use an existing one. You'll use an existing file.

3. Click the **Create from file** option button, click the **Browse** button to open the Browse dialog box, change the Look in folder to the **Tutorial.04\Tutorial** folder included with your Data Files, click the Word filename **GalaTabl**, and then click the **OK** button. See Figure 4-9.

Insert Object dialog box ◄ **Figure 4-9**

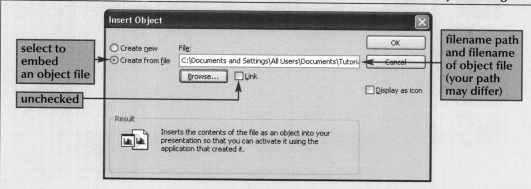

In Figure 4-9, the path and name of the file appear in the File text box. (Note that the path shown on your computer might be different.)

4. Make sure the **Link** check box is not selected, as shown in Figure 4-9, and then click the **OK** button. The embedded table appears in Slide 13.

5. Resize the table by dragging the corner sizing handles so that the table is as large as possible and still fits on the slide below the slide title, and then click a blank area of the slide, outside the table, to deselect it. You can barely read the table with its current colors, so you fix the colors next.

6. Save the presentation.

Norma asks you to modify the embedded table by changing the table color scheme. Because you embedded the table, you will use the program that created the object (in this case, Word) to make this change.

To modify an embedded object:

▶ **1.** Double-click anywhere in the table in Slide 13. The embedded table object becomes active in Word; the Word ruler appears above and to the left of the table, and the Word menu bar and toolbars replace the PowerPoint menu bar and toolbars. See Figure 4-10.

Figure 4-10	Slide 13 with embedded Word table made active

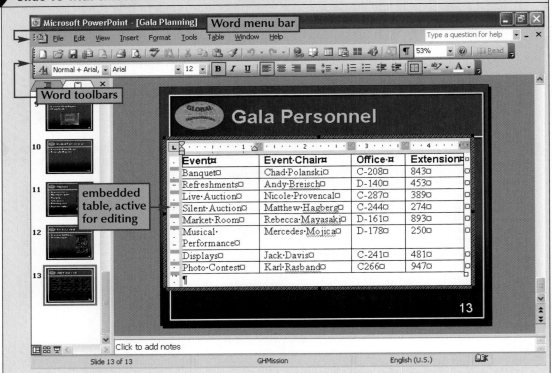

▶ **2.** Click **Table** on the menu bar (which is now Word's menu bar), click **Table AutoFormat** to open the Table AutoFormat dialog box, click **Table Colorful 1** in the Table styles list, and then click the **Apply** button. The table color scheme changes so that the table text will be legible and attractive on the PowerPoint slide.

▶ **3.** Click a blank area of the slide, outside the table, to return to PowerPoint with the object selected.

▶ **4.** Click a blank area of the slide again to deselect the object. Now you'll see how the table looks in Slide Show view.

▶ **5.** Switch to Slide Show view. As you can see, the table is attractive and legible. See Figure 4-11.

Embedded and modified table in Slide Show view ◄ **Figure 4-11**

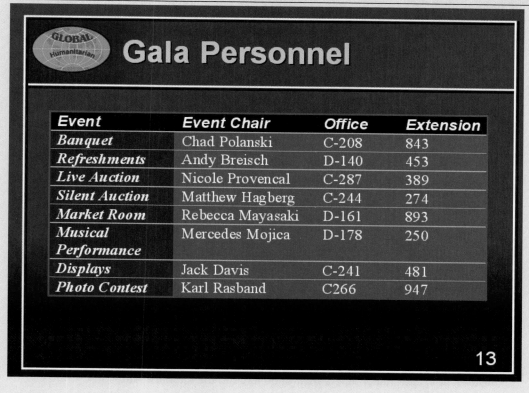

6. Press the **Esc** key to return to Normal view, and then save the presentation using the default filename.

You have now completed Slide 13, which contains the embedded object. Next, you'll link an Excel chart to the presentation.

Linking and Modifying an Excel Chart

Now you know how to insert objects into a PowerPoint slide by importing them and by embedding them. What if you needed to include in your presentation data that might change? For example, you might need to include data from an Excel worksheet, but you know that the final numbers won't be available for a while or that the numbers will change over time. In this case, you can link the data. Then, when the source file is updated, you can automatically update the linked object in the destination file so that it reflects the changes made to the source file.

Linking an Object

Reference Window

- In Normal view, click Insert on the menu bar, and then click Object to open the Insert Object dialog box.
- Click the Create from file option button, click the Browse button, navigate to the location of the file you want to insert, click it, and then click the OK button.
- Click the Link check box.
- Click the OK button.

Norma decides to include a bar graph of past and projected income and expenses from the fundraising activities at the gala. She chooses a bar graph because it emphasizes the earnings over the designated time period (the past five years), and shows trends that might help project income from this year's gala.

Miriam Schwartz already created a chart showing this data in an Excel workbook. Norma anticipates that she might have to modify Miriam's workbook after she creates the PowerPoint presentation. For example, the estimates for costs of the current gala might change as more exact values on rental fees, setup costs, celebrity appearance honoraria, auctioneer fees, and other expenses become available. Norma wants any changes made to the workbook to be reflected in the PowerPoint file, so rather than retype or import the data into a PowerPoint chart, she asks you to link Miriam's Excel workbook to the PowerPoint presentation.

You'll link Miriam's Excel graph of income and expenses to a new Slide 14 in Norma's presentation now.

To insert the chart and link the Excel worksheet:

1. With Slide 13 in the slide pane, insert a new Slide 14, set the layout to **Title Only**, and then type **Projected Income** as the slide title. (Remember to close the task pane.)

2. Click **Insert** on the menu bar, click **Object**, click the **Create from file** option button, click the **Browse** button, and then change the Look in folder to the **Tutorial.04\Tutorial** folder included with your Data Files.

   Ordinarily, you would now simply select the Excel file you want to link; however, because in this instance you'll be modifying a Data File, you'll first make a copy in case you make a mistake, or in case you or others want to go through the tutorial again.

3. Right-click the filename **GHChart**, then click **Copy** on the shortcut menu.

4. Right-click a blank area of the file list in the Browse dialog box to bring up another shortcut menu, and then click **Paste** on this shortcut menu. A copy of the income and expenses worksheet, with the filename **Copy of GHChart**, appears in the filename list.

   Because "Copy of GHChart" isn't a particularly descriptive filename, you'll change the filename to Gala Projected Income.

5. Right-click the filename **Copy of GHChart**, and then click **Rename** on the shortcut menu.

6. Type **Gala Projected Income**, and then press the **Enter** key. The copy is renamed.

   Trouble? If you get an error message that you're changing the filename extension, click the No button, repeat Step 5, type "Gala Projected Income.xls," and then press the Enter key.

7. Make sure **Gala Projected Income** is highlighted, and then click the **OK** button. The path and filename of the selected file appears in the File text box of the Insert Object dialog box. You need to select the Link check box in order to link, rather than embed, the file.

8. Click the **Link** check box to select it, and then click the **OK** button. After a few moments, the chart appears in Slide 14. You have linked the Excel workbook to the PowerPoint presentation.

9. Click anywhere in the slide outside the chart to deselect the object. See Figure 4-12. Some of the text on the chart is barely legible, but you'll soon fix that.

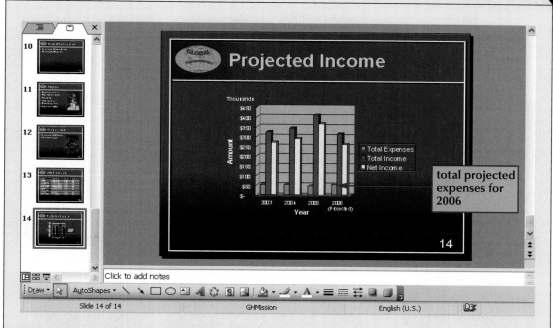

10. Save the presentation using the default filename.

Another method for linking a file to a PowerPoint presentation is to use the Paste Special command on the Edit menu in PowerPoint. You select the object in the source file that you want to link, and then click the Copy button on the Standard toolbar in the source program. Then you switch to the destination file in PowerPoint, and use the Paste Special command on the Edit menu. In the Paste Special dialog box that opens, you can choose to paste the copied object as a link. The Paste Special method is especially handy when you don't want to link an entire file to a PowerPoint presentation.

After you linked the chart, Norma received new information about the projected expenses of the gala. She asks you to make changes to the worksheet data, which will then be reflected in the chart.

To modify the linked chart:

1. Notice on the chart that the Total Expenses for 2006 (Projected) is approximately $50 thousand, and then double-click anywhere on the chart. Excel starts and opens the Gala Projected Income workbook.

2. Click the **Maximize** button on the Excel window so that Excel fills the entire screen.

3. Click the **Income Data** sheet tab near the bottom of the Excel window to display the data on the income and expenses of the gala.

4. Click cell **F4**, which currently contains the number $22,558, type **34,684**, which is the newly projected administrative salary, and press the **Enter** key. The new value is now $34,684, and the total expenses for 2006, in cell F19, changes from $54,614 to $66,740.

5. Click the **Chart** sheet tab near the bottom of the Excel window, save the worksheet using the default filename, and then exit Excel. The change you made in the chart in Excel is automatically reflected in the increased height of the Total Expenses column for the year 2006 in the PowerPoint slide.

6. Resize the chart as large as possible on the slide, and then click a blank area of the slide to deselect the chart.

7. Click the **Slide Show from current slide** button 🖳 to see how the chart looks in full-screen view. See Figure 4-13.

| Figure 4-13 | Linked and modified chart in Slide Show view |

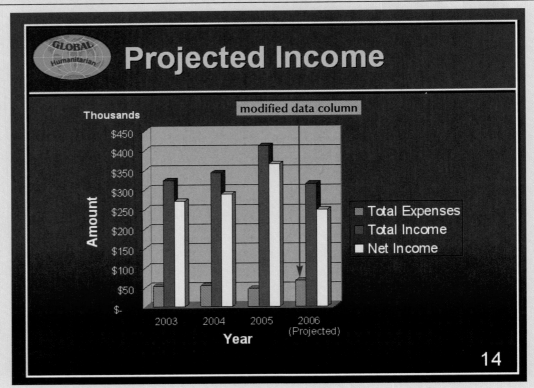

Trouble? If your chart doesn't have the approximate size and position of the chart shown in Figure 4-13, press the Esc key to return to Normal view, adjust the size or position of the chart, and then return to Slide Show view.

8. Press the **Esc** key to exit Slide Show view and return to Normal view.

9. Save the presentation using the default filename.

You have now linked and edited an Excel chart from PowerPoint. If you decide later to make further changes to the data in the workbook, you can do so either by directly starting Excel and opening Gala Projected Income or by double-clicking the chart in PowerPoint. Either way, any changes made to the workbook will be reflected in the linked object in the PowerPoint slide.

If you close and then reopen the presentation, you will see a message telling you that the presentation contains links, and asking you if you want to update them. To have PowerPoint update the links for the latest version of the source files, click the Update Links button. To have PowerPoint use the information currently in the destination file, click the Cancel button.

Session 4.1 Quick Check

1. How does applying a design template from another presentation differ from applying a design template from the Templates folder?
2. Describe how you use a Word outline to create slides in PowerPoint.
3. How do you save the text of a PowerPoint presentation in the form of a Word outline?
4. Define or describe:
   a. import
   b. embed
   c. link
   d. OLE
5. If you modify the source file of a linked object, such as an Excel chart linked to a PowerPoint slide, what happens to the linked object in the PowerPoint slide?
6. If you insert a picture created with scanning software and hardware, is the picture file imported, embedded, or linked?
7. Why would you link an object rather than embed it?

Session 4.2

Creating and Editing Hyperlinks

As you know, a **hyperlink** (or **link**) is a word, phrase, or graphic image that you click to "jump to" (or display) another location, called the **target**. The target of a link can be a location within the document (presentation), a different document, or a page on the World Wide Web. Graphic hyperlinks are visually indistinguishable from graphics that are not hyperlinks. The mouse pointer changes to a hand with a pointing finger when it is positioned over a link. In a presentation, text links are underlined and are a different color than the rest of the text, unless you have made a change to the color scheme. Once you've click a text link during a slide show, the link changes to another color to reflect the fact that it has been clicked, or **followed**.

Norma wants to easily move from Slide 4, which lists the major events and activities of the Global Humanitarian gala, to any slide dealing with a particular activity. Therefore, she asks you to create hyperlinks between each item in Slide 4 and the corresponding slides in the presentation, and then to create hyperlinks from each slide back to Slide 4.

To create a hyperlink to another slide in the presentation:

1. If you took a break after the last session, open the **Gala Planning** presentation located in the **Tutorial.04\Tutorial** folder included with your Data Files, and then switch to Normal view and close the task pane, if necessary.

2. Go to **Slide 4**.

   First, you'll link the text "Banquet" with the slide that describes the banquet.

3. Double-click the word **Banquet** to select the entire word, and then click the **Insert Hyperlink** button 🖳 on the Standard toolbar. The Insert Hyperlink dialog box opens. See Figure 4-14.

Figure 4-14 | Insert Hyperlink dialog box

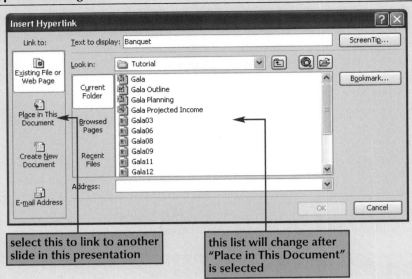

select this to link to another slide in this presentation

this list will change after "Place in This Document" is selected

You need to identify the file or location to which you want to link. Clicking each of the buttons in the Link to panel on the left side of the dialog box changes the rest of the dialog box so that you can then specify the exact location to jump to. For example, as you can see in Figure 4-14, the current item selected in the Link to panel is Existing File or Web Page. But in this presentation, you want to link to another location within the presentation, that is, within the current document.

▶ **4.** Click the **Place in This Document** button in the Link to panel on the left side of the dialog box. The dialog box changes to list all of the slides in the presentation.

▶ **5.** Click **5. Banquet** in the Select a place in this document list. The Slide preview area on the right side of the dialog box shows Slide 5. See Figure 4-15.

Figure 4-15 | Insert Hyperlink dialog box after selecting a slide in current document

selected Link to button

target slide number and name

preview of selected slide

▶ **6.** Click the **OK** button in the Insert Hyperlink dialog box. The word "Banquet" remains selected in the slide pane, but it is now underlined.

▶ **7.** Click a blank area of the slide to deselect the text. The word "Banquet" now appears as light-blue, underlined text, indicating that the word is a hyperlink. (Recall that you can specify the hyperlink color when you set the presentation color scheme.)

8. Repeat this procedure to add hyperlinks for each of the other bulleted items in Slide 4 so that each item is a hyperlink to its corresponding slide. Slide 4 should then look like Figure 4-16.

Slide 4 after inserting hyperlinks | **Figure 4-16**

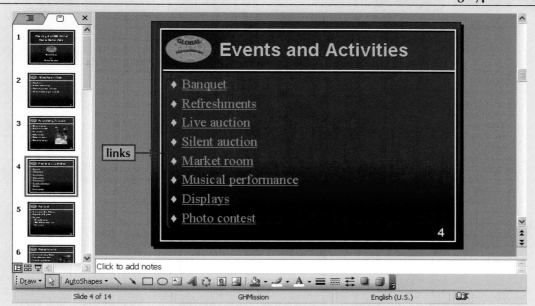

Trouble? If you make a mistake, repeat the procedure. The Edit Hyperlink dialog box will open in place of the Insert Hyperlink dialog box. You can then change the target of the hyperlink.

9. Save the presentation.

Now that you have added hyperlinks from the text in Slide 4 to the corresponding slides, you need hyperlinks from all the other slides back to Slide 4. This way, Norma can easily jump to an event slide, jump back to Slide 4, and then jump to another event slide. To create a link back to Slide 4, you will insert text on the target slide that will become the hyperlink.

To create hyperlinks from the slides back to Slide 4:

1. Go to **Slide 5**, click the **Text Box** button 🔲 on the Drawing toolbar, click the text pointer ⌐ near the lower-right corner of the slide (just to the left of the slide number), click the **Align Right** button 🔳 on the Formatting toolbar, and then type **Return to Event List**. Clicking the Align Right button causes the text to move to the left instead of to the right, so the text won't cover the slide number.

2. Select the text **Return to Event List**, click the **Insert Hyperlink** button 🔲, set the hyperlink target to Slide 4 ("Events and Activities"), and then click the **OK** button to return to Slide 5.

3. Click the slanted-line border of the text box to select the entire text box object, drag the text box by its border to position it as shown in Figure 4-17, if necessary, and then deselect the text box.

Figure 4-17 | **Slide with new link text added**

Now you'll add the links back to Slide 4 from the rest of the slides. Because all of the links will jump to the same slide, you can copy the text box and the link you created on Slide 5 to the other slides.

To copy a link:

1. Click the **link** text in Slide 5 to make the text box active, click the text box border to select the entire text box object, and then click the **Copy** button 🗐 on the Standard toolbar.

2. Go to **Slide 6**, and then click the **Paste** button 🗐 on the Standard toolbar. The link text is copied to the same position on Slide 6 as it was on Slide 5. Now you'll verify that the pasted link on Slide 6 has the same target as the original link on Slide 5.

3. Right-click the newly pasted link text, click **Edit Hyperlink** on the shortcut menu to open the Edit Hyperlink dialog box, verify that **4. Events and Activities** is selected in the Select a place in this document list, and then click the **Cancel** button.

   Trouble? If you don't see Edit Hyperlink on the shortcut menu, you clicked the text box border instead of the link text. Repeat Step 3, but make sure you right-click the link text.

4. Repeat Step 2 to paste the link text to Slides 7 through 12 (that is, all the slides that are targets of the hyperlinks on Slide 4).

5. Save the presentation.

With all the items on Slide 4 hyperlinked to the other slides and then back again, you're ready to test the results.

To use a hyperlink to jump to a specific slide:

1. Go to **Slide 4**, and then click the **Slide Show from current slide** button 🖵.

2. Click the **Refreshments** hyperlink. PowerPoint immediately displays Slide 6 ("Refreshments").

3. Click the **Return to Event List** hyperlink. PowerPoint again displays Slide 4. See Figure 4-18. The Refreshments link text is now light yellow, indicating that the hyperlink was followed.

Slide Show view of slide with followed hyperlink ◄ | **Figure 4-18**

Events and Activities

- ◆ Banquet
- ◆ Refreshments ——— followed link
- ◆ Live auction

4. Try all the other hyperlinks to make sure they work, and then return to Slide 4 in Normal view.

In addition to creating hyperlinks among the slides, you can add action buttons that have essentially the same effect. For Norma's presentation, you'll insert an action button that will add a link to another presentation.

Adding Action Buttons

An **action button** is a ready-made icon for which you can easily define a hyperlink to other slides or documents, as well as several other actions. You can use one of the 12 action buttons in PowerPoint, such as Action Button: Sound.

Adding an Action Button as a Link to Another Presentation | Reference Window

- In Normal view, click Slide Show on the menu bar, point to Action Buttons, and then click the desired button.
- Click the pointer at the location on the slide where you want the action button to appear.
- In the Action Settings dialog box, click the Hyperlink to option button, click the Hyperlink to list arrow, and then click Other PowerPoint Presentation to open the Hyperlink to Other PowerPoint Presentation dialog box.
- Select the presentation to which you want to jump, and then click the OK button.
- Click the OK button in the Action Settings dialog box.
- Resize and reposition the action button icon as desired.

Norma wants you to add a link between her presentation and the **GHMission** presentation, which gives the objectives and mission of Global Humanitarian. You'll create a hyperlink to that presentation by adding an action button.

To add an action button to link to another presentation:

1. Go to **Slide 2** ("Objectives of Gala").
2. Click **Slide Show** on the menu bar, point to **Action Buttons**, and then click the **Action Button: Document** button ▭ (the second button in the third row). The pointer changes to +.

3. Click ╋ roughly centered between the last bulleted item in Slide 2 and the bottom of the slide. A button appears on the slide and the Action Settings dialog box opens with the Mouse Click tab on top. (The dialog box covers the button.) See Figure 4-19. You can choose one of five actions to occur when you click the action button, or you can switch to the Mouse Over tab and choose an action to occur when you position the mouse pointer over the button. You will set the button so that you jump to another presentation when you click the button.

| Figure 4-19 | Action Settings dialog box |

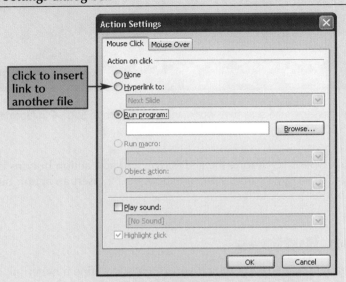

4. Click the **Hyperlink to** option button, click the **Hyperlink to** list arrow, scroll down, and then click **Other PowerPoint Presentation**. The Hyperlink to Other PowerPoint Presentation dialog box opens. It is similar to the Open dialog box.

5. Change the Look in folder, if necessary, to the **Tutorial.04\Tutorial** folder included with your Data Files, click **GHMission**, and then click the **OK** button.

6. Make sure **Global Humanitarian: Our Objectives and Mission** is selected in the Hyperlink to Slide dialog box, and then click the **OK** button. The path and filename of the file you selected appear in the Hyperlink to text box.

7. Click the **OK** button to close the Action Settings dialog box.

8. If necessary, drag the action button to the location shown in Figure 4-20, and then deselect the button.

| Figure 4-20 | Slide 2 with action button |

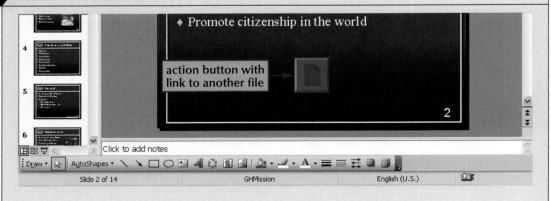

9. Switch to Slide Show view with Slide 2 ("Objectives of Gala"), on the screen, and then click the action button. Slide 1 of the GHMission presentation appears on the screen.

   Trouble? If a warning appears telling you that hyperlinks can be harmful to your computer and asking if you want to continue, click the Yes button.

10. Go through the entire GHMission presentation until you reach the blank slide at the end, and then press the **spacebar** once more. (You could also press the Esc key or right-click any slide followed by clicking End Show, and PowerPoint would return to the original presentation.) PowerPoint returns to Slide 2 of the Gala Planning presentation.

11. Return to Normal view, and then save the presentation using the default filename.

Norma looks at your work so far and is pleased with your progress. The presentation now includes an imported table from Word, an Excel chart, text links to other slides in the presentation, and an action button with a link to another presentation. In the next session, you'll help Norma ensure that her presentation will run smoothly and be available to all of her intended audience.

Viewing a Slide Show with Embedded or Linked Objects

When you present a slide show using a presentation with linked files, those files must be available on a disk so that PowerPoint can access them; and when you embed a file, the source program must be available if you want to edit the embedded object. This is because a copy of the linked file or source program for an embedded file is not included within the PowerPoint file itself; only the path and filename for accessing the linked file are there. Therefore, you should view the presentation on the system that will be used for running the slide show to make sure it has the necessary files. If embedded or linked objects don't work when you run the slide show, you'll have to edit the object path so that PowerPoint can find the objects on your disk.

To view the slide show:

1. Go to **Slide 1**, and then click the **Slide Show from current slide** button 🖵. Slide 1 appears in Slide Show view.

2. Click the **left mouse button** (or press the **spacebar**) to go to Slide 2, and then click the action button to jump to the other slide show.

3. Press the **Esc** key to return to the Gala Planning presentation.

4. Advance to **Slide 4** ("Events and Activities") and test some of the hyperlinks, using the "Return to Event List" link on each linked slide to jump back to Slide 4.

5. After viewing all the slides and testing the hyperlinks, return to Slide 1 in Normal view.

Norma is pleased with how well the embedded and linked objects work in her slide show. She now asks you to print a hard copy of the slides.

To print the presentation:

▶ **1.** Switch to Print Preview and preview the slides in grayscale. The slide title is difficult to read.

▶ **2.** Click the **Options** button on the Preview toolbar, point to **Color/Grayscale**, and then click **Pure Black and White**. The slide title is now legible.

▶ **3.** Scroll through the slides to make sure that all the slides are legible, and stop at Slide 14. The labels on the Excel chart on Slide 14 are hidden. This is because they were formatted with white text to make them visible on the blue presentation background.

▶ **4.** Click the **Close** button on the Preview toolbar, make sure Slide 14 is in the slide pane, click the **Color/Grayscale** button ▦ on the Standard toolbar, and then click **Pure Black and White**. The slide changes to black and white and the Grayscale View toolbar opens.

▶ **5.** Click the **Setting** button on the Grayscale View toolbar, and then click **Light Grayscale**. The labels are now legible. See Figure 4-21.

Figure 4-21 ▶ **Slide 14 in Print Preview with grayscale settings applied**

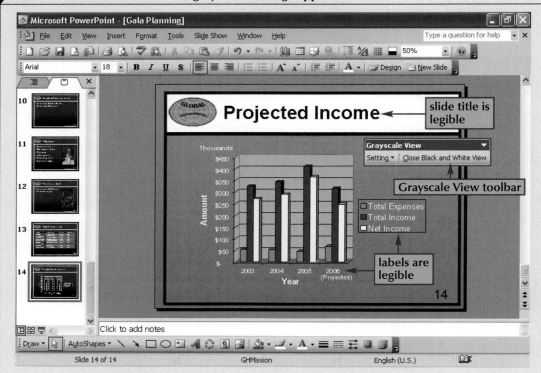

▶ **6.** Click the **Close Black and White View** button on the Grayscale View toolbar, switch back to Print Preview, and then go to **Slide 14**. The grayscale settings you set in Normal view are applied in Print Preview as well.

▶ **7.** Close Print Preview, go to **Slide 1**, change the subtitle to your name, and then save the presentation.

▶ **8.** Print the slides as handouts, six slides per page.

▶ **9.** Switch to Slide Sorter view, and then change the zoom, if necessary, to **50%** so you can see all the slides on your screen at once. See Figure 4-22.

Completed presentation in Slide Sorter view ◄ **Figure 4-22**

**The Internet:
World Wide
Web**

Publishing Presentations on the World Wide Web

As you probably know, the **Internet** is the largest and most widely used computer network in the world. In fact, it's really a network of thousands of smaller networks, all joined together electronically. Part of the Internet is a global information-sharing system called the **World Wide Web** (also called the Web or WWW). The Web allows you to find and view electronic documents called **Web pages**. Organizations and individuals make their Web pages available by placing them on a **Web server**, a dedicated network computer with high-capacity hard disks. The Web, then, is a connected network of these Web servers. The location of a particular set of Web pages on a server is called a **Web site**. You can access a particular Web site by specifying its address, also called its **Uniform Resource Locator** (**URL**). To specify URLs and to view Web pages, you use a **Web browser**, a software program that sends requests for Web pages, retrieves them, and then interprets them for display on the computer screen. Two of the most popular browsers are Microsoft Internet Explorer and Netscape Navigator.

Most Web sites contain a **home page**, a Web page that contains general information about the site. Home pages are like "home base"—they are starting points for online viewers. They usually contain links to the rest of the pages in the Web site.

Publishing a Web page usually means copying HTML files to a Web server so that others can view the Web page. In PowerPoint, however, the Publish command opens a dialog box in which you can customize the Web page you are saving.

Normally, you and the organization for which you work would create Web pages using a **Web page editor**, software specifically designed for this purpose, such as Microsoft FrontPage. But sometimes you want to publish a PowerPoint presentation, for example, as a link from the organization's home page. Global Humanitarian, similar to most large organizations, has its own Web site, but Norma thinks the pictures and information in the Gala Planning presentation would make an excellent resource for all those who help organize the gala.

To prepare Norma's PowerPoint presentation (or any presentation) for viewing on the World Wide Web, first you have to convert it to a file format called HTML, with the filename extension .htm or .html. **HTML** stands for **Hypertext Markup Language**, a special language for describing the format of a Web page so that Web browsers can interpret and display the page. The HTML markings in a file tell the browser how to format the text, graphics, tables, and other objects. Fortunately, you don't have to learn Hypertext Markup Language to create HTML documents; PowerPoint does the work for you. You can easily save any PowerPoint presentation as an HTML (or related) document using PowerPoint's Publish as Web Page command. This command allows you to create a set of HTML documents (or pages)—one HTML page (with the filename extension .htm) for each slide, various graphics files, an index page, and other supporting files—or to create a single Web page file (with the file-name extension .mht) that includes within it all the supporting documents and information.

If you want to edit a resulting .htm document, you'll have to use either a word proces-sor that supports HTML editing (for example, Microsoft Word) or, better still, a dedicated HTML editor (for example, Microsoft FrontPage). PowerPoint doesn't support direct editing of HTML documents. If you want to edit a resulting .mht file, you'll have to edit the origi-nal presentation file in PowerPoint, and then save it again as a .mht file.

Publishing the Web Pages

Norma wants you to save the Gala Planning presentation as a Web page so that she can copy it to the company's Web site. You remember that you added an action button to link to the GHMission presentation, so that presentation will need to be saved as a Web page as well. You'll do this first.

To save a presentation as a Web page:

1. Open **GHMission** from the **Tutorial.04\Tutorial** folder included with your Data Files, click **File** on the menu bar, and then click **Save as Web Page**. The Save As dialog box opens, with the Save as type automatically set to Single File Web Page. See Figure 4-23.

| Figure 4-23 | Save As dialog box for saving a single file Web page |

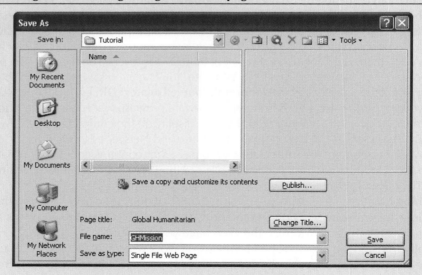

2. Change the filename in the File name text box to **GlobalHumanitarianMission** (all one word, no spaces).

3. Click the **Save** button. PowerPoint creates the Web page file GlobalHumanitarianMission in the default (Tutorial.04\Tutorial) folder.

4. Close the **GlobalHumanitarianMission** presentation without saving changes.

Having saved GlobalHumanitarianMission (from GHMission) as a Web page file, you now need to fix the hyperlinked action button in the Gala Planning presentation so that its target is the Web page file GlobalHumanitarianMission rather than the presentation file GHMission. You need to do this before you save Gala Planning as a Web page because you cannot edit Web page files within PowerPoint.

To change the hyperlink target and save the presentation as a Web page:

1. With Gala Planning in the PowerPoint window, go to **Slide 2** in Normal view.

2. Right-click the **action button**, and then click **Edit Hyperlink** on the shortcut menu. The Action Settings dialog box appears on the screen with the Mouse Click tab on top. Now you want to change the target file from GHMission to the Web page GlobalHumanitarianMission.

3. Click the **Hyperlink to** list arrow, click **Other File**, change the Look in location to the **Tutorial.04\Tutorial** folder (if necessary), click **GlobalHumanitarianMission**, and then click the **OK** button.

4. Click the **OK** button in the Action Settings dialog box. Now you're ready to save Gala Planning as a Web page.

5. Publish the Gala Planning presentation as a single file Web page, using the procedure previously described, except in the Save As dialog box, change the filename from Gala Planning (with a space) to **GalaPlanning** (without a space). This ensures that any type of browser can open the file, even browsers that don't accept spaces in the filenames.

Now that you saved the presentation as a single Web page, you're ready to see how it looks in a Web browser.

Viewing a Presentation in a Web Browser

It's always a good idea to see exactly what the presentation looks like in a browser before you actually publish it to a Web server. You can, of course, start your browser and then open the Web page, but you can also do this from within PowerPoint. You'll do this now.

To view the presentation in a Web browser from within PowerPoint:

1. With GalaPlanning still open in the PowerPoint window, click **File** on the menu bar, and then click **Web Page Preview**. PowerPoint starts your browser with the Web page open in the browser window. (In this book, we used Internet Explorer 6.0.)

   Trouble? If your computer uses a version of Internet Explorer other than 6.0, your pages will look slightly different than those shown here. If your computer uses Netscape Navigator, you will not be able to view the Web page because Navigator does not support single file Web pages at this time.

2. If necessary, maximize the browser window so it fills the screen. See Figure 4-24.

| Figure 4-24 | Presentation Web page in browser |

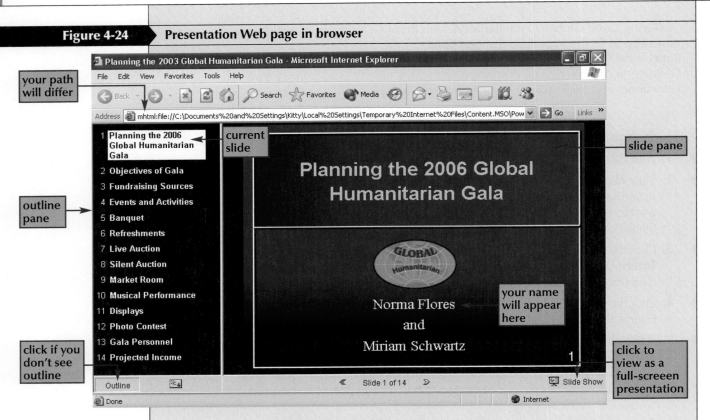

As you can see, the first slide of your presentation appears in the main frame of the browser, and an outline of the slides appears along the left edge of the outline pane. Each outline item is a hyperlink to its corresponding slide. Also, a navigation toolbar appears at the bottom of the window. These hyperlinks and the toolbar help you navigate through the presentation. Now you'll see how the navigation works.

Trouble? If you don't see the outline, click the Outline button at the bottom of the screen.

3. Click the **Next Slide** button ▷ on the navigation toolbar at the bottom of the Web page. The slide pane now displays Slide 2 of the presentation.

4. Click **4 Events and Activities** in the outline pane of the Web preview. The slide pane now displays Slide 4 ("Events and Activities").

5. Click the **Silent auction** hyperlink in Slide 4 in the contents pane. The slide pane now displays Slide 8.

6. Click the **Previous Slide** button ◁ on the browser toolbar. Slide 7 ("Live Auction") appears on the screen. As you can see, the navigation buttons help you easily move one slide forward or backward, whereas the outline hyperlinks allow you to jump from one slide to any other—in any order.

7. Click **2 Objectives of Gala** in the outline pane, and then click the **action button** on the slide. Slide 1 of the GlobalHumanitarianMission Web page appears in the browser window, or in a new window of the browser.

Trouble? If Slide 1 of the GlobalHumanitarianMission Web page does not appear, start Internet Explorer, click File on the menu bar, click Open to open the Open dialog box, browse to the file GalaPlanning, click the OK button in the Open dialog box, and then repeat Step 7.

8. Go through the slides of GlobalHumanitarianMission as desired.

9. After going through GlobalHumanitarianMission in your browser, click the **Back** button ◁ Back on the browser toolbar as many times as necessary to return to Slide 2 of the GalaPlanning presentation. (You can't just press Esc to exit the GlobalHumanitarianMission Web page and return to the GalaPlanning Web page.)

10. Look through the GalaPlanning Web page as you desire, and then exit your Web browser.

   Trouble? If you had to start Internet Explorer to use the action button on Slide 2, close both Internet Explorer windows.

11. Close the presentation without saving any changes.

Norma is pleased with how the presentation looks in the browser and sends the files to the company's technical support person to publish to the Global Humanitarian Web site. Next, she wants to schedule a specific time to broadcast her presentation over the Internet to get feedback from others.

Sharing and Collaborating with Others

PowerPoint provides a wide variety of methods for delivering your presentations and collaborating with others, including sending presentations via e-mail, broadcasting a presentation over the Internet, and making a presentation available on the World Wide Web. You're probably already familiar with e-mail, and you just learned about publishing a presentation as a Web page. This section will focus on holding online meetings and broadcasting a presentation.

An **online meeting** is a method of sharing and exchanging information with people at different locations in real time (the actual time during which an event takes place) as if all the participants are together in the same room. To hold an online meeting, you can use Microsoft NetMeeting, which is installed as part of Office 2003 and is accessible within the Office 2003 programs. **NetMeeting** is a program that manages online meetings. It allows participants to write notes on an electronic "whiteboard," send and receive typed messages, and exchange files. You can also record the results of your meeting, archive the results, and put them on a Web server so that those who missed the meeting can "replay" it at a later time.

An **online broadcast** is a method for showing a PowerPoint presentation online. It may or may not include an online meeting. A broadcast in its simplest form is analogous to the broadcast of a television show: The presentation is sent electronically to all the participants at a prearranged time. To run an online broadcast in PowerPoint 2003, you need to download the presentation broadcast feature from the Microsoft Office Online Web site.

Scheduling and Hosting an Online Meeting

Reference Window

- As the presenter, click Tools, point to Online Collaboration, click Schedule Meeting, and then enter the appropriate information in the NetMeeting dialog box, including your first and last name, your e-mail address, your physical location, and the URL of the Web server you will use to host the meeting.
- Click the OK button to close the NetMeeting dialog box and open the Outlook 2003 Meeting window.
- Schedule the meeting and choose the meeting participants using the Outlook 2003 Meeting window, and then click the Send button on the Meeting window toolbar.
- Click the View This NetShow button, when, as the presenter using Outlook, an Outlook Reminder window will open a few minutes before the meeting.
- Type in the chat area or draw on the whiteboard.
- End the online meeting by clicking the End Meeting button.

Reference Window

Setting Up and Running an Online Broadcast

- If necessary, download and install the Microsoft PowerPoint 2003 broadcast feature from the Microsoft Office Online Web site.
- As presenter, schedule an online meeting with the people who you want to view the online broadcast.
- At the designated time, open the presentation you want to broadcast, click Slide Show on the menu bar, point to Online Broadcast, and then click Begin Broadcast. Your presentation is automatically saved as a Web page, and then appears in the Web browsers of the participants.
- Run the slide show as you normally would, typing notes in the chat and whiteboard areas to communicate points to the viewers.

Norma decides to arrange an online broadcast of her presentation for the people in the Peru office. Then, she and Miriam, along with the help of their staff and many volunteers, successfully plan and carry out the Global Humanitarian gala, which is a huge success.

Review

Session 4.2 Quick Check

1. What is a hyperlink?
2. What are two examples of hyperlink targets?
3. What is an action button?
4. How do you save a presentation as a single Web page?
5. Describe what a presentation looks like in your browser.
6. Describe how to broadcast a presentation over the Internet.

Review

Tutorial Summary

In this tutorial, you learned how to import, modify, and export a Microsoft Word outline to your presentation and import a digital photograph. You learned how to embed and modify a Word table in your presentation and link and modify an Excel chart. You also learned how to create and edit hyperlinks, add action buttons, create and customize a toolbar, and publish a presentation on the World Wide Web.

Key Terms

action button	link	target
destination file	NetMeeting	Uniform Resource Locator
embed	object	(URL)
follow	object linking and	Web browser
home page	embedding (OLE)	Web page
hyperlink	online broadcast	Web page editor
HTML (Hypertext Markup	online meeting	Web server
Language)	publish	Web site
import	source file	World Wide Web
Internet		

Practice

Get hands-on practice of the skills you learned in this tutorial using the same case scenario.

Review Assignments

Data Files needed for the Review Assignments: LoanOtln.doc, Loan.ppt, Mentor.jpg, ProjTabl.doc, Chicken.jpg, Crafts.jpg, Dolls.jpg, Guide.jpg, Herd.jpg, Taxi.jpg, Weave.jpg, and Loans.xls

Norma and Miriam earmarked about $50,000 of the over $400,000 raised during the Global Humanitarian gala for the Global Humanitarian Entrepreneurial Support Program. This program provides small, low-interest loans and assistance for home and family businesses in less developed countries. It also provides training and mentoring in basic business practices. Norma and Miriam want you to help prepare a presentation reporting on recent entrepreneurial projects in Peru. Complete the following:

1. Open a new, blank presentation, and then import the Word outline **LoanOtln** located in the Tutorial.04\Review folder included with your Data Files.
2. Type "Entrepreneurial Support Programs in Peru" as the title in the title slide, and type your name as the subtitle in the title slide.
3. Apply the design template from the presentation file **Loan**, located in the Tutorial.04\Review folder.
4. Turn on slide numbering in the Header and Footer dialog box.
5. Save the presentation to the Tutorial.04\Review folder using the filename **Entrepreneurial Support Programs**.
6. Switch to Slide Sorter view, select Slides 4 through 10, and then apply the Title, Text, and Content layout to the selected slides.
7. In Slide 2, change the slide layout so an object will appear below the bulleted list, and then import the digital image **Mentor**, located in the Tutorial.04\Review folder. Resize the picture so it's as large as possible without covering the slide border lines or slide number.
8. In Slide 3, embed the Word table from the file **ProjTabl**, located in the Tutorial.04\Review folder, and then resize the table so it appears as large as possible without covering the brown border lines of the slide.
9. Import the appropriate pictures from the Tutorial.04\Review folder to Slides 4 through 10.
10. In Slide 5, set the white background of the Dolls picture to be transparent.
11. In the Tutorial.04\Review folder, make a copy of the Excel file **Loans**, change the name of the copy to **Loans Chart**, and then link it to Slide 11.
12. Double-click the chart on Slide 11, edit the number of loans given in 2005 to 48, edit the number successful to 29, switch back to the worksheet containing the chart, save and close the file and exit Excel. Make sure the chart was updated on Slide 11. (Resize the chart on Slide 11 if necessary.)
13. In Slide 3, below the table, create a text box and type "[Chicken] [Dolls] [Guide] [Herd] [Crafts] [Taxi] [Weaves]," including the brackets and a space between each bracketed word. Each bracketed word corresponds to one of the entrepreneurial projects covered in the presentation. Position the text box so it's centered below the table.
14. Select "Chicken" (but not the brackets around it) and make it a link to Slide 4, select "Dolls" and make it a link to Slide 5, and so forth for the other five words in the text box so that each word is a hyperlink to the corresponding project.
15. In Slides 4 through 10, create a text hyperlink "Return to Projects List" back to Slide 3. Position the hyperlink text box in the lower-left corner of each slide, and adjust the position of the text box or the graphic so they don't overlap. (*Hint*: Remember that you can copy the hyperlink from Slide 4 to the other slides.)
16. Add a document action button to Slide 11 in the lower-left corner of the slide, and link it to Slide 3. (*Hint*: Click the Hyperlink to list arrow in the Action Settings dialog box, and then click Slides.) Add an action button to Slide 3 to jump to Slide 11.

17. After completing the slide show, save the presentation.
18. Switch to Slide Show view and test the links you added.
19. View the presentation in grayscale, make any adjustments necessary so that all the elements are legible, then print the presentation as handouts with four slides per page.
20. Save the presentation as a single Web Page named **EntrepreneurialSupportPrograms** (no spaces). Test the Web page in your browser, and then close your browser.

Apply

Apply the skills you learned in this tutorial to modify a presentation for a national programming consulting firm.

Case Problem 1

Data Files needed for this Case Problem: PPCOtln.doc, PPCDes.ppt, PPCTbl.doc, PPCData.xls, Temp.jpg, and HeadQ.jpg

Programming-Plus Corporation Donald Van Pelt of Chicago is CEO of a large national consulting firm called Programming-Plus Corporation (P+C). P+C provides freelance programming in C++, Java, and other languages; supplies temporary employees with expertise in programming; and trains corporate programmers in advanced programming techniques. Donald asks you to help prepare a PowerPoint presentation to give to sales personnel so they can present information about P+C services. Compplete the following:

1. Open a new, blank presentation, type "Programming Plus Corp." as the title in the title slide, and then type your name as the subtitle in the title slide.
2. Import the Word outline **PPCOtln**, located in the Tutorial.04\Cases folder included with your Data Files.
3. Apply the design template from the presentation file **PPCDes**, located in the Tutorial.04\Cases folder.
4. Reapply the Title and Text Slide layout to all the slides with bulleted lists. (*Hint*: Switch to Slide Sorter view, select Slides 2 through 9, open the Slide Layout task pane, click the Slide Layout list arrow for the desired layout, and then click Reapply Layout.)
5. Save the presentation to the Tutorial.04\Cases folder using the filename **PPCServices**. (You won't include any spaces in the filename in anticipation of creating a Web page because some browsers don't accept spaces in filenames.)
6. In Slide 3, embed a Word table from the file **PPCTbl**, located in the Tutorial.04\Cases folder. Resize the table so it appears as large as possible.
7. In Slide 4, change the slide layout to Title and Content, and then click the Insert Chart button to create a chart.

Explore

8. Import data from an Excel file to the chart. Click the gray square in the upper-left corner of the datasheet to select all the cells, and then press the Delete key to delete all the current data. Start Microsoft Excel, open the Excel file **PPCData**, located in the Tutorial.04\Cases folder, select all the data in the spreadsheet, click the Copy button, and then exit Excel. Return to Slide 4 in the presentation, click the cell above the unlabeled column—the cell above and to the left of cell A1—and then click the Paste button on the Standard toolbar.
9. Click Chart on the menu bar, click Chart Options, click the Titles tab, type "Amount in $Millions" as the Value (Z) axis title, click the OK button, and then deselect the chart.
10. In Slide 7, import the digital image **Temp**, located in the Tutorial.04\Cases folder. Position the image to the right of the bulleted list.
11. In Slide 2, import the digital image **HeadQ**, located in the Tutorial.04\Cases folder. Position the image below the bulleted list.
12. Still in Slide 2, insert a text box to the right of the image with the text "Contact Us" with 24-point Arial font, and then make that text a hyperlink to Slide 9.

13. In Slide 9, insert the action button titled Home and make it a hyperlink to the first slide. This will allow Donald to easily jump from the end to the beginning of the slide show.
14. After completing the slide show, save the presentation using the default filename.
15. View the slide show in Slide Show view and test the links that you inserted.
16. Omit the background graphics from the master, preview the presentation in grayscale, make any adjustments necessary, and then print the presentation as handouts with six slides per page.
17. Save the presentation as a Web page, and then view the slide show in your browser.

Case Problem 2

Apply

Use your PowerPoint skills to create a presentation for a small Internet discussion management company.

Data Files needed for this Case Problem: GCDes.ppt, GCOtln.doc, GCChat.jpg, and GCGroup.jpg

GlobalChat   Crystal Bennett of Columbus, Ohio, is president of GlobalChat, a small but growing company that specializes in managing Internet discussion groups. The company sells software to individuals, families, schools, companies, and other organizations to help them set up and conduct electronic chat rooms and other types of discussion groups. Crystal asks you to help her prepare and publish a presentation on the services offered by her company. Complete the following:

1. Open a new, blank presentation, type "GlobalChat" on the first line of the title in the title placeholder, type "Bringing the World Together" on the second line in the title placeholder, and then type your name in the subtitle placeholder.
2. Apply the design template **GCDes**, located in the Tutorial.04\Cases folder included with your Data Files.
3. Select "GlobalChat" in Slide 1, increase the font size to 72 points, and change the font color to the blue color in the color scheme.
4. Import the Word outline in the file **GCOtln**, located in the Tutorial.04\Cases folder.
5. Save the presentation as **GlobalChat** in the Tutorial.04\Cases folder.
6. In Slide 2, change the slide layout to Title and Text over Content, and then import the clip art **GCChat**, located in the Tutorial.04\Cases folder.
7. Also in Slide 2, make each of the software names a hyperlink to the corresponding slide that describes the software feature.
8. On each of the three slides that describe software features, import the clip art **GCGroup**, change the slide layout to Title and Text over Content, change the size of the clip art to a height of one inch, move the clip art to the lower-right corner of the screen, and then increase the size of the bulleted list text box so it fills the remaining blank area.

Explore

9. Select the GCGroup clip art on each of the three slides, and make it a hyperlink back to Slide 2.
10. In Slide 7, insert Action Button - Home, and then set its hyperlink target to the first slide.

Explore

11. Change the color of the action button in Slide 7 to the bright-blue Follow Shadows Scheme Color. (*Hint*: Right-click the action button, and click Format AutoShape.)
12. Check all the hyperlinks in Slide Show view.
13. Set the slide transition for all the slides to Comb Horizontal.
14. Give Slides 2 through 7 the Exciting animation scheme called Float.
15. Start with Slide 1 and run the presentation in Slide Show view.
16. Save the presentation using the default filename, and then print the presentation as handouts with four slides per page.
17. Save the completed presentation as a single file Web page, and then view the slide show in your browser.

Create

Create a presentation using the skills you learned in this tutorial for a company selling products and services for outdoor activities.

Case Problem 3

Data Files needed for this Case Problem: HAOServ.ppt, HAOTempl.ppt, and HAOHikes.doc

High Adventure Outfitters High Adventure Outfitters (HAO) is a small business in Jackson, Wyoming, a center for many types of outdoor activities, including hiking, backpacking, camping, canoeing, hunting, and river running. The owner and president of HAO, Matthew Steinberg, provides guided tours for various types of activities in western Wyoming. Matthew asks you to set up a PowerPoint presentation on his company's supplies and services. Create the finished presentation as shown in Figure 4-25, and then create a Web page of the presentation.

Figure 4-25

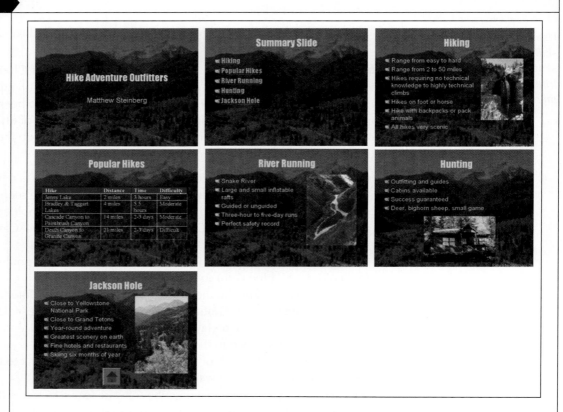

Read all the steps before you start creating your presentation.

1. The presentation is created from **HAOServ**, located in the Tutorial.04\Cases folder included with your Data Files. Change the name "Matthew Steinberg" on Slide 1 to your name, and save it as **HAOServices**.
2. The presentation uses the design template from the file **HAOTempl**, located in the Tutorial.04\Cases folder.
3. The information for the table of hikes on Slide 4 comes from the file **HAOHikes**, located in the Tutorial.04\Cases folder. You will have to modify the table later so that its size, fonts, and borders are legible and attractive. Keep this in mind and decide whether to embed or link the table.
4. Slide 2 is a summary slide featuring all the slides except the first one.
5. Slide 2 has hyperlinks from each of the bulleted items to the other slides (except Slide 1).
6. Slides 3 through 7 have a text hyperlink called "Return to Summary Slide" that links back to Slide 2.
7. Slide 7 includes an Action Button - Home, with a hyperlink to the first slide.
8. Save your final presentation, and then save it as a Web page using the filename **HAOServices**.

Research

Use the Internet to col-lect information about your favorite music and prepare a presentation on the topic.

Explore

Case Problem 4

Data File needed for this Case Problem: Music.ppt

My Favorite Music   Prepare a presentation to your classmates on your favorite type of music, whether it's classical or popular, rhythm and blues or Broadway, jazz or rap. Do the following:

1. Using Microsoft Word, create an outline of your presentation on your favorite music. Include at least six titles, which will become slide titles. (Remember to switch to Outline view in Word to type your slide titles.) Use books and magazines from your college library, encyclopedia, the Internet, CD slipcovers and booklets, or other sources of information to get backgrounds, biographies, lyrics, reviews, and analyses on your chosen topic. If you haven't covered Microsoft Word in your courses and don't know how to create an outline with heading styles, use the Help feature of Word.
2. Save the Word file using the filename **My Music Outline** to a high-capacity disk.
3. In another Word document, create a table. Your table might list the names of musical compositions, their composers, their performers, the types of music, the years of release, or other information.
4. Save the Word file with the table using the filename **My Music Table** to the Tutorial.04\Cases folder included with your Data Files.
5. Open a new, blank presentation, and include an appropriate title of your choosing and a subtitle with your name as the presenter.
6. Import the Word outline into PowerPoint.
7. Apply the design template from the presentation file **Music**, located in the Tutorial.04\Cases folder.
8. Reapply the slide layouts to each slide, as needed, so it uses the proper font and has the proper format. (*Hint*: Switch to Slide Sorter view, select the relevant slides, open the Slide Layout task pane, click the Slide Layout list arrow for the desired layout, and then click Reapply Layout.)
9. Embed your table into a slide of your presentation. Resize and reposition it as needed to maximize its readability.
10. Insert at least two action buttons into your presentation with links to other slides within your presentation.
11. Include at least one text hyperlink in your presentation, with a link to another slide. The text of the hyperlink can be a bulleted item, the text in a table cell, or a text box.
12. Add graphics, sound effects, slide transitions, and animations to the slide show, as desired.
13. Save your presentation using the filename **MyMusic**, and print the presentation as handouts with four slides per page.
14. Save your presentation as a single file Web page and then view the slide show in your browser.

Research

Go to the Web to find information you can use to create presentations.

Internet Assignments

The purpose of the Internet Assignments is to challenge you to find information on the Internet that you can use to work effectively with this software. The actual assignments are updated and maintained on the Course Technology Web site. Log on to the Internet and use your Web browser to go to the Student Online Companion for New Perspectives Office 2003 at **www.course.com/np/office2003**. Click the Internet Assignments link, and then navigate to the assignments for this tutorial.

Assess

SAM Assessment and Training

If you have a SAM user profile, you may have access to hands-on instruction, practice, and assessment of the skills covered in this tutorial. Log in to your SAM account and go to your assignments page to see what your instructor has assigned.

Reinforce

Lab Assignments

The New Perspectives Labs are designed to help you master some of the key concepts and skills presented in this text. The steps for completing this Lab are located on the Course Technology Web site. Log on to the Internet and use your Web browser to go to the Student Online Companion for New Perspectives Office 2003 at **www.course.com/np/office2003**. Click the Lab Assignments link, and then navigate to the assignments for this tutorial.

Review

Quick Check Answers

Session 4.1

1. They are the same, except that the presentation file will usually not be found in the Templates folder, whereas the design template file will be.
2. In PowerPoint, click Insert on the menu bar, click Slides from Outline, select the Word file with the outline, and then click the Insert button.
3. Click File on the menu bar, point to Send To, click Microsoft Word, select the desired Word page layout, click the OK button, specify the filename, and then click the OK button.
4. a. Import means to insert a file that was created using one program into another program's file.
   b. Embed means to insert a file so that a connection with the source program is maintained.
   c. Link means to insert a file so that a connection between the source file and the destination file is maintained, and changes made to the source file are reflected in the linked object in the destination file.
   d. OLE means object linking and embedding.
5. The object is updated to reflect the changes made to the source file.
6. imported
7. so that modifications you make to the source file are reflected in the destination file

Session 4.2

1. A hyperlink is a word, phrase, or graphic that you click to display an object at another location.
2. Hyperlink targets can be other slides within the presentation or other presentations.
3. An action button is a ready-made icon for which you can easily define hyperlinks to other slides or documents.
4. Click File, and then click Save as Web Page.
5. A frame on the left contains an outline of the slides, the slide itself appears in a frame on the right, and navigation buttons appear at the bottom of the slide.
6. Announce to the participant the time and place of the broadcast, open the presentation that you will broadcast, click Slide Show, point to Online Broadcast, and then click Begin Broadcast.

New Perspectives on

Microsoft® Office PowerPoint® 2003

Tutorial 5   PPT 187
Applying Advanced Special Effects in Presentations
Adding More Complex Sound, Animation, and Graphics to a Presentation

Tutorial 6   PPT 231
Creating Special Types of Presentations
Giving Presentations with Transparencies, 35mm Slides, Posters, and Banners

Additional Case 1   ADD 1
Creating a Presentation on Local Folklore

Additional Case 2   ADD 5
Creating a Presentation for the Director of a Museum or Hall of Fame

Read This Before You Begin: Tutorials 5–6

To the Student

Data Files

To complete the Level III PowerPoint Tutorials (Tutorials 5 and 6), you need the starting student Data Files. Your instructor will either provide you with these Data Files or ask you to obtain them yourself.

The Level III PowerPoint tutorials require the folders shown in the next column to complete the Tutorials, Review Assignments, and Case Problems. You will need to copy these folders from a file server, a standalone computer, or the Web to the drive and folder where you will be storing your Data Files. Your instructor will tell you which computer, drive letter, and folder(s) contain the files you need. You can also download the files by going to www.course.com; see the inside back or front cover for more information on downloading the files, or ask your instructor or technical support person for assistance.

If you are storing your Data Files on floppy disks, you will need **two** blank, formatted, high-density disks for these tutorials. Label your disks as shown, and place on them the folder(s) indicated.

▼**PowerPoint 2003 Level III: Data Disk 1**
   Tutorial.05 folder
▼**PowerPoint 2003 Level III: Data Disk 2**
   Tutorial.06 folder

When you begin a tutorial, refer to the Student Data Files section at the bottom of the tutorial opener page, which indicates which folders and files you need for the tutorial. Each end-of-tutorial exercise also indicates the files you need to complete that exercise. For Tutorials 5 and 6, you should save all your work to a high-capacity disk, such as a Zip disk or the hard disk on your computer. Because of the file sizes generated, you will not be able to save all the files back to your data disks if you are working from floppy disks. If you have any questions about the Data Files, see your instructor or technical support person for assistance.

To the Instructor

The Data Files are available on the Instructor Resources CD for this title. Follow the instructions in the Help file on the CD to install the programs to your network or standalone computer. See the "To the Student" section above for information on how to set up the Data Files that accompany this text.

You are granted a license to copy the Data Files to any computer or computer network used by students who have purchased this book.

System Requirements

If you are going to work through this book using your own computer, you need:

- **Computer System** Microsoft Windows 2000, Windows XP, or higher must be installed on your computer. These tutorials assume a complete installation of Microsoft PowerPoint 2003.

- **Data Files** You will not be able to complete the tutorials or exercises in this book using your own computer until you have the necessary starting Data Files.

Objectives

Session 5.1
- Copy a slide to another application
- Copy a slide to another slide as a picture object
- Apply complex animation and sound effects to a presentation
- Download clip art from Microsoft Office Online
- Insert an audio track from a CD into a presentation
- Record a narration
- Manipulate background objects on a slide

Session 5.2
- Set up a self-running presentation
- Use drawings and diagrams from other applications in a PowerPoint presentation
- Apply callouts to a diagram
- Create and edit a custom show

Applying Advanced Special Effects in Presentations

Adding More Complex Sound, Animation, and Graphics to a Presentation

Case

Global Humanitarian, Student Internships

Consuela Jennings is the director of student internships in the Austin, Texas office of Global Humanitarian. As part of her duties, she encourages faculty of colleges and universities throughout Canada and the United States to initiate and maintain service-learning courses—that is, credit or noncredit courses in which students serve others while gaining knowledge and developing skills—in cooperation with Global Humanitarian. Consuela also helps recruit students to participate in these courses. Most of the service-learning courses are in standard disciplines, such as foreign languages, linguistics, history, geology, and geography, and involve off-campus internships in third-world countries.

Consuela is preparing a recruitment trip to talk to faculty and students on various campuses. She asks you to help her prepare a PowerPoint presentation and hand-outs regarding service-learning courses through Global Humanitarian. She wants to be able to run the slide show herself while she gives a presentation, and she wants to be able to set it up at college internship fairs as a self-running slide show.

Student Data Files

▼**Tutorial.05**

▽ **Tutorial folder**

Abstract.doc
SAmer.jpg
ServLern.ppt

▽ **Review folder**

Bolivia.jpg
Students.jpg
StuRep.ppt

▽ **Cases folder**

Arizona.jpg
Arteries.jpg
GrndCan.ppt
GrndCan0.jpg
GrndCan1.jpg
GrndCan2.jpg
GrndCan3.jpg
GrndCan4.jpg
Heart.jpg
Heart.ppt

In this tutorial, you'll copy a slide into a Word document, make picture thumbnails, animate a background object, animate a process diagram, and download clip art and music over the Internet. You'll also apply a sound clip, insert a CD audio track, and add action buttons to your slides. Finally, you'll set up a self-running presentation, insert a graphic produced with illustration software, and create a custom show.

Session 5.1

Planning the Presentation

Before creating the presentation, Consuela and you sit down to plan the presentation using the following guidelines:

- **Purpose of presentation**: to provide information about service-learning courses and internships through Global Humanitarian
- **Type of presentation**: Product/Services Overview
- **Audience**: students and faculty of colleges and universities in Canada and the United States
- **Audience needs**: to understand the opportunities and responsibilities of participating in service-learning courses and internships through Global Humanitarian
- **Location of presentation**: college and university classrooms and lecture halls
- **Format**: electronic slide show for oral and self-running presentations

With the above general plan for the presentation, Consuela started to create a presentation using the AutoContent Wizard and selected Product/Services Overview as the type of presentation under Sales/Marketing. She modified the text created by the wizard, and then applied a custom-designed template to the presentation. She needs to send an abstract (summary) to colleges and universities to advertise her presentation. She wants you to copy one of the slides that briefly describes an aspect of the Global Humanitarian internship program into a Word document to create the abstract. You'll do this first.

Using PowerPoint Slides as Picture Objects

To copy a slide as a picture object, you select the slide in Slide Sorter view, and then copy the slide to the clipboard. The slide is copied as a picture object. Then you can switch to another slide in Normal view or open another file and paste the slide; it will be pasted as a picture.

Reference Window	**Copying and Modifying a Slide as a Picture Object**

- Switch to Slide Sorter view.
- Select the slide from which you want to make a picture image.
- Click the Copy button on the Standard toolbar.
- Go to the document or slide (in Normal view) into which you want the picture object inserted.
- Click the Paste button on the Standard toolbar.
- Modify the picture object as desired.

Pasting a PowerPoint Slide into a Word Document

Consuela informs you that Global Humanitarian must send an abstract (summary), consisting of one paragraph and one graphic, to colleges and universities to advertise the presentation. To create the abstract, you'll open the presentation that Consuela started, select one of the slides, and then copy it as a picture object into a Microsoft Word document.

To copy a slide into a Word document:

► **1.** Open the file **ServLern** from the Tutorial.05\Tutorial folder included with your Data Files, maximize the PowerPoint window, if necessary, and then close the task pane, if necessary. The title page of the Global Humanitarian presentation appears in the slide pane.

► **2.** Save the presentation file as **Global Humanitarian Service Learning** to a high-capacity disk (your hard disk, a Zip disk, or the like).

   Trouble? If you're using a floppy disk for your Data Files, you won't have enough space to save the files in this tutorial. If you don't have access to a hard drive or some other high-capacity disk, you should read and work through the steps anyway to learn the material in this tutorial; just skip the steps that require you to save your work. (Consult with your instructor—you may be required to print out your work at different stages.)

► **3.** Quickly go through the presentation to get an idea of its content and design, and then go to **Slide 2** ("Presentation Contents"). See Figure 5-1. As you can see, the presentation includes a custom design (slide color scheme, background, color, fonts, and background graphics) developed by a graphic designer under Consuela's direction.

Slide 2 of the Global Humanitarian Service Learning presentation ◄ **Figure 5-1**

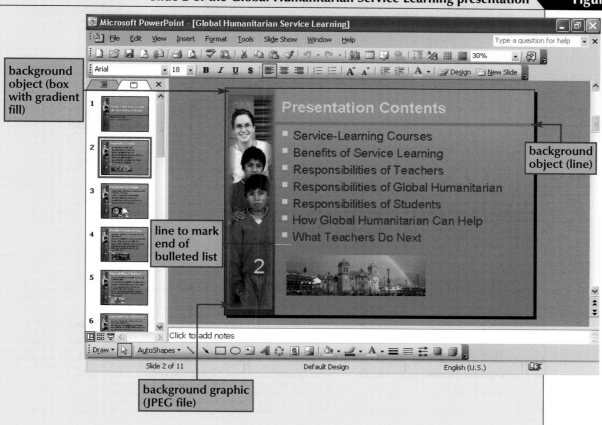

4. Switch to Slide Sorter view, and make sure Slide 2 is still selected. Consuela wants you to put a copy of Slide 2 into the Global Humanitarian abstract.

5. Click the **Copy** button 📋 on the Standard toolbar. Slide 2 is placed as a picture object on the clipboard.

6. Start Microsoft Word, open the file **Abstract** from the Tutorial.05\Tutorial folder included with your Data Files, and save it to a high-capacity disk using the filename **Global Humanitarian Abstract**.

7. With the insertion point at the beginning of the Word document, click the **Paste** button 📋 on the Standard toolbar. The image of Slide 2 appears at the beginning of the Word document. See Figure 5-2.

Figure 5-2 ▶ **Word document with Slide 2 pasted as a graphic**

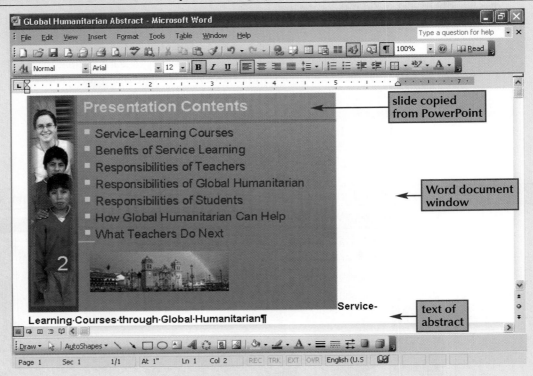

With the picture object in the Word document, you'll want to resize and position it so that it appears to the left of the text paragraph, rather than above it.

To modify the picture object in Word:

1. Right-click the image to select it and to display the shortcut menu.

2. Click **Format Object** on the shortcut menu, click the **Size** tab, make sure the **Lock aspect ratio** check box is selected, and then change the value in the Height text box to **2** inches. This will decrease the size of the image in the document. Remember, the aspect ratio is the relationship between the height and width of the picture, so if you lock it, changing the width causes the height to be resized proportionately.

3. Click the **Layout** tab in the Format Object dialog box, and then click the **Square** wrapping style icon. This will wrap the text to the right of the image.

4. Click the **Left** option button in the Horizontal alignment section. Selecting this option places the picture on the left side of the page.

5. Click the **OK** button. After a moment, the image is resized and the text wraps around the right side of the image.

6. Click anywhere in the document text to deselect the picture. See Figure 5-3.

Word document after adjusting graphic ◄ **Figure 5-3**

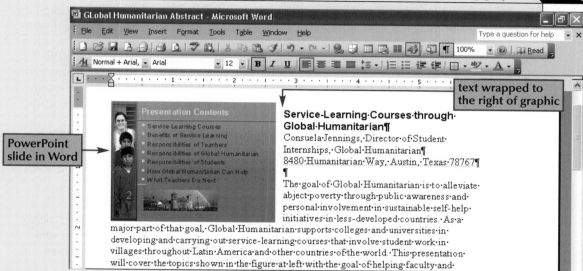

7. Add your name to the end of the revised Word document, save and print the document, and then exit Word.

Having added the picture to the Global Humanitarian abstract, you can now give the document to Consuela so she can mail it to colleges and universities to include in their publicity about the presentation.

Pasting Slides into Another Slide as Pictures

Next, Consuela wants you to modify the Presentation Contents slide by deleting the bulleted list and pasting images of other slides in the presentation as picture objects to create thumbnails. She then would like you to make each thumbnail a hyperlink to its respective, full-size slide. To do this, you'll change the slide layout and delete the bulleted list and other items in the slide.

Copying a Slide as a Picture into Another Slide	Reference Window

- Switch to Slide Sorter view, and select the slide you want to copy.
- Click the Copy button 📄 on the Standard toolbar.
- Switch to Normal view, and go to the slide onto which you want to paste the picture of the copied slide.
- Click Edit on the menu bar, click Paste Special, and then click one of the Picture options in the As list box.
- Click the OK button in the Paste Special dialog box.

To modify Slide 2 in preparation for slide miniatures:

▶ **1.** Delete **Slide 2** ("Presentation Contents") in Slide Sorter view, and then switch to Normal view.

▶ **2.** Insert a new Slide 2 with the **Title Only** layout, and then close the task pane.

▶ **3.** Click the title placeholder and type **Presentation Contents**. Now Slide 2 has the same title as the old Slide 2, which you deleted, but has a blank area where you can insert the thumbnails.

The slide is almost ready for you to paste the thumbnails. To make it easier to align the thumbnails on the slide, you will modify the slide grid. A **grid** is an array of dotted vertical and horizontal lines that can make positioning objects easier. Usually the grid is hidden, but you can make it visible. You can also change the spacing of the dots on the gridlines to make it easier to position small or large objects. Another handy feature of the grid is the Snap to Grid option, which is selected by default. With this option selected, objects you place on the slide will automatically align with a gridline, even if the gridlines are not visible.

Now you'll display and then adjust the grid so that the spacing between the dotted gridlines is larger. This will make it easier to align the thumbnails.

To modify the grid settings and make the grid visible:

▶ **1.** Click **View** on the menu bar, click **Grid and Guides** to display the Grid and Guides dialog box, note that the Spacing text box is set to the default value of 0.25 inches, make sure that the **Snap objects to grid** check box is selected, click the **Display grid on screen** check box, and then click the **OK** button. A representation of the gridlines appears on the screen. See Figure 5-4.

Figure 5-4	Grid visible on new Slide 2

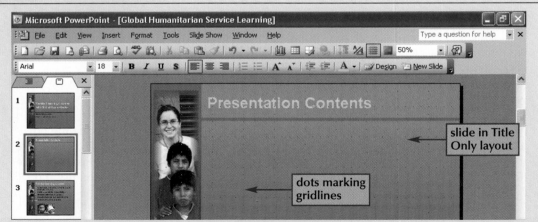

Each gridline is 0.25 inches apart. When you insert a picture into the slide or resize a picture, the edge of the picture will "snap" to an intersection of two gridlines (seen or unseen). PowerPoint doesn't allow the picture to be part way between two gridlines. Now, you'll change the spacing between the gridlines.

▶ **2.** Open the Grid and Guides dialog box again, click the **Spacing** list arrow, and then click **1/5"**. The value in the Spacing text box changes to 0.2 inches. (You could also simply type 0.2 in the Spacing text box.)

▶ **3.** Click the **OK** button. The dots in the visible gridlines move closer together. In fact, they changed from 0.25 to 0.2 inches apart. See Figure 5-5.

Slide 2 with new gridline dimensions ◄ **Figure 5-5**

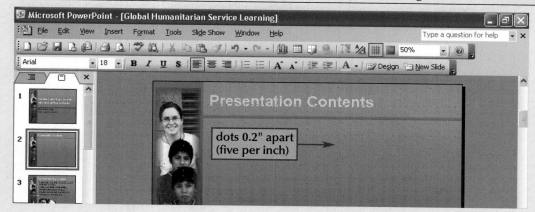

Now you're ready to copy and paste the slide pictures into Slide 2. To do this, you first copy each slide to the clipboard as you did when you copied a slide to paste it into a Word document. To paste the slide as a picture in another slide, however, you cannot use the Paste command; you need to use the Paste Special command, available on the Edit menu. If you use the Paste command, PowerPoint will insert the copied slide as a new slide in the presentation.

To make thumbnails by copying slides:

1. Switch to Slide Sorter view.

2. Click **Slide 3** to select it, and then click the **Copy** button 🗐 on the Standard toolbar.

3. Double-click **Slide 2** to switch to Slide 2 in Normal view, click **Edit** on the menu bar, and then click **Paste Special**. The Paste Special dialog box opens. You want to paste the slide as a picture, so you will use one of the Picture options in the As list box. You'll use the Windows Metafile picture file type, although any of the other picture types would work just as well.

4. Click **Picture (Windows Metafile)** in the As list box, and then click the **OK** button. The dialog box closes and Slide 3 is inserted as a picture in Slide 2. See Figure 5-6.

Slide after inserting copied slide image ◄ **Figure 5-6**

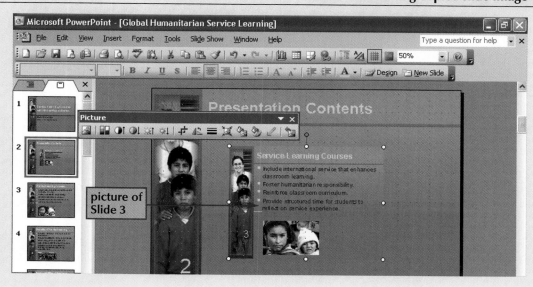

Now you'll resize and reposition the slide thumbnail.

5. With the picture still selected, click the **Format Picture** button on the Picture toolbar, click the **Size** tab, make sure the **Lock aspect ratio** check box is selected, and then change the value in the Width text box in the Size and rotate section at the top of the dialog box to **2.5"**. See Figure 5-7.

| Figure 5-7 | Size tab in the Format Picture dialog box |

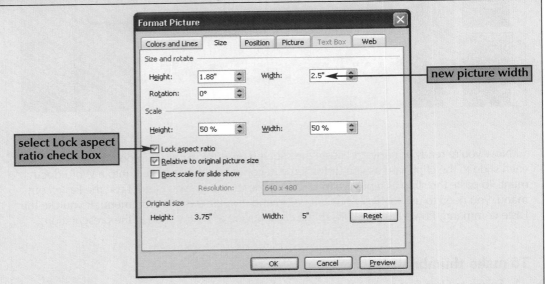

Trouble? If the Picture toolbar is not visible, click View on the menu bar, point to Toolbars, and then click Picture.

6. Click the **OK** button. The picture is resized to approximately half its original size.

7. Drag the thumbnail so it snaps to the gridline in the upper-left corner of the blank area of the slide, as shown in Figure 5-8.

| Figure 5-8 | Slide 2 after resizing and positioning thumbnail of Slide 3 |

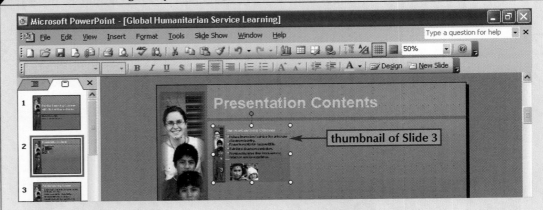

Trouble? If the size and position of the thumbnail of Slide 3 are different from the one shown in Figure 5-8, make sure you have adjusted the picture width (not the height) to 2.5 inches and positioned the slide as shown.

▶ **8.** Repeat Steps 1 through 7 to insert Slides 4 and 5, positioning them to the right of the previous slide, so that the first three thumbnails are in a row.

You'll skip Slide 6 ("Responsibilities of Teachers (cont.)") because it's a continuation of the Slide 5 topic, but you'll insert Slides 7 through 11.

▶ **9.** Insert Slides 7 through 11 as thumbnails below the first three thumbnails. See Figure 5-9.

Slide 2 with eight slide thumbnails ◀ **Figure 5-9**

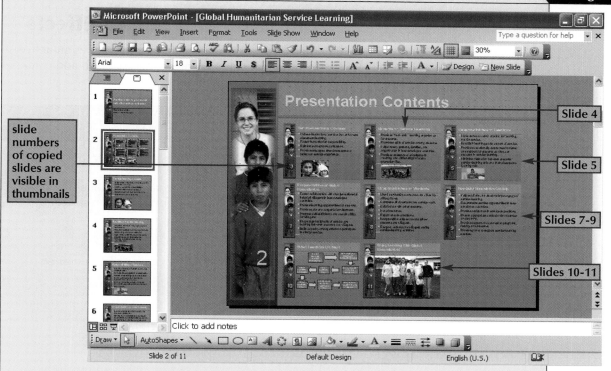

▶ **10.** Click **View** on the menu bar, click **Grid and Guides**, click the **Display grid on screen** check box to clear it, and then click the **OK** button. The gridlines are no longer visible on the screen.

Now you'll make the thumbnails hyperlinks to their respective slides in the presentation.

To create hyperlinks from the thumbnails:

▶ **1.** With Slide 2 in the slide pane in Normal view, select the **Slide 3** thumbnail, and then click the **Insert Hyperlink** button 🖳 on the Standard Toolbar. The Insert Hyperlink dialog box appears.

▶ **2.** Click the **Place in This Document** button in the Link to panel, click **3. Service-Learning Courses** in the Select a place in this document list of slides, and then click the **OK** button. Now, when you run the slide show and click the picture of Slide 3 on Slide 2, PowerPoint will jump to Slide 3.

▶ **3.** Repeat Steps 1 and 2 to make each picture a hyperlink to its respective slide in the presentation. (Remember that you skipped Slide 6.)

▶ **4.** Save your presentation. You'll test the hyperlinks later.

In this example, you used the picture objects of the slides as hyperlinks to the actual slides in the presentation, but you can design any PowerPoint slide and use it as a picture of any type on any other slide, or in any other Windows program. You can also save any or all of the slides in a presentation as picture files (in GIF, JPEG, PNG, TIF, BMP, or WMF file format) by displaying the desired slide in the slide pane in Normal view, clicking File on the menu bar, clicking Save As, and then selecting one of the picture formats as the file type.

Next, you'll add interest to the presentation by inserting animations and sound effects.

Applying Complex Animation and Sound Effects

Consuela wants you to make the presentation for the colleges and universities as attractive and eye-catching as possible. You decide that one way to achieve this goal is to add complex animation and sound effects to the presentation.

Reference Window	**Animating an Object**

- Click Slide Show on the menu bar, and then click Custom Animation to open the Custom Animation task pane.
- Select the object or objects that you want to animate using the same animation effect.
- Click the Add Effects list arrow, point to the desired type of effect, and then select the effect.
- Change the Start, Direction, and Speed options, as desired.
- To add sound effects, click the object list arrow in the animation list in the Custom Animation task pane, click Effect Options, click the Sound list arrow, click the desired sound effect, and then click the OK button.
- To change the timing, click the object list arrow in the animation list, click Timing, change the Delay time, and then click the OK button.

Animating a Background Object

You'll begin by animating a background graphic. When you animate a background graphic, the animation will occur on every slide in the presentation because the background is part of the slide master. The steps for applying a custom animation to an object on the slide master are the same as the steps for applying a custom animation to objects on slides. You'll animate the green line under the slide title.

To animate a background graphic:

1. Shift-click the **Normal View** button 🔲 to switch to Slide Master view, and then click Slide 1 in the Slides tab, if necessary.

2. Click **Slide Show** on the menu bar, and then click **Custom Animation**.

3. Click the green horizontal line below the title placeholder.

   Trouble? If you have trouble selecting the line, click the right end of the line to select it without selecting the text placeholders.

4. Click the **Add Effect** button in the Custom Animation task pane, point to **Entrance**, and then click **Fly In**. See Figure 5-10. PowerPoint previews the animation of the line. Now you'll change the direction and speed of the animation.

Animating the green line ◄ Figure 5-10

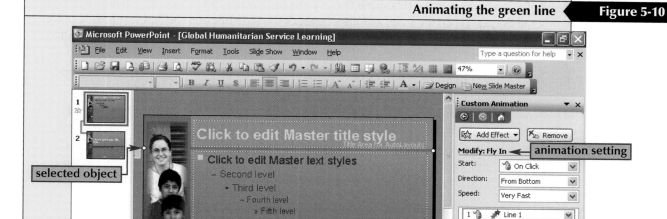

Trouble? If you don't see Fly In on the Entrance list, click More Effects to open the Add Entrance Effect dialog box, click Fly In, and then click the OK button.

5. Click the **Start** list arrow in the Modify: Fly In section of the task pane, click **After Previous** to set the animation to run immediately after the slide appears on the screen, click the **Direction** list arrow, and then click **From Left** so that the line flies in from the left side of the slide. Notice that as you make each change to the animation, PowerPoint usually plays the animation automatically.

6. Click the **Speed** list arrow, and then click **Medium**.

7. Click the **Play** button at the bottom of the task pane to watch the graphic animate.

8. Click Slide 2 in the Slides tab to switch to the title master, and then repeat Steps 3 through 6 for the horizontal brown line.

9. Return to Normal view.

This animation is subtle but adds a touch of professionalism to your presentation. Remember not to overdo custom animations. Excessive animation can detract from your presentation.

Next, you'll animate the process diagram on Slide 10. The diagram illustrates the steps involved in setting up a service-learning course with Global Humanitarian.

Animating a Process Diagram

The graphic artist, under Consuela's direction, already created most of the graphics for the process diagram, so you'll just create the animation. You should understand, however, that anyone familiar with PowerPoint drawing tools can create this slide; you just have to know how to add text boxes, change the border and fill color of the text boxes, and insert AutoShapes.

The goal of animating the process diagram is to make each object appear on the screen one at a time, in the sequence of the process. Now you'll animate the process illustrated on Slide 10.

To animate the process diagram:

1. Go to **Slide 10** ("What Teachers Do Next"). First, you need to select all of the objects on the slide except for the slide title and the first box in the diagram.

2. Click anywhere in the slide pane to make the pane active, press the **Ctrl + A** keys to select all the objects on the slide, and then Ctrl-click the slide title and the first text box, "Contact Consuela Jennings," to deselect them. All text boxes and arrows, except the slide title and the first text box, are selected.

3. Click the **Add Effect** list arrow, point to **Entrance**, and then click **More Effects**. The Add Entrance Effect dialog box opens.

4. Click **Wipe** in the Basic effect section, and then click the **OK** button. All of the selected objects are assigned the Wipe animation.

5. In the task pane, click the **Start** list arrow, click **After Previous**, click the **Direction** list arrow, click **From Left**, click the **Speed** list arrow, and then click **Fast**. A preview of the animation appears in the slide pane for each of the selected slides. See Figure 5-11.

Figure 5-11   **Slide with custom animation applied**

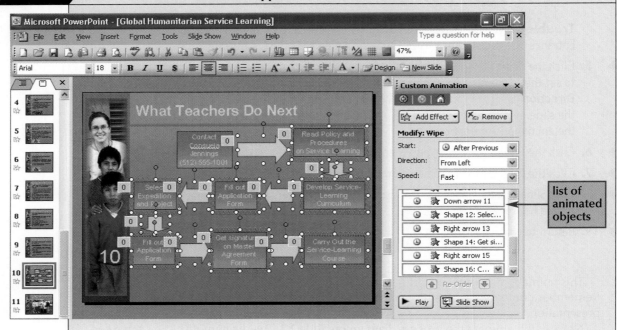

The animation should have proceeded in the order shown by the arrows, but this wasn't the case because the objects currently are set to animate in the order they were added to the slide. Now, you'll change the animation order of the objects. First, you'll play the animation and watch the animation order of the objects, and then you'll modify the animation to correct anything that is animating out of order.

To change the order of animating objects:

1. Click the **Play** button in the task pane and observe the order in which the objects animate. As you can see, the first four objects animate in the proper order. These are referred to as Right arrow 3, Shape 4, Down arrow 5, and Shape 6 in the Custom Animation task pane. But the next object that should animate is the left arrow referred to as Left arrow 10 in the Custom Animation task pane. You'll move up Left arrow 10 to the location just below Shape 6 in the task pane.

2. Drag **Left arrow 10** up until it's positioned just below Shape 6, as shown in Figure 5-12, and then release the mouse button. Now you'll drag other objects so that they animate in the proper order.

Reordering the animated objects ◀ **Figure 5-12**

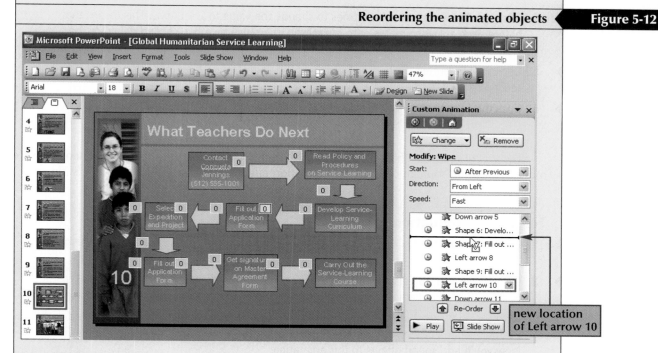

3. Drag **Shape 12: Select. . .** up until it's positioned just below Left arrow 8, drag **Down arrow 11** up until it's just below Shape 12, drag **Right arrow 15** up until it's below Shape 9, and drag **Shape 14** up until it's below Right arrow 15. When you are done, look through the list of objects in the Custom Animation task pane and make sure they are in the following order: Right arrow 3, Shape 4, Down arrow 5, Shape 6, Left arrow 10, Shape 7, Left arrow 8, Shape 12, Down arrow 11, Shape 9, Right arrow 15, Shape 14, Right arrow 13, and Shape 16.

4. When you're done reordering the items, click the **Play** button in the task pane again to verify that all items are in the correct order.

Having reordered the animation, you'll now want to customize the animation further by changing the direction of some of the objects so that they wipe in the direction that you want them to appear. You'll also change the timing of the animation for the arrows so that they appear on the screen after a delay. This will allow the viewer to read the information in the text box before the next arrow appears.

To change the direction and timing of animation for some objects:

1. Deselect all the objects, Ctrl-click the two block arrows that point down, and then change the Direction to **From Top**.

2. Deselect the down arrows, Ctrl-click all five objects in the second row (the two block arrows that point left and the three text boxes), and then change the Direction to **From Right**. Next, you'll change the timing of some of the animations.

3. Deselect the items in the second row, Ctrl-click all the block arrows, click the **Right arrow 13** list arrow (the final selected object) in the animation list in the task pane to display a menu, and then click **Timing**. The Wipe dialog box opens with the Timing tab on top.

4. Click the **Delay** up arrow four times to change the value to **2** seconds. This means that before each arrow animates onto the screen, there will be a two-second delay for the viewer to read the information in the text box just before the next arrow animates.

5. Click the **OK** button. PowerPoint previews the animation of the block arrows, with a two-second delay before each one.

6. Click the **Play** button in the task pane to see the entire animation.

Now you're ready to change the animation of the final objects to make the presentation more interesting. You can change any animation effect applied to the objects on a slide.

To edit the animation effects:

1. Click the final text box (the text box beginning with "Carry Out . . ."). The object named **Shape 16** is selected in the animation list.

2. Click the **Shape 16** list arrow in the task pane, and then click **Remove** on the menu to remove the current animation effect.

3. With the final object still selected, add the **Swivel** Entrance animation effect (located in the Exciting section of the Add Entrance Effect dialog box), and change its speed to **Medium**. Now you'll add sound effects to this animation.

4. Click the **Shape 16** list arrow, click **Effect Options** on the menu to open the Swivel dialog box with the Effect tab on top. Note that this is the same dialog box that opens when you click Timing in the object menu in the animation list, except the Effect tab is on top instead of the Timing tab.

5. Click the **Sound** list arrow, click **Applause**, and then click the **OK** button.

   Trouble? If a message appears telling you that sound effects are not installed, check with your instructor or technical support person if you are working in a lab. If you are working on your own computer, click the Yes button to install the feature now. If you cannot install the sound effects, skip Step 5.

6. With the text box still selected, change the Start option for Shape 16 to **After Previous**.

7. Add the sound effect **Drum Roll** to the last block arrow (Right arrow 13). These changes add a dramatic effect to the last two objects in the diagram.

8. Deselect the arrow object, click the **Slide Show** button in the task pane to view this slide as it will appear when Consuela gives her presentation. Make sure all aspects of the animation are correct—that is, each object animates in the proper order and direction, with the desired delay, and with the added sound effect (where applicable).

9. Press the **Esc** key to exit the slide show and return to Normal view.

10. Close the task pane, and save the presentation.

You've completed the complex animation effects for Slide 10. Next, Consuela wants to add background music and an animated GIF to the slide. Unfortunately, the standard Office Clip Gallery doesn't include the desired music and GIF files that you need. Therefore, you decide to download some clip files from the Microsoft Office Online Web site.

Downloading Clips from Microsoft Office Online

Microsoft provides a Web site called Office Online that contains many images and sound clips for you to use in your PowerPoint presentations. Consuela wants you to add an animated GIF and background music to Slide 10. Recall that an animated GIF is a video clip, identified with the filename extension .gif. To add background music, you'll add a sound clip to the slide and set it to replay over and over again until you go to the next slide.

Reference Window

Downloading Clips from Microsoft Office Online

- Display the slide into which you want to insert a picture, motion, or sound clip.
- Click the Insert Clip Art button 🖼 on the Drawing toolbar to open the Clip Art task pane.
- Click the Clip art on Office Online link.
- Use the search feature on the Office Online page to find the clips that you want, and then click the check box below each clip that you want to download.
- Click the Click to Download button.

You'll connect to Office Online and search for an animated GIF and music file to use in the current presentation.

To download an animated GIF over the Internet:

1. Make sure your computer is connected to the Internet. This might require you to connect your computer modem to an outside phone line, unless your computer is equipped with direct or wireless Internet access.

2. Make sure you're still viewing Slide 10 in Normal view, and then click the **Insert Clip Art** button 🖼 on the Drawing toolbar. The Clip Art task pane opens.

3. Click the **Clip art on Office Online** link near the bottom of the task pane. The Microsoft Office Clip Art and Media page of the Microsoft Office Online site appears in your Web browser.

   Trouble? If you see a page with an addendum to the Microsoft End User License Agreement, read the agreement, and then click the Accept button.

   Trouble? If you get an error message telling you that the Internet connection failed, start your browser, and then repeat Steps 1 through 3.

   Now you'll search the online Microsoft Office Clip Art and Media page for animated GIF and sound files.

4. Click the **Search** list arrow in the upper-right corner of the Microsoft Office Clip Art and Media page, and then click **Animations**. You want to search for an animated GIF that relates to the service-learning courses offered by Global Humanitarian.

5. Click in the **Search** text box to the right of the Search category you just selected, and then type **academic**.

6. Click the **green arrow** button ➡ to the right of the Search text box. This initiates the search. After a minute or two (depending on your connection speed), Office Online displays and animates a group of pictures.

7. Click the **Next right arrow** button, if necessary, until you see the picture of a woman reading a book in a library, as shown in Figure 5-13. Because Microsoft continually updates the Office Online pages, the picture might not be in the same place as in the figure.

Figure 5-13 | **Microsoft Office Clip Art and Media page after searching for animated clips**

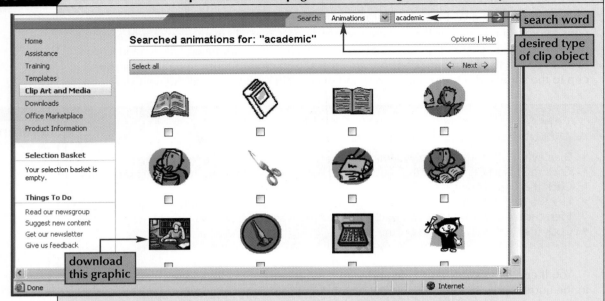

Trouble? If you can't find the animated picture of a woman reading in a library, select a different animated picture file to download.

8. Click the check box below the animation picture to select it, and then click the **Download 1 item** link in the pane on the left. The Download window appears identifying the number of items you have selected to download and the total file size.

Trouble? If Microsoft displays a "Terms of Use" screen, click the Accept button.

Trouble? If you now see a Security Warning dialog box, click the Yes button to install the Microsoft Office Template and Media Control, and then click the Continue button once the installation is complete.

Trouble? If you see a window informing you that Microsoft Office Template and Media Control has been installed, click the Continue button.

9. Click the **Download Now** button in the window. The File Download dialog box opens.

10. Click the **Open** button. The Communications - Microsoft Clip Organizer dialog box opens, showing the clip you just downloaded added to the Communications folder in the Downloaded Clips folder. "Communications" in the title bar of the dialog box is the category name of the selected clip.

Trouble? If the Add Clips to Organizer dialog box also opens, click the Now button. Microsoft then organizes the clip art within your Organizer. This might take a few minutes. Once the clip art is organized, the Add Clips to Organizer dialog box won't open again when you download clip art.

11. Close the Communications - Microsoft Clip Organizer dialog box, but leave the browser open to the Microsoft Office Clip Art and Media page.

You've successfully downloaded the desired animated GIF picture into your Organizer. Now you'll download a music clip.

To download a music clip over the Internet:

1. In the browser window, change the Search type to **Sounds**, click in the **Search** text box, and then type **waltz** to search for waltz music.

2. Click the **green arrow** button to the right of the Search text box button to initiate the search.

3. Go through the pages of sound clips, if necessary, until you see the sound clip titled **Classical Waltz**. (There might be only one page of clips.) See Figure 5-14.

Waltz music files found in Microsoft Office Clip Art and Media page ◄ **Figure 5-14**

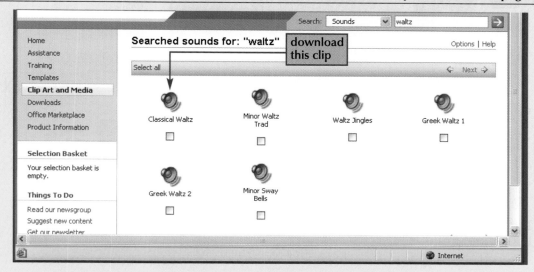

Trouble? If you can't find the Classical Waltz sound clip, download a different waltz.

Trouble? If PowerPoint displays a security warning and asks if you want to install the Microsoft Office on the Web Control, click the Yes button, click the Continue button, and then click the Download Now button.

4. Download the sound clip the same way you downloaded the motion clip, and then close the Clip Art Organizer dialog box.

5. Exit your Web browser, and then, if you manually connected to the Internet, disconnect now.

Having downloaded a motion clip and a sound clip, you're ready to apply them to your PowerPoint presentation.

Applying the Downloaded Motion and Sound Clips

Consuela wants the animated GIF and the background music to "play" while potential clients view the animation that you added to the process diagram on Slide 10. You'll begin by applying the motion clip.

To apply the motion clip to the slide:

▶ **1.** Make sure Slide 10 is in the slide pane, select any text in the Search for text box of the Clip Art task pane and type **academic**, click the **Results should be** list arrow, click the **All media types** check box, if necessary, to select it, and then click the **Go** button in the task pane. The task pane displays a set of pictures similar to the ones shown in Figure 5-15.

Figure 5-15 | Downloaded graphic in Clip Art task pane

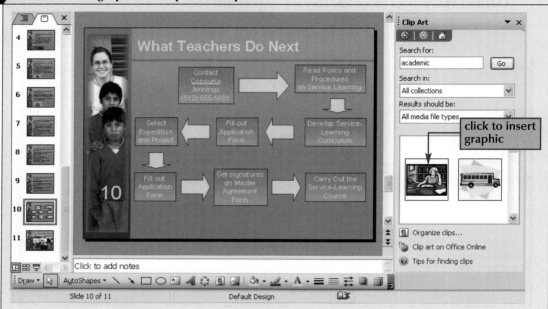

▶ **2.** Click the picture of a woman reading in a library (or the picture you downloaded). The picture is inserted into the center of Slide 10.

▶ **3.** Position the image to the left of the first text box, resize it so that it fits in the space, and then deselect the image. See Figure 5-16.

Figure 5-16 | Slide with animated graphic

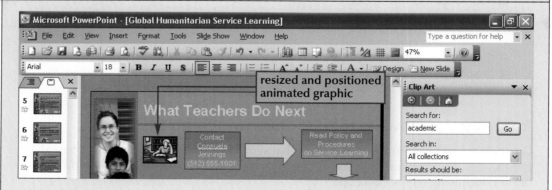

You don't need to do anything special to an animated GIF to make it play continuously in Slide Show view; it does this by default. You'll test this now.

▶ **4.** Click the **Slide Show from current slide** button 🖵 at the bottom of the Slides tab. Slide 10 appears in Slide Show view and the clip of the person reading a book animates automatically, and stays animated, even after the process diagram animation has finished.

▶ **5.** Press the **Esc** key to end the slide show.

Now you'll insert the sound clip and set it up to play as background music while the slide is on the screen in Slide Show view.

To apply a sound clip as background music:

1. Select the text in the Search for text box in the task pane, type **waltz**, and then click the **Go** button. The Clip Art task pane displays one or more clips with the word "waltz" in the title.

2. Scroll the list of clips in the task pane as necessary until you see the icon for Classical Waltz (you might see only "Classical. . ."), and then click it. A dialog box opens asking how you want the sound to start in the slide show.

3. Click the **Automatically** button to indicate that you want the sound clip to play as soon as the slide appears on the screen. PowerPoint inserts the sound icon in the middle of the slide.

4. Drag the sound icon to the lower-right corner of the slide.

5. Start the slide show from Slide 10. The animated GIF appears and plays and the diagram animates, but the sound doesn't start until after all of the images in the process diagram appear. Also, the sound clip plays once, and then stops.

   Because you've animated the other objects on the screen, the sound clip won't play until all the objects appear because the sound clip is the last object. You can solve that problem by moving the sound object to the top of the animation list in the Custom Animation task pane.

6. Press the **Esc** key to stop the slide show, click the **Other Task Panes** list arrow ▼ at the top of the Clip Art task pane, and then click **Custom Animation** to open the Custom Animation task pane. The sound icon is selected in the animation list. The name of the item, j0388613.wav, is the name of the sound file you downloaded.

   Trouble? If you downloaded a sound file other than Classical Waltz, the filename listed in the animation list will be different.

7. Drag the **sound object** animation item to the top of the animation list (above Right arrow 3). Now you'll change the effect options for the sound object.

   Trouble? If your list of animation objects lists Media 17 instead of a filename for the sound object, drag Media 17 to the top of the animation list, and make the changes in the next step to Media 17.

8. Click the **j0388613.wav** list arrow, click **Effect Options** to open the Play Sound dialog box, and, if necessary, click the **Effect** tab.

9. Make sure the **From beginning** option button is selected in the Start playing section of the dialog box, and then click the **After current slide** option button in the Stop playing section. See Figure 5-17.

Figure 5-17 ▶ **Play Sound dialog box**

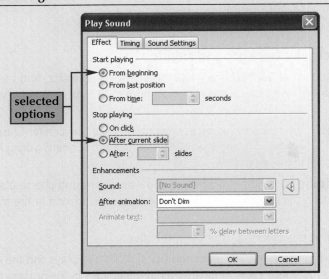

10. Click the **OK** button. To make sure the animation proceeds as the tune (sound object) is being played, you need to change one of the options of Right arrow 3.

11. Click the **Right arrow 3** animation item, click the **Right arrow 3** list arrow in the animation list, and then click **Start With Previous**. Now the animation will start at the same time the tune plays. Next you'll set the background music to play continuously while the slide is on the screen, and you'll hide the sound icon because it has no function on the screen and might distract those who view the slide show.

12. Right-click the **sound** icon, click **Edit Sound Object** on the shortcut menu, click the **Loop until stopped** check box to select it, click the **Hide sound icon during slide show** check box to select it, and then click the **OK button**.

13. Click the **Slide Show** button in the task pane to see the animations and hear the background music of Slide 10. After the animation ends, but while the tune is still playing, press the **Esc** key to return to Normal view.

14. If everything worked correctly, save your presentation. If you notice any problems, fix them and then save the presentation.

This completes the animation and sound effects for Slide 10.

Inserting a CD Audio Track into a Slide

Just as you can insert a music clip into a slide, you can also insert a CD audio track into a slide. Consuela wants you to insert some CD music into Slide 2 ("Presentation Contents") of your presentation. You'll do that now.

Inserting a CD Track into a Slide

- Click Insert on the menu bar, point to Movies and Sounds, and then click Play CD Audio Track.
- Select the starting and ending track in the Play CD Audio Track section of the dialog box, and specify other options, as desired.
- Click the OK button.
- Place a music CD into your computer's CD-ROM or DVD drive before you run the slide show to play the selected track during the slide show.

To insert a CD audio track into a slide:

1. Go to **Slide 2** ("Presentation Contents").

2. Select a music CD that has a track you want to play in the background of Slide 2.

    Trouble? If you don't have a music CD, continue with the steps, using 1 as the track number in Steps 5 and 6.

3. Click **Insert** on the menu bar, point to **Movies and Sounds**, and then click **Play CD Audio Track**. The Insert CD Audio dialog box opens.

4. Click the **Loop until stopped** and the **Hide sound icon during slide show** check boxes to select them.

5. Double-click the value in the Start at track text box, and then type the track number of the song you want to apply. You can play two or more consecutive tracks, but you want to play only one track.

6. Double-click the value in the End at track text box, type the same track number that you typed in the Start at track text box, and then click the **OK** button. A dialog box opens asking how you want the sound to start in the slide show.

7. Click the **Automatically** button in the dialog box that opens asking how you want the sound to start in the slide show. PowerPoint inserts a CD icon in the middle of the slide.

8. Drag the **CD** icon from the middle of the slide to near the lower-left corner, below the large yellow slide number. Now you want to tell PowerPoint to start playing the CD track before any animation, and to stop after this slide.

9. Click the **Media 10** list arrow in the animation list in the Custom Animation task pane, click **Effect Options** to open the Effect tab in the Play CD Audio dialog box, and then click the **After current slide** option button. The CD will stop playing after this slide. You want the CD to start playing immediately when the slide appears.

10. Click the **Timing** tab, click the **Start** list arrow, and then click **With Previous**.

11. Click the **OK** button, close the task pane, and then save the presentation. To test the music you just added, you need to insert the CD you want to use.

12. Place the music CD you chose into the drive, verify that the music plays properly, verify the track number of the track you want to add, and then close the music program window to stop the music.

    Trouble? If you don't have a CD, skip Steps 12 and 13.

13. Run the slide show from Slide 2, listen to the CD track, click a link or a blank area of the slide to move to another slide, notice that the CD track stops playing, and then press the **Esc** key to end the slide show.

Your slide is ready to play a CD music track. Now you just have to make sure your music CD is inserted into the drive whenever you start the slide show. If the CD is not inserted when you run the slide show, the music simply will be omitted. Note that the CD icon is not linked to the specific CD that was in the CD drive when you set the options. The track number you specified will play from any CD.

Adding Action Buttons to a Slide

You're already familiar with action buttons. Action buttons, sometimes called **navigation buttons**, help a person viewing a presentation to navigate through it. You'll add action buttons to some of the slides in the current presentation for Global Humanitarian. You'll use buttons that will help indicate to the viewer or presenter what will happen when he or she clicks the button; for example, you'll use a button with a right-pointing arrow to indicate that clicking it will move to the next slide. These action buttons will help viewers navigate the slide show, without necessarily having to proceed in a specific order.

To add action buttons to the slides:

1. Go to **Slide 3** ("Service-Learning Courses"). You'll add three action buttons to this slide, and then copy them to the other slides in the presentation.

2. Click **Slide Show** on the menu bar, point to **Action Buttons**, click the **Action Button: Forward or Next** button ▷, and then position the pointer anywhere in the slide. The pointer changes to ┼.

3. Drag ┼ while holding down the **Shift** key, so that you draw a small square near the bottom-right corner of the slide. Pressing the Shift key causes you to draw a square button instead of a rectangle. PowerPoint displays the Action Settings dialog box, with the default setting of Hyperlink to: Next Slide, which is the setting you want.

4. Click the **OK** button, and then deselect the action button.

5. Insert the **Action Button: Home** button 🏠 immediately to the left of and the same size as the Forward or Next button.

6. In the Action Settings dialog box, click the **Hyperlink to** list arrow, click **Slide**, click **2. Presentation Contents**, and then click the **OK** button twice to close the two dialog boxes.

7. Insert the **Action Button: Back or Previous** button ◁ to the left of the Home action button, and set the hyperlink to **Previous Slide**. Compare your screen to Figure 5-18.

Figure 5-18	Slide 3 with action buttons

Trouble? If the action buttons don't have essentially the same sizes and positions shown in Figure 5-18, adjust them now.

▶ **8.** Position the pointer above the upper-left corner of the Back or Previous action button, and then drag down and to the right to draw a selection box around all three action buttons. As you drag, a rectangle with a dotted-line border appears around the objects you dragged over. When you release the mouse button, the three buttons are selected.

▶ **9.** Copy the selected buttons to all the other slides (including Slides 1 and 2) using the **Copy** 🗎 and **Paste** 🖺 buttons on the Standard toolbar. As you paste the action buttons in a slide, make sure they don't overlap or bump into text; if they do, drag them down below the text.

▶ **10.** Go to **Slide 1**, and then delete the **Back** and **Home** action buttons (leaving only the Forward action button).

▶ **11.** Go to **Slide 2**, delete the **Home** action button (leaving the Back and Forward action buttons), and then drag the **Back** action button closer to the Forward button.

▶ **12.** Go to **Slide 11** ("Enjoy Learning with Global Humanitarian!"), delete the **Next** action button (leaving only the Back and Home action buttons), and then drag the two buttons to the right by the space of one button.

▶ **13.** View the slide show starting at Slide 1 to ensure that all the action buttons work properly; if necessary, stop the slide show and fix any buttons that do not work correctly.

▶ **14.** Save your presentation.

Having set up action buttons, you're ready to add narration to the slides to help potential clients understand how to run the slide show.

Recording a Narration

Consuela told you that she would use the PowerPoint presentation not only for oral presentations, but also as a self-running presentation. A **self-running presentation** runs without human interruption, but it can accept human intervention to advance to another slide or return to a previous one. Consuela wants to set up the self-running presentation on a computer at college internship fairs and similar events. At these events, students and faculty can come by and run through the presentation on their own. So that the attendees will know how to navigate through the presentation, Consuela suggests that you add narration to the slides. Before you record narration for a presentation, you should always write a brief script for each slide so you won't hesitate while recording. We'll assume that you already did that, and you're ready to record the narration.

Recording a Narration

Reference Window

- In Normal view, go to the slide where you want to start recording a narration, click Slide Show, click Record Narration, click the Set Microphone Level button, position the microphone where you want it while you record the slide show narration, read the text shown in quotes in the dialog box, and then click the OK button.
- Leave the Link narration in check box unselected if you want to save the narration with the presentation; select it if you want to save the narration in another file that is linked to the presentation file.
- Click the OK button.
- Speak into the microphone to record the narration for the current slide.
- Press the spacebar to go to the next slide (if desired), record the narration for that slide, and then continue, as desired, to other slides.
- After completing the narrations, press the Esc key to end the slide show.
- Click the Save button to save the timing of the presentation, or click the Don't Save button to save only the narration.

To record a narration:

▶ **1.** Make sure your computer is equipped with a microphone.

   Trouble? If your system doesn't have a microphone, find a computer that does, connect a microphone to your computer, or check with your instructor or technical support person. If you cannot connect a microphone to your computer, read the following steps but do not do them.

▶ **2.** Go to **Slide 1**, click **Slide Show** on the menu bar, and then click **Record Narration**. The Record Narration dialog box opens.

▶ **3.** Click the **Set Microphone Level** button, position the microphone where you want it while you record the narration, and then read the text in quotes in the Microphone Check dialog box. PowerPoint automatically adjusts the microphone level for you.

▶ **4.** Click the **OK** button in the Microphone Check dialog box. The Microphone Check dialog box closes.

▶ **5.** Make sure the **Link narrations in** check box is not selected. The recorded sound files will be saved within the presentation rather than in separate files.

   When you click the OK button to close the Record Narration dialog box, PowerPoint will automatically start the slide show. You should start talking as soon as each slide appears, without waiting for the animation to finish. If you want to comment on each bullet as it appears, time your narration to coincide with the animations.

▶ **6.** Click the **OK** button in the Record Narration dialog box. PowerPoint automatically starts the slide show.

▶ **7.** As soon as the slide appears (without waiting for the animation to finish), talk into the microphone, using a clear and steady voice: "Welcome to Service Learning with Global Humanitarian. After you read the contents of this title slide, click the yellow Forward button at the bottom of the screen to advance to the next slide."

▶ **8.** Press the **spacebar** to go to Slide 2, and then immediately say into the microphone, "This is the Presentation Contents slide, or Home slide. To jump directly to another location in the slide show, click one of the miniature slides on the screen. To go to the next slide, click the Forward button. To go back to the previous slide, click the Back button."

▶ **9.** Press the **spacebar** to go to Slide 3, and then immediately say into the microphone, "After looking over this slide, or any subsequent slide, click the Home button to return to the Presentation Contents slide, or click the Back or Forward button to go to the previous or next slide."

▶ **10.** Press the **Esc** button to halt the recording before going to the next slide. PowerPoint displays a message asking if you want to save the timing that you set for each slide when you recorded your narration. You don't want the slide show to advance on its own, so you won't save the timing.

▶ **11.** Click the **Don't Save** button. You've now recorded a narration for your slide show.

▶ **12.** Go back to **Slide 1**, run the slide show to test your narration, and then press the **Esc** key after listening to your narration for Slide 3.

   Trouble? If the narration has mistakes, return to Normal view, click the sound icon in the lower-right corner of the slide, press the Delete key, and re-record the narration for that slide. Note that to save a narration of a particular slide, you must advance to the next slide, or the narration won't be saved. After re-recording your narration, repeat Steps 10 and 11.

▶ **13.** Save the presentation.

You've recorded the narration for the presentation. Next, you'll remove the background on one slide in the presentation.

Manipulating Background Objects

The next task that Consuela wants you to perform to improve the Global Humanitarian presentation is to remove the background on Slide 11, the final slide. As the slide now appears, the background picture of the student with the Peruvian children on the left side of the slide interferes with the larger picture of service-learning students that appears on the main part of the slide. You'll first remove the entire background, and then adjust the size and location of the large graphic. Later you'll see how to add part of the background back into the slide.

To remove the background of a slide:

1. Go to **Slide 11**, click **Format** on the menu bar, and then click **Background**. The Background dialog box opens.

2. Click the **Omit background graphics from master** check box to select it, and then click the **Apply** button. All three background objects on Slide 11 disappear: the image of the student with Peruvian children, the green-to-brown gradient box, and the horizontal green bar below the title.

   Trouble? If you accidentally click the Apply to All button, click the Undo button 🔄 on the Standard toolbar, and then repeat Step 2.

3. Resize the title text box so it spans the width of the slide, and then position the text box closer to the top of the slide.

4. Click the text box border to select the entire text box object, if necessary, and then click the **Center** button 🔳 on the Standard toolbar to center the text within the text box.

5. Resize the graphic so it fills the entire width of the slide and comes close to the text at the top. Compare your screen to the one shown in Figure 5-19.

Slide 11 after modifications ◀ **Figure 5-19**

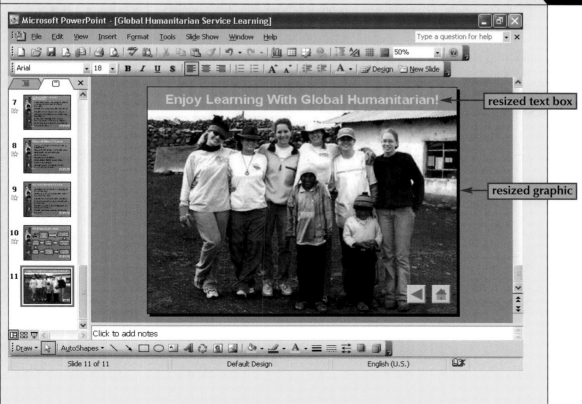

The appearance of the slide still needs improvement, so you decide to re-insert the horizontal green bar below the slide title. Because PowerPoint doesn't allow you to add part of a background, you must copy the background object from the master slide into the current slide.

▶ **6.** Shift-click the **Normal View** button ⊞ to switch to Slide Master view.

▶ **7.** Click the horizontal green bar to select it, click the **Copy** button 📋 on the Standard toolbar, return to Normal view, and then click the **Paste** button 📋. The green bar appears on the slide.

▶ **8.** Drag the horizontal green bar so it rests just on top of the digital picture and below the title, and then deselect the bar. See Figure 5-20.

Figure 5-20 | **Slide 11 with background object copied to slide**

▶ **9.** Save the presentation.

You've omitted the background objects from one slide, copied a background object, and used it in a slide.

You've almost completed the presentation. Your last set of tasks is to set up the presentation as a self-running slide show, so that it will run unattended.

Review

Session 5.1 Quick Check

1. Give two methods for inserting a PowerPoint slide into another program.
2. If the Clip Art task pane on your computer doesn't have any picture, motion, or sound clips that you want, where can you get additional clips?
3. True or False: PowerPoint provides a facility for omitting some background objects while displaying other background objects.
4. True or False: While a sound clip associated with a slide is playing, PowerPoint can proceed with the animations of that slide.
5. True or False: If you add several objects to a slide and want to animate them one at a time, they must always animate in the same order in which you added them.
6. Describe how to set up a slide to play a CD music track.
7. Describe how to record a narration for a presentation.

Session 5.2

Setting Up a Self-Running Presentation

Consuela likes the presentation so far. She will use it in its current state to give slide show presentations to groups of faculty members and students. Now she would like you to set up the presentation so that it is self-running; however, she wants people who view the show to be able to control the presentation if they choose (for example, if they want to review a slide that has already gone by). This means that you need to set up the slide show as a self-running presentation, but with features that allow for human intervention. This often includes one or more of the following:

- **Automatic timing**: This feature tells PowerPoint to display slides for a certain amount of time before moving to the next slide.
- **Hyperlinks**: These allow users to speed up or change the order of viewing. You can set up a slide show so that, if users don't use the hyperlinks, the slide show will proceed automatically.
- **Narration**: This gives the users more information or instructions for overriding the automatic timing.
- **Kiosk browsing**: This feature tells PowerPoint that, when the slide show reaches the last slide, the presentation should start over again at the beginning.

Looking at the above list of items typically involved in a self-running presentation, you've already added hyperlinks and narration. The only items left to add are automatic slide timing and kiosk browsing. You also want to add slide transitions. You'll add transitions and manually set the timing next.

Setting the Slide Timing Manually

You can set the slide timing manually or you can rehearse the presentation and save the timing from your rehearsal. You will set the timing manually.

To set the slide timing:

1. If you took a break at the end of the previous session, open the presentation **Global Humanitarian Service Learning**.

2. Click the **Slide Sorter View** button 🔲 to switch to Slide Sorter view.

3. Click the **Transition** button on the Slide Sorter toolbar to open the Slide Transition task pane, scroll down the list of transitions, and then click **Dissolve**.

4. Click the **Automatically after** check box in the task pane to select it. A time of zero minutes and zero seconds appears in the Automatically after text box.

5. Click the **Automatically after** up arrow five times to set the slide timing to five seconds, and then click the **Apply to All Slides** button in the task pane. The transition effect and manual timing are applied to all of the slides, and the time appears below each slide in Slide Sorter view. See Figure 5-21.

Figure 5-21 Slides after manually setting the timing

6. Click **Slide 1**, if necessary, to make it the current slide, and then click the **Slide Show** button in the task pane, and then watch as the slide show advances through the first several slides. Notice that when a slide has an animation, the slide show advances as soon as the animation finishes because the animations take longer than five seconds.

7. Press the **Esc** key, and then save the presentation.

The manual timing you set is not helpful because the viewer does not have enough time to read all of the information on the slide after the last item animates. Instead, you'll rehearse the slide show and record the slide timing.

Rehearsing and Recording the Slide Timing

You can rehearse a slide show and have PowerPoint keep track of the time you spend on each slide as you rehearse the presentation. You can then use those times for automatic timing of a self-running slide show. You'll rehearse the slide show now.

Get ready to read and look over each slide in the presentation, listening to any narration, watching animations, and reading the text. Take the amount of time that you think a student or teacher would take to view each slide or bulleted item. You'll use the spacebar to advance from one one slide to the next, according to your desired timing of each item. Don't use the action buttons. You should move along at a speed for moderately slow readers. Keep in mind that if you move too slowly, your viewers will become bored or wonder if the slide show is working properly; if you move too quickly, viewers will not have enough time to read and absorb the information on each slide.

To determine the timing of slides for a self-running slide show:

1. Click **Slide 1** in Slide Sorter view, if necessary.

2. Click the **Rehearse Timings** button 🕓 on the Slide Sorter toolbar. PowerPoint automatically starts the slide show, and the Rehearsal dialog box appears on the screen in the upper-left corner.

3. Leave Slide 1 on the screen until the narration you recorded finishes playing, and then press the **spacebar**. Slide 2 appears on the screen.

4. Continue through the slide show using the guidelines discussed prior to this set of steps. If you need to stop the rehearsal, click the **Pause** button ⏸ on the Rehearsal toolbar to pause the timer; click it again to start the timer again. If you think you have spent too long on a slide, click the **Repeat** button ↺ on the Rehearsal toolbar to restart the timer for the current slide.

After you press the spacebar to set the timing for Slide 11 (the last slide), a black screen appears and a dialog box asks if you want to save the timing.

5. Click the **Yes** button. PowerPoint saves the timing and returns you to Slide Sorter view with Slide 1 selected. The rehearsed time appears below each slide thumbnail, and the exact timing for the selected slide appears in the Automatically after text box in the Slide Transition task pane. (Your rehearsed timings override the manual timings you set.) See Figure 5-22.

Slides with recorded display times | Figure 5-22

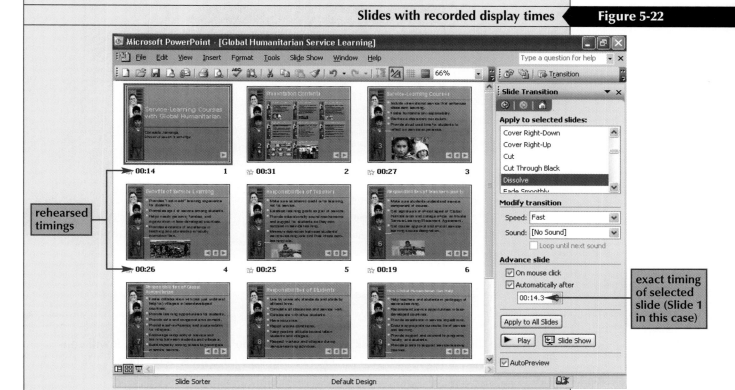

6. Run the slide show to check the animation and timing. If you feel that a slide stays on the screen for too much or too little time, stop the slide show, click the slide to select it in Slide Sorter view, and then change the time in the Automatically after check box.

Trouble? If the times you selected are significantly different from those shown in Figure 5-22, you might want to adjust them.

7. Close the task pane, and then save the presentation.

Applying Kiosk Browsing

The browse-at-a-kiosk feature in PowerPoint allows you to set up a presentation to continually start over. It also disables the spacebar and left mouse-click functions to advance through the slide show. A viewer can, however, click hyperlinks on the screen, including action buttons. You can also still press the Esc key to end the slide show.

Now you'll set up the Global Humanitarian presentation for kiosk browsing.

To set up the presentation for browsing at a kiosk:

► **1.** Click **Slide Show** on the menu bar, and click **Set Up Show** to open the Set Up Show dialog box.

► **2.** Click the **Browsed at a kiosk (full screen)** option button in the Show type section of the dialog box. See Figure 5-23.

Figure 5-23	Set Up Show dialog box

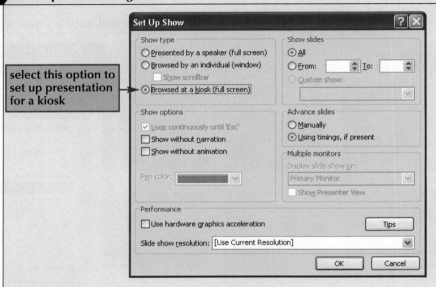

select this option to set up presentation for a kiosk

► **3.** Click the **OK** button, and then save the presentation.

With the slide show set for kiosk browsing, when you run the slide show, it will continue to run until someone presses the Esc key. Now you'll test the slide show.

To test the self-running slide show:

► **1.** Start the slide show from Slide 8. Watch as the slide show progresses to Slide 9 and then to Slide 10.

► **2.** On Slide 10, click the **Back** action button. Slide 9 appears on the screen. Because you moved back in the slide show, the slide show will not continue on its own; the timings are paused until you move past the slide where you initially clicked the Back button.

► **3.** Click the **Next** action button on Slide 9. Slide 10 appears and remains on the screen, but the background music does not play. If you waited for the animation to complete before you clicked the Back button, you will see the entire process diagram. If you did not wait for the animation to complete before you clicked the Back button, the process diagram will animate now.

► **4.** Click the **Next** action button on Slide 10. The slide show progresses to Slide 11 and then continues running itself. After the rehearsed time, Slide 1 appears because the slide show was set to run continuously.

► **5.** Press the **Esc** key to end the slide show.

Next, you'll add an additional graphic to the presentation.

Adding Illustrations and Callouts

Consuela is pleased with the presentation. After looking it over once more, she decides that she would like you to add a new slide with a graphic showing a map of the South American countries in which Global Humanitarian sponsors service-learning project sites. She wants the colors of the map to match the color scheme of the presentation, and she would like to include something on the map to graphically tie it to the service-learning trips. To accomplish this, she hired a graphic artist.

You're already familiar with the PowerPoint drawing tools. For example, Consuela used the Block Arrows (types of AutoShapes) and text boxes (with borders and gradient fills) to create the diagram in Slide 10 of your presentation. If you want more sophisticated diagrams or illustrations, however, you'll have to use a more sophisticated drawing software package. The more popular high-end drawing software includes Adobe Illustrator and CorelDraw. Because this type of software is complex and difficult to learn, it's meant primarily for skilled artists and draftspersons. People with moderate artistic ability, however, might also find sophisticated illustration software useful in creating complex drawings.

The graphic artist hired by Consuela scanned a map of South America, and then used drawing software to recolor the countries on the map with shades of green so that the map would match the color scheme of the presentation. The artist then edited and merged two photographs of Peruvian children with the map. The artist saved the final image in JPEG format. You'll import this image into PowerPoint, resize it, and then label it using PowerPoint drawing tools.

To insert a graphic produced with illustration software:

1. Double-click **Slide 7** ("Responsibilities of Global Humanitarian") to switch to that slide in Normal view, click the **New Slide** button ⊡ on the Formatting toolbar, click the **Title and Content** layout, close the task pane, click the slide title placeholder, and then type **Countries with Global Humanitarian Projects**. The new Slide 8 and its title are now part of the presentation.

2. Click the **Insert Picture** button ⊡ in the placeholder, navigate to the **Tutorial.05\Tutorial** folder included with your Data Files, click **SAmer**, and then click the **Insert** button. The picture of the map appears in the slide. Now, you'll resize the picture and remove the dark background on the graphic.

3. Drag the sizing handles so that the top of the map is just below the horizontal green bar below the slide title and the bottom of the map is near the bottom of the slide.

4. Click the **Set Transparent Color** button ⊿ on the Picture toolbar, and then click anywhere in the dark area around the map of South America. The dark background disappears so that the picture blends better with the slide background. See Figure 5-24.

| Figure 5-24 | Illustration inserted into slide |

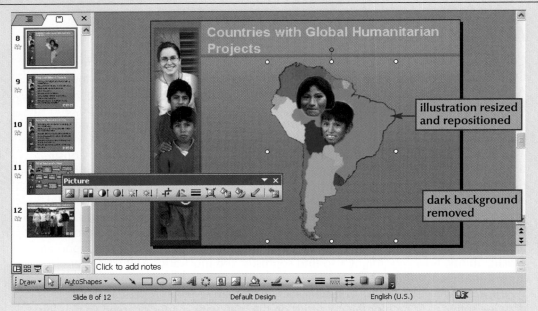

Trouble? If the color of the map becomes distorted when you apply the Set Transparent Color tool, don't worry. The picture will look fine in Slide Show view.

Trouble? If the Picture toolbar isn't visible on your screen, click View on the menu bar, point to Toolbars, and then click Picture.

With the illustration in the new slide, you'll create callouts for the illustration. **Callouts** are labels that include a text box and a line (with or without an arrowhead) between the text box and the item being labeled.

To add callouts to the illustration:

1. Click the **AutoShapes** button on the Drawing toolbar, point to **Callouts**, and then click the **Line Callout 2 (No border)** button located on the fourth row, second column, of the callout icons.

2. Click ┼ to the left of Peru (the large, light-green country on the left). A callout box is inserted on the slide with the blinking insertion point inside it.

3. Type **Peru**, and then click the edge of the callout text box to select the entire object. As you can see, the word "Peru" is light yellow on a darker yellow background, which makes the word hard to read. You'll remove the background color, increase the font size, and change the thickness and location of the callout line.

4. Click the **Fill Color** list arrow on the Drawing toolbar, click **No Fill**, click **Format** on the menu bar, click **Font** to open the Font dialog box, change the font size to **32**, click the **OK** button, and then drag the sizing handles of the callout text box so that the entire word "Peru" just fits inside the box.

5. With the callout box object still selected, click the **Line Style** button on the Drawing toolbar, and then click **2¼ pt**.

6. Drag the adjustment handle (the small, yellow diamond at the end of the callout line) to the center of the country of Peru, drag the text box so that it's positioned as shown in Figure 5-25, and then click a blank area of the slide to deselect the callout.

Slide 8 after adding and editing callout ◀ **Figure 5-25**

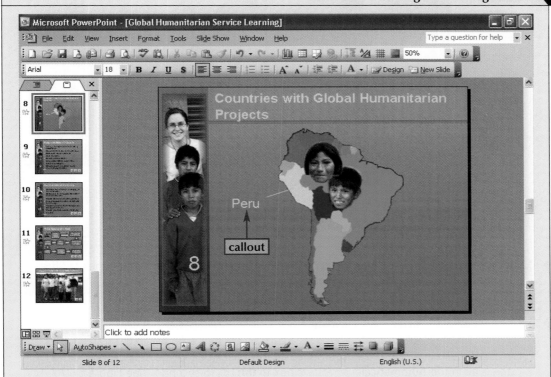

Trouble? If your callout doesn't look like the one shown in Figure 5-25, make the necessary adjustments now.

7. Press and hold the **Shift** key, click the callout to select the entire object, release the **Shift** key, click the **Copy** button 🖺 on the Standard toolbar, and then click the **Paste** button 🖺 on the Standard toolbar. A copy of the callout with the same format applied appears on the slide.

8. Drag the callout to reposition it below the Peru callout, and then drag the adjustment handle on the copied callout so the line points to Bolivia, the dark green country southeast of Peru.

9. Double-click **Peru** in the copied callout, type **Bolivia**, and then resize the callout box to fit the text.

10. Add the following two callouts to the slide, using the same callout style, fill, text format, and line thickness as the first two callouts you added: **Ecuador**, which is the small country just above the top of Peru, and **Paraguay**, the small, bright green country southwest of Bolivia.

11. Position the callouts as shown in Figure 5-26.

Figure 5-26 | Slide 8 with callouts

12. Go to **Slide 7**, copy the three action buttons at the bottom of the screen, go back to **Slide 8**, and then paste the action buttons onto the slide.

You need to apply a transition and set the timing for the new slide.

13. Switch to Slide Sorter view, click **Slide 8** to select it, if necessary, click the **Transition** button on the Slide Sorter toolbar, make sure **Dissolve** is selected in the transition list in the task pane and that the **Automatically after** check box is selected, and then change the time in the Automatically after text box to **00:15** (15 seconds). See Figure 5-27.

Figure 5-27 | Slide 8 set to 15-second display and Dissolve transition

14. Close the task pane and save your presentation. See Figure 5-28.

Completed presentation in Slide Sorter view | **Figure 5-28**

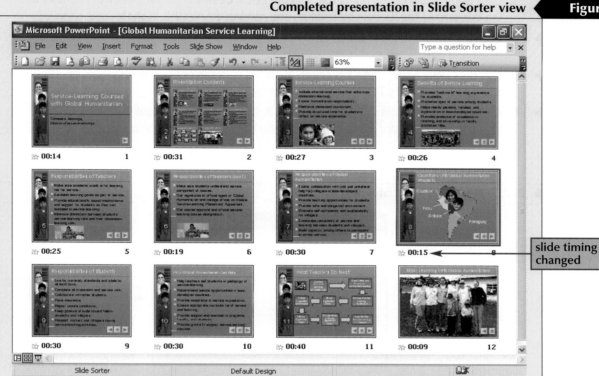

slide timing changed

The graphic and callouts you added to Slide 8 demonstrate the power of combining illustration software, clip art, photographs, and PowerPoint drawing tools to make a complete illustration.

Your presentation is complete. You send a copy to Consuela, who is pleased with the final result. She uses the presentation at many colleges and universities, both for her oral presentations and as a self-running presentation at college internship fairs, and gets many favorable responses from students and faculty.

Creating and Editing a Custom Show

After Consuela had used the Global Humanitarian Service Learning presentation at various colleges and universities, she decided that not all the slides were applicable to presentations to school administrators. Specifically, she felt that during oral presentations to administrators, she didn't need Slide 2 ("Presentation Contents") because she always proceeded from one slide to the next, Slide 11 ("What Teachers Do Next") because the teachers weren't actually in the audience, or Slide 12 ("Enjoy Learning With Global Humanitarian!") because it was more student oriented. Furthermore, Consuela would like the current Slide 8 ("Countries with Global Humanitarian Projects") to appear as the last slide in the presentation. Consuela therefore asks you to create a custom show with those changes. A **custom show** is a presentation in which selected slides are left out of the presentation or the order of slides is changed without actually deleting or moving slides within the PowerPoint file. You'll create a custom show now.

To create and run a custom show:

▶ **1.** Click **Slide Show** on the menu bar, and then click **Custom Shows**. The Custom Shows dialog box opens. You'll begin by creating and naming a new custom show.

▶ **2.** Click the **New** button, and then type **Presentation to Administrators** in the Slide show name text box.

▶ **3.** Ctrl-click **Slide 1** and **Slide 3 through 10** in the Slides in presentation list box, and then click the **Add** button. The selected slides are added to the Slides in custom show list box.

▶ **4.** In the Slides in custom show list box, click **7. Countries with Global Humanitarian Projects** (although you'll be able to read only the first part of the slide name), and then click the down arrow to the right of the list box twice to move that slide to the end of the list (so it becomes Slide 9). See Figure 5-29.

Figure 5-29	Define Custom Show dialog box

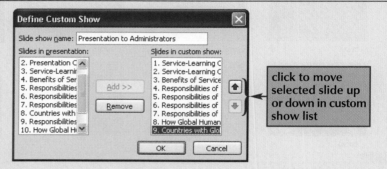

▶ **5.** Click the **OK** button. The custom show you just created is added to the Custom shows list box in the Custom Shows dialog box. Now, with the Custom Show dialog box open, you can give a presentation using the custom show.

▶ **6.** Click the **Show** button to switch to Slide Show view, and then use the action buttons to go through the presentation. Notice that the slides appear in the order you set in the Slides in custom show list box in the Custom Shows dialog box, and that this order is different from the original presentation.

▶ **7.** Press the **Esc** key to end the presentation.

▶ **8.** Print the presentation as handouts, 4 slides per page.

▶ **9.** Save and close the presentation.

From now on, when Consuela wants to give a presentation of the custom show, she clicks Slide Show on the menu bar, clicks Custom Shows, selects "Presentation to Administrators" in the Custom shows list box, and then clicks the Show button.

If Consuela decides to include additional slides, remove slides, or change the order of the slides in the custom show, she can modify the custom show she created. She would open the Custom Show dialog box, click the name of the custom show in the Custom shows list, and then click the Edit button in the dialog box to open the Define Custom Show dialog box.

Consuela thanks you for your help in preparing these presentations.

Review

Session 5.2 Quick Check

1. List five typical features of a self-running presentation.
2. If you use the PowerPoint feature to rehearse slide timing and you make a mistake in the timing, how can you fix the mistake without redoing the entire slide show rehearsal?
3. Why might you want to use illustration software to make a diagram or illustration, instead of the PowerPoint drawing tools?
4. How do you end a slide show running at a kiosk?
5. True or False: When you create a custom show, you create a new file that is linked to the original presentation.
6. True or False: You can apply transitions, animations, and timings to the same slide.

Review

Tutorial Summary

In this tutorial, you learned how to use PowerPoint slides in other applications by copying a slide into a Word document and then modifying the slide as a picture object. You also learned to make thumbnails of slides and paste them in another slide, and then to create hyperlinks from the thumbnails. You learned how to apply complex animation and sound effects by animating a background object, and editing and reordering animation effects. You learned how to download animated pictures and music clips from the Microsoft Office Online Web site, insert a CD audio track into a slide, add action buttons to a slide, and record a narration as part of a presentation. You also learned how to set up and run a self-running presentation. Next, you learned how to insert an illustration and add callouts. Finally, you learned how to create a custom show.

Key Terms

automatic timing	grid	navigation button
callout	kiosk browsing	self-running presentation
custom show		

Practice

Review Assignments

Get hands-on practice of the skills you learned in the tutorial using the same case scenario.

Data Files needed for the Review Assignments: StuRep.ppt, Bolivia.jpg, Students.jpg

After the success of the self-running presentation at colleges and universities, Consuela thinks it would be a good idea to set up a kiosk in the lobby of the Global Humanitarian office in Austin. She asks you to design a presentation based on a student report of the experience in a service-learning expedition sponsored by Global Humanitarian. The purpose of the kiosk will be to show visitors a sample of the courses students take and the volunteer work they perform. The visitors are often potential donors or expedition participants, so it's important to create an attractive, meaningful presentation. Do the following:

1. Open the presentation **StuRep** from the Tutorial.05\Review folder included with your Data Files, and then save it to the same folder as **Student Report on Service Learning**.
2. On Slide 1, change the name of the student from "Haley Knudsen" to your name. If you have a digital photograph of yourself or can create one, insert it next to your name.
3. To Slide 2, add AutoShape block arrows to show the flow of the steps in preparation for the service-learning experience in Bolivia. Add custom animation to the text boxes and arrows so they fly in onto the slide in the order of the steps, and modify

the animation so that the objects fly in from the appropriate direction and so that the text box following each arrow appears immediately after the arrow. Make sure each text box appears for a few seconds before the next arrow appears.

4. To Slide 3, add the animated clip art of a Spanish accordion player and fiddler. This is available from the Microsoft Office Clip Art and Media page on Microsoft Office Online. Change the layout of the slide as necessary.

5. Also to Slide 3, add the sound clip "agriculture" (some of its other keywords are accordion, banjoes, and music), which you can find in the Microsoft Office Clip Art and Media page on Microsoft Office Online. Set up the sound clip to play as soon as the slide appears in Slide Show view and repeats until the slide no longer appears in the slide show, and hide the sound icon during the slide show.

6. To Slide 5, add the image **Bolivia**, located the Tutorial.05\Review folder included with your Data Files, which was created using a combination of a drawing program and a photo-editing program, and make the blue background transparent.

7. Add a callout with the text "Bolivia" to the country of Bolivia, which is highlighted with a black outline, and reformat the callout so the text is 32 points and yellow, the callout line is yellow and 2¼ points, and there is no fill on the callout text box.

8. Create a new Slide 10 with the Title and Content layout. Remove the background images, and then insert the picture file **Students**, located the Tutorial.05\Review folder included with your Data Files. This is a picture of a group of students taking the service-learning courses.

9. Add the title "Student Participants," resize the title text box as wide as possible, center the title text, re-insert the line graphic that was on the slide master, and then resize the graphic as large as possible.

10. Create a new Slide 2 with the Title Only layout, give it the title "Contents," insert thumbnails of the subsequent slides in the presentation, and then make the thumbnails hyperlinks to their respective slides.

11. Add Back, Next, and Home action buttons to all of the slides, except the first and last slides. For the first slide, include only Home and Next action buttons. To the last slide, include only Home and Back action buttons. Also, don't include a Home action button on Slide 2, which you should make the Home location. On Slide 2, arrange the action buttons vertically on the right if you don't have enough space to fit them in the lower-right corner.

12. Record the narration for Slide 1: "Welcome to Service Learning in Oruro, Bolivia, sponsored by Global Humanitarian."

13. Apply an audio CD track to Slide 1. Choose any desired track from your CD collection. If you don't have any audio CDs, set the track to track 1. Hide the CD icon during slide shows.

14. Record timing for the slides so that when the slide show runs on its own, each slide is on the screen an appropriate amount of time. Your timing should be about 14 seconds for each slide without a bulleted list and about 20 seconds for those with a bulleted list.

15. Edit the timing of Slide 1 so it stays on the screen for 10 seconds, and then edit the timing of Slide 11 so it stays on the screen for 12 seconds.

16. Set up the presentation as a self-running slide show (for kiosk browsing).

17. Create a custom show called Brief Report using Slides 4, 5, 6, 7, and 11, and then reorder the custom show slides so that the Student Participants slide comes first.

18. Run the slide show, save the presentation, and then print a copy as handouts with four slides per page. You can print the presentation in black and white or in color.

19. Close the presentation.

Case Problem 1

Data Files needed for this Case Problem: Heart.ppt, Heart.jpg, Arteries.jpg

Mount Pleasant Regional Hospital   Dr. Andrea Raffensbarger of Greeley, Colorado, is chief cardiologist at Mount Pleasant Regional Hospital. She just hired you as her part-time assistant. Your first assignment is to develop a PowerPoint presentation for heart patients being released from the hospital. Your supervisor gave you the necessary material on rehabilitating the heart, which you've organized into a text-only presentation. Your task now is to make the presentation attractive and more educational by including graphics, animation, and sound.

1. Open the file **Heart** from your Tutorial.05\Cases folder included with your Data Files, and save the file to the same folder as **Rehab Heart Program**.
2. To both the slide master and title master, add a graphic that shows a red heart on an electrocardiogram chart. To find the graphic, search the Microsoft Office Clip Art and Media page on Microsoft Online using the keywords "heart healthcare chart" (without punctuation between the words). In the title master, place the graphic above the Master title style placeholder; in the slide master, place the graphic to the left of the title placeholder. You'll need to decrease the width of the title placeholder and reduce the size of the graphic to make it fit.
3. Insert the graphic file **Heart**, located in the Tutorial.05\Cases folder included with your Data Files, into Slide 3 ("What Is Heart Disease?"). Place the graphic to the right of the bulleted list. Label the parts of the heart with callouts, formatted to be clear, as follows:
   - **superior vena cava**: the light-blue tube on the left as you face the heart (actually on the right side of the heart)
   - **right atrium**: the violet item in front of the superior vena cava
   - **aorta**: the large red item at the top of the heart with the three outlet tubes
   - **pulmonary trunk**: the light-brown structure that comes out of the upper-center part of the heart
   - **left atrium**: the yellow-green structure below and to the right of the pulmonary trunk
   - **right coronary artery**: the large red artery next to the right atrium (on the left side as you face the heart)
   - **anterior interventricular artery**: the large red artery going down the middle of the heart
4. Animate the callouts on the heart diagram so that they appear in the slide one at a time during the slide show.
5. Insert the graphic file **Arteries**, located in the Tutorial.05\Cases folder included with your Data Files, into Slide 3 ("What Is Heart Disease") so that you now have two graphics on the slide. Place the second graphic below the bulleted list. (You'll have to reduce the size of the bulleted-list placeholder to accommodate the graphics. Label, using callouts, the top artery "Normal artery" and the bottom one "Diseased artery."
6. Still in Slide 3, remove all the background objects and add the clip art (located to the left of the title placeholder) back into the slide.
7. To Slide 1, add the sound clip called Heart Thuds from Microsoft Office Online. Set the sound to loop as long as the slide is displayed, and set the sound icon to be hidden during the slide show.
8. Animate all of the slides with bulleted lists so that the lists use progressive disclosure.
9. Record timing for the slides so that when the slide show runs on its own, each slide is on the screen an appropriate amount of time.
10. Set up the presentation as a self-running slide show (for kiosk browsing).
11. Carefully go through the presentation to make sure all the animations, sounds, and graphics appear as they should, and correct any problems.
12. Save your presentation and print your slides as a handout with four slides per page.

Create

Create a presentation on the Grand Canyon using the skills you learned in the tutorial.

Case Problem 2

Data Files needed for this Case Problem: GrndCan.ppt, GrndCan0.jpg, GrndCan1.jpg, GrndCan2.jpg, GrndCan3.jpg, GrndCan4.jpg, Arizona.jpg

Scenic North America Travel Club Scenic North America Travel Club is an organization that helps people learn from their travels to scenic locations in North America (Canada, Mexico, and the United States). The club offers information about vacation sites and provides discounts on hotels, motels, campsites, RV parks, and restaurants. Thomas Smith, the director of your local chapter of Scenic North America, asks you to give a presentation to his local chapter on the Grand Canyon, one of the most popular scenic travel sites. Your task is to prepare a PowerPoint presentation that includes graphics and information using the five JPEG photos of the Grand Canyon, **GrndCan0** through **GrndCan4**, located in the Tutorial.05\Cases folder included with your Data Files. The eight slides in your presentation should look like the slides in Figure 5-30.

Figure 5-30

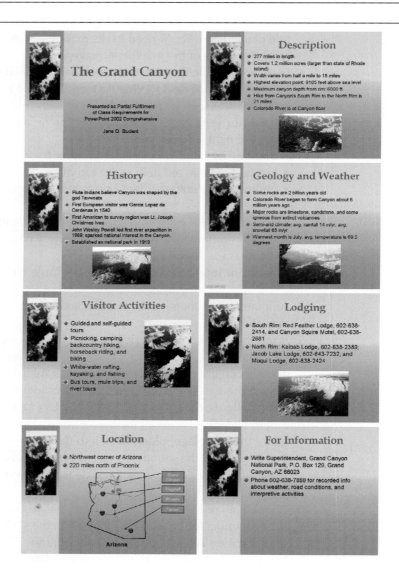

The following information will help you in creating the slide show. Read all the steps before you start creating your presentation.

1. The presentation is created from **GrndCan**, located in the Tutorial.05\Cases folder included with your Data Files. Add your name as the subtitle on Slide 1, and then save it as **Scenic North America**.
2. Create a custom color scheme by setting the Background color to yellow, the Text and lines color to black, the Shadows to gray, the Title text to brown, the Fills to tan, the Accent to blue, the Accent and hyperlink to light blue, and the Accent and following hyperlink to light gray. Match the colors as best you can from Figure 5-30, but don't worry if your colors aren't exactly like those shown.
3. To create the background, use a two-color gradient fill, with yellow on top and tan on the bottom. Add a rectangle (using the Rectangle drawing tool) on the left side (see Figure 5-30), set its Line color to No line, and color it with a two-color gradient fill, with tan on top and yellow on the bottom. In the upper part of the rectangle on the left, insert the graphic **GrndCan0**.
4. The title font is Book Antiqua bold and the body text is Arial, but you may choose any font that you think matches the theme of the presentation.
5. Slide 1 should include your name as author of the presentation.
6. Slides 2 through 5 contain images. You'll find all these images in the Tutorial.05\Cases folder included with your Data Files. You should use each image at least once.

Explore

7. To create the bullets, use picture bullets that are included with PowerPoint 2003. (*Hint*: On the Bullets and Numbering dialog box, click the Picture button, and select the large, round, gold-colored picture bullet.)
8. In Slide 7, insert the map of Arizona (the graphics file **Arizona**, located in the Tutorial.05\Cases folder included with your Data Files). Make the background transparent.

Explore

9. In Slide 7, add callouts (Line Callout 2) as shown in Figure 5-30, change the font and fill colors as shown, and use PowerPoint's align feature to right-align the four text boxes of the callouts. (*Hint*: Select all four text boxes, click Draw, point to Align or Distribute, and click Align Right. You'll then have to adjust the position of the ends of the lines of the callouts.)
10. To Slide 7, add the sound file named Desert Theme, which you can find on Microsoft Office Online, searching for sounds that match the term "mood music." Set the Sound Options so that the sound icon doesn't appear on the screen during the slide show.
11. Add a recorded narration to Slide 8. For the text of the narration, use the information on the slide. Save the slide timing.
12. Manually set the timing to 10 seconds for Slide 1 and 25 seconds for Slides 2 through 7. Do this in preparation for when the slide show runs on its own (in kiosk browsing).
13. Set up the presentation as a self-running slide show (for kiosk browsing).
14. Create a custom show named **Vacation Information** using only Slides 1, 2, 5, 6, and 8.
15. Save your presentation, and print your slides as a handouts with four slides per page.

Challenge

Explore other PowerPoint features associated with what you learned in this tutorial.

Case Problem 3

There are no Data Files needed for this Case Problem.

Games Night at Western North Dakota State University Each year, on a cold night during the winter semester, dozens of students at Western North Dakota State University get together at the student union building to enjoy Annual Games Night. There, the students not only play their favorite board and card games, but often learn new games. This year, the organizer of the event asks you to set up a stand-alone (but not self-running) PowerPoint presentation on how to play a game, or how to play part of the game. (For example, in chess, you might just want to explain all the moves and show what checkmate is, without going into all the details of stalemate, draws by repetition, en passant pawn capture, pawn promotion, etc.) The requirement is that the presentation be a pictorial guide—including step-by-step, how-to pictures (with text and recorded words) on how to play the game. Do the following:

1. Select a board game, card game, dice game, or party game that you enjoy. You must pick a game for which you know the rules well, or have access to the rules booklet or instructions.

Explore

2. Acquire photos, diagrams, figures, or clips for use in explaining how to play the game. Ideally, you have access to both a scanner and digital camera. With the camera, take actual pictures of the game setup and the play. If you don't have a digital camera, here are some simple ways of acquiring images (in some cases, you'll need a scanner):

   a. **Chess**. The Microsoft Office Online Web site has many clip art images and photos dealing with chess, including photo clips of each of the chess pieces, checkmate positions, chessboards and clocks, and chess players (including animated graphics). You can also scan a small chessboard, or create one using the PowerPoint drawing tools. You can also scan the printed symbols of chess pieces from a book on chess.

   b. **Cards**. The Microsoft Office Online Web site has several pages of clips that deal with playing cards. You also can scan the cards directly or use the card symbols found in the Symbols font: ♣, ♦, ♥, ♠.

   c. **Dice**. You can find clips (including animated graphics) of dice on the Microsoft Office Online Web site, or you can scan dice or draw dice using the PowerPoint drawing tools.

   d. **Other games**. Think creatively of how to acquire images to explain a game. Using a flat-bed scanner, you can scan any flat items, such as cards (face cards, Trivial Pursuit® question cards, Monopoly® deed cards), sections of the game board, play money, or even tokens and tiles (like the tiles in Scrabble®). You can also scan pictures of the pieces from the instruction booklet or the game box. In some cases, you can easily draw game pieces—like Boggle® letter dice, Scrabble letter tiles, checkers, and marbles for Chinese checkers—using the PowerPoint drawing tools.

3. Create an appropriate presentation design or use one of PowerPoint's built-in design templates.

4. Prepare PowerPoint slides that include the images you created and appropriate text. The text can be in bulleted lists and text boxes.

Explore

5. Use callouts of type Line Callout 3 to label figures and diagrams. (*Hint*: Drag the three little yellow diamond positioning handles to properly position the callout lines.)

6. Use custom animation to step through the instructions on playing the game, so that pictures and text appear only as the viewer needs them.

Explore

7. Apply appropriate sound effects, such as cards being shuffled and dice being thrown. You can also record your own sound effects, such as moving a chess piece. (*Hint*: You can use the Record Narration feature of PowerPoint to record sound effects.)

8. Record narrations to help explain the game, and include background music, if you desire.

9. Include action buttons so those unfamiliar with the normal PowerPoint navigation keys can easily navigate through the instructions.

10. Apply transitions to the slides. (Because of the fun nature of games, you can be more creative in transition effects, sounds, and animations than with a formal business presentation.)

11. Test the slide show with the narration and animation.

Explore

12. Show the slide show without narration and animation. (*Hint*: Click Slide Show on the menu bar, click Set Up Show, and click the check boxes "Show without narration" and "Show without animation." Use the navigation buttons to advance each slide.) After going through the slide show with that setup, uncheck the two check boxes before you save the presentation.
13. Save your presentation using the filename **Game**, and then print the presentation as a handout with four slides per page.
14. Close the presentation file.

Research

Use the Internet to collect information about a job and create a new presentation based on this information.

Case Problem 4

There are no Data Files needed for this Case Problem.

Student Employment Most students have had several jobs over the years while going to high school and college. Most of these jobs are entirely forgettable. But did you have a particularly good or bad job? Your task here is to prepare a presentation telling other students about your best or worst job. (If you didn't have a best or worst, pick any job. If you haven't had a job, give a presentation on some other long-term activity, such as volunteer service, an internship, military training, a scouting jamboree, or a laboratory class.) Do the following:

1. Select a part-time or full-time job (or some other activity) that you particularly liked or disliked and prepare an outline for a presentation about it. Include a job title in your outline. Elements you could include in your outline are: job description, hours worked each day or each week, duties performed, pay, description of bosses and co-workers, advantages and disadvantages of the job, why you loved/hated the job, and future plans relative to that job.
2. Connect to the Internet and go to **www.monster.com**, **www.hotjobs.com**, or **www.careerbuilder.com** to find any jobs fitting the description of your job title. Find information about the pay scale and what skills employers are looking for to complete this job.
3. Create a creative descriptive title for the presentation; for example: "Latrine Janitor: The Ins and Outs of Toiletry" or "Mule Tour Guide at the Grand Canyon: My 'Hottest' Job." Include your name on the title slide.
4. Prepare at least six slides, with a graphic on every slide.
5. Include at least one digital photograph of the job you performed. Find an appropriate picture of that job on the Web.
6. Download and use at least one graphic and one sound clip from the Microsoft Office Online Web site.
7. Prepare the presentation to be attractive and eye-catching, as well as informative.
8. Create and animate at least one diagram. For example, you might prepare a flow diagram showing how products are developed or assembled, or how sales are made.
9. Apply slide transitions and, where appropriate, animations and built-in sound.
10. Set up the presentation to be self-running. You don't need to include action buttons unless you feel they are appropriate.
11. Set up the presentation to play one or more CD music tracks in the background for two or more slides. Don't have the CD play when a sound clip plays.
12. Save the presentation using the filename **My Best Job**, **My Worst Job**, or **My Typical Job**, and print the presentation as a handout with four slides per page.
13. Close the presentation file.

Research

Go to the Web to find information you can use to create presentations.

Internet Assignments

The purpose of the Internet Assignments is to challenge you to find information on the Internet that you can use to work effectively with this software. The actual assignments are updated and maintained on the Course Technology Web site. Log on to the Internet and use your Web browser to go to the Student Online Companion for New Perspectives Office 2003 at **www.course.com/np/office2003**. Click the Internet Assignments link, and then navigate to the assignments for this tutorial.

Assess

SAM Assessment and Training

If you have a SAM user profile, you may have access to hands-on instruction, practice, and assessment of the skills covered in this tutorial. Log in to your SAM account and go to your assignments page to see what your instructor has assigned.

Review

Quick Check Answers

Session 5.1

1. From Slide Sorter view, select the slide and click the Copy button, and then paste the slide elsewhere in the presentation or in another program. Or from Normal view, save the slide presentation as a graphic file (such as a JPEG file), and then insert the file into another program.
2. the Microsoft Office Clip Art and Media page on the Microsoft Office Online Web site
3. False. If you want to display other background objects, you must copy them from the master slide into the desired slide.
4. True, but you have to set it up to do so.
5. False. You can change the order of animation, regardless of the order in which the objects were applied to the slide.
6. You would "insert" the CD music track much as you would a clip from the Office Clip Gallery, except you would select a particular track on the CD.
7. You would turn on the Narration feature, record the narration into a microphone attached to your computer, and press the Esc key when you're done recording.

Session 5.2

1. automatic timing, manual timing, hyperlinks, narration, and kiosk browsing
2. Select the slide in Slide Sorter view, open the Transition task pane, and then change the timing.
3. because the illustration might be too complex for the simple PowerPoint drawing tools
4. press the Esc key (you cannot click on the slide to open the shortcut menu to end the slide show)
5. False. The custom show is saved as part of the original presentation file.
6. True.

Objectives

Session 6.1
- Create design templates using the slide masters
- Make overhead transparencies in black and white (grayscale) and in color
- Save a presentation as an outline in Rich Text Format

Session 6.2
- Create a banner and prepare a multiple-page and single-page poster
- Insert revision marks and comments
- Compare presentation versions
- Review revisions to a presentation
- Create a Web presentation using custom, animated action buttons

Creating Special Types of Presentations

Giving Presentations with Transparencies, 35mm Slides, Posters, and Banners

Case

Global Humanitarian, Professional Presentations

Global Humanitarian is a charter member of the Pan-American Association of Humanitarian Organizations (Asociación Panamericana de Organisaciones Humanitarias, APOH), which helps set up, train, coordinate, and certify humanitarian organizations throughout North, Central, and South America. Every other year, APOH holds its Conference on Humanitarian Services in Latin America, at which representatives of member organizations are invited to give oral and poster presentations.

The upcoming conference will be held in Guadalajara, Mexico, and Global Humanitarian plans to send two of its full-time staff to give presentations. William Marzardo, director of public relations for Global Humanitarian, will give an oral presentation using overhead transparencies (no computer projection system will be available in the conference meeting rooms). His topic will be Global Humanitarian's major successes in South America. Harriet Siebert, director of special projects at Global Humanitarian, will give an oral presentation using 35mm slides. Her topic will be on the process of building adobe homes in Peru. William and Harriet ask you to help them prepare their presentations.

Student Data Files

▼**Tutorial.06**

▽ **Tutorial folder**
- Bullet.jpg
- GHLogo2.tif
- GHOver.ppt
- GHSlides.ppt
- HomeButn.jpg
- MPDark.jpg
- NextButn.jpg
- PrevButn.jpg

▽ **Review folder**
- Costa.jpg
- MnBut.jpg
- Montan.jpg
- PeruGeo.jpg
- PeruGeo.ppt
- PeruLogo.jpg
- Puna.jpg
- Selva.jpg
- Sierra.jpg
- StoneWrk.jpg

▽ **Cases folder**
- BkgrValy.jpg
- Bullet.tif
- Jayhawk.ppt
- NavBack.jpg
- NavNext.jpg
- PalmAddr.jpg
- PalmAlrm.jpg
- PalmCalc.jpg
- PalmGame.jpg
- PalmSchd.jpg
- ParkJog.jpg
- ParkPic.jpg
- ParkRivr.jpg
- ParkShow.ppt
- ParkSign.jpg
- SFBridge.jpg
- SFCblCar.jpg
- SFCtyHll.jpg
- SFDwnTwn.jpg

In this tutorial, you'll create a design template for overheads and 35mm slides. You'll make overhead transparencies, save a presentation as an outline in Rich Text Format (RTF), and use a film recorder to prepare 35mm slides. You'll create a poster presentation and create and print a banner. You'll also publish a Web presentation with custom action buttons.

Session 6.1

Creating a Design Template for Overheads

As you already know, a design template is a file that contains a color scheme; attributes and formats for the titles, main text, and other text; and the background design for the slides in a presentation. You'll also recall that to make a custom design template, you prepare a PowerPoint presentation with the desired color scheme, font attributes, and background objects, and then save the file as a design template, rather than as a normal presentation file. You can then use your custom-designed templates in other presentations.

William and Harriet asked you to prepare design templates for them to use in making their **overhead transparencies** (transparent sheets containing text that can be projected onto a screen) and 35mm slides. They know that these are two common media for presentations at professional meetings, so they want to have design templates to use not only at this conference, but at other events as well. Designs that work well for on-screen slide presentations may not work as well for presentations using an overhead transparency or 35mm slide. In this tutorial, you'll learn more about the principles and practices of design templates.

The following are some things you should keep in mind as you prepare the template:

- PowerPoint is an excellent vehicle for preparing overhead transparencies. It works better than a word processor because it's specifically designed for preparing presentations, especially those that include graphics as well as text.
- Overhead transparencies offer several advantages over 35mm slides or on-screen electronic slide shows. First, most classrooms and lecture halls are equipped with overhead projectors, but not with 35mm slide projectors or computer projection systems, so overheads will almost always work without arranging (and paying extra) for special audio-visual equipment. Second, overhead projectors tend to be more reliable than 35mm projectors or computer projection systems. Third, overhead projection usually doesn't require the room to be darkened, or at least not as much as with other projection methods, so the audience can more easily take notes and participate in group discussions. And fourth, overhead projection allows the speaker to see the visuals without turning away from the audience, thus maintaining better eye contact.
- The more ink required to print a transparency sheet, the more expensive the sheet is to print, and the longer it takes. So if you have limited resources (some inkjet cartridges are expensive) or limited time (you're in a hurry to print your visuals), use color sparingly. This means that you should generally print black (or dark) text on a white background and limit the number of background objects.
- You can design your overhead transparencies in color and print them in grayscale. So if you aren't sure which type of printer you'll use, don't be afraid to set up the PowerPoint presentation in color.
- Overhead transparencies should normally be printed in portrait orientation, not landscape, because most overhead projectors are better at fitting sheets that are tall and narrow, rather than short and wide.

Preparing the Template

You begin by creating a design template for overhead transparencies, which William will use to create his presentation on Global Humanitarian. You'll prepare the design template for the overhead transparency with the above concepts in mind. The template will include a limited amount of color and appropriate background objects. You will also change the orientation to portrait.

To create a design template for overhead transparencies:

1. Open a new, blank presentation in Normal view, and then close the task pane. Next, you'll modify the page layout for 8½ × 11-inch transparency film.

2. Click **File** on the menu bar, and then click **Page Setup**. The Page Setup dialog box appears on the screen with On-screen Show in the Slides sized for text box.

3. Click the **Slides sized for** list arrow, scroll down and click **Overhead**, and then click the **Portrait** option button in the Orientation/Slides section. See Figure 6-1. Notice that the width adjusts to 7.5 inches and the height to 10 inches rather than to 8.5 and 11, respectively. This is because PowerPoint sets the size to the typical printable area on the page, not to the actual size of the transparency film.

Page Setup dialog box ◄ **Figure 6-1**

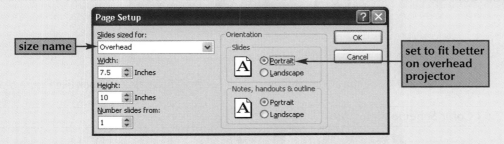

4. Click the **OK** button. The title slide in the slide pane changes size and orientation to reflect the changes you made to the page setup.

Your next task is to modify the master slides to include a color scheme, a picture bullet, and background objects. You'll keep the majority of the background blank (white) to avoid printing excessive ink on the transparency film sheets.

To create a color scheme:

1. Shift-click the **Normal View** button ▣ to display Slide Master view. First, you'll set the color scheme to an attractive color combination: green, red, orange, yellow, and brown.

2. Click the **Design** button on the Formatting toolbar to open the Slide Design task pane, click the **Color Schemes** link near the top of the task pane, click the **Edit Color Schemes** link near the bottom of the task pane to open the Edit Color Scheme dialog box, and then make sure the **Custom tab** is selected. As you recall, to change a color, select the scheme color item you wish to change, and then click the Change Color button to access the color palette.

3. Click the **Shadows** color box, click the **Change Color** button to open the Shadow Color dialog box, click the yellow color cell on the Standard tab indicated for shadows in Figure 6-2, and then click the **OK** button.

4. Repeat this process for the rest of the colors in the color scheme as indicated below. The background color and the text and lines color will remain the default of white and black, respectively.

- **Title text:** dark green
- **Fills:** red
- **Accent:** brown
- **Accent and hyperlink:** light green
- **Accent and followed hyperlink:** medium green

| Figure 6-2 | Presentation color scheme |

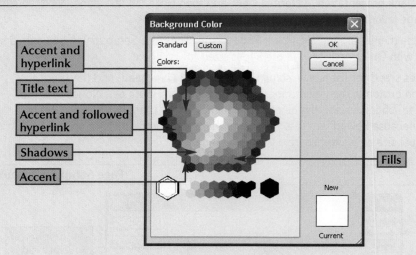

5. Once you have set all the colors, your Edit Color Scheme dialog box will look like Figure 6-3.

| Figure 6-3 | Edit Color Scheme dialog box |

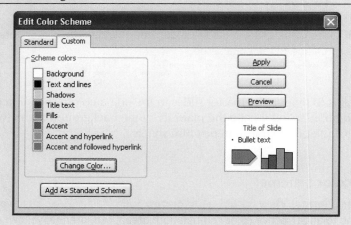

6. Click the **Apply** button in the Edit Color Scheme dialog box, and then close the task pane. Now you'll change the fonts and bullets in the text boxes.

7. Click the edge of the **title text box** placeholder to select the entire text box, change the font to **36-point Arial bold**, and then change the text alignment to **Align Left**. The body text is already 20-point Arial, which is what you want.

That completes the changes in the color scheme and the fonts. Now, you'll modify the bullets.

Using a Digital Image as a Bullet

Next, you'll set the level-one bullets to a digital image—a JPEG picture of a piece of woven wool taken from a digital photograph of a Peruvian in traditional costume. You can make your own bullets by cropping and resizing all or a portion of a picture you take with a digital camera or scan from a printed photograph.

To use a picture as a bullet:

1. Click to the right of the level-one bullet within the Master text style placeholder so that the insertion point appears to the left of the word "Click," click **Format** on the menu bar, click **Bullets and Numbering** to open the Bullets and Numbering dialog box with the Bulleted tab on top, and then click the **Picture** button in the dialog box. The Picture Bullet dialog box opens.

   Trouble? If the text of the level-one bullet is selected, position the pointer between the bullet and the word "Click," making sure that the pointer changes to the I-beam pointer and not a four-headed arrow, and then click again.

2. Click the **Import** button to open the Add Clips to Organizer dialog box, change the Look in folder to the **Tutorial.06\Tutorial** folder included with your Data Files, and then double-click the JPEG file **Bullet**. The picture bullet is added as the first bullet in the Picture Bullet dialog box. See Figure 6-4.

Picture Bullet dialog box | **Figure 6-4**

imported picture (Peruvian design)

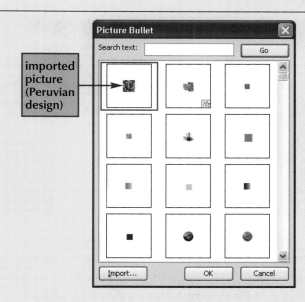

3. With the imported bullet still selected, as shown in Figure 6-4, click the **OK** button. The reddish, woven wool bullet appears as the level-one bullet in the body text box placeholder.

4. Click to the right of the level-two bullet (currently a dash), open the **Bullets and Numbering** dialog box, click a filled square bullet, click the **Color** list arrow, click the fourth color tile (the dark green color), and then click the **OK** button. The level-two bullet changes to a dark green square.

You've made important progress in designing an appropriate design template for overhead transparencies. Next, you'll add background objects to the slide masters.

Adding Background Objects to the Slide Masters

To complete your custom design template, you'll add a drawn rectangle to the background, behind the title text box. You might want to keep the image small to avoid excessive ink on the transparency film.

When you draw the rectangle, you'll draw it on top of the title text box, and then you'll send it to the back, behind the title text box. Remember that objects on a slide are in an order from front to back, and if you place one object on top of another, you can send either object forward or back.

To add background objects to the slide masters:

1. Click the **Insert Picture** button 🖾 on the Drawing toolbar, and insert the file **GHLogo2** from the Tutorial.06\Tutorial folder included with your Data Files. This is a new logo designed for Global Humanitarian using illustration software and clip art.

   Trouble? If you don't see the file GHLogo2, which is a TIFF graphics file, in the Insert Pictures dialog box, click the Files of type list arrow, and then select All Files.

2. Drag the logo to the upper-left corner of the screen, and then resize and move the **title text box** placeholder so it fits to the right of the logo. Compare your screen to Figure 6-5 and make any necessary adjustments. Notice the size, shape, and position of the title placeholder; the placeholder is narrower and higher up on the page, yielding a smaller top margin.

Figure 6-5	Slide master with logo and resized title text box

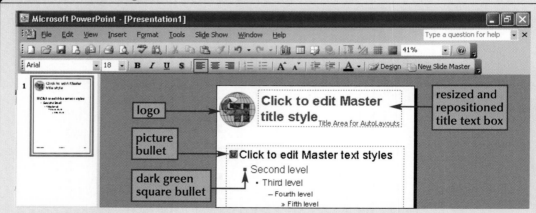

3. Click the **Rectangle** button 🔲 on the Drawing toolbar, and draw a rectangle that fits over the entire top part of the slide (logo and title), with its edges against the edges of the slide.

4. Click the **Fill Color** list arrow 🔶 ▾ on the Drawing toolbar, click the yellow color tile, click the **Line color** list arrow ✏ ▾ on the Drawing toolbar, and then click **No line**.

5. With the yellow rectangle still selected, click the **Draw** button on the Drawing toolbar, point to **Order**, and then click **Send to Back**. Now you'll add a brown line.

6. Click the **Line** button ＼ on the Drawing toolbar, draw a line across the bottom of the rectangle, change the line color to brown in the color palette, click the **Line Style** button ☰ on the Drawing toolbar, and then click **6 pt**.

7. Resize the **body text** placeholder so that the top of it is closer to the brown line. The complete background objects should appear as shown in Figure 6-6.

Slide master after adding background graphics ◀ **Figure 6-6**

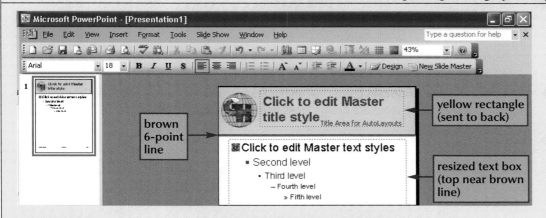

Trouble? If the objects on your screen do not match those shown in Figure 6-6, modify them now.

You're almost finished. You need to add a title master and modify the footer so that only the slide number appears in it. Note that when you use the default blank design template, it lacks a title master. So if you want to modify the appearance of the title page, you need to insert a title master. Similarly, you can insert other masters, including multiple slide masters and title masters. You would do this, for example, if you want two or more slide layouts rather than just one.

To add a title master and modify the footer:

▶ 1. Click the **Insert New Title Master** button 🔲 on the Slide Master View toolbar to create a title master.

▶ 2. On the title master, use Figure 6-7 as a guide to move the logo, change the size of the yellow rectangle, move the brown line to the bottom edge of the rectangle, change the size and position of the title placeholder, and change the title text box alignment to **Center**. Your only task left on the master slides is to make sure that the date, time, and footer do not appear, but that the page number is visible.

Title master after adjusting background elements ◀ **Figure 6-7**

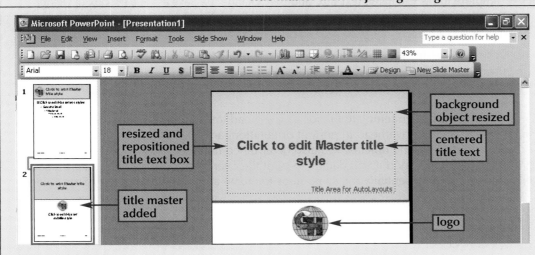

3. Click **View** on the menu bar, click **Header and Footer**, click the **Slide number** check box to select it, click the **Footer** and **Date and time** check boxes to uncheck them, and then click the **Apply to All** button. The title master does not change, but you will see the changes when you return to Normal view.

   Now you should make sure that the colors and background objects would be readable and attractive if printed in grayscale.

4. Click the **Color/Grayscale** button ▣ on the Standard toolbar, and then click **Grayscale**. See Figure 6-8. The template design looks fine in grayscale.

Figure 6-8 | **Grayscale preview of overhead template design**

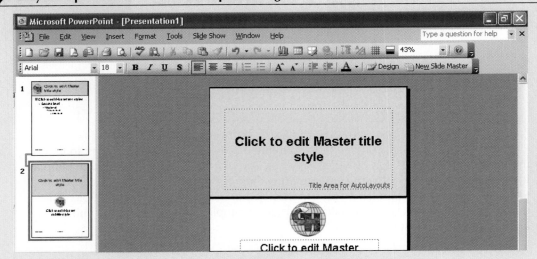

5. Click the **Color/Grayscale** button ▣ again, and then click **Color** to view the slide in color again.

   Now you've completed the slide masters and are ready to save the PowerPoint file as a design template.

To save the presentation as a design template:

1. Return to Normal view, click **File** on the menu bar, click **Save As**, type **GH Overheads Template** in the File name text box, and then change the Save as type list box to **Design Template**. You'll want to save this to your hard disk, a Zip disk, or some other high-capacity disk because it might not fit on your disk. Do not save it to the default Templates folder.

2. Click the **Save in** list arrow, navigate to the desired folder or your high-capacity disk, and then click the **Save** button. The template file is saved to your disk.

   You created a design template file for an overhead transparency presentation by changing the page setup to overhead in portrait orientation, and then specifying the color scheme and background objects. You also determined that the color scheme and background objects look good if you decide to print the overhead transparencies in grayscale. Next, you'll follow essentially the same steps to create a design template for 35mm slides.

Creating a Design Template for 35mm Slides

Most modern presentation halls and conference rooms come equipped with computer projection systems, so nowadays most PowerPoint presentations are made on-screen (electronically). However, under some circumstances you might need to prepare 35mm slides. To do this, you would create a PowerPoint presentation and then use a **film recorder**, an instrument that takes pictures of computer graphics files, including PowerPoint presentations, using 35mm film. You would then develop the film as 35mm slides.

In our example, the audience for Harriet's presentation will be a small, professional group in a more formal setting than William's presentation, so Harriet wants to use a computer projector to display her PowerPoint presentation. But she's not sure that the conference room will have a computer projector, and might instead have a 35mm slide projector. Even though 35mm slides aren't used much any more, Harriet feels that she'll use them enough to warrant creating a design template for that purpose. So she asks you to create a design template for Global Humanitarian professional slide presentations.

To give Global Humanitarian a consistent image in all presentations given by its employees, you'll use the same color scheme and logo as you did for the overhead transparency design, but the slide design will have some significant differences. For example, 35mm slides usually look better with white or light-colored text on a dark background. Moreover, you'll use a picture for the background instead of just color fills. You can use a photo in the background of 35mm slides to add interest and an artistic flare. And, of course, you'll set up the page for 35mm slides.

If you decide to use a picture background in your other presentations, keep in mind the following:

- Make sure the picture is very light overall (for use with dark-colored text) or very dark (for use with light-colored text). If you use a picture with normal colors (usually the case in correctly exposed digital photographs), the text won't be legible.
- Make sure the picture is low contrast. If you use a picture with normal contrast, it will distract from the text.
- Make sure that even though the picture is low contrast, the viewers can still tell what the picture represents without actually having to get information from the picture. In the case of your slide template, the viewers will see that the background is Machu Picchu, the ancient city in Peru, but they don't have to be able to distinguish, for example, the mountains and hills behind the ruins.
- If you're not absolutely sure that a particular picture fulfills the above three criteria, don't use it. Instead, pick a solid-color, gradient, textured, or patterned background.

Setting up the Template for 35mm Slides

Just as you changed the page setup to overheads for the transparencies, you'll now change the page setup for 35mm slides. You need to change the setup or else the PowerPoint slides won't fit properly on the 35mm film.

To set up the design template for 35mm slides:

▶ 1. Click **File**, click **Page Setup**, set the Slides sized for text box to **35mm Slides**, set the slide orientation to **Landscape**, and then click the **OK** button. The width of the slide increases relative to its height. Don't worry now that the logo is distorted; you'll fix it later.

▶ 2. Save the file as a design template file to a high-capacity disk, just as you did with the overhead transparency master, but this time use the filename **GH 35mm Slides Template**.

▶ 3. Shift-click the **Normal View** button ▣ to display the slide masters. As noted, the logo graphic was distorted (stretched too wide) when you changed the relative dimensions of the height and width. It's usually easiest to reset the picture to its original dimensions, and then, if necessary, resize it.

▶ 4. On the title master, click the distorted **GHLogo2**, and then click the **Reset Picture** button ▣ on the Picture toolbar.

▶ 5. Delete the yellow background box behind the title.

▶ 6. Reposition and resize the graphic, the title and subtitle placeholders, and the brown line so they appear as shown in Figure 6-9. You don't have to be exact.

| Figure 6-9 | Title master slide with modified background objects |

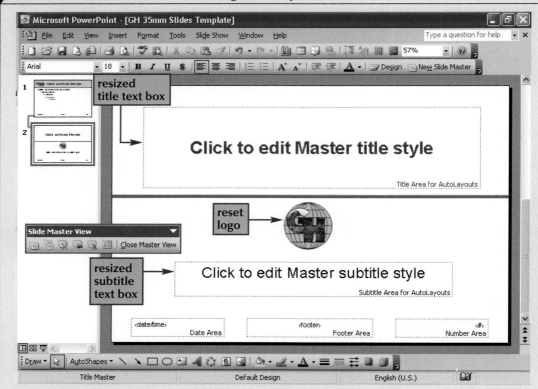

▶ 7. Drag the vertical scroll bar up to display the slide master, reset the logo graphic, resize the logo so it fits properly to the left of the title placeholder, and then delete the yellow background box behind the title just as you did on the title master.

▶ 8. Resize and reposition the text placeholders so they appear as shown in Figure 6-10.

Resizing for 35mm slides and adjusting text boxes ◀ **Figure 6-10**

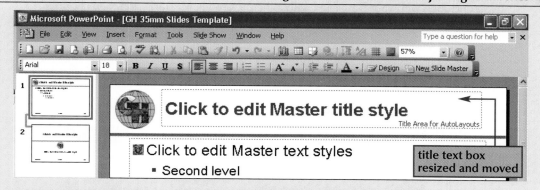

Trouble? If you have trouble positioning an object exactly where you want, press and hold the Alt key while you drag the object to temporarily turn off the Snap to Grid feature.

▶ **9.** Change the font color of the title text boxes on both the slide and title masters to the yellow color in the color palette, and then change the font color of the subtitle text box in the title master and the body text box in the slide master to white. Note that when you do this, you won't be able to read the placeholder text.

▶ **10.** Save the design template.

You're now ready to add the dark background picture.

Adding a Picture Background to the Slide Masters

Up until now, you created presentations with plain white, plain colored, or gradient fill backgrounds, but now you'll use a picture as the background. The picture file that you'll use is a digital photograph of Machu Picchu that was darkened using photo-editing software. The picture is similar to those you saw in previous tutorials, and it repeats the theme in the new Global Humanitarian logo that appears on each slide.

Adding a Picture Background   Reference Window

- In Normal view or Slide Master view, click Format on the menu bar, and then click Background.
- Click the Background Fill list arrow, click Fill Effects, and then click the Picture tab.
- Click the Select Picture button, select the desired picture file, and then click the Insert button.
- Click the OK button in the Fill Effects dialog box, and then click the Apply or the Apply to All button.

To add a picture background:

▶ **1.** Click the slide master in the Slides tab, click **Format** on the menu bar, and then click **Background**. The familiar Background dialog box appears on the screen.

▶ **2.** Click the **Background Fill** list arrow, click **Fill Effects**, and then click the **Picture** tab. This tab in the Fill Effects dialog box allows you to select a picture—in this case, an edited digital photograph—as the background to the slide.

▶ **3.** Click the **Select Picture** button, change the Look in location to the **Tutorial.06\Tutorial** folder included with your Data Files, select the picture file **MPDark**, and then click the **Insert** button.

▶ **4.** Click the **OK** button in the Fill Effects dialog box, and then click the **Apply to All** button in the Background dialog box. The picture is now part of the background for the slides. See Figure 6-11.

Figure 6-11 **Slide master after adding background picture**

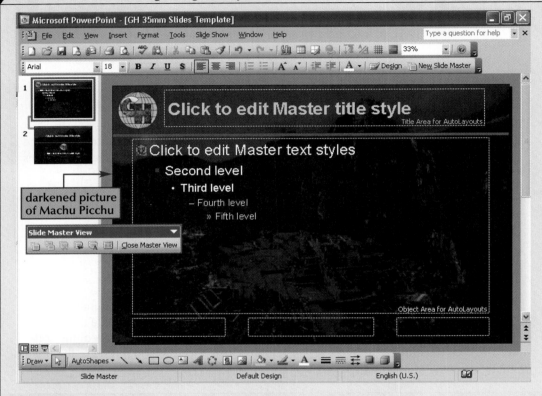

As you can see, the slide number is not visible because the text is black on a dark background. Instead of changing the font to white or a light color, you'll simply remove the page numbering. Slide numbers are not typically included on 35mm slides because it's easier to write page numbers on the slide frame (the casing around the film) so that you can keep the slides in order as you place them in a slide carousel. This also gives you the flexibility of reusing and reordering slides for different presentations. This is significant because slides can be expensive and time consuming to produce.

To remove the slide numbers from the slide masters:

▶ **1.** Click **View** on the menu bar, click **Header and Footer**, and then click the **Slide number** check box to deselect it.

▶ **2.** Click the **Apply to All** button to remove the page numbers from both the slide and title masters.

▶ **3.** Click the **Normal View** button ▣. Your slide should appear as shown in Figure 6-12.

Title slide of 35mm slide design template   **Figure 6-12**

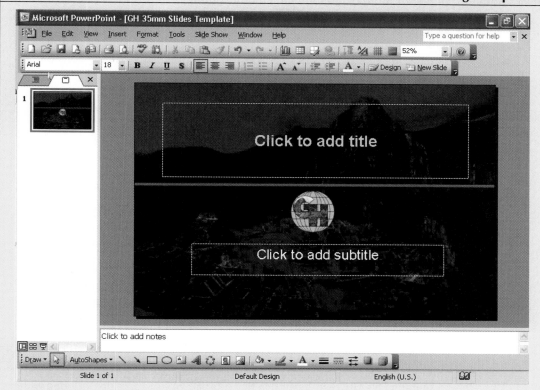

4. Save the template file, and then close the presentation.

You asked Harriet and William to check your two design templates. They're pleased with the results and instruct you to go ahead and use them to make the overhead and 35mm presentations.

Making Overhead Transparencies

William wants you to apply your overhead transparency design template to the current version of his presentation, and then print the overheads. Before doing so, you must make sure you purchase and use the right type of transparency film in 8½ × 11-inch sheets. Carefully read the specifications on the package of transparency sheets before you purchase or print them. Make sure the package says that the film is designed specifically for your type of printer—laser or inkjet—because the two are not interchangeable. Furthermore, ordinary transparency film sheets designed for color felt-tip pens and markers are not acceptable for printers; the film can melt inside the printer, and it doesn't properly hold printer ink.

When you apply a design template to an existing presentation, keep in mind that you must often make one or more of the following modifications:

- Change the page setup. PowerPoint doesn't change an existing presentation to the same page setup as the design template.
- Reset and resize the imported graphics. This is essential if the relative dimensions of the new design are significantly different from the old design. You saw this when you converted the overhead transparency template to the 35mm slide template; you originally imported the new Global Humanitarian logo with the pages set up in portrait orientation, and then the graphics became distorted when you applied landscape orientation.
- Recolor or select different clip art, digital photographs, and other imported graphics so that they match the design template color scheme.
- Recolor organization charts, data charts, graphs, and other graphic objects created in PowerPoint so that these objects are visible.
- Resize text boxes or change font sizes. When the presentation undergoes a font change (in size and style), sometimes the font doesn't fit properly, or the hard returns are in the wrong place. Fortunately, all the text fit properly when you applied the 35mm design template to Harriet's original presentation.

Now you'll apply the overhead transparency design template to William's presentation—which he already prepared using the default design template—as well as insert some pictures supplied by William.

To apply the overhead transparency design template to a presentation:

▶ 1. Open the presentation file **GHOver**, located in the Tutorial.06\Tutorial folder included with your Data Files.

▶ 2. Click the **Design** button on the Formatting toolbar to open the Slide Design task pane. You will apply the custom template that you designed for Global Humanitarian overheads.

▶ 3. Click the **Browse** link at the bottom of the task pane, change the **Look in** location to the folder or high-capacity disk where you saved the design templates, click the template filename **GH Overheads Template**, and then click the **Apply** button in the Apply Design Template dialog box. The design is applied to the presentation, but PowerPoint doesn't change the page setup.

▶ 4. Change the page setup to **Overhead** with **Portrait** orientation.

▶ 5. Save the presentation to the location where you saved your custom design templates using the filename **GH Overheads**.

Now you'll check the slides to make sure that no graphics in the presentation were distorted when you applied the new page setup.

▶ 6. Go through the slide presentation until you reach **Slide 8** ("Villages Helped in South America Since the Year 2000"), and then fix the distorted graphic by resizing it with the approximate aspect ratio shown in Slide 8 in Figure 6-13. You cannot reset this picture, because the location of the dots on the map will become misaligned.

▶ 7. Go to **Slide 9**, and then switch to Slide Sorter view. See Figure 6-13.

Completed overhead transparency presentation ◄ **Figure 6-13**

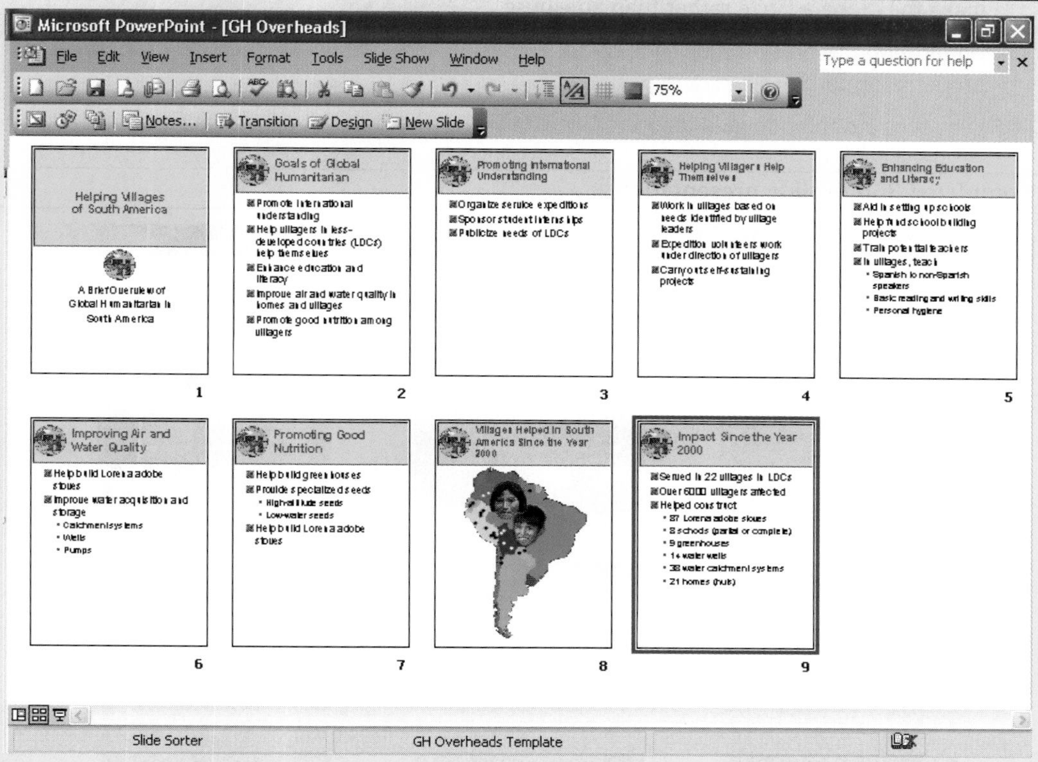

8. Add your name as the fourth line in the subtitle on Slide 1, and then save and print the presentation on normal paper as handouts with four slides per page.

William likes the look of his presentation overheads. He will complete all the slides in the presentation by adding more graphics, and then print the presentation. He may choose to print the presentation on color inkjet transparency film, or he might decide to save time and money and print the presentation on black-and-white transparency film in grayscale using his laser printer. Either way, he has a professional look for his presentation overheads, and one that is consistent with other Global Humanitarian presentations.

Preparing 35mm Slides

Now you'll apply your 35mm slide template to Harriet's presentation file on building adobe huts in villages of less-developed countries.

To apply the 35mm slide design template to a presentation:

1. Open the presentation file titled **GHSlides** from the Tutorial.06\Tutorial folder included with your Data Files, and then save the file to a high-capacity disk using the filename **GH 35mm Slides**.

2. Apply the design template **GH 35mm Slides Template** located in the folder or on the high-capacity disk where you saved it, and then close the task pane.

3. Change the page setup to **35mm Slides**.

4. Reset the picture of the Global Humanitarian logo on the slide masters, if necessary, to make the globe a circle rather than an ellipse.

5. Go through the presentation slide by slide, making sure that all the text and graphics are properly formatted, sized, and positioned.

6. View the presentation in Slide Sorter view to see all the slides at once. See Figure 6-14.

| Figure 6-14 | Completed 35mm slide presentation |

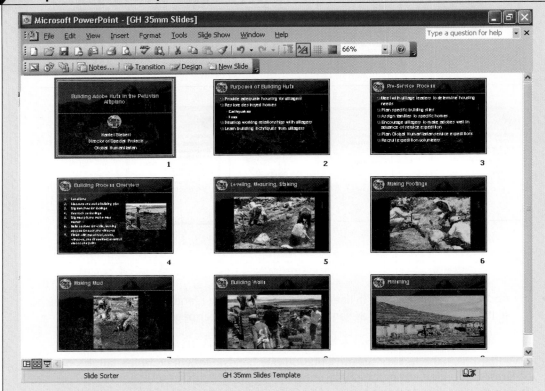

7. Return to Normal view, replace Harriet's name on Slide 1 with your name, save the completed 35mm slide presentation, and then print the presentation as handouts with four slides per page. (Note that the figures in this tutorial will continue to show Harriet's name on Slide 1.)

You give the GH 35mm Slides presentation file to Harriet, who uses a film recorder to make 35mm slides. She could also send the PowerPoint presentation to a service bureau (a company that can print 35mm slides, banners, posters, and other types of media) to convert the PowerPoint file into 35mm slides. Service bureaus are located in almost all major cities in the United States, and online service bureaus, such as Genigraphics, are available everywhere.

Saving a Presentation as an RTF Outline

William decided he wants to use the outline of his presentation with other applications, including word processors (such as Word), illustration software (such as Adobe Illustrator or CorelDRAW), or page layout (desktop publishing) software (such as Microsoft Publisher or Adobe PageMaker). To give him the flexibility of importing the outline text from this presentation into any software, he asks you to save the outline in **Rich Text Format (RTF)**, a file format that many types of software can open and read.

To save the presentation as an RTF outline:

1. Click **Window** on the menu bar, and then click **GH Overheads** to switch to that open presentation.

   Trouble? If you don't see GH Overheads on the Window menu, you probably closed the presentation after you saved it last. Open it from the folder or disk to which you saved it.

2. Click **File** on the menu bar, click **Save As** to open the Save As dialog box, and then make sure the Save in folder is the location to where you saved your custom design templates.

3. Click the **Save as type** list arrow, and then click **Outline/RTF**.

4. Click the **Save** button. PowerPoint saves the document into the default folder using the current filename, except it automatically changes the filename extension from .ppt to .rtf, so that the complete filename is **GH Overheads.rtf**.

5. Close the file.

Now William can use the outline of this presentation as text with other applications.

Session 6.1 Quick Check

Review

1. List four advantages that overhead transparencies offer over 35mm slides and electronic slide shows.
2. True or False: It's easy to print overheads in grayscale even when the presentation was designed in color.
3. Give three reasons why you usually want to print overhead transparency film with a white (blank) background.
4. Describe how to use a digital photograph as a slide background.
5. What are two attributes of a good background picture for slides with text?
6. How do you save a presentation in Rich Text Format (RTF)?

Session 6.2

Creating a Poster Presentation

A **poster presentation** is generally given at a professional meeting, and the information is formatted as a poster, or in the space of a poster. The poster size is usually about 6 × 4 feet in landscape orientation. Often the presenters or authors stand by their mounted posters at a designated time and place—during the so-called "poster session" of the conference—to answer questions, pass out business cards, and distribute handouts.

Harriet has been invited to give a poster presentation at an upcoming conference of the APOH. She asks you to help her prepare a PowerPoint poster presentation.

You can format PowerPoint poster presentations in two ways: as a multiple-page poster (with the title slide and each information slide printed on separate sheets of paper) or as a single-page poster with multiple frames (or slides) on one large printout.

A single-page poster has two advantages over a multiple-page poster:

- It's easy to set up. You don't have to bother with different sheets of paper and numerous thumbtacks (you usually need only four to six) to hang and display your poster.
- It looks professional. Usually a service bureau prints the poster on high-gloss paper, which has a photographic-quality appearance.

A multiple-page poster has three advantages over a single-page poster:

- It's less expensive. A service bureau can charge from $70 to $250 to print a one-page poster, depending on its size and complexity.
- It doesn't take as long to prepare.
- It is less cumbersome to carry. For example, you can easily slip a multiple-page poster in your briefcase or carry-on luggage, but a large, single-page poster has to be rolled up and stored in a long tube, which is awkward to carry when traveling on an airplane or other mode of transportation.

If you ever have to give a professional presentation at a poster session, check with the session chair for recommendations about which type of presentation to prepare.

Harriet asks you to prepare both formats so that she can choose which she wants to use for her presentation.

Creating a Multiple-Page Poster Presentation

You'll start by preparing a multiple-page poster. Many of the same principles that you learned regarding overhead transparencies apply to poster presentation slides. As a general rule, you'll want dark text on a light background. So for Harriet's presentation, you use her current 35mm slide presentation and modify it with a light background and dark text.

To create a multiple-page poster presentation:

1. If you took a break after the previous session, make sure PowerPoint is running, open the presentation file **GH 35mm Slides** from the folder or disk where you saved your files.

2. Save the file with a new filename to your high-capacity disk using the filename **GH Multiple-page Poster**. You'll first adjust the page setup, and then remove the background graphic from the presentation.

3. Change the page setup to **Letter Paper (8.5 × 11 in)** so that the slides fit properly on normal paper when you print the individual slides. You'll leave the orientation set to landscape because there is no reason to change it.

4. Click **Format**, click **Background** to open the Background dialog box, click the **Background fill** list arrow, click the white tile in the color palette, and then click the **Apply to All** button. The background for all the slides turns white, and the picture background disappears.

   Now you need to adjust the logo. Even though you didn't change the orientation, the slide dimensions for slides printed on 8½ × 11-inch paper are different from those for 35mm slides, so the graphics may be distorted.

5. Display the slide master, adjust the aspect ratio of the logo to its original setting by clicking the **Reset Picture** button 🖼 on the Picture toolbar, and then adjust its size so it fits properly next to the title text box. Now you must change the font colors so they are more legible.

6. Change the title text style font to brown, and then change the body text font to black.

7. Display the title master, and reset the picture to its original size and shape.

8. Return to Normal view, and then go through the presentation to make sure all the slides are attractive and readable.

9. Switch to Slide Sorter view. See Figure 6-15.

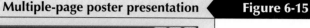

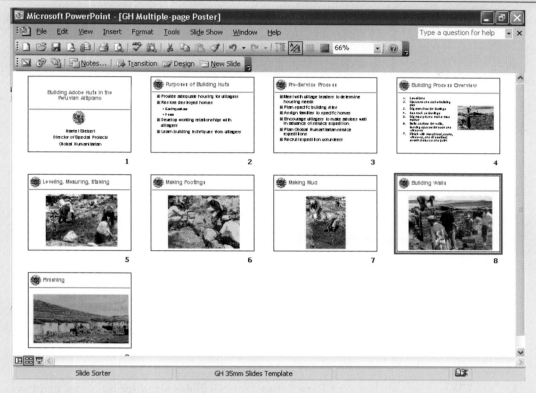

10. Save the presentation.

Before you print the slides on individual pieces of paper, you'll delete the current title slide, and print a banner with the information from the title slide.

Creating a Banner

Poster presentations need a title so the viewers know the subject of the presentation. You can create a **banner**, which is a large sign or page that typically has dimensions of 4 feet wide by 8½ inches high. Most inkjet printers can print banners, but most software, including PowerPoint, cannot print banners directly to an inkjet printer. If you design a banner in PowerPoint, you must take the file to a service bureau, which can print large banners as well as large posters. If you want to print your own banners, you'll need access to a specialty printing program that supports banner printing, such as Microsoft Greetings Workshop or Mindscape PrintMaster. You also must buy banner paper.

Reference Window

Using PowerPoint to Create a Banner

- Click File on the menu bar, click Page Setup, click the Slides sized for list arrow, click Banner, and then click the OK button.
- Adjust the title and subtitle placeholders to the desired size and location on the banner slide.
- Adjust the font size, as desired, so that the title and subtitle text fit in the banner.
- Type the text, insert graphics, and make other desired modifications and enhancements.
- Save the banner file to a disk, and then send the file to a service bureau for printing, or use a specialty printing program to print the banner yourself.

Harriet wants you to prepare a banner for her multiple-page poster presentation. You'll prepare the banner in PowerPoint, but you can't print directly from PowerPoint onto banner paper, so you must submit the PowerPoint file to a service bureau for printing.

To prepare a banner in PowerPoint:

1. Click **Slide 2**, shift-click **Slide 9**, and then press the **Delete** key. All the slides except the first one are deleted.

2. Save the presentation using the new filename **GH Banner**.

3. Switch to Normal view, click **Format** on the menu bar, click **Background**, click the **Omit background graphics from master** check box, and then click the **Apply** or **Apply to All** button. (It doesn't matter which button you click because the presentation has only one slide.) Now you'll change the page setup for a banner.

4. Click **File** on the menu bar, click **Page Setup**, click the **Slides sized for** list arrow, and then click **Banner**. This sets the width to 8 inches and the height to 1 inch. Of course, you don't really want an 8 × 1-inch banner, but the aspect ratio is typical for a banner. The service bureau needs a computer picture file with the desired aspect ratio, not necessarily the absolute size.

5. Click the **OK** button in the dialog box. The slide is reformatted for a banner. Now you need to change the text so that it fits properly within the banner dimensions.

6. Select the **title text box** object, resize it as wide as possible, change its font to **24 pt**, select the **subtitle text box** object, and then resize it as wide as possible.

   When Harriet created the title slide, she pressed the Enter key after typing her name and after her job title. You want all the text in the subtitle text box to appear on one line.

7. Click just before "Director," press the **Backspace** key to delete the paragraph after your name, type a **comma**, and then press the **spacebar**.

8. Click just before "Global," press the **Backspace** key, type a **comma**, and then press the **spacebar**. The author's name, title, and organization are now all on one line.

9. Draw a 1½-point brown rectangle around the banner with no fill. Compare your screen to Figure 6-16.

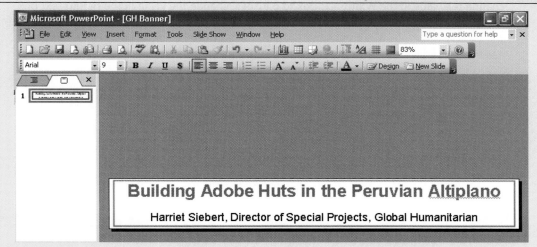

▶ **10.** Save the banner using the default filename and location, print a copy of it onto regular-sized paper so that William can see what it will look like when you print it out in full size, and then close the presentation.

You can now take this file to a service bureau for printing onto a 4 × ½-foot page. You could also use Microsoft Greetings Workshop or Mindscape PrintMaster to prepare and print a banner.

The multiple-page poster presentation, including the title banner, is now complete. Next, you'll create the single-page poster.

Creating a Single-Page Poster

To create a single-page poster, you'll copy all of the individual slides onto one slide, create a banner-style title for that slide, and then delete all the other slides in the presentation. You can then take that one-slide presentation file to a service bureau to print onto a large poster sheet. To copy the slides to the banner-style title slide, you'll set up the presentation to be a single-page poster by deleting all of the slides except the title slide and then changing the dimensions to poster size. You'll then save it with a new filename, open the original presentation, and then copy each of the slides except the title slide to the new banner-style slide.

Now you're ready to create Harriet's "Building Adobe Huts" presentation as a single-page poster.

To set up a presentation for a single-page poster:

▶ **1.** Open the presentation **GH Multiple-page Poster**, switch to Normal view, and then save the file to your high-capacity disk using the new filename **GH Single-page Poster**. Because you'll paste, resize, and position each of the eight subsequent slides into this Slide 1, you'll find it easier if you turn on the Snap to Grid feature and change the grid size.

▶ **2.** Click the **Draw** button on the Drawing toolbar, click **Grid and Guides** to open the Grid and Guides dialog box, click the **Snap objects to grid** check box to select it, if necessary, change the Grid setting to a spacing of **0.2** inches, and then click the **OK** button.

▶ **3.** Switch to Slide Sorter view, select all the slides except the first, and then delete them.

▶ **4.** Open the **Page Setup** dialog box, click the **Slides sized for** list arrow, click **Custom**, change the value in the Width text box to **6** inches, change the value in the Height text box to **4** inches, and then click the **OK** button. Obviously, the poster will not be 6 × 4 inches; it will be 6 × 4 feet. As with the banner, you only need to make sure that your presentation has the desired width-to-height ratio.

▶ **5.** Switch to the title master in Slide Master view, change the title text box font size to **10 pt**, resize the title text box placeholder so it is almost the width of the slide, resize the title text box so it's a little taller than the title text, and then drag it near the top of the slide.

▶ **6.** Delete the brown horizontal line and the Global Humanitarian logo, change the subtitle text box font size to **8 pt**, and then resize and reposition the subtitle text box placeholder as shown in Figure 6-17. Compare your screen to Figure 6-17.

Figure 6-17 ▶	Title master of single-page poster presentation

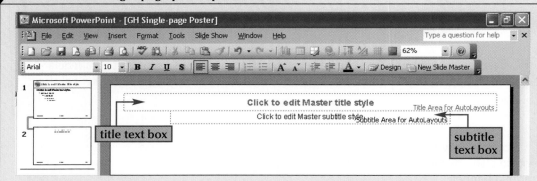

▶ **7.** Click the **Normal View** button ⊞, and then edit the subtitle as before so all the text is on one line. (Don't forget to insert a comma and space after each line to separate the author's name, title, and organization.)

▶ **8.** Save the presentation using the default name.

You're now ready to insert a miniature copy of all the slides into this one slide.

To copy slides from the multiple-page poster presentation to the single-page poster presentation:

▶ **1.** Open the file **GH Multiple-page Poster**. It opens in Slide Sorter view because that's the view you saved it in. Now you'll copy Slides 2 through 9 from this presentation to the other one.

▶ **2.** Select **Slide 2**, and then press the **Ctrl+C** keys to copy it to the Clipboard. You'll paste the slide in the single-page poster as a GIF picture file.

▶ **3.** Click **Window** on the menu bar, click **GH Single-page Poster**, click **Edit** on the menu bar, click **Paste Special** to open the Paste Special dialog box, click **Picture (GIF)** in the As list, and then click the **OK** button.

▶ **4.** Make sure the Picture toolbar is open, click the **Format Picture** button 🖼 on the Picture toolbar, click the **Size** tab, make sure the **Lock aspect ratio** check box is checked, and then change the value in the Width text box in the Size and rotate section to **1.25** inches.

Trouble? If the Picture toolbar is not visible, right-click the slide you just copied, and then click Show Picture Toolbar on the shortcut menu.

Now you'll draw a brown border around the slide miniature to make it stand out as a separate slide.

5. Click the **Colors and Lines** tab in the Format Picture dialog box, click the **Color** list arrow in the Line section, click the **brown** color tile in the row below Automatic, and then click the **OK** button. The picture of the slide is resized and has a brown border around it.

6. Drag the slide to the position of the first slide shown in Figure 6-18.

Slide show view of single-page poster presentation | Figure 6-18

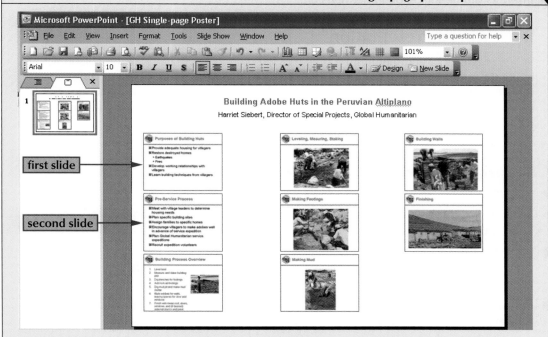

7. Repeat the above procedure to copy, paste, resize, draw a border around, and reposition the other seven slides from the GH Multiple-page Poster slide show, until Slide 1 of the file GH Single-page Poster looks like the slide shown in Figure 6-18. You have completed the single-page poster presentation. You can now save it and print a copy.

8. Save the presentation using the default filename, and then print a copy of the poster on an 8½ × 11-inch sheet of paper, either in color or grayscale.

9. Close both files in the PowerPoint presentation window.

You give a copy of both poster presentation files to Harriet. She decides she wants a single-page poster presentation, so she takes the file to a local service bureau, where she has it printed on a 6 × 4-foot sheet of glossy poster paper. The result is clear, easy to read, attractive, and professional. Harriet successfully uses the poster during her presentation at the poster session of the next APOH conference.

Reviewing a Presentation and Comparing Revisions

Harriet decides that she'd like another Global Humanitarian employee to review her 35mm slide presentation. For that purpose, she sets up a **review cycle**, which is a system for sending out a presentation file for others to review, having them make changes (revisions) and add comments to the presentation, getting back the copies of the files with the revisions and comments, combining the revised files into one document so that PowerPoint marks the revisions, and then accepting or rejecting the revisions.

Harriet sends the file GH 35mm Slides to Patricia Tuesta for review. She will make revisions and add comments to the presentation. A **comment** in PowerPoint is the electronic equivalent of an adhesive note that you can "attach" to a slide. You can use comments, for example, to remind yourself to verify information in a report, but comments are most useful when multiple people are reviewing a single presentation. For example, one person might receive a copy of the presentation via e-mail, delete or change a bullet, and then insert a comment to explain her revision.

Reviewing a Presentation

When you insert a comment into a slide, PowerPoint notes the name of the person who made the comment. How does PowerPoint know this? When a person edits and saves a file, PowerPoint also saves the name and initials located under User Information on the General tab of the Options dialog box. You'll see how this works because you'll make revisions to the GH 35mm Slides file as if you were Patricia Tuesta.

To specify the user name and initials in PowerPoint:

1. Open the file **GH 35mm Slides**. This is the file you'll edit as if you were Patricia.

2. Click **Tools** on the menu bar, click **Options** to open the Options dialog box, and then click the **General** tab, if necessary.

3. Write down the current Name and Initials (which are your name and initials if you're using your own computer) under User Information. You must restore this information when you complete this procedure.

4. Select the name in the Name text box, type **Patricia Tuesta**, select the text in the Initials text box, and then type **PT**. See Figure 6-19.

Figure 6-19 | **General tab of the Options dialog box**

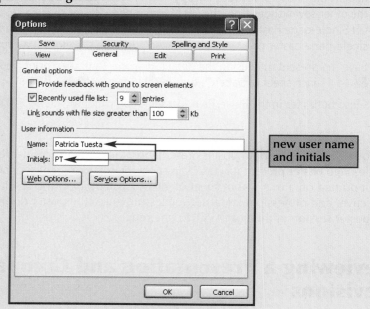

5. Click the **OK** button.

From now on, as you make changes in the presentation and save the results, PowerPoint will save the new version of the file with the name Patricia Tuesta and the initials PT. Now you'll make revisions and insert comments as if you were Patricia.

To make revisions and insert comments into the presentation:

▶ 1. Go to **Slide 4**, select the phrase "adobes for walls" in item 6, and then type **walls with adobes**. Patricia will now explain in a comment why she made this change.

▶ 2. Click **View** on the menu bar, point to **Toolbars**, click **Reviewing** to open the toolbar, and then click the **Insert Comment** button on the Reviewing toolbar. PowerPoint opens an empty comment box with the blinking insertion point in it. See Figure 6-20.

Inserting a comment into Slide 4 ◀ **Figure 6-20**

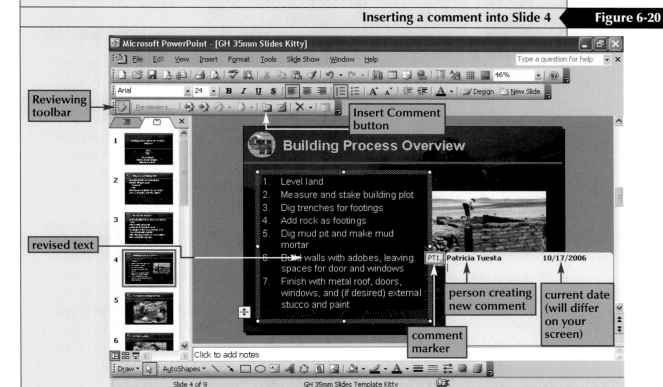

▶ 3. With the insertion point in the comment box, type **You build the walls, not the adobes here.**, and then click anywhere in a blank area of the slide. PowerPoint closes the comment box, but leaves a little rectangle with the text "PT1," meaning the first comment by "PT" (Patricia Tuesta).

▶ 4. Go to **Slide 7**, click to the right of the title "Making Mud," insert a space and an open parenthesis "**(**", type **Mortar**, and then insert a close parenthesis "**)**".

▶ 5. Click the **Insert Comment** button on the Reviewing toolbar, and type **Add this for clarification.** (Include the period at the end of the sentence.) See Figure 6-21.

Figure 6-21 | **Slide 7 with revision and comment**

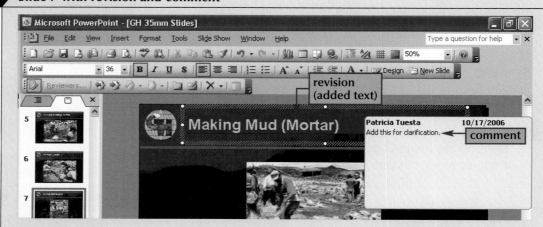

6. Click in a blank part of the slide to close the comment box. The comment rectangle with "PT2" appears in the slide. That completes Patricia's changes to the presentation.

   Now that your completed presentation contains comments, you'll print the comments pages of the PowerPoint presentation.

7. Click **File** on the menu bar, click **Print** to open the Print dialog box, click the **Slides** option button in the Print range section, type **4,7** in the Slides text box, click the **Print what** list arrow, click **Handouts**, set the **Slides per page** to **2**, make sure the **Print comments and ink markup** check box is selected, and then click the **OK** button. PowerPoint prints the slides as two miniatures on a page and prints a separate page with the two comments.

8. Save the presentation using the new filename **GH 35mm Slides Revised** to the same folder or high-capacity disk where you saved the other presentations you created in this tutorial, and then close the file. Now you'll change the user name back to what it was originally.

9. Click **Tools** on the menu bar, click **Options**, change the Name and Initials in the User Information of the General tab on the Options dialog box back to their original settings—the name and initials that you wrote down in Step 3 in the previous set of steps or your name and initials if you're using your own computer—and then click the **OK** button.

Merging and Comparing Presentations

Having made revisions on behalf of Patricia, now you'll compare and merge the two versions of the GH 35mm Slides presentation file. When you compare and merge two presentation files, PowerPoint opens the Revisions pane, which lists all the changes to the current slide and all the comments in that slide. PowerPoint notes the name and initials of the person who made each revision and comment.

Comparing and Merging Presentations From Different Reviewers

- Open your original presentation in the PowerPoint window.
- Click Tools on the menu bar, click Compare and Merge Presentations, select another edited file, and then click the Merge button. PowerPoint merges the second file into the first, creating a revision marker for each difference in the two presentations. PowerPoint also combines all comments into the original presentation file.
- Repeat this procedure for all edited copies of the presentation file.
- After merging all the files, you can review the changes and accept or reject each of them.

To merge and compare two presentations:

1. Open the file **GH 35mm Slides**, the version of the file before Patricia made changes and added comments.

2. Click **Tools** on the menu bar, and then click **Compare and Merge Presentations**.

3. Change the Look in folder to the location where you saved the file GH 35mm Slides Revised, if necessary, click **GH 35mm Slides Revised**, and then click the **Merge** button. PowerPoint displays a message explaining that the presentation wasn't sent anywhere, and provides other information. If you had actually e-mailed or otherwise sent the original file to a reviewer, received it back, and not opened it since, PowerPoint wouldn't display this message. Read over the information in the message, but because you simulated making changes on another computer, you can ignore the message and proceed with the merge.

4. Click the **Continue** button. PowerPoint merges the two files, noting any differences, opening the Revisions pane and the Reviewing toolbar.

Having merged the original and revised versions of the presentation, you're now ready to review the changes and comments.

Reviewing Changes

To review changes in a presentation, you can scroll through the presentation and click the change icons on the slides or click the Next Item button on the Reviewing toolbar to jump to each changed item. When you review changes to a presentation, you decide whether to accept or reject the changes. You also usually delete the comments so that they don't appear in the final presentation. If you leave comments in the presentation, they will not appear in the slide show.

To review changes:

1. Click the **Next Item** button ⧉ on the Reviewing toolbar. PowerPoint displays Slide 4, the location of Patricia's first revision. PowerPoint lists the revision and comment made on this slide in the Revisions pane. The change Patricia made is also denoted by the revision marker on the slide. The first item in the Revisions pane is the comment, which PowerPoint opens for you to read. See Figure 6-22. After you read the comment, you delete it so that your final presentation contains no comments or revision markers.

Figure 6-22 | Presentation file after comparing and merging with revised file

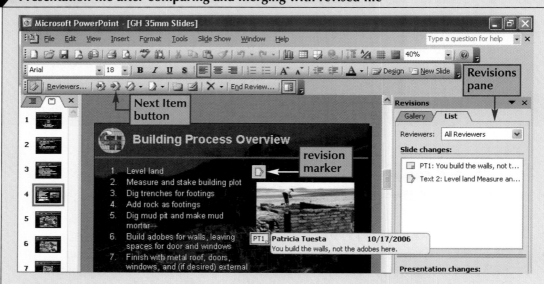

▶ **2.** Click the **Delete Comment** button ✕ ▾ on the Reviewing toolbar.

▶ **3.** Click the **Next Item** button 🔁 on the Reviewing toolbar. PowerPoint moves to the next revision, the edit that Patricia made to the text on the slide. A description of the change appears in a box next to the revision marker. See Figure 6-23. You can now accept or reject the change. You decide to accept this revision.

Figure 6-23 | Slide 4 with revisions

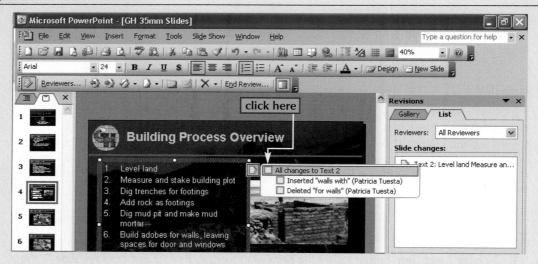

▶ **4.** Click the check box to the left of "All changes to Text 2." PowerPoint makes the changes in the numbered list, per Patricia's suggestions. After you accept or reject a change, you can leave the revision marker in the slide or delete it. You'll leave the marker here (which won't appear in Slide Show view).

▶ **5.** Click the **Next Item** button 🔁 on the Reviewing toolbar. PowerPoint displays Patricia's comment on Slide 7. This time you decide to leave the comment in the presentation.

6. Click the **Next Item** button ⊡ on the Reviewing toolbar to display the revision Patricia made to Slide 7, the addition of "(Mortar)." You decide to reject this change because you already explained that the mud is the mortar used in building the huts. To reject a change, you can ignore it, and the change will not be incorporated, or you can delete the marker without clicking the check box to accept the change. You will delete the marker.

7. Click the **Delete Marker** button ⊠ ▾ on the Reviewing toolbar. You don't have to delete the marker to reject the change; you can just ignore it.

8. Save the presentation with the new filename **GH 35mm Slides New Version**, and then close both open presentations.

The file you just saved still contains a comment and a revision marker, but those items don't affect how the presentation will look when shown using Slide Show view, when printed, or when made into 35mm slides.

Publishing a Web Presentation with Custom Action Buttons

After Harriet makes her presentation on building huts in the Peruvian altiplano, she decides she will post the presentation on the Global Humanitarian company Web site. She asks you to add navigation (action) buttons to the slides, but instead of using the PowerPoint built-in action buttons, she wants you to use customized ones to give the presentation a more unique look. Furthermore, she wants you to set the action buttons to animate and make a sound when a user passes the pointer over them.

Reference Window

Applying Mouse-Over Action Settings to an Action Button

- Select the action button.
- Click Slide Show on the menu bar, click Action Settings to display the Action Settings dialog box, and then click the Mouse Over tab.
- If desired, click the Play sound check box, click the Play sound list arrow, and select a sound.
- If desired, click the Highlight when mouse over check box.
- Click the OK button.

You asked the company artist to create two small JPEG files, using pictures of stones, as pointers to go to the previous or next slide. The artist creates the two JPEG files using a photo-imaging program, so now you're ready to import them into the slide show, resize the custom action buttons, and link them to the previous or next slide. Then when you publish the presentation as a Web page, you'll specify that you want to use your own navigation buttons, not the ones normally created by PowerPoint.

To add custom action buttons to the slides:

1. Open the file **GH 35mm Slides**, change the page setup to **On-screen Show**, reset the logos on the slide masters to their original aspect ratio, and resize as necessary.

2. On Slide 1, insert the graphics (JPEG) file **NextButn**, located in the Tutorial.06\Tutorial folder included with your Data Files, and move it to the lower-right corner of the slide. See Figure 6-24.

Figure 6-24 Slide 1 with custom action button

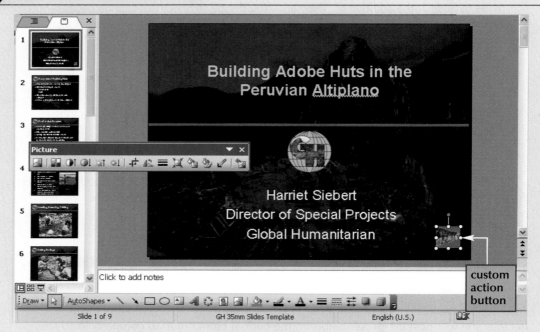

3. With the graphic still selected, click the **Insert Hyperlink** button 🔗 on the Standard tool-bar, click the **Place in This Document** button in the Link to section of the dialog box, select **Next Slide** in the Select a place in this document section of the dialog box (you might have to scroll up to see it), and then click the **OK** button. The graphic is now an action button, which, during a slide show or Web presentation, will cause the presentation to advance to the next slide. Now you'll add one more feature to the customized action button: to become highlighted and make a sound when a user moves the pointer over it.

4. With the custom action button still selected, click **Slide Show** on the menu bar, click **Action Settings** to display the Action Settings dialog box, and then click the **Mouse Over** tab. See Figure 6-25.

Figure 6-25 Mouse Over tab in Action Settings dialog box

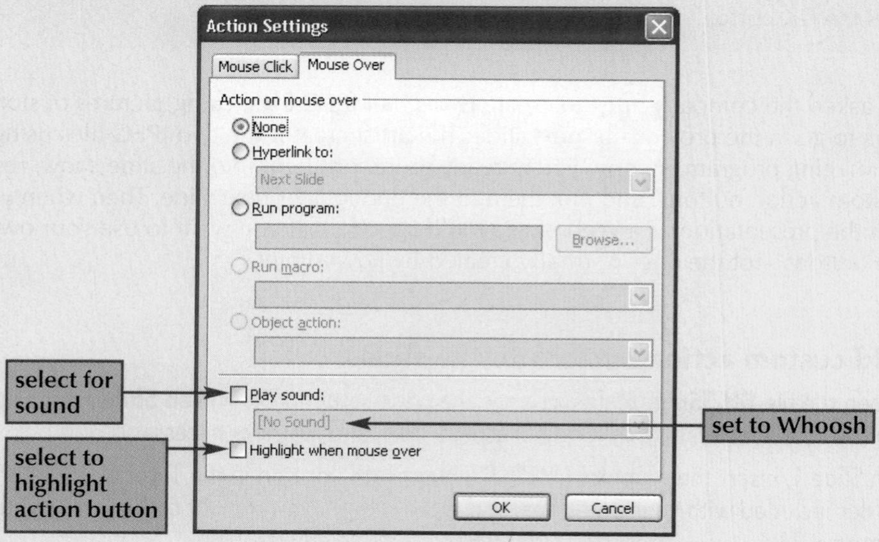

▶ **5.** Click the **Play sound** check box to select it, click the **Play sound** list arrow, and then click **Whoosh**. This becomes the sound effect when a user moves the pointer over the button.

   Trouble? If a dialog box opens telling you that this feature is not installed, ask your instructor or technical support person for help if you are working in a lab, or click the Yes button to install the sound if you are working on your own computer.

▶ **6.** Click the **Highlight when mouse over** check box to select it. The button will now highlight when a user moves the pointer over the button.

▶ **7.** Click the **OK** button.

▶ **8.** Insert the graphics file **HomeButn**, located in the Tutorial.06\Tutorial folder included with your Data Files and position it to the left of the NextButn button.

▶ **9.** Set the HomeButn button to hyperlink to Slide 1, and then set it so that it highlights and makes a Whoosh sound when a user moves the mouse pointer over it.

▶ **10.** Repeat Steps 8 and 9, except this time insert, position, link, and set the action for the button **PrevButn**, positioning it to the left of the HomeButn, and setting it to link to the previous slide. See Figure 6-26.

Slide with three custom action buttons **Figure 6-26**

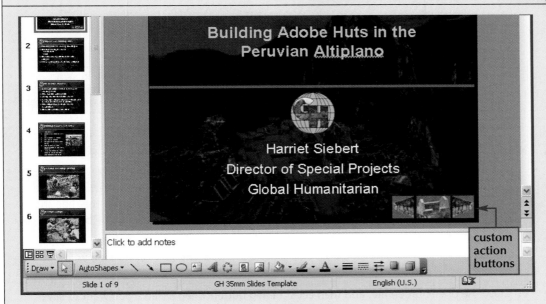

   Trouble? If the three image buttons don't fit on the slide without overlapping the slide subtitle, move the subtitle text box up a little higher so all the text is legible.

▶ **11.** Copy the three customized action buttons to all the other slides, shrinking and moving to the left the digital photographs in the slides, as necessary, so that they don't overlap with the action buttons.

▶ **12.** Delete the Previous and Home buttons from Slide 1, delete the Next button from the last slide, and then reposition the buttons on the last slide so they appear in the lower-right corner.

▶ **13.** Go through the presentation in Slide Show view to make sure the action buttons work properly (including the change in appearance and the sound when you pass the mouse over the buttons), and then save the presentation file to your high-capacity disk using the filename **GH Web Presentation**.

Now you're ready to publish this presentation as a Web page.

To publish the presentation as a Web page:

1. Click **File** on the menu bar, click **Save as Web Page** to open the Save As dialog box, and then make sure the Save as type list box is set to **Single File Web Page**.

2. Rather than clicking the Save button at this point, click the **Publish** button in the Save As dialog box. This allows you to customize the Web page. The Publish as Web Page dialog box opens.

3. Deselect the **Display speaker notes** check box, make sure the File name text box includes the file **GH Web Presentation**, and make sure all the other options are like those in Figure 6-27. (Note that your file location will vary from that shown here.)

Figure 6-27	Publish as Web Page dialog box

4. Click the **Web Options** button, deselect the **Add slide navigation controls** so that PowerPoint doesn't create the navigation bar with its own action buttons on the Web page, and then click the **Show slide animation while browsing** check box to select it. Those who view the Web page will see all the animation, just as they would when viewing the slide show in a presentation, and they will be able to use your custom-animated navigation buttons.

5. Click the **OK** button in the Web Options dialog box, and then click the **Publish** button in the Publish as Web Page dialog box. The file is saved as a single-file Web page with the filename extension .mht.

6. Close the presentation file, and then click the **No** button when asked if you want to save the presentation (because you already saved it).

7. Start your Web browser. The browser doesn't have to be connected to the Internet because you'll open your GH Web Presentation file in the browser from the folder or disk where you saved the files you created in this tutorial.

8. On your browser, click **File** on the menu bar, click **Open**, click the **Browse** button, navigate to the folder or disk where you saved the files you created in this tutorial, click **GH Web Presentation**, click the **Open** button, and then click the **OK** button. See Figure 6-28.

Slide 1 viewed in Web browser ◄ Figure 6-28

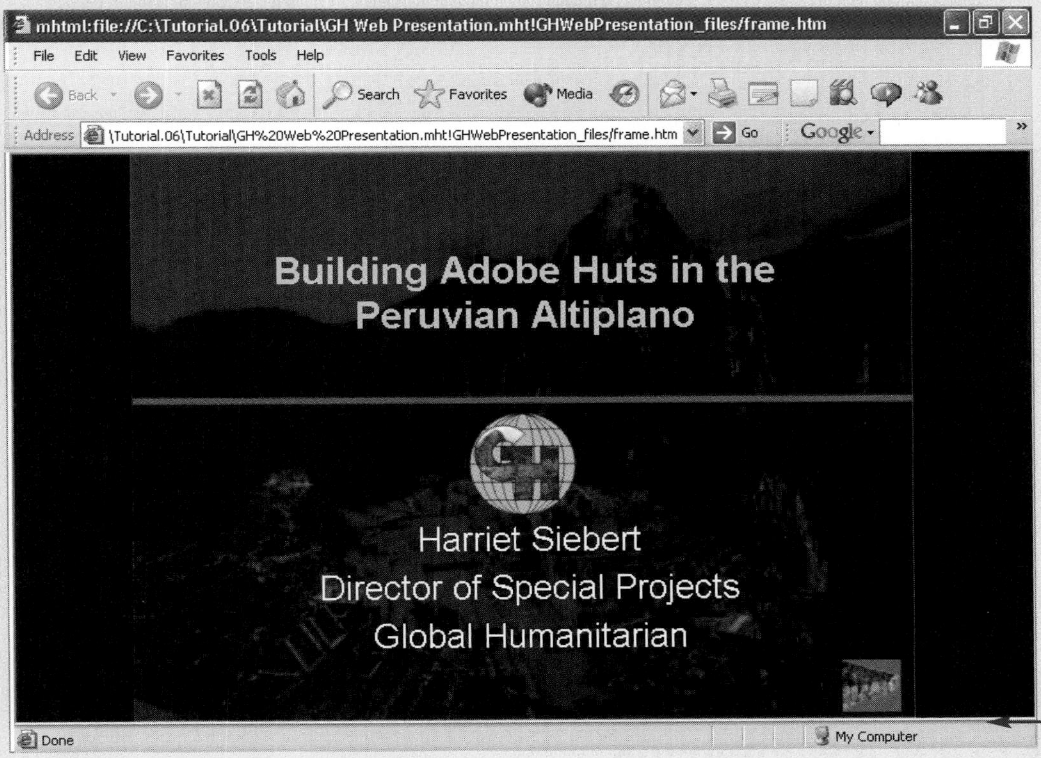

navigation
bar not
included

9. Click the custom Next Slide button to go to the next slide in the Web presentation, and then continue clicking the action buttons to review all the slides in the presentation.

Trouble? If your animation of the action buttons doesn't work, don't worry. This type of animation often doesn't translate well to a Web page.

10. Exit the Web browser.

Harriet is pleased with your work in creating a Web version of her slide presentation. She gives the HTML file and accompanying folder to the Global Humanitarian network administrator to post on the company Web page.

William thanks you for all your help in making the presentations at the APOH meetings so successful.

Session 6.2 Quick Check

Review

1. What are the general steps required to prepare a banner using PowerPoint?
2. List three instances when you might need to prepare a poster presentation.
3. What are the differences between a multiple-page poster presentation and a single-page poster presentation?
4. List one advantage and one disadvantage of a single-page poster over a multiple-page poster.
5. In general terms, how do you compare an original PowerPoint presentation file with a revised one?

6. True or False: If you want action buttons to advance one slide forward or one slide back, you must use the PowerPoint action buttons found on the Slide Show menu.
7. In general terms, how do you set up a hyperlink object (text or graphic) to become highlighted and make a sound when a user passes the pointer over it?

Review

Tutorial Summary

In this tutorial, you learned how to create a design template for overheads. You created a color scheme, used a digital image as a bullet, and added background objects to the slide master. You also created a design template for 35mm slides and added a picture background to the slide masters. You made overhead transparencies and saved a presentation as an RTF outline. You created a multiple-page poster, created and printed a banner, and created a single-page poster. You learned how to make revisions, insert comments into a presentation, and merge and compare two versions of a poster. You also published a Web presentation with custom action buttons.

Key Terms

banner	overhead transparency	review cycle
comment	poster presentation	Rich Text Format (RTF)
film recorder		

Practice

Practice the skills you learned in the tutorial using the same case scenario.

Review Assignments

Data Files needed for the Review Assignments: PeruGeo.ppt, StoneWrk.jpg, PeruGeo.jpg, Costa.jpg, Sierra.jpg, Puna.jpg, Montana.jpg, Selva.jpg, PeruLogo.jpg, and MntBut.jpg

After William and Harriet enjoyed success in their presentations at the meetings of the APOH, they start to think about future presentations at professional conferences. They decide to make a joint presentation, which they'll use to educate expedition leaders and volunteers. After they create the text and graphics for the presentation, you need to do the following:

1. Start PowerPoint, open the file **PeruGeo** from the Tutorial.06\Review folder the Data Files, and save the file as **Peru Geography 35mm Slides** to a high-capacity disk.
2. In the subtitle text box of Slide 1, add a new line with the phrase "Presented by," followed by a space and your name.
3. Change the page setup to 35mm slides.
4. Add the background picture **StoneWrk**, located in the Tutorial.06\Review folder, to all the slides in the presentation.
5. Change the color scheme so that the title text is yellow and the text and lines are white.
6. In Slides 2 through 7, insert the picture (JPEG file) **PeruGeo**, **Costa**, **Sierra**, **Puna**, **Montana**, and **Selva**, respectively (all located in the Tutorial.06\Review folder included with your Data Files). Based on the shape of the picture, change the slide layout, and adjust the size and position of the pictures to maximize the visibility of the picture and the readability of the slide.
7. Switch to Master view, insert a title master, and then add the logo file **PeruLogo** to the title master and slide master. Size and position it to look attractive and readable. Adjust the size and position of the text boxes so all the text is still legible. Set appropriate fonts, font colors, and font sizes.

8. Change the level-one bullet to the picture **MntBut** (located in the Tutorial.06\Review folder), and the level-two bullet to a yellow square.

9. Complete the presentation design by adding any other appropriate background objects, such as lines and squares. Be creative and tasteful.

10. Review all the slides in the presentation to make sure they are attractive and well-formatted. Make any adjustments to improve the appearance and readability of the presentation.

11. Save the presentation using the current filename.

12. Print the presentation as handouts with four slides per page.

13. Delete all but the first slide in the presentation, delete the text in the first slide so it contains only the background objects, and save the presentation as a design template file to your high-capacity disk using the filename **GH Geography 35mm Template**. Harriet and William now have another choice for a design template for Global Humanitarian presentations.

14. Modify the template that you just saved so it works well for creating overhead transparencies. (For example, remove the background picture, set the background color to white, fix any distortions in the background objects, and change the page setup.)

15. Save this as a design template file using the new filename **GH Geography Overhead Template**. Make sure you save it to the location where you are saving your Data Files and not to the Templates folder.

16. Open the presentation file **Peru Geography 35mm Slides** again.

17. Apply the GH Geography Overhead Template to the presentation. Change the page setup, if necessary, to 7.5 × 10-inch, portrait-oriented overheads. Delete the distorted graphic in the masters.

18. Review the presentation one slide at a time to make sure all the text and graphics are readable, attractive, and well-formatted. Adjust the aspect ratio of any distorted image.

19. Save the presentation as **Peru Geography Overheads**.

20. Print the overhead transparency presentation as a handout with four slides per page.

Apply

Apply the skills you learned in the tutorial to create a new presentation and publish it as a Web page.

Case Problem 1

Data Files needed for this Case Problem: BkgrValy.jpg, ParkSign.jpg, Bullet.tif, ParkShow.ppt, ParkJog.jpg, ParkPic.jpg, ParkRivr.jpg, NavNext.jpg, and NavBack.jpg

Canyon Glen Park Harvey McNaughton is superintendent of parks in Whistler, British Columbia, Canada, which is a town famous for its skiing, but which also hosts numerous conferences and festivals during the summer. Locals and visitors alike take advantage of the city parks, including the largest one, Canyon Glen. This park has facilities for picnicking, volleyball, and softball, as well as a small amphitheatre. Harvey is also in charge of the Whistler jogging trail that passes through Canyon Glen. The jogging trail is 22 miles of paved path, not only for jogging, but also for walking, biking, and roller skating (or in-line skating). Harvey was invited to give a presentation at the Annual Canadian Conference on Parks and Recreation, and he asks you to help him prepare his presentation graphics. Harvey will give his presentation using 35mm slides, but he also wants you to create custom navigation (action) buttons for the presentation and publish it as a Web page on the Whistler Web site. Do the following:

1. Create a design template for 35mm slides using the graphic file **BkgrValy** (located in the Tutorial.06\Cases folder included with your Data Files) as a picture background (mountains and valley) for all the slides.

2. Choose your color scheme based partly on the colors in the background picture and partly on the colors in the other graphics you'll use, which are the JPEG files that begin with the word "Park," located in the Tutorial.06\Cases folder. In other words, the color scheme should include greens, yellows, grays, and possibly other colors.

3. Use the JPEG file **ParkSign** as a logo that goes on all the slides.

4. On your slide masters, select appropriate, attractive, and readable fonts, font sizes, and font attributes, as well as appropriately sized and positioned text boxes.

5. Use the picture file **Bullet** (a picture of a stone at Canyon Glen), located in the Tutorial.06\Cases folder, to make bullets for all the level-one bulleted items in the presentation.

6. Select a normal round bullet, but color it gray for the level-two bullets.

7. If you want, apply any other background objects that you think would look attractive.

8. Save the presentation as a design template to your high-capacity disk using the filename **Canyon Glen Slide Template**, and close the file.

9. Open the file **ParkShow**, located in the Tutorial.06\Cases folder, and save it as the presentation file **Canyon Glen Slide Presentation**.

10. Change the name on Slide 1 to your name. Apply the Canyon Glen Slide Template to the presentation.

11. Add the graphics files **ParkJog** (picture of the jogging trail), **ParkPic** (picture of one of the covered picnic areas), and **ParkRivr** (picture of the river that passes through the park) to the presentation—selecting the appropriate slide into which each picture should be inserted.

12. Go through all the slides to make sure they are attractive and legible. Make sure the graphics don't overlap the text.

13. If necessary, adjust the font size of the organization chart so the text is more legible.

14. Save the 35mm slide presentation using the default filename (Canyon Glen Slide Presentation).

15. Print a copy of the presentation as a handout with four slides per page.

16. Prepare the presentation for publication as a Web page by adding custom navigation (action) buttons **NavNext** and **NavBack** to each slide. Don't include a Home navigation button.

17. Make the navigation buttons cyclical—the Back button on Slide 1 should link to the last slide, and the Next button on the last slide should link to Slide 1.

18. Set the custom navigation buttons to become highlighted and to make a sound when the pointer passes over them.

19. Save the file as a Web page using the filename **Canyon Glen Slide Presentation**. Tell PowerPoint to omit putting in its own navigation objects.

20. Review the Web page in your Web browser. If you notice problems, fix them, and then save the Web page again.

21. Close the file.

Case Problem 2

Research

Use the Internet to research information on personal digital assistants, and create a new slide presentation using the skills you learned in the tutorial.

Data Files needed for this Case Problem: PalmAddr.jpg, PalmAlrm.jpg, PalmCalc.jpg, PalmGame.jpg, and PalmSchd.jpg

PDAs for College Students The teacher in your Computer Applications class asks you to prepare a presentation on personal digital assistants (PDAs) (for example, Palm Pilot, Visor, and Clié) for college students. (These are sometimes also called palm-held or handheld computers.) The presentation should answer the following questions: Who should buy a PDA? Why should a student use a PDA? What are some of the applications on a PDA?

What are the advantages? What are the disadvantages and inconveniences? Do the following:

1. Talk to students who have PDAs. Ask them the above questions. If you use one yourself, you can answer the questions. Go into a PDA chat room on the Internet, and ask the participants to provide information for your presentation.
2. Do an Internet search for Web pages on PDAs, and gather information. Reviews of new PDA products are a good source of information on the pros and cons of PDAs.
3. Organize your presentation in PowerPoint overhead transparency format, 7.5 × 10 inches in size, and in portrait orientation.
4. Include at least eight pages, one of which can be the title page. Include you name on the title page.
5. You can also use the five graphics files about PDAs (which all begin with the word "Palm") located in the Tutorial.06\Cases folder of your Data Files. You should include at least five pictures (photos, clip art, GIF animation files) in your presentation. You can get many pictures of PDAs from the Internet.
6. Use pictures for the level-one bullets on your bulleted list slides.
7. Design the presentation with a white background and other colors that match the figures.
8. After you determine the color scheme, make sure the slides are still legible in grayscale.
9. Prepare, as desired, appropriate background objects, including a logo, if you have access to graphics software.
10. After completing the presentation, save it using the filename **PDA Multiple-Page Overhead**.
11. Change the format and layout of the presentation so that each slide is in landscape orientation.
12. Go through each slide to make sure the graphics, background objects, text boxes, etc., are not distorted, but are attractive and readable.
13. Copy all the individual slides to one large slide in preparation to make a single-page poster presentation.
14. On your single-page poster presentation, don't include a separate title page, but rather make the title (and byline) large-font headings at the top of the page.
15. Save the presentation using the filename **PDA Single-Page Poster**.
16. Print the single-page poster presentation on a single piece of 8½ × 11-inch paper, unless your instructor tells you to print it on large, poster-sized paper.
17. Close the presentation.

Case Problem 3

Data File needed for this Case Problem: Jayhawk.ppt

Jayhawk Foreign-Language Institute You recently accepted employment at the Jayhawk Foreign-Language Institute headquartered in Lawrence, Kansas. This company has on-site language-training institutes in six countries. Your task is to prepare a 35mm slide presentation and a single-page poster presentation on the language institute in Guadalajara, Mexico. Do the following:

1. Open the presentation file named **Jayhawk**, and save it to your disk using the filename **Jayhawk in Guadalajara**.
2. Set up and format the presentation for 7.5 × 10-inch (portrait) overhead transparency film.

3. Using the slide master and creating a new title master, apply an appropriate design to the presentation with an attractive color scheme, background objects, fonts, font size, and font colors.

4. Include a picture of a hawk in the logo that should go on every slide.

5. Include at least one picture bullet for the bulleted lists.

6. In addition to the current slide master, create a new slide master. Change the format of the second slide master to exclude the logo and to have a different font color in the title. Apply the new slide master to at least one slide in your presentation. (*Hint*: Create a second slide master by clicking the Insert New Slide Master Button on the Slide Master View toolbar. To apply the new slide master, display the Slide Design task pane, click the Custom Design list arrow, and click Apply to Selected Slides.)

7. Using clip art and digital photographs, apply one or more pictures per slide. If your on-disk clip gallery doesn't have the appropriate pictures, download pictures from the Clip Art and Media page on the Microsoft Office Online Web site.

8. Save the completed presentation, change the User Information name as if you are a different person reviewing the file, make at least two revisions to the text of the presentation, and insert at least two comments into the presentation using the Reviewing toolbar.

9. Include your name on Slide 1, and then save the presentation using the filename **Jayhawk in Guadalajara Revised**.

10. Print the speaker notes (Notes Pages) of the presentation. In the process, print a page with the comments. (*Hint*: Click the Include comment pages check box, and then use essentially the same procedure for printing Notes Pages as you would for printing handouts.)

11. Compare and merge the Jayhawk in the Guadalajara presentation with the revised version. Use the Reviewing toolbar to accept all the changes and delete all the markers and comments.

12. Save the presentation using the filename **Jayhawk in Guadalajara Final**.

13. Save the outline of the final presentation as an RTF outline using the default filename. (PowerPoint will automatically add the .rtf filename extension.)

14. Print the presentation as a handout with four slides per page.

15. Using the same design and format, create an attractive, legible, single-page poster presentation.

16. Don't include the title slide as one of the slide panes, but rather prepare a title banner that spans the top of the single-page poster.

17. Save the poster presentation using the filename **Jayhawk Poster**.

18. Print the poster onto one regular sheet of 8½ × 11-inch paper.

19. Close the presentation.

Research

Use the Internet to research a town or city, and create a collaborative presentation geared for tourists.

Case Problem 4

Data Files needed for this Case Problem: SFBridge.jpg, SFCblCar.jpg, SFCtyHll.jpg, and SFDwnTwn.jpg

Group Presentation on a Town or City You and some of your fellow students have accepted jobs as assistants to travel agents at a large local travel agency. The travel agents ask you to work together on preparing information that might be of interest to tourists about a town or city in the United States or abroad.

According to your teacher's instructions, you become part of a three- to five-person group that will collaborate on preparing a presentation on a town or city. None of the members of the group actually has to be from or live in that town or city, although it might be a good idea to select a location with which at least one member of your group is familiar. You can get further information about the city from travel guides, tourist brochures, Web sites, encyclopedias, and personal visits, all of which are also sources of graphics for your presentation. Do the following:

1. Select a town or city for your presentation, and then get your teacher's approval. If your teacher allows you or instructs you to do so, you can select the city of San Francisco, for which your Data Files contains four photographs. These photographs are JPEG files that begin with the letters "SF." **SFBridge** is a picture of the Golden Gate Bridge; **SFCblCar** is a picture of a cable car; **SFCtyHll** is a picture of San Francisco's City Hall; and **SFDwnTwn** is a picture of downtown San Francisco, as viewed from the Twin Peaks area.
2. Gather information about your city and organize it into PowerPoint slides with titles and bulleted lists.
3. Include at least eight slides, not counting the title.
4. Create an original design template for your presentation. Design the template as a multiple-page poster presentation. You might want to design a group or course logo for the presentation. You'll want to use a color scheme that fits the flavor of the town or city on which you are reporting. (If you don't have a color printer, you can use a grayscale scheme, or a color scheme that produces attractive grayscale output.)
5. Include picture bullets in the presentation.
6. Save the design template using the filename **City Template**.
7. Include at least four pictures in your presentation, preferably photographs of your town or city. Add your name to Slide 1.
8. Create a title banner named **City Banner** to go with your poster presentation. (*Hint*: If you don't have access to banner software or a service bureau, you can still print the banner as separate sheets of paper, and then cut and tape the pages together.)
9. Save your completed presentation using the filename **City Poster Presentation**.
10. Print each slide on a separate piece of paper.
11. Close the presentation.
12. Mount each printed slide with colored construction paper to give it a colored border.
13. If your teacher instructs, hold a class poster session in which all the groups display their posters to the other class members.

Research

Go to the Web to find information you can use to create presentations.

Internet Assignments

The purpose of the Internet Assignments is to challenge you to find information on the Internet that you can use to work effectively with this software. The actual assignments are updated and maintained on the Course Technology Web site. Log on to the Internet and use your Web browser to go to the Student Online Companion for New Perspectives Office 2003 at **www.course.com/np/office2003**. Click the Internet Assignments link, and then navigate to the assignments for this tutorial.

Assess

SAM Assessment and Training

If you have a SAM user profile, you may have access to hands-on instruction, practice, and assessment of the skills covered in this tutorial. Log in to your SAM account and go to your assignments page to see what your instructor has assigned.

Review

Quick Check Answers

Session 6.1

1. Advantages: (a) The room can stay lighter, (b) you can more easily face the audience, (c) most classrooms and conference rooms come equipped with overhead projectors, and (d) overhead projectors seem to be more reliable than 35mm slide projectors. Disadvantage: They don't look as professional as 35mm slides.
2. True
3. cheaper (less ink), faster (less printing), and the presentation room stays lighter
4. Open the Background dialog box, select Fill Effects, click Picture tab, and then select a photograph file from the disk.
5. The background picture should be dark (if the text is light) or light (if the text is dark) and have low contrast.
6. Click File on the menu bar, click Save As to open the Save As dialog box, click the Save as type list arrow, click Outline/RTF, and click the Save button.

Session 6.2

1. Set up the page for banners, and then take the PowerPoint file to a service bureau to print on a large sheet of paper.
2. professional meetings, academic meetings, and informal meetings
3. A multiple-page poster presentation includes many slide panes and a title banner on just one page, whereas a single-page poster presentation includes one printed page for each slide.
4. Advantages: easy to set up, looks professional. Disadvantages: expensive, takes longer to prepare, cumbersome to carry
5. Open the original PowerPoint file, and use the Compare and Merge Presentations feature to compare and merge the revised PowerPoint file. This adds revision marks to the original file.
6. False
7. Select the action button, open the Action Settings dialog box (from Slide Show on the menu bar), click the Mouse Over tab, and then make your selections.

Objectives

In this case you will:
- Complete a Purpose and Outcomes Worksheet for your presentation
- Complete an Audience Analysis Worksheet for your presentation
- Complete a Situational Assessment Worksheet for your presentation
- Create an attention-getting introduction, an advance organizer or overview, and a summary for your presentation
- Complete a Focus and Organization Worksheet for your presentation
- Complete a Presentation Visuals Worksheet for your presentation
- Insert photographs acquired with a digital camera or scanner into your presentation
- Insert graphic, motion, and sound clips downloaded from the Online Design Gallery Live
- Complete a Presentation Delivery Worksheet for your presentation
- Copy slides as miniatures to be included on another slide

Student Data Files

There are no Data Files needed for this Case Problem.

Creating a Presentation on Local Folklore

Case

Family, Business, or Community Folklore

Folklore is the study of the traditions of people as they appear in popular fiction, customs, and beliefs. Folklore includes myths, legends, stories, riddles, proverbs, nursery rhymes, popular ballads, cowboy songs, and community customs. Folklore is more than entertainment; it tells us about the worldviews of groups of people, and helps us understand their traditions and history.

Your assignment is to prepare a presentation on one or more stories (or other types of folklore) from a family, business, community, or your school. According to your teacher's instructions, you should do this presentation on your own or as a group.

Here are some examples of the types of stories you might research and present:

- **Stories from the George Hamilton family of Sugar City, Idaho.** For example, George was traveling in his automobile along a back road near his hometown when he saw a man whose car was disabled. He helped the man, who then asked George his name. When the man heard "Hamilton," he replied, "Are you related to Grant Hamilton? Why, that good-for-nothing owes me $20." George immediately reached for his wallet and pulled out a $20 bill. "The good name of Hamilton is worth more than $20," he said as he handed the man the money.

- **Business (company) stories from Hewlett-Packard.** The company prides itself on doing things the "HP way"—meaning that HP has a certain culture, and that culture propagates because of company folklore. For example, when HP faced hard times and layoffs of 10 percent, company officers went to the employees and asked them to take a 10 percent salary cut, work nine of 10 days, and in return, there would be no layoffs. This story, known as the "nine-day fortnight," became part of company lore, and in fact, was repeated in later years. Such company folklore breeds employee loyalty.
- **Community stories from southwestern Utah (red-rock desert country).** For example, around 1950, after a road had just been refurbished, a motorcade of VIPs was traveling the roadway north of the town of St. George. As a prank, some youth ignited tires and inner tubes inside one of the volcano cinder cones that dot the landscape of this rugged desert area. Because the burning materials were out of sight, the VIPs thought that the ancient volcano might erupt, and they became frightened. They called in geologists from California before the prank was uncovered.

Complete the following:

1. Talk to older family members, longtime company employees, longtime community residents, or alumni from your university. Ask them to share commonly told stories. In folklore terminology, the people who supply you with folklore stories are called **informants**.
2. Compile as much information as you can about your informants, including places and dates of birth and upbringing, jobs, marital status (if relevant), religion (if relevant), hobbies, and childhood memories. This information will help you better understand the significance of the folklore they provide.
3. After gathering the stories and backgrounds of your informants, interpret these stories and reflect upon their significance. To begin, you might ask yourself (or your informants) the following questions: Who generally tells these stories? What are the personality characteristics of the teller? When and where are the stories told? Who is generally the audience for the stories? How does the audience receive these stories? Do they like them? Why? Do they know the stories already and participate in the telling? How are the stories told? (Try to get a feel for the storyteller's tone, dialect, and voice.) How does the informant feel about these stories? What values or cultural characteristics do the stories demonstrate or communicate?

4. Complete a Purpose and Outcomes Worksheet for your presentation.

5. Complete an Audience Analysis Worksheet for your presentation. Keep in mind that your audience will probably be your classmates.

6. Complete a Situation and Media Assessment Worksheet for your presentation.

7. Begin preparing a PowerPoint presentation on your folklore stories by creating bulleted lists and, if desired, other paragraphs. Leave space for appropriate graphics.

8. Plan the PowerPoint presentation to include at least eight slides, including the title slide, contents slide, and summary slide.

9. Create an appropriate, attention-getting introduction for your presentation.

10. Complete a Focus and Organization Worksheet, and organize the text in your PowerPoint presentation accordingly.

11. Create an advance organizer or overview for your PowerPoint presentation.

12. Include a summary recapping the key ideas of your PowerPoint presentation.

13. Using the Presentation Delivery Worksheet, decide on an appropriate presentation style.

14. Complete a Presentation Visuals Worksheet. Include in the PowerPoint presentation at least two pictures that you acquired by scanning a photograph or taking a photograph with a digital camera. Also include at least one appropriate clip art graphic that you downloaded from the Online Design Gallery Live.

15. Include at least one motion clip and one sound clip in your PowerPoint presentation.

16. Design the PowerPoint presentation with an attractive color scheme, background objects, fonts, font sizes, and font colors.

17. Add appropriate slide transitions and slide animation effects with built-in sounds to your PowerPoint presentation.

18. Copy two or more slides to a contents slide and hyperlink them to their respective slides in the presentation.

19. Save your completed PowerPoint presentation using the filename "Folklore".

20. Print the presentation as handouts with four slides per page.

21. Practice your presentation in front of one or more classmates or family members, and ask them to complete the evaluation section of the Presentation Delivery Worksheet.
22. Complete a Facilities Checklist for your presentation.
23. Set up your classroom for your presentation.
24. Give your presentation to your classmates or some other audience, as indicated by your instructor.

Objectives

In this case you will:
- Complete a Purpose and Outcomes Worksheet for your presentation
- Complete an Audience Analysis Worksheet for your presentation
- Complete a Situational Assessment Worksheet for your presentation
- Create an attention-getting introduction, an advance organizer or overview, and a summary for your presentation
- Complete a Focus and Organization Worksheet for your presentation
- Complete a Presentation Visuals Worksheet for your presentation
- Insert photographs acquired with a digital camera or scanner into your presentation
- Insert graphic, motion, and sound clips downloaded from the Online Design Gallery Live
- Complete a Presentation Delivery Worksheet for your presentation
- Copy slides as miniatures to be included on another slide

Student Data Files

There are no Data Files needed for this Case Problem.

Creating a Presentation for the Director of a Museum or Hall of Fame

Case

Exhibit Consulting, Inc.

Judith Golovenko is president of Exhibit Consulting, Inc. (ECI), a large consulting firm headquartered in Washington, DC. She recently hired you to help prepare and deliver presentations to museums in the DC area and other towns and cities in the Mid-Atlantic states. Your assignment is to prepare a presentation explaining the services provided by ECI. You'll give your presentation to a director of a museum, or sports or music hall of fame. According to your teacher's instructions, you should prepare this presentation on your own or as a group.

Some of the services that ECI might provide include the following:

- Arrange traveling exhibits. For example, ECI could arrange for a museum to display a traveling exhibit of artifacts from an Egyptian pharaoh's tomb, or artworks from French impressionist painters.
- Negotiate with professional athletes or musicians for personal items to be displayed in a hall of fame.
- Design and develop advertising and marketing campaigns for special or permanent exhibits.
- Provide financial development services to obtain funding from individuals and local corporations.

- Write funding proposals to the National Endowment for the Arts, the Federal Council on the Arts and Humanities, the Andrew W. Mellon Foundation, and other public and private granting agencies.
- Coordinate special lectures from art historians, sports historians, university professors, art curators, and other experts in the field of a particular exhibit.
- Publish brochures, guides, slides, postcards, calendars, books, and other print matter dealing with special or permanent exhibits.
- Coordinate the preparation of audio tours of museum exhibits and halls of fame.
- Develop family programs and extension programs for museums and halls of fame.

Complete the following:

1. Visit a local museum or hall of fame; attend exhibits; look through brochures and other printed materials; view films; participate in other activities associated with a special or permanent exhibit; view the Web pages of a museum or hall of fame; and do anything else you can to learn about exhibits and prepare a knowledgeable presentation.
2. Complete a Purpose and Outcomes Worksheet for your presentation.
3. Complete an Audience Analysis Worksheet for your presentation. Keep in mind that your audience will be the director (or board of directors) of a museum or hall of fame.
4. Complete a Situation and Media Assessment Worksheet for your presentation.
5. Using the information you glean from your visit and the above list of services provided by ECI, prepare the text portion of a PowerPoint presentation with at least nine slides, including the title slide, contents slide, introduction slide, and summary slide.
6. Complete a Focus and Organization Worksheet to determine an appropriate organizational pattern for your presentation, and organize the text in your PowerPoint presentation accordingly.
7. Create an advance organizer or overview for your presentation.
8. Include a summary recapping the key ideas of your presentation.
9. Using the Presentation Delivery Worksheet, decide on an appropriate presentation style.

10. Complete a Presentation Visuals Worksheet. Include at least one appropriate graphic on each slide of the presentation. You can obtain your graphics by taking digital photographs of local museums, downloading pictures from Web sites, scanning pictures from art history or sports books and magazines, or downloading graphics from the Online Design Gallery Live.

11. Using the Presentation Delivery Worksheet, decide on an appropriate presentation style for your presentation.

12. Design the presentation with an attractive color scheme, background objects, fonts, font sizes, and font colors.

13. Add appropriate slide transitions and slide animation effects with built-in sounds to your presentation.

14. Save your completed presentation using the filename "Exhibit Consulting".

15. Print the presentation as handouts with four slides per page.

16. Practice your presentation in front of one or more classmates or family members, and ask them to complete the evaluation section of the Presentation Delivery Worksheet.

17. Complete a Facilities Checklist for your presentation.

18. Set up the room for your presentation.

19. Give your presentation to your classmates or some other audience, as indicated by your instructor.

Glossary/Index

Note: Boldface entries include definitions.

Special Characters

35mm slides Photographic transparencies that are projected onto a screen. PRES 16–17, PRES 18
    adding picture background to slide masters, PPT 241–243
    preparing, PPT 245–246
    setting up design template, PPT 239–241

A

accents, color, PPT 95
Access. See Microsoft Access 2003
action button(s) A ready-made icon for which you can easily define a hyperlink to other slides or documents, as well as several other actions. PPT 169–171
    adding to slices, PPT 208–209
    changing target, PPT 175
    custom, in Web presentations, PPT 259–263
Action Settings dialog box, PPT 170, PPT 260–261
active cell(s) The cell in which you are entering data in a datasheet. PPT 115
Address bar, FM 8
adjustment handle(s) A yellow handle that appears when an AutoShape is selected that you can drag to resize an element of the AutoShape without changing the overall size of the object. PPT 73
advance organizers, PRES 26
alignment of text, PPT 56–57
anecdotes Short stories or experiences that demonstrate a specific point.
    in introductions, PRES 23
animated GIF A single file that contains a series of images that are quickly displayed one after another; these files are identified with the file extension .gif. PPT 108
animation scheme(s) A special visual or audio effect applied to an object, such as a graphic or a bulleted list, on a slide. PPT 126–128
animation(s) The association of the elements on the slide with a special look or sound effect. PPT 7
    applying downloaded clips, PPT 203–206
    background objects, PPT 196–197
    custom, PPT 128–133
    downloading clips from Microsoft Office Online, PPT 201–202
    process diagrams, PPT 197–200
appearance of speaker, PRES 66–67
audience
    analyzing needs and expectations, PRES 9–11
    commenting about, in introductions, PRES 24

    establishing eye contact, PRES 64–65
    establishing rapport with, PRES 26
    getting attention of, PRES 23
    questions from, preparing for, PRES 60–61
    selecting appropriate visuals for, PRES 51
audience participation When your audience is actively involved in a presentation, adding their ideas, rather than simply sitting and listening. PRES 24–25
audio tracks, inserting into slides from CDs, PPT 206–208
authorities as information sources, PRES 28–29
AutoContent Wizard, PPT 10–12
AutoFit Options button, PPT 107
automatic timing A PowerPoint feature that displays slides for a certain amount of time before moving to the next slide. PPT 213
AutoShapes, PPT 72–74
    fill color, PPT 73
    inserting shapes in slides, PPT 72–73

B

background(s)
    color, PPT 95
    custom, PPT 97–98
    textured, PPT 112–113
background graphics
    adding to custom template, PPT 101–104
    changing on title master, PPT 55
background objects, PPT 211–212
    animating, PPT 196–197
    removing from slides, PPT 211–212
backup copies, FM 7
banner(s) A large sign or page that typically has dimensions of 4 feet wide by 8½ inches high. PPT 249–251
bar graph(s) A graph that uses horizontal bars to represent specific values; bar graphs, like column graphs, are useful in comparing the value of one item to another over a period of time, or a range of dates or costs. PRES 46, PRES 51
bitmap image(s) A grid (or "map") of colored dots that form a picture. PPT 50
    background, changing on title master, PPT 55
    changing order of objects, PPT 54
    inserting on slides, PPT 52–53
    repositioning, PPT 53
    resizing, PPT 53–54
    setting color to transparent, PPT 54
body (of presentation), PRES 27–30

body text A large text box on a slide in which you type a bulleted or numbered list; also called main text. PPT 14
borders, tables, PPT 68
broadcast(s), online, PPT 177–178
browse-at-a-kiosk feature, PPT 213, PPT 215–216
built-in animation schemes, PPT 126–128
bullet(s)
    digital images as, PPT 235
    modifying, PPT 100–101
Bullet tab, Bullets and Numbering dialog box, PPT 100
bulleted item(s) One paragraph in a bulleted list. PPT 13
    adding, PPT 15–16
bulleted list(s) A list of paragraphs with a special character, such as a dot, to the left of each paragraph. PPT 13
Bullets and Numbering dialog box, PPT 100

C

callouts Labels on a slide that include a text box and a line (with or without an arrowhead) between the text box and the item being labeled.
    illustrations, PPT 218–221
CDs
    inserting audio tracks into slides, PPT 206–208
    running presentations from, PPT 136–137
cell(s) The intersection of a row and a column in a data sheet or a table. PPT 114
    active, PPT 115
chalkboards, PRES 13–14, PRES 18
changes, reviewing, PPT 257–259
chart(s) A visual depiction of data in a datasheet that uses lines, arrows, and boxes (or other shapes) to show relationships, parts, steps, or processes; when a chart uses a coordinate system to show the relationship between two variables, it is known as a graph. PRES 47–49, PRES 51, PPT 66, PPT 114–124
    changing chart type, PPT 117–118
    creating, PPT 114
    Excel, linking, PPT 161–164
    inserting, PPT 114–115
    inserting data into datasheet, PPT 116
    label font, PPT 118–119
    modifying, PPT 115–116
    organization. See organization chart(s)
chart labels, PPT 118–119
Chart Type dialog box, PPT 117

chronological organization An organizational style in which a presenter presents things according to a time sequence. PRES 32, PRES 33

clip art Images in the Clip Art Organizer accompanying Office 2003 or available from the Clip and Media Page on the Microsoft Office Online Web site. PRES 50, PPT 46–50
  inserting, PPT 46–47
  moving, PPT 47–48
  recoloring, PPT 48–50
  resizing, PPT 47–48
closing files, OFF 21–22

collaborative presentation(s) A presentation given as part of a group or team. PRES 68–69
collapse icon, FM 7
color
  clip art, changing, PPT 48–50
  fill, AutoShapes, PPT 73
  fonts, PPT 56
  setting to transparent, PPT 54

color scheme(s) A set of matching colors that makes up the background, fonts, and other elements of a presentation.
  creating, PPT 233–234
  custom, PPT 42, PPT 95–97
Colors dialog box, PPT 56

column graph(s) A graph that uses vertical bars to represent specific values; column graphs, like bar graphs, are useful in comparing the value of one item to another over a period of time, or a range of dates or costs. PRES 46

comment(s) The electronic equivalent of an adhesive note that you "attach" to a slide. PPT 254
  inserting into presentations, PPT 255–256
common window elements, OFF 9
compact disc(s) (CDs), FM 4
comparing presentations, PPT 256–257
compressed (zipped) folder(s), FM 18–20
conclusion, PRES 34–35

content layout(s) A predetermined slide layout for holding charts, diagrams, images, tables, or movie clips. PPT 19
copying
  files and folders, FM 14–16
  hyperlinks, PPT 168
  slides as picture objects, PPT 188–196
corporate documents, PRES 28
correcting errors. *See* error correction
custom animation, PPT 128–133
custom design templates, PPT 95–106
  applying, PPT 105–196
  background, PPT 97–98
  background images, PPT 101–104

bullets, PPT 100–101
color scheme, PPT 95–97
fonts, PPT 99
saving, PPT 104–105

custom show(s) A presentation in which selected slides are left out of the presentation or the order of slides is changed without actually delete or moving slides within the PowerPoint file. PPT 221–222
cycle diagrams, PPT 69

D

data disks, PPT 3
data files, navigating to, FM 10

database(s) The file you create in Access. OFF 4

datasheet(s) A grid of cells, similar to a Microsoft Excel worksheet. PPT 114
  for creating charts, PPT 116

deductive organization An organization style in which a presenter presents conclusions or solutions first, and then explains the information that led to those conclusions. PRES 31, PRES 33
definitions in introductions, PRES 24
deleting
  files, FM 17–18
  folders, FM 17–18
  organization chart boxes, PPT 121
  slides, PPT 17–19
  text boxes, PPT 63
delivery, PRES 64–66
  establishing eye contact, PRES 64–65
  voice, PRES 65–66

delivery method The approach for a presentation. PRES 56–60
  extemporaneous presentations, PRES 50, PRES 58–59
  impromptu presentations, PRES 59–60
  written or memorized presentations, PRES 57–58, PRES 60
demographic characteristics, PRES 9–10

demonstration(s) A specific type of presentation that shows an audience how something works or helps them to understand a process or procedure. PRES 6–8

demoting To decrease the level of an item in an outline. PPT 21
  outline text, PPT 22–23

design template(s) A file containing the color scheme, text formats, background colors and objects, and graphics in the presentation. PPT 10, PPT 42–45
  from another presentation, applying, PPT 150–152
  applying, PPT 44–45, PPT 58–60

creating presentations, PPT 42–44
custom. *See* custom design templates
modifying in Slide Master view, PPT 50–52
multiple, PPT 58–60
for overhead transparencies, PPT 232–238
saving presentations as, PPT 238
for 35mm slides, PPT 239–243

destination file The program into which objects are imported, embedded, or linked. PPT 152

diagram(s) A simple illustration using lines and shapes to represent parts, objects, and processes, that can be used to show how to assemble a piece of equipment, or how the parts of an item or process are related to each other; also called line drawing. PPT 69–71, PRES 49–50
  adding and modifying text, PPT 71
  creating, PPT 70

digital movie(s). *See* video clip(s)
digital photos, adding to presentations, PPT 107–108
disk(s), FM 4

document(s) The file you create in Word. FM 4, OFF 4
downloading
  applying downloaded motion and sound clips, PPT 203–206
  clips from Microsoft Office Online, PPT 201–203
  music clips from Internet, PPT 203
Drawing toolbar, PPT 5
drive(s), FM 4

E

Edit Color Scheme dialog box, PPT 234
editing
  movie objects, PPT 110
  presentations, PPT 18
  slides. *See* editing slides
editing slides, PPT 14–17
  adding bulleted items, PPT 15–16
  creating sub-bullets, PPT 16–17
  text, PPT 15

electronic on-screen presentation(s) Presentations created with Microsoft PowerPoint, Corel Presentations, or other presentation software and projected onto a screen. PRES 17–18
embedded objects
  modifying, PPT 160–161
  viewing slide shows with, PPT 171–173

embedding To import an object while allowing a one-way connection to be maintained with the source program so that you can make changes to the object in the destination file using the source

program's commands; the changes you make do not appear in the source file. PPT 153
  Word tables, PPT 158–161
error correction
  spell checking, PPT 24–25
  Style Checker, PPT 25–27
Excel. *See* Microsoft Excel 2003
Excel charts, linking, PPT 161–164
exiting programs, OFF 30
expand icon, FM 7, FM 11
experts as information sources, PRES 28–29
Explorer bar, FM 7
exporting outlines to Word, PPT 156–157
extemporaneous presentation(s) A presentation in which the presenter speaks from a few notes or an outline. PRES 50, PRES 58–59
extension(s), FM 16, FM 17
extracting files, FM 18
eye contact, PRES 64–65

F

Facilities Checklists, PRES 71–73
familiar phrases in introductions, PRES 24
file(s), FM 4, OFF 18–23
  backup copies, FM 7
  closing, OFF 21–22
  compressed (zipped), FM 18–20
  creating, OFF 19
  deleting, FM 17–18
  destination, PPT 152
  extracting, FM 18
  naming and renaming, FM 16–17
  opening, OFF 22–23
  organizing, FM 4–7
  printing, OFF 29–30
  saving, OFF 19–21
  source, PPT 152
file extension(s) A three character code that Office appends to a filename, which identifies the program in which that file was created. The file extensions are .doc for Word, .xls for Excel, .ppt for PowerPoint, and .mdb for Access. FM 16, FM 17, OFF 19
file path(s), FM 10
file system, FM 5
file window sizing buttons, OFF 9–11
filename(s) A descriptive name you give a file the first time you save it. FM 16–17, OFF 19
fill color, PPT 95
  AutoShapes, PPT 73
  organization charts, PPT 124
Fill Effects dialog box, PPT 98, PPT 112

film recorder(s) An instrument that takes pictures of computer graphics files, including PowerPoint presentations, using 35mm film. PPT 239
first-level bullet(s) The main paragraph in a bulleted list. PPT 13
flip chart(s) Previously prepared pictures and visuals that are bound together and shown one at a time. PRES 14, PRES 18
flipping objects, PPT 74
floppy disk(s), FM 4
flowchart(s) A chart that uses lines, arrows, and boxes or other shapes to show sequence; flowcharts are useful for describing the steps in a procedure, or stages in a decision-making process. PRES 49
focus Narrowing a topic to make it manageable for a presentation. PRES 20–22
folder(s) A container for your files. FM 4, OFF 19
  compressed (zipped), FM 18–20
  creating, FM 12–13
  deleting, FM 17–18
  moving and copying, FM 14–16
  organizing, FM 4–7
  subfolders, FM 5
Folders pane, FM 7
followed link(s) A text link that has been clicked; followed links usually change to another color to reflect the fact that it has been clicked. PPT 165
font(s) The design of a set of characters. PPT 55
  chart labels, PPT 118–119
  color, PPT 56
  modifying, PPT 99
  organization charts, PPT 123
  tables, PPT 68–69
font size, organization charts, PPT 123
font style A special attribute applied to the characters of a font. PPT 55
footer(s) Text that appears at the bottom of every slide in a presentation. PPT 7
  inserting, PPT 62–63
Formatting toolbar, PPT 5

G

General tab, Options dialog box, PPT 254
gestures, PRES 67
GIF files, PPT 108
gradient fill A type of shading in which one color blends into another or varies from one shade to another. PPT 97, PPT 98
Gradient tab, Fill Effects dialog box, PPT 98
grammar, PRES 66
graph(s) A visual representation of data that shows the relationship between two variables along two axes or reference lines: the independent variable

on the horizontal axis, and the dependent variable on the vertical axis; if a graph does not use a coordinate system to show a relationship, it is known as a chart. PRES 46–47, PRES 51
graphic(s) A picture, clip art, photograph, shape, graph, chart, or diagram added to a slide. PPT 42, PPT 45–50
  background, adding to custom template, PPT 101–104
  bitmap images, PPT 50
  clip art. *See* clip art
  importing, PPT 157–158
grid(s) An array of dotted vertical and horizontal lines on a slide that can make positioning objects easier; the grid is usually hidden from view.
  slides, PPT 192–193

H

handout(s) A printout of a slide that is given to the audience; usually summarizes key points of your presentation or numerical data that you distribute to an audience. PRES 16, PRES 18, PPT 29
handout master, PPT 50
hard disk(s), FM 4
header(s) Text that appears at the top of each slide. PPT 62
Header and Footer dialog box, PPT 62–63
Help Information in Office that you can use to find out how to perform a task or obtain more information about a feature. OFF 23–29
  Help task pane, OFF 25–27
  Microsoft Office Online, OFF 27–29
  ScreenTips, OFF 23
  Type a question for help box, OFF 23–25
Help task pane A task pane that enables you to search the Help system using keywords or phrases to obtain more in-depth help. OFF 25–27
hiding slides, PPT 134–135
home page(s) A Web page that contains general information about the site and usually contain links to the rest of the pages in the Web site. PPT 173
hyperlink(s) A word, phrase, or graphic image that you click to "jump to" (or display) another location, called the target; also known as a link. PPT 165–169, PPT 213
  action buttons, PPT 169–171
  changing target, PPT 175
  color, PPT 96
  copying, PPT 168
  creating from thumbnails, PPT 195
  followed, PPT 165
  jumping to specific slides, PPT 168–169
HTML (Hypertext Markup Language) A special language for describing the format of a Web page

so that Web browsers can interpret and display the page. PPT 173–174

Hypertext Markup Language (HTML), PPT 173–174

I

illustration(s) A pictorial way to represent parts and processes, consisting of diagrams, drawings, maps, photographs, and clip art. PRES 49–51

    callouts, PPT 218–221

    inserting in slides, PPT 217–221

importing A method of copying a file that was created using one program into another program's file. PPT 153

    graphics, PPT 157–158

    Word outlines, PPT 154–155

impromptu presentation(s) A presentation in which the presenter speaks without notes, an outline, or memorized text. PRES 59–60

inductive organization An organizational style in which the presenter begins with the individual facts and saves the conclusions until the end of the presentation. PRES 30–31, PRES 33

information gathering, PRES 27–30

informative presentation(s) Presentations that provide your audience with background information, knowledge, and specific details about a topic that enable them to make informed decisions, form attitudes, or increase their expertise on a topic. PRES 5

Insert Diagram or Organization Chart button, PPT 120

Insert Hyperlink dialog box, PPT 166

Insert Media Clip button, PPT 109

Insert New Title Master button, PPT 102

Insert Object dialog box, PPT 159

integration The ability to share information between programs. OFF 5

Internet The largest and most widely used computer network in the world; actually a network of thousands of smaller networks, all joined together electronically. PPT 173

Internet sites, searching using Research pane, PPT 27–28

Internet sources, PRES 29–30

interviews, as information sources, PRES 29

introduction(s) The opening statements of a presentation. PRES 22–27

    common mistakes in, PRES 26–27

K

keyboard shortcut(s) A combination of keys you press to perform a command. OFF 11

kiosk browsing A PowerPoint feature that makes a slide show run continuously. PPT 213, PPT 215–216

L

layout(s) A predetermined way of organizing the text and objects on a slide. PPT 10

library resources, PRES 28

light bulb symbol, PPT 15, PPT 26

line(s), color, PPT 95

line drawing(s) *See* diagram(s). PRES 49–50, PRES 51

line graph(s) A graph that uses points to represent the specific values and then joins the points by a line; line graphs are effective for illustrating trends. PRES 46, PRES 51

link(s) A connection between a source file and a linked object so that the object exists in only the source file, but the link displays the object in the destination file; you can edit the object in the source file, and the edits will appear in the destination file. *See also* hyperlink(s)

linked objects

    modifying, PPT 163–164

    viewing slide shows with, PPT 171–173

linking, PPT 153–154

    Excel charts, PPT 161–164

lists

    bulleted, PPT 13

    numbered, PPT 13

M

main ideas The key points of a presentation. PRES 21

    supporting, PRES 33

main text *See* body text.

mannerism(s) A recurring or unnatural movement of your voice or body, that can be annoying. PRES 67–68

map(s) A visual that shows the spatial relationships (position and location) in a geographic area. PRES 50, PRES 51

master(s) Slide containing the elements and styles of the design template, including text and other objects that appear on all the slides of the same type. PPT 50. *See also specific masters*

media The presentation methods you use to support and clarify your oral presentation. PRES 13–19

    strengths and weaknesses compared, PRES 18

meetings, online, PPT 177

memorized presentation(s) A presentation that is memorized in advance. PRES 57–58, PRES 60

menu(s) A group of related commands. OFF 11–13

    full, OFF 12–13

    personalized, OFF 11–12

menu bar A collection of menus for commonly used commands. OFF 9, PPT 5

menu command(s) A word on a menu that you click to execute a task. OFF 11

merging presentations, PPT 256–257

Microsoft Access 2003 A database program you use to enter, organize, display, and retrieve related information. OFF 4

Microsoft Excel 2003 A spreadsheet program you use to display, organize, and analyze numerical data. OFF 4

    charts, linking, PPT 161–164

    starting, OFF 6–7

Microsoft Office 2003 A collection of the most popular Microsoft programs: Word, Excel, PowerPoint, Access, and Outlook.

    common window elements, OFF 9

    overview, OFF 4–5

Microsoft Office Online, OFF 27–29

    downloading clips, PPT 201–203

Microsoft Outlook 2003 An information management program you use to send, receive, and organize e-mail; plan your schedule; arrange meetings; organize contacts; create a to-do list; and jot down notes. You can also use Outlook to print schedules, task lists, phone directories, and other documents. OFF 4

Microsoft PowerPoint 2003 A presentation graphics program you use to create a collection of slides that can contain text, charts, and pictures. OFF 4

    overview, PPT 4

    starting, PPT 4

Microsoft Word 2003 A word-processing program you use to create text documents. OFF 4

    outlines, importing, PPT 154–155

    starting, OFF 7–8

    tables, embedding, PPT 158–161

movements of speaker, PRES 67

movie(s)

    adding to presentations, PPT 106, PPT 108–110

    editing, PPT 110

Movie Options dialog box, PPT 110

moving

    bitmap images, PPT 53

    clip art, PPT 47–48

    files and folders, FM 14–16

    slides in Slide Sorter view, PPT 23–24

    text boxes, PPT 63–65, PPT 76–77

    text in Outline tab, PPT 22

multiple-page poster presentations, PPT 248–249

music clips

    applying downloaded clips, PPT 203–206

    downloading from Internet, PPT 203

My Computer, FM 7, FM 8–9

    copying files and folders, FM 16

My Documents folder, FM 9–10

N

naming presentations, PPT 12

narration(s), PPT 213
    recording, PPT 209–210

navigating
    to data files, FM 10
    presentations, PPT 6

navigation buttons. *See* action button(s)

nervousness, PRES 61–63

NetMeeting A program that manages online meetings. PPT 177

nonverbal communication Conveying a message in ways other than through words. PRES 66–68

Normal View button, PPT 5

note(s) Information on the slide for the presenter; also called speaker notes. PPT 29

notepads, PRES 13–14, PRES 18

notes master, PPT 50

notes pane The area of the PowerPoint window that contains speaker notes. PPT 5, PPT 6

numbered list(s) Paragraphs that are numbered consecutively within the body text. PPT 13

O

object(s) Anything on a slide you can manipulate as a whole, including clip art, photos, text boxes, graphics, diagrams, and charts. PPT 13, PPT 152. *See also specific objects*
    changing order, PPT 54
    embedding, PPT 153
    flipping, PPT 74
    importing, PPT 153
    linking, PPT 153–154

object linking and embedding (OLE) A process by which programs let you embed or link objects from one program to another. PPT 154

observations as information sources, PRES 29

occasion, commenting about, in introductions, PRES 24

Office. *See* Microsoft Office 2003

Office on Microsoft.com A Web site maintained by Microsoft that provides access to additional Help resources such as current Help topics, how-to articles, and tips for using Office. OFF 27–29

OLE (object linking and embedding), PPT 154

online broadcast(s) A method for showing a PowerPoint presentation online; it may or may not include an online meeting. PPT 177–178

online meeting(s) A method of sharing and exchanging information with people at different locations in real time (the actual time during which an event takes place), as if all the participants are together in the same room. PPT 177

online services, searching using Research pane, PPT 27–28

on-screen presentations
    electronic, PRES 17–18

opening
    existing presentations, PPT 5–6
    files, OFF 22–23

Options dialog box
    General tab, PPT 254

order, objects on slides, changing, PPT 54

organization chart(s) A chart that shows relationships using boxes and lines in a horizontal and vertical pattern; organizational charts are effective for showing hierarchy, such as the structure of a company or other organization, or illustrating the relationship between departments. PRES 48–49, PRES 51, PPT 69, PPT 119–124
    creating, PPT 120–121
    modifying, PPT 121–124

organizing files and folders, FM 4–7
    need for, FM 5–6
    planning, FM 7
    strategies, FM 6–7

organizing information, PRES 30–33
    chronologically, PRES 32, PRES 33
    deductively, PRES 31, PRES 33
    inductively, PRES 30–31, PRES 33
    by problem and solutions, PRES 33
    spatially, PRES 32, PRES 33

organizing presentations, PRES 21–22

outcome What you want to happen as a result of giving your presentation, or what you want the audience to do as a result of hearing your presentation. PRES 8

outcome statements, PRES 8–9

outline(s)
    exporting to Word, PPT 156–157
    Word, importing, PPT 154–155

Outline tab The area of the PowerPoint window that shows the title and text of each slide. PPT 4, PPT 6
    moving text, PPT 22

outline text
    demoting, PPT 22–23
    promoting, PPT 21–22

Outlook. *See* Microsoft Outlook 2003

overhead transparency A transparent sheet containing text that can be projected onto a screen; also called overheads. PPT 232–238, PRES 15–16, PRES 18
    adding background objects to slide masters, PPT 236–238
    creating design template, PPT 233–234
    digital images as bullets, PPT 235
    making, PPT 243–245

overviews Advance organizers or previews of a presentation. PRES 26

P

Package for CD A PowerPoint command that places the entire presentation on a CD so you can take the presentation and show it on any computer with the PowerPoint Viewer. PPT 136–137

Page Setup dialog box, PPT 233

pane(s), Windows Explorer window, FM 7

personalized menus, OFF 11–12

personalized toolbars, OFF 13–14

persuasive presentations Presentations with the specific goal of influencing how an audience feels or acts regarding a particular position or plan. PRES 5–6

photograph(s) A visual that shows what something looks like. PRES 50, PRES 51

picture(s), adding to slides, PPT 50

Picture Bullet dialog box, PPT 235

pie chart(s) A chart shaped like a circle or pie; pie charts are best for showing percentages or proportions of the parts that make up a whole. PRES 47–48, PRES 51

pixel(s) A colored dot that, when combined with other pixels, forms a picture; stands for picture element. PPT 50

placeholder(s) A region of a slide, or a location in an outline, reserved for inserting text or graphics. PPT 13

planning presentations, PPT 10, PPT 32, PPT 92, PPT 150, PPT 188, PRES 4

Play Sound dialog box, PPT 206

point(s) The unit used to measure the size of the characters in a font. PPT 55

pointer pen A PowerPoint mouse pointer icon that allows you to draw lines on the screen during a slide show. PPT 133–134

poster(s) Written summaries of your presentation that can be displayed on stationary blackboards or attached to the walls of a room. PRES 14–15, PRES 18

poster presentation(s) A presentation formatted as a poster, or in the space of a poster, usually given at a professional meeting. PPT 247–253
    banners, PPT 249–251
    multiple-page, PPT 248–249
    single-page, PPT 251–253

posture of speaker, PRES 66–67

PowerPoint. *See* Microsoft PowerPoint 2003

PowerPoint Viewer A separate program that you can use to give your slide show on any Windows 95/98/2000/NT/XP computer. PPT 136

PowerPoint window, PPT 4, PPT 5

practicing presentations, PRES 63–64
presentation(s) The file you create in PowerPoint. OFF 4
actions buttons, linking, PPT 169–171
design templates. *See* design template(s)
determining outcome, PRES 8–9
determining purpose, PRES 4–8
editing, PPT 18
existing, opening, PPT 5–6
naming, PPT 12
navigating, PPT 6
planning, PPT 10, PPT 32, PPT 92, PPT 150, PPT 188, PRES 4
preparing to run on another computer, PPT 136–137
previewing, PPT 30–31, PRES 26
printing, PPT 172–173
publishing on Web, PPT 173–177
reviewing, PPT 253–256
saving, PPT 12, PPT 19
selecting type, PPT 10–11
slides. *See* slide(s)
spell checking, PPT 24–25
Style Checker, PPT 25–27
viewing in Slide Show view, PPT 7–9
viewing in Slide Sorter view, PPT 32
viewing in Web browsers, PPT 175–177
previewing presentations, PPT 30–31, PRES 26
Print dialog box, PPT 31
Print Preview, grayscale settings, PPT 172
printing
files, OFF 29–30
presentations, PPT 172–173
problem-solution organization An organizational style in which the presenter presents a problem, outlines various solutions to the problem, and then explains the recommended solution. PRES 33
process diagrams, animating, PPT 197–200
program(s). *See also* Microsoft Office 2003; *specific programs*
exiting, OFF 30
open, switching between, OFF 9
program window sizing buttons, OFF 9–11
progressive disclosure An animation effect in which bulleted items are displayed on a slide one item at a time. PPT 7, PPT 126
promoting To increase the level of an item in an outline. PPT 21
outline text, PPT 21–22
pronunciation, PRES 66
publishing In PowerPoint, to open a dialog box in which you can customize the Web page you are saving; generally, to copy HTML files to a Web

server so that others can view the Web page. PPT 173–177
purpose statements, PRES 8–9
stating, PRES 25
pyramid diagrams, PPT 69

Q

quantitative data in introductions, PRES 23
questions in introductions, PRES 24
quotations in introductions, PRES 24

R

radial diagrams, PPT 69
rapport How the audience responds to a presenter and a presentation. PRES 26
Recolor Picture dialog box, PPT 48–49
recoloring clip art, PPT 48–50
recording narrations, PPT 209–210
Recycle Bin, FM 17
rehearsing, PRES 63–64
Research task pane, OFF 16–18, PPT 27–28
resizing
bitmap images, PPT 53–54
clip art, PPT 47–48
text boxes, PPT 57–58
resizing buttons Buttons that resize and close the program window or the file window. OFF 9
review cycle A system for sending out a presentation file for others to review, having them make changes (revisions) and add comments to the presentation, getting back the copies of the files with the revisions and comments, combining the revised files into one document so that PowerPoint marks the revisions, and then accepting or rejecting the revisions. PPT 253
reviewing
changes, PPT 257–259
presentations, PPT 253–256
rhetorical questions Questions that you don't expect the audience to answer. PRES 24
Rich Text Format (RTF) A file format that many types of software can open and read. PPT 246
saving presentations as RTF outlines, PPT 246–247
root directory, FM 5
rotate handle(s) The small green circle above an object that you can drag to rotate the object. PPT 73
rotating text boxes, PPT 75–76
RTF outlines, saving presentations as, PPT 246–247
rulers, changing tab stops, PPT 60–62

S

Save As dialog box, OFF 20–21
saving
custom design templates, PPT 104–105
files, OFF 19–21
presentations, PPT 12, PPT 19
presentations as design templates, PPT 238
presentations as RTF outlines, PPT 246–247
presentations as Web pages, PPT 174
ScreenTip(s) A yellow box that appears when you position the mouse pointer over a toolbar button. The yellow box displays the button's name. OFF 23
searching using Research pane, PPT 27–28
second-level bullet(s) A bullet beneath (and indented from) a first-level bullet; also called a sub-bullet. PPT 13
creating, PPT 16–17
selecting title text, PPT 15
self-running presentation(s) A presentation that runs without human interruption, although it can accept human intervention to advance to another slide or return to a previous one. PPT 209
kiosk browsing, PPT 213, PPT 215–216
recording narrations, PPT 209–210, PPT 213
setting up, PPT 213–216
Send to Microsoft Word dialog box, PPT 156–157
setup The physical arrangements for a presentation. PRES 70–71
shading style The direction in which shading will be applied to a slide. PPT 97
shadows, color, PPT 95
shapes. *See* AutoShapes
single-page poster presentations, PPT 251–253
situation The unique setting, time frame, or circumstances (such as the size of your audience) for your presentation.
assessing, PRES 11–13
selecting appropriate visuals for, PRES 52
size, changing. *See* resizing
sizing buttons
file window, OFF 9–11
program window, OFF 9–11
sizing handle(s) A small square on the edge of an object that you can drag to increase or decrease the size of the object. PPT 13
slide(s)
adding action buttons, PPT 208–209
adding pictures, PPT 50
adding text, PPT 20
bitmap images. *See* bitmap image(s)
changing order of objects on slides, PPT 54
charts. *See* chart(s)

copying and modifying as picture objects, PPT 188–196

creating by promoting outline text, PPT 21–22

custom action buttons, PPT 259–261

deleting, PPT 17–19

diagrams, PPT 69–71

editing. *See* editing slides

graphics. *See* bitmap image(s); clip art

grids, PPT 192–193

hiding, PPT 134–135

hyperlinks between. *See* hyperlink(s)

inserting CD audio tracks, PPT 206–208

inserting from another presentation, PPT 92–94

moving in Slide Sorter view, PPT 23–24

new, adding to presentations, PPT 19–20

pasting into another slide as pictures, PPT 191–196

pasting into Word documents, PPT 189–191

summary, PPT 77–78

tables. *See* table(s)

text. *See* text

Slide Design task pane, PPT 96

Slide Finder dialog box, PPT 93–94

slide layout, changing, PPT 46

slide master(s) Contains the objects that appear on all the slides except the title slide. PPT 50

adding background objects, PPT 236–238

adding picture background, PPT 241–243

modifying, PPT 51–52

Slide Master view

modifying slide master, PPT 51–52

modifying title master, PPT 51

switching to, PPT 50–51

slide pane The area of the PowerPoint window that shows the current slide as it will look during the slide show. PPT 4, PPT 5, PPT 6

slide show(s)

custom, PPT 221–222

viewing, PPT 29

Slide Show view, viewing presentations, PPT 7–9

Slide Sorter view

moving slides, PPT 23–24

viewing presentations, PPT 32

Slide Sorter View button, PPT 5, PPT 125

slide timing

rehearsing and recording, PPT 214–215

setting manually, PPT 213–214

slide transition(s) The manner in which a new slide appears on the screen during a slide show. *See also* transition(s). PPT 7, PPT 125–126

Slides tab The area of the PowerPoint window that shows a column of numbered slide thumbnails so that you can *see* a visual representation of several slides at once. PPT 6

slide-title master pair The slide master and the title master that appear in Slide Master view as a set. PPT 51

sound clips, adding to presentations, PPT 106, PPT 110–112

sound icon, PPT 131, PPT 132

source file The file in which objects you import, embed, or link are created. PPT 152

spatial organization An organizational style in which a presenter provides a logical and effective order for describing the physical layout of an item or system. PRES 32, PRES 33

speaker notes, PPT 29

special effects Animations, such as one slide fading out as another slide appears, animated (moving) text, and sound effects. PPT 124–128

built-in animation schemes, PPT 126–128

slide transitions, PPT 125–126

spell checking, PPT 24–25

Standard Buttons toolbar, FM 8

Standard toolbar, PPT 5

starting

PowerPoint, PPT 4

programs, OFF 5–9

statistics in introductions, PRES 23

status bar An area at the bottom of the program window that contains information about the open file or the current task on which you are working. OFF 9

storyboard(s) A table or map of instructions and visuals that explains how to complete a process or describe a series of events. PRES 53–54

student data files, PPT 3, PPT 41

Style Checker A tool that checks your presentation for consistency in punctuation, capitalization, and visual elements, and marks problems on a slide with a light bulb. PPT 25–27

Style Options dialog box, PPT 25–26

sub-bullet(s). *See* second-level bullet(s).

subfolder(s), FM 5

summary, PRES 34–35

summary slide(s) A slide that contains the slide titles of selected slides in the presentation. PPT 77–78

supporting main points, PRES 33

surveys as information sources, PRES 29

switching

between open programs, OFF 8–9

views, PPT 6–7

T

tab(s) Space between the left margin and the beginning of the text on a particular line, or between the text in one column and the text in another column. PPT 60

tab stop(s) The location where the insertion point moves (including any text to the right of it) when you press the Tab key. PPT 60–62

changing, PPT 60–62

inserting, PPT 61

table(s) A visual method of organizing words and numerical data in horizontal rows and vertical columns. PRES 44–46, PRES 51, PPT 66–69

adding information, PPT 67

cells, PPT 66

creating, PPT 66–67

drawing borders, PPT 68

inserting on slides, PPT 66

modifying font, PPT 68–69

Word, embedding, PPT 158–161

target(s) A location you go to when you click a link within a presentation.

hyperlinks, changing, PPT 175

target diagrams, PPT 69

task pane(s) A window that provides access to commands for common tasks you'll perform in Office programs. FM 8, OFF 9, OFF 14–18, PPT 4

navigating among, OFF 15–16

opening and closing, OFF 14–15

searching reference materials, OFF 16–18

team presentations, PRES 68–69

template(s) A specific organizational pattern for a presentation. PRES 30

built-in. *See* design template(s)

text

adding to slides, PPT 20

alignment, PPT 56–57

body (main), PPT 14

boxes, modifying format of text in, PPT 55–57

color, PPT 95

editing in slides, PPT 15

font, PPT 55

font style, PPT 55

modifying format on slides, PPT 55–57

moving in Outline tab, PPT 22

outline. *See* outline text

title, PPT 14

text and content layout(s) A predetermined slide layout that includes placeholders for body text and objects including charts, diagrams, images, tables, or movie clips. PPT 19

text box(es) A container on the slide for text. PPT 13

deleting, PPT 63

inserting on slides, PPT 74–75

moving, PPT 63–65, PPT 76–77

resizing on slides, PPT 57–58

rotating, PPT 75–76

text box border, PPT 15

text layout(s) A predetermined slide layout that includes a placeholder for body text. PPT 19

Texture tab, Fill Effects dialog box, PPT 112

textured backgrounds, PPT 112–113

thesaurus A list of words and their synonyms, antonyms, and other related words. PPT 27–28

thumbnail(s) A miniature image of a slide as it appears in the presentation. PPT 6
 creating hyperlinks from, PPT 195
 making by copying slides, PPT 193–195

title bar A bar at the top of the window that contains the filename of the open file, the program name, and the program window resizing buttons. OFF 9, PPT 5

title master Contains the objects that appear on the title slide. PPT 50
 changing background graphic, PPT 55
 modifying, PPT 51

title text The text box at the top of the slide that describes the information on that slide. PPT 14
 color, PPT 95
 selecting, PPT 15

Title Text Color dialog box, PPT 97

toolbar(s) A collection of buttons that correspond to commonly used menu commands. OFF 9, OFF 11
 personalized, OFF 13–14

training presentations Presentations that provide audiences with an opportunity to learn new skills, or to be educated on how to perform a task. PRES 6–8

transition(s) An organizational signpost that indicates the organization and structure of a presentation; also, a method of moving one slide off the screen and bringing another slide onto the screen during a slide show. *See also* slide transition(s). PRES 33–34, PPT 7, PPT 125–126

transition icon, PPT 125

Type a question for help box Located on the menu bar of every Office program; finds answers to specific questions from information in the Help system. Type a question using everyday language about a task you want to perform or a topic you need help with, and then press the Enter key to search the Help system. The Search Results task pane opens with a list of Help topics related to your query. OFF 23–25

U

unhiding slides, PPT 135

Uniform Resource Locator(s) (URLs) The address of a Web site. PPT 173

V

variant(s) A variation of a particular shading style; there are four variants of each shading style. PPT 97

Venn diagrams, PPT 69
 adding and modifying text, PPT 71
 creating, PPT 70

video clip(s) An animated picture file; also known as digital movie.
 adding to presentations, PPT 106, PPT 108–110
 editing, PPT 110

view(s). *See also specific views*
 switching, PPT 6–7

viewing presentations
 Slide Show view, PPT 7–9
 Slide Sorter view, PPT 32
 Web browsers, PPT 175–177

viewing slide shows, PPT 29

visuals Tables, charts, graphs, and illustrations in a presentation. PRES 42–56. *See also* chart(s); graph(s); illustration(s); table(s)
 appropriate for audience, selecting, PRES 51
 appropriate for presentation, selecting, PRES 44–51
 appropriate for situation, selecting, PRES 52
 benefits, PRES 42–44
 crating, PRES 52–53
 effective use, PRES 53–56

voice, PRES 65–66

W

Web. *See* World Wide Web (WWW)

Web browser(s) A software program that sends requests for Web pages, retrieves them, and then interprets them for display on the computer screen. PPT 173
 viewing presentations, PPT 175–177

Web page(s) Electronic documents displayed by a Web browser. PPT 173
 publishing, PPT 174–175, PPT 262–263

Web page editor(s) Software specifically designed for creating Web pages. PPT 173

Web presentations, publishing with custom action buttons, PPT 259–263

Web server(s) A dedicated network computer with high-capacity hard disks used by organizations to make their Web pages available to others on the World Wide Web. PPT 173

Web site(s) The location of a particular set of Web pages on a server. PPT 173

whiteboards, PRES 13–14, PRES 18

window(s), resizing, OFF 10–11

window elements, common to Office programs, OFF 9

window sizing buttons, OFF 9–11

Windows Explorer, FM 7–8, FM 9–10
 copying files and folders, FM 16

Windows Explorer window, FM 7

Word. *See* Microsoft Word 2003

word choice, using thesaurus for, PPT 27–28

Word documents, pasting slides into, PPT 189–191

workbook(s) The file you create in Excel. OFF 4

World Wide Web (WWW) A global information-sharing system that is part of the Internet; also called the Web.
 publishing presentations, PPT 173–177

written presentation(s) A presentation that is completely written out and then read word for word. PRES 57–58, PRES 60

WWW. *See* World Wide Web (WWW)

Z

Zip disk(s), FM 4

zipped folders, FM 18–20

Presentation Concepts Photo Credits

FIGURE	SOURCE/CREDIT LINE
Fig 1-1	© Getty Images
Fig 1-2	© Real Life/Getty Images
Fig 1-3	© PhotoDisc/Getty Images
Fig 1-4	© Getty Images
Fig 1-6	© Getty Images
Fig 1-8	© David Oliver/Getty Images
Fig 1-9	© Kaluzny-Thatcher /Getty Images
Fig 1-10	© Getty Images
Fig 1-11	© Getty Images
Fig 1-12	© Getty Images
Fig 1-13	© Ken Reid/Getty Images
Fig 1-14	© Steve McAlister Productions/Getty Images
Fig 1-15	© Walter Hodges/Getty Images
Fig 1-18	© PhotoDisc
Fig 1-19	© PhotoDisc
Fig 1-20	© Steve Dunwell/Getty Images
Fig 1-21	© Getty Images
Fig 1-22	© Getty Images
Fig 1-23	© Getty Images
Fig 1-24	© Getty Images
Fig 2-11	Courtesy of the author
Fig 2-14	© Getty Images
Fig 2-15	© John Waterman/Getty Images
Fig 2-16	© Walter Hodges/Getty Images
Fig 2-17	© Getty Images
Fig 2-18	James Lafayette/IndexStock
Fig 2-19	© ADAMSMITH/Getty Images
Fig 2-20	© Steve Niedorf Photography/Getty Images
Fig 2-21	© Getty Images
Fig 2-22	© Getty Images
Fig 2-23	© Getty Images
Fig 2-25	© Peter Gridley/Getty Images

Task Reference

TASK	PAGE #	RECOMMENDED METHOD
Action button, insert	PPT 169	In Normal view, click Slide Show, point to Action Buttons, click a button, click at the desired location in the slide, select the action setting (for example, hyperlink or sound), click OK
Animation order, change	PPT 198	In Normal view with Custom Animation in Task Pane, click object in slide, click Up or Down Re-Order Arrow
Animation Scheme, built-in, apply	PPT 127	See Reference Window: Applying an Animation Scheme
Animation, change features	PPT 199	In Normal view, click Slide Show, click Custom Animation, click object in slide, click object list arrow in Task Pane, click Effect Options; add sounds, change timing, or make other changes, click OK
Animation, custom, apply	PPT 128	In Normal view, click Slide Show, click Custom Animation, click object that you want to animate in slide pane, click Add Effects list arrow, point to animation category, select desired animation, select desired direction of animation, set animation order, set animation timing, specify animation path, add sound effect, or make other modifications as desired
Animation, object	PPT 196	See Reference Window: Animating an Object
AutoContent Wizard, run	PPT 10	Click File, click New, click From AutoContent Wizard on New Presentation task pane, follow instructions
Background, gradient, create	PPT 98	Click Format, click Background, click Background fill list arrow, click Fill Effects, click Gradient tab, set the desired gradient effects, click OK, click Apply or Apply to All
Background, picture, add	PPT 236	In Normal view or Slide Master view, click Format, click Background, click Background Fill list arrow, click Fill Effects, click Picture tab, click Select Picture, select desired picture file, click Insert, click OK, click Apply or Apply to All
Background, texture, add	PPT 112	See Reference Window: Applying a Textured Background
Border of table, draw	PPT 68	Click 🖉, set desired border style and border width on Tables and Borders toolbar, drag 🖉 along border
Bullet style, modify	PPT 99	Click in text of bulleted item, click Format, click Bullets and Numbering, select desired bullet (including color and size), click OK
Bullet, insert picture as	PPT 235	Click in text of bulleted item, click Format, click Bullets and Numbering, click Picture, select picture bullet, click OK, or in Picture Bullet dialog box, click Import, select folder with picture, click picture file, click Add, click OK
CD Audio Track, insert into slide	PPT 207	See Reference Window: Inserting a CD Track into a slide
Chart, insert	PPT 114	See Reference Window: Creating a Chart (Graph)
Clip Art, insert	PPT 16	Change slide layout to a Content layout, click 🖼 in content placeholder, click clipart image, click OK
Clip Art, recolor	PPT 47	Click clipart image, click 🖼, click color list arrow of color to change, click desired color, click OK
Clip, download from Microsoft Online	PPT 201	See Reference Window: Downloading Clips from Microsoft Office Online
Clip, insert from the Clip Organizer	PPT 204	Click 🖼, type search word in Search box in task pane, click Search button, click desired clip
Color Scheme, create	PPT 96	Click the Design button, click Color Schemes, click Edit Color Schemes, click Custom tab, change color of elements as desired, click Apply

TASK	PAGE #	RECOMMENDED METHOD
Design Template, apply	PPT 43	Click the Design button, click design thumbnail in task pane
Design Template, apply from other presentation	PPT 151	Click the Design button, click Design Templates, click Browse, select folder and presentation filename, click Apply
Design Template, apply to one slide or selected slides	PPT 58	Click the Design button, select slide(s), click design thumbnail list arrow, click Apply to Selected Slides
Diagram, create	PPT 70	Change slide layout to a Content layout, click [icon], click desired diagram type, click OK, modify diagram as desired
Fill color, change	PPT 73	Click object to select it, click [icon], select desired color
Font color, modify	PPT 56	Click edge of text box, click [icon], click color (or click More Colors and click color, click OK)
Font, modify	PPT 56	Click edge of text box, click Font list arrow, click font
Footers, create	PPT 62	Click View, click Header and Footer, make sure there is a check mark in the Footer Check box, click ⌶ in Footer text box, type text, click Apply to All
Graphics, import	PPT 107	Click [icon], change to desired folder, click picture filename, click Insert
Grayscale, preview presentation in	PPT 30	Click [icon], click Grayscale
Handouts, print	PPT 31	Click File, click Print, click Print what list arrow, click Handouts, click Slides per page list arrow, click number, click OK
Hyperlink, create	PPT 165	Select phrase or object, click [icon], click desired Link to button, select the desired slide in this presentation or select a folder and file or a URL, click OK
Kiosk browsing, set up	PPT 216	Click Slide Show, click Set Up Show, Click Browsed at kiosk (full screen), click OK
Layout, slide, change	PPT 46	Click Format, click Slide Layout, click desired layout
Master, slide or title, modify	PPT 51	Shift-click [icon], make modifications, click [icon]
Mouse Over Action Settings, apply	PPT 259	See Reference Window: Applying Mouse-Over Action Settings to an Action Button
Movie clip, insert	PPT 109	Click Insert, point to Movies and Sounds, click Movie from File, select folder and movie file (video clip) filename, click OK, choose to play automatically or on mouse click
Narration, record	PPT 209	See Reference Window: Recording a Narration
Notes, create	PPT 29	Click ⌶ in Notes pane, type text
Notes, print	PPT 31	Click File, click Print, click Print what list arrow, click Notes Pages, click OK
Numbering, slide	PPT 62	Click View, click Header and Footer, click Slide Number check box, click Apply or Apply to All
Object, change order	PPT 54	Click object, click the Draw button, point to Order, click desired layering order
Object, embed	PPT 159	Click Insert, click Object, click Create from file option button, make sure Link check box is not selected, select folder and filename, click OK
Object, link	PPT 161	See Reference Window: Linking an Object
Object, resize	PPT 47	Click object, drag sizing handle
Object, rotate	PPT 76	Click object to select it, drag rotate handle with [icon]
Organization chart, insert	PPT 120	See Reference Window: Creating an Organization Chart
Outline text, demote	PPT 23	Click Outline tab (if necessary), click paragraph, click [icon]
Outline text, promote	PPT 21	Click Outline tab (if necessary), click paragraph, click [icon]

TASK	PAGE #	RECOMMENDED METHOD
Outline, export	PPT 156	Click File, point to Send to, click Microsoft Office Word, click Outline only (or select other option), click OK
Picture, insert	PPT 107	Click 🖼, change to desired folder, click picture filename, click Insert
Pointer pen, mark slides during slide show with	PPT 133	Click ✏, click desired pen type, draw lines with pen pointer
PowerPoint, exit	PPT 12	Click ☒ on PowerPoint window
PowerPoint, start	PPT 4	Click Start button, point to All Programs, point to Microsoft Office, click Microsoft Office PowerPoint 2003
Presentation, close	PPT 9	Click ☒ on presentation window
Presentation, open	PPT 5	Click 📂, select disk and folder, click filename, click Open
Presentation, print	PPT 30	Click File, click Print, select options, click OK
Process diagram, animate	PPT 197	In Normal view, display desired slide, click Slide Show, click Custom Animation, select objects in diagram, select desired effect, start time, direction, and speed for each object, modify animation order as necessary
Reviewers, comparing and merging presentations	PPT 257	See Reference Window: Comparing and Merging Presentations from Different Reviewers
RTF Outline, save presentation as	PPT 247	Click File, click Save As, change Save as type to Outline/RTF, click Save
Ruler, view (or hide)	PPT 60	Click View, click Ruler
Self-running presentation, set up	PPT 216	Click Slide Show, click Set Up Show, click Browsed at a kiosk (full screen), click OK
Shape, create	PPT 72	Click the AutoShapes button, point to shape type, click desired shape, drag ╀ in slide
Slide Show, view	PPT 8	Click 🖳
Slide Sorter View, switch to	PPT 7	Click 🔡
Slide Transitions, apply	PPT 125	See Reference Window: Applying Slide Transitions
Slide, add new	PPT 19	Click the New Slide button
Slide, copy as image	PPT 188	See Reference Window: Copying and Modifying a Slide as a Picture Object
Slide, copy to Word	PPT 189	In Slide Sorter view, select slide, click 📋, switch to Word document, click 📋
Slide, delete	PPT 17	In Slide Pane, click Edit, click Delete Slide. In Outline tab, click ▦, press Delete. In Slide tab, click slide, press Delete
Slide, go to next	PPT 6	Click ⮟
Slide, go to previous	PPT 6	Click ⮝
Slides, hide	PPT 135	In Normal view, click (or Ctrl-click) slides in Slide tab to select one or more slides, click Slide Show, click Hide Slide
Slides, insert from other presentation	PPT 92	See Reference Window: Inserting Slides from Another Presentation
Slides, unhide	PPT 135	In Normal view, click (or Ctrl-click) hidden slide(s) in Slide tab to select one or more slides, click Slide Show, click Hide Slide
Sound clip, insert	PPT 111	Click Insert, point to Movies and Sounds, click Sound from File, select folder and sound filename, click OK
Speaker Notes, create	PPT 29	Click I in Notes Pane, type text

TASK	PAGE #	RECOMMENDED METHOD
Style Checker, fix style problem	PPT 26	Click light bulb, click option to fix style problem
Style Checker, set options	PPT 25	Click Tools, click Options, click Spelling and Style tab, click Style Options, set options, click OK, click OK
Style Checker, turn on	PPT 25	Click Tools, click Options, click Spelling and Style tab, select Check style check box, click OK
Summary Slide, add	PPT 77	Switch to Slide Sorter view, select desired slides, click ▨
Tab stop, add	PPT 61	Select text box, click View, click Ruler, click tab stop alignment selector button to select desired tab stop style, click location on ruler
Tab stop, delete	PPT 62	Drag the tab stop off the ruler
Tab stop, move	PPT 62	Select text box, click View, click Ruler, drag tab stop to new location on ruler
Table, create	PPT 66	Change slide layout to a Content layout, click ▦, set number of columns and rows, fill in and format cells as desired
Text box, add	PPT 74	Click ▨, click ↓ in slide, type text
Text box, move	PPT 76	Click text box, drag edge (not sizing handle) of text box
Text box, resize	PPT 75	Click text box, drag sizing handle
Timing, rehearse	PPT 214	In Slide Sorter view, click Slide 1, click ▨, advance from slide to slide with desired timing, click Yes to save timings
Transparent color, picture, set	PPT 54	Click picture, click ◪, click color in picture
Video clip, insert	PPT 109	Click Insert, point to Movies and Sounds, click Movie from File, select folder and movie file (video clip) filename, click OK, choose to play automatically or on Mouse click
Web page, publish	PPT 174	Click File, click Save as Web Page, select Save as type, click Save
Word Outline, import	PPT 154	Click Insert, click Slides from Outline, select folder and Word document filename, click Insert

Microsoft Office Specialist Certification Grid

Standardized Coding Number	Certification Skill Activity	Courseware Requirements	Tutorial: Pages
PP03S-1	**Creating Content**		
PP03S-1-1	Create new presentations from templates	Creating presentations using automated tools (e.g., AutoContent Wizard)	Tutorial 1: 10–12
		Creating presentations using templates	Tutorial 2: 42–44
PP03S-1-2	Insert and edit text-based content	Adding text to and deleting text from slides	Tutorial 1: 14–17, 20
		Checking spelling and grammar	Tutorial 1: 24–25
		Checking usage (e.g., Thesaurus)	Tutorial 1: 28
		Importing text from other sources	Tutorial 4: 154–155
PP03S-1-3	Insert tables, charts and diagrams	Creating tables, charts and diagrams	Tutorial 2: 66–67, 70–71 Tutorial 3: 114–124
PP03S-1-4	Insert pictures, shapes and graphics	Adding pictures, shapes and other graphics to slides (e.g., ClipArt, AutoShapes, WordArt)	Tutorial 2: 46–47, 53, 72–73 Tutorial 3: 107–108
PP03S-1-5	Insert objects	Inserting objects (e.g., Excel charts, media clips, Paintbrush pictures)	Tutorial 2: 46–47 Tutorial 3: 109–111 Tutorial 4: 159, 162–163 Tutorial 5: 201–205
PP03S-2	**Formatting Content**		
PP03S-2-1	Format text-based content	Modifying font typeface, style, color and size	Tutorial 2: 56–57 Tutorial 3: 99
		Aligning text	Tutorial 2: 60–62
PP03S-2-2	Format pictures, shapes and graphics	Changing the size and color of pictures, shapes and other graphics	Tutorial 2: 47–49, 73–74 Tutorial 3: 102, 109
		Aligning, connecting and rotating pictures, shapes and other graphics	Tutorial 2: 74, 76 Tutorial 5: 192–195
		Adding effects to pictures, shapes and other graphics	Tutorial 5: 196–200
PP03S-2-3	Format slides	Customizing slide backgrounds	Tutorial 1: 31 Tutorial 2: 51–55 Tutorial 3: 98, 112–113 Tutorial 5: 196–197 Tutorial 6: 236–237, 242
		Modifying slide layout	Tutorial 1: 19–20 Tutorial 2: 46, 66
		Applying design templates	Tutorial 2: 45, 58–59 Tutorial 3: 105–106 Tutorial 4: 151–152
		Modifying page setup	Tutorial 6: 233, 240, 244
PP03S-2-4	Apply animation schemes	Applying an animation scheme to a single slide, group of slides, or an entire presentation	Tutorial 3: 127–132
PP03S-2-5	Apply slide transitions	Applying transition effects to a single slide, group of slides, or an entire presentation	Tutorial 3: 125–126

Microsoft Office Specialist Certification Grid

Standardized Coding Number	Certification Skill Activity	Courseware Requirements	Tutorial: Pages
PP03S-2-6	Customize slide templates	Customizing templates	Tutorial 2: 50–58 Tutorial 3: 96–103
PP03S-2-7	Work with masters	Inserting content in headers and footers	Tutorial 2: 62–63
		Creating and managing multiple masters	Tutorial 2: 58–59, 64
		Adding, deleting and modifying placeholders	Tutorial 2: 57–58, 63–64 Tutorial 3: 102–103 Tutorial 6: 242
PP03S-3	**Collaborating**		
PP03S-3-1	Track, accept and reject changes in a presentation	Tracking, accepting, and rejecting changes in a presentation	Tutorial 6: 255–256, 257–259
PP03S-3-2	Add, edit and delete comments in a presentation	Adding, editing and deleting comments in a presentation	Tutorial 6: 255–256, 258
PP03S-3-3	Compare and merge presentations	Comparing and merging presentations	Tutorial 6: 257
PP03S-4	**Managing and Delivering Presentations**		
PP03S-4-1	Organize a presentation	Adding, deleting and rearranging slides	Tutorial 1: 17, 19, 21–24 Tutorial 2: 77
		Using normal, slide sorter, note pages and zoom views	Tutorial 1: 6–7, 32
		Adding hyperlinks to slides	Tutorial 4: 165–168 Tutorial 5: 195
		Setting grids and guides	Tutorial 5: 192–193
PP03S-4-2	Set up slide shows for delivery	Creating and editing custom shows	Tutorial 5: 222
		Adding and modifying Action buttons	Tutorial 4: 169–171 Tutorial 6: 259–261
		Hiding slides	Tutorial 3: 135
PP03S-4-3	Rehearse timing	Rehearsing and saving timing of presentations	Tutorial 5: 214–215
PP03S-4-4	Deliver presentations	Navigating presentations in Slide Show view	Tutorial 1: 8–9
		Using pens, highlighters, arrows and pointers for emphasis	Tutorial 3: 133–134 Tutorial 5: 218–220
PP03S-4-5	Prepare presentations for remote delivery	Packaging presentations to folders for storage on a Compact Disc (e.g., Package for CD)	Tutorial 3: 136–137
		Scheduling and defining settings for Online Broadcasts	Tutorial 4: 177–178
PP03S-4-6	Save and publish presentations	Creating and using folders for presentation storage	"Managing Your Files" Tutorial: 12–18
		Saving slides in different folders and with different file names	"Managing Your Files" Tutorial: 12–18 Tutorial 1: 12
		Saving presentations as Web pages	Tutorial 4: 174–175
		Publishing slides and presentations as Web pages and setting publishing options	Tutorial 4: 174–175 Tutorial 6: 262

Microsoft Office Specialist Certification Grid

Standardized Coding Number	Certification Skill Activity	Courseware Requirements	Tutorial: Pages
PP03S-4-7	Print slides, outlines, handouts, and speaker notes	Printing slides, outlines, handouts and speaker notes	Tutorial 1: 31
		Previewing slides for printing and changing preview options	Tutorial 1: 30–31 Tutorial 4: 172
		Modifying printing options	Tutorial 1: 31
PP03S-4-8	Export a presentation to another Microsoft Office program	Sending presentations to Microsoft Word	Tutorial 4: 156–157 Tutorial 5: 189–190